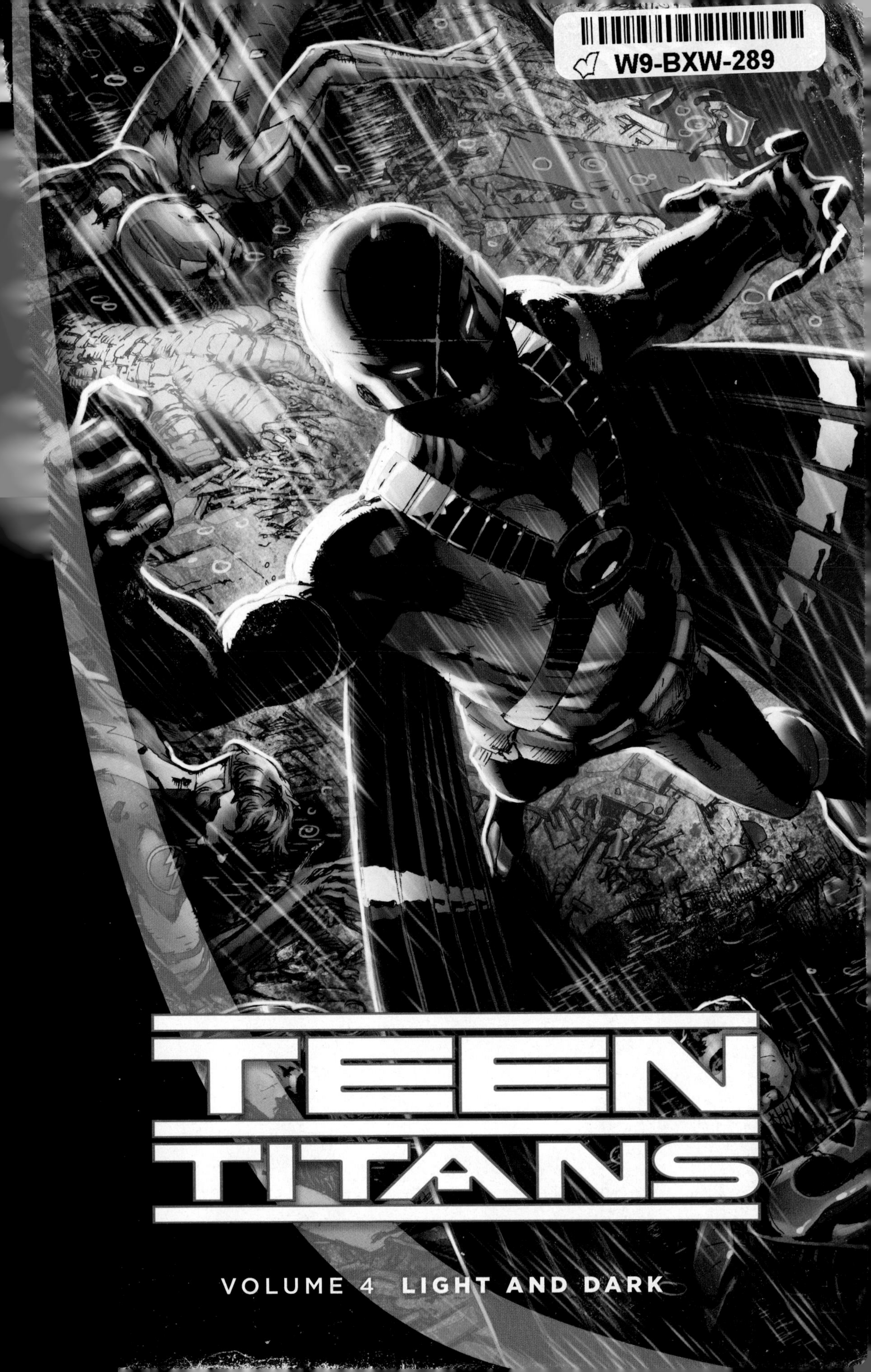

TEEN TITANS

VOLUME 4 **LIGHT AND DARK**

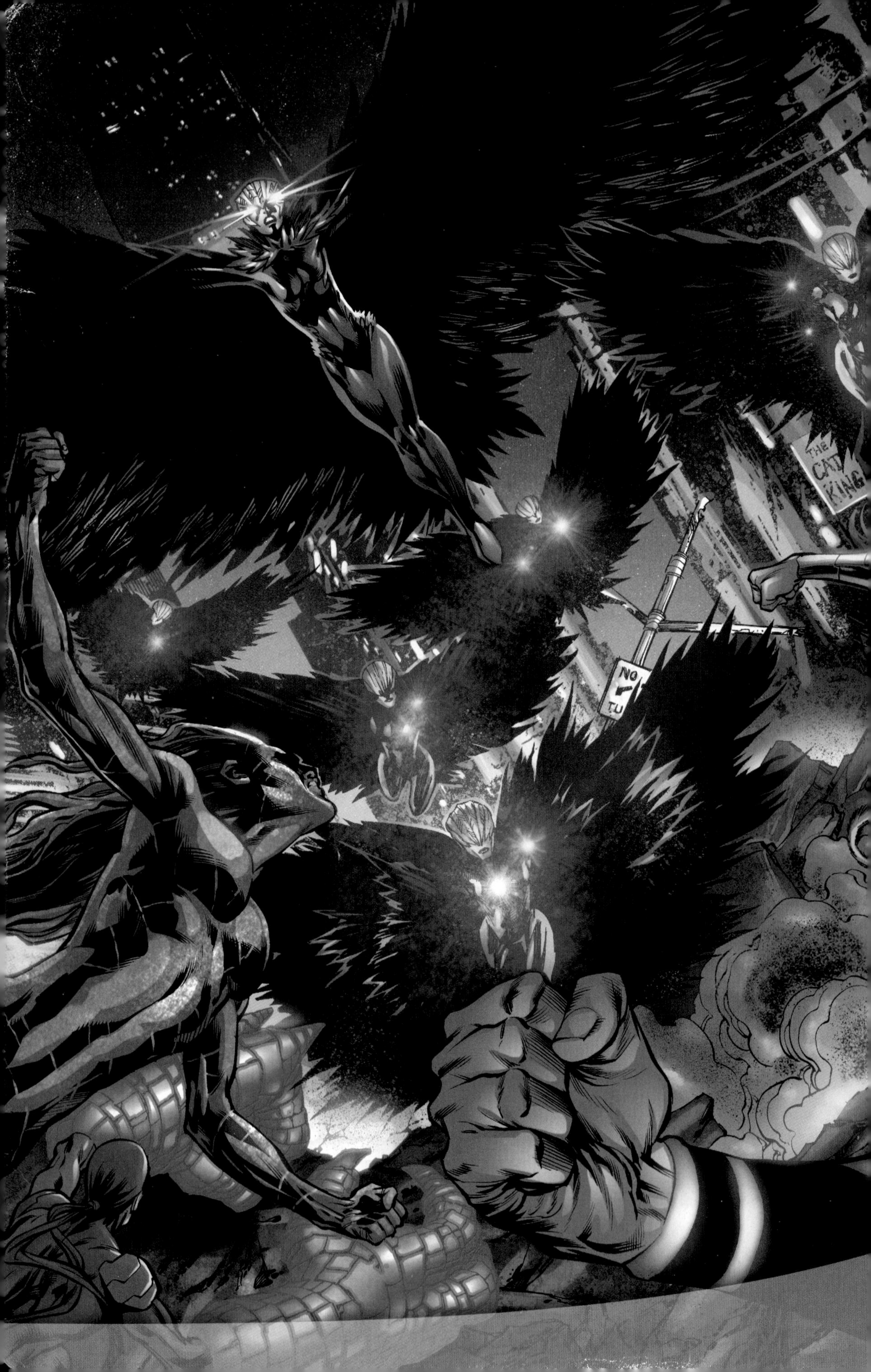
THE CAT KING
NO
TU

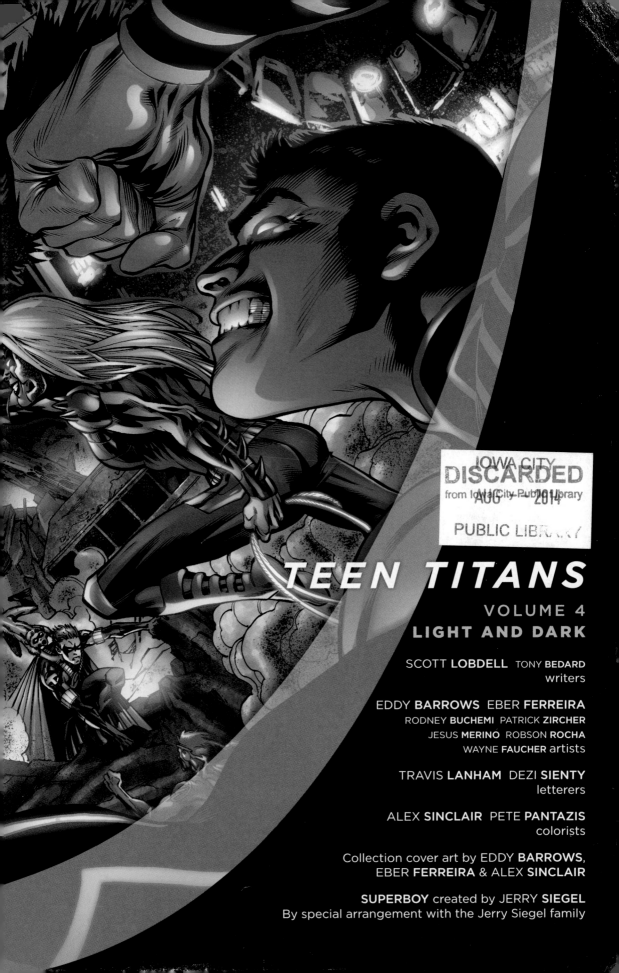

TEEN TITANS

VOLUME 4
LIGHT AND DARK

SCOTT **LOBDELL** TONY **BEDARD**
writers

EDDY **BARROWS** EBER **FERREIRA**
RODNEY **BUCHEMI** PATRICK **ZIRCHER**
JESUS **MERINO** ROBSON **ROCHA**
WAYNE **FAUCHER** artists

TRAVIS **LANHAM** DEZI **SIENTY**
letterers

ALEX **SINCLAIR** PETE **PANTAZIS**
colorists

Collection cover art by EDDY **BARROWS**,
EBER **FERREIRA** & ALEX **SINCLAIR**

SUPERBOY created by JERRY **SIEGEL**
By special arrangement with the Jerry Siegel family

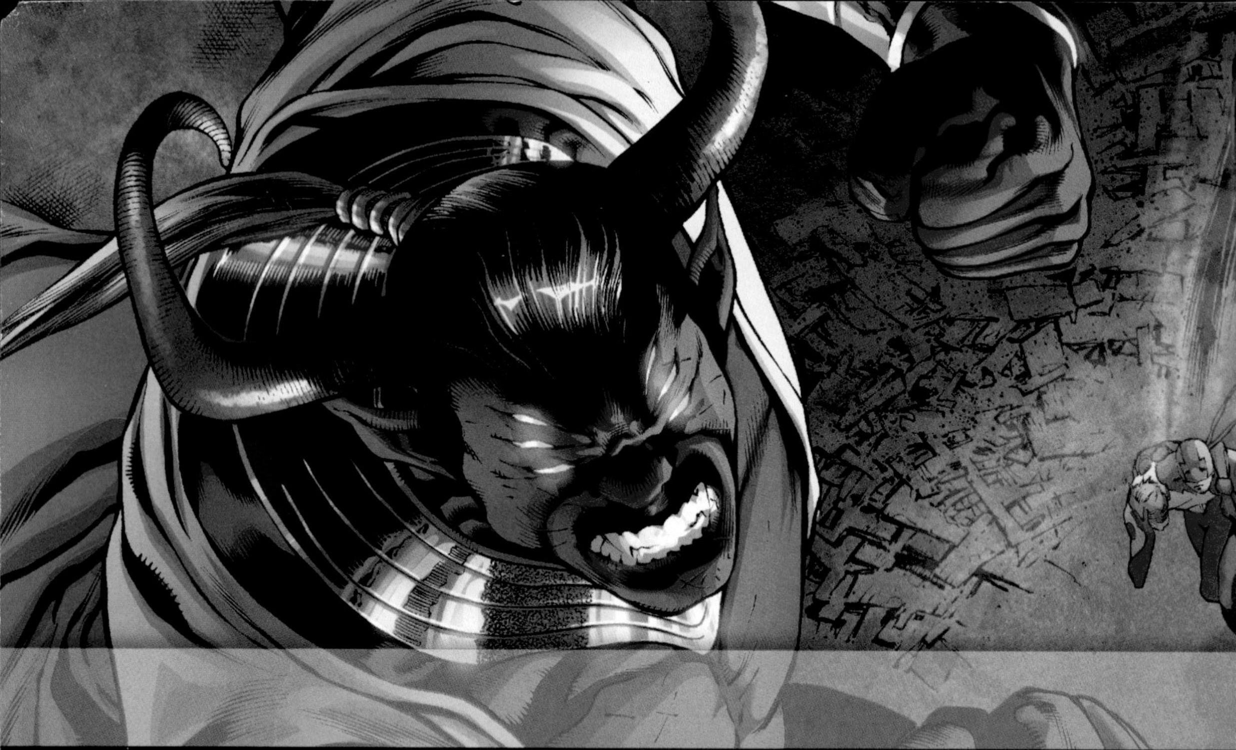

MIKE COTTON Editor - Original Series ANTHONY MARQUES Assistant Editor - Original Series
ROWENA YOW Editor ROBBIN BROSTERMAN Design Director - Books
ROBBIE BIEDERMAN Publication Design

BOB HARRAS Senior VP - Editor-in-Chief, DC Comics

DIANE NELSON President DAN DIDIO and JIM LEE Co-Publishers GEOFF JOHNS Chief Creative Officer
AMIT DESAI Senior VP - Marketing & Franchise Management AMY GENKINS Senior VP - Business & Legal Affairs
NAIRI GARDINER Senior VP - Finance JEFF BOISON VP - Publishing Planning MARK CHIARELLO VP - Art Direction & Design
JOHN CUNNINGHAM VP - Marketing TERRI CUNNINGHAM VP - Editorial Administration
LARRY GANEM VP - Talent Relations & Services ALISON GILL Senior VP - Manufacturing & Operations
HANK KANALZ Senior VP - Vertigo & Integrated Publishingm JAY KOGAN VP - Business & Legal Affairs, Publishing
JACK MAHAN VP - Business Affairs, Talent NICK NAPOLITANO VP - Manufacturing Administration
SUE POHJA VP - Book Sales FRED RUIZ VP - Maufacturing Operations
COURTNEY SIMMONS Senior VP - Publicity BOB WAYNE Senior VP - Sales

TEEN TITANS VOLUME 4: LIGHT AND DARK

DC Comics, 1700 Broadway, New York, NY 10019
A Warner Bros. Entertainment Company.
Printed by RR Donnelley, Owensville, MO, USA. 6/18/14. First Printing.

ISBN: 978-1-4012-4624-2

Library of Congress Cataloging-in-Publication Data

Lobdell, Scott, author.
Teen Titans. Volume 4, Light and Dark / Scott Lobdell, Eddy Barrows.
pages cm. — (The New 52!)
ISBN 978-1-4012-4624-2 (paperback)
1. Graphic novels. I. Barrows, Eddy, illustrator. II. Title. III. Title: Light and Dark.
PN6728.T34L66 2014
741.5'973—dc23
2014010812

SUSTAINABLE FORESTRY INITIATIVE
Certified Chain of Custody
20% Certified Forest Content, 80% Certified Sourcing
www.sfiprogram.org
SFI-01042
APPLIES TO TEXT STOCK ONLY

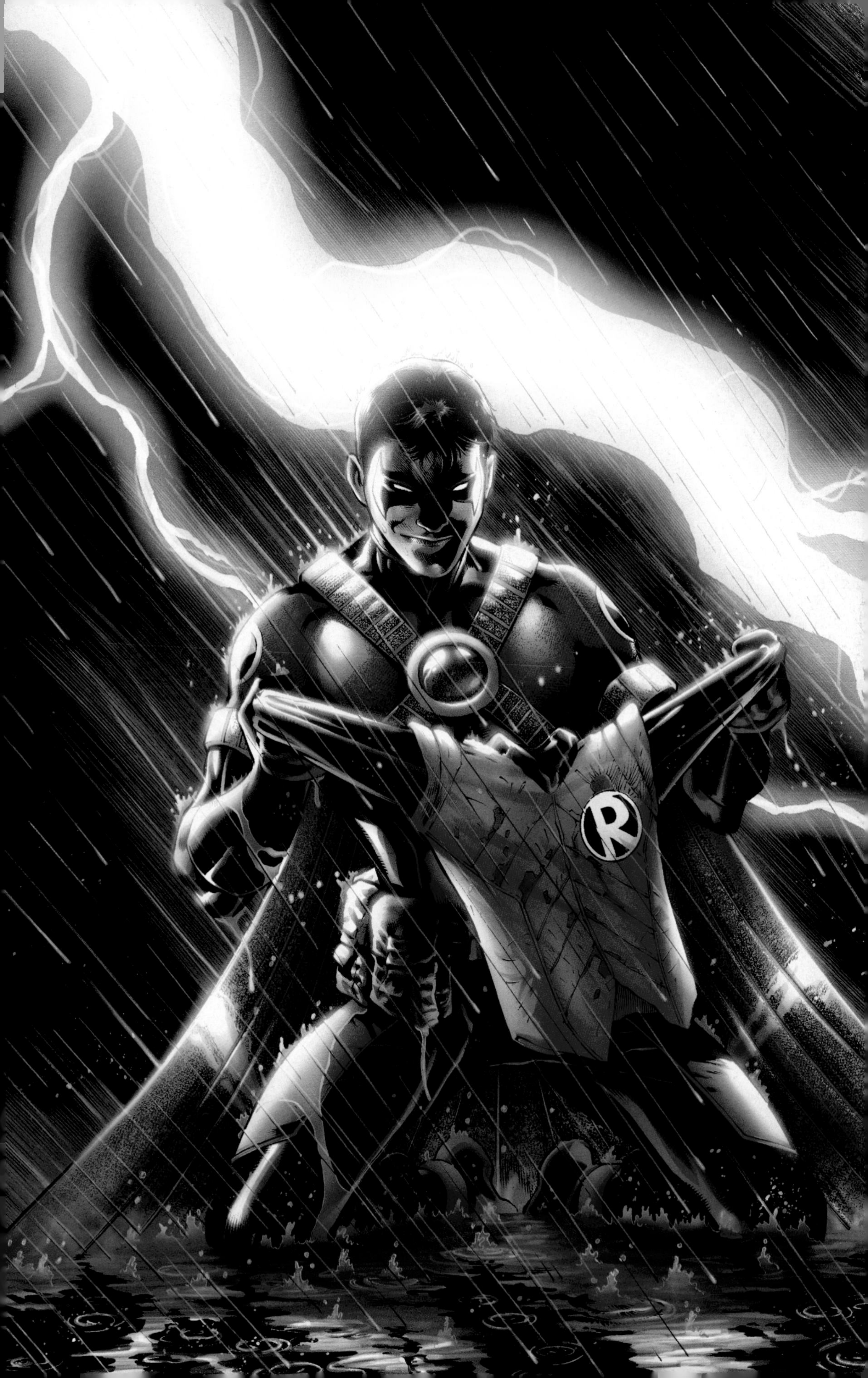

TO BELLE AND BACK

SCOTT LOBDELL writer EDDY BARROWS (pages 1-16) RODNEY BUCHEMI (pages 17-20) pencillers EBER FERREIRA (pages 1-16) RODNEY BUCHEMI (pages 17-20) inkers cover art by EDDY BARROWS, EBER FERREIRA & ALEX SINCLAIR

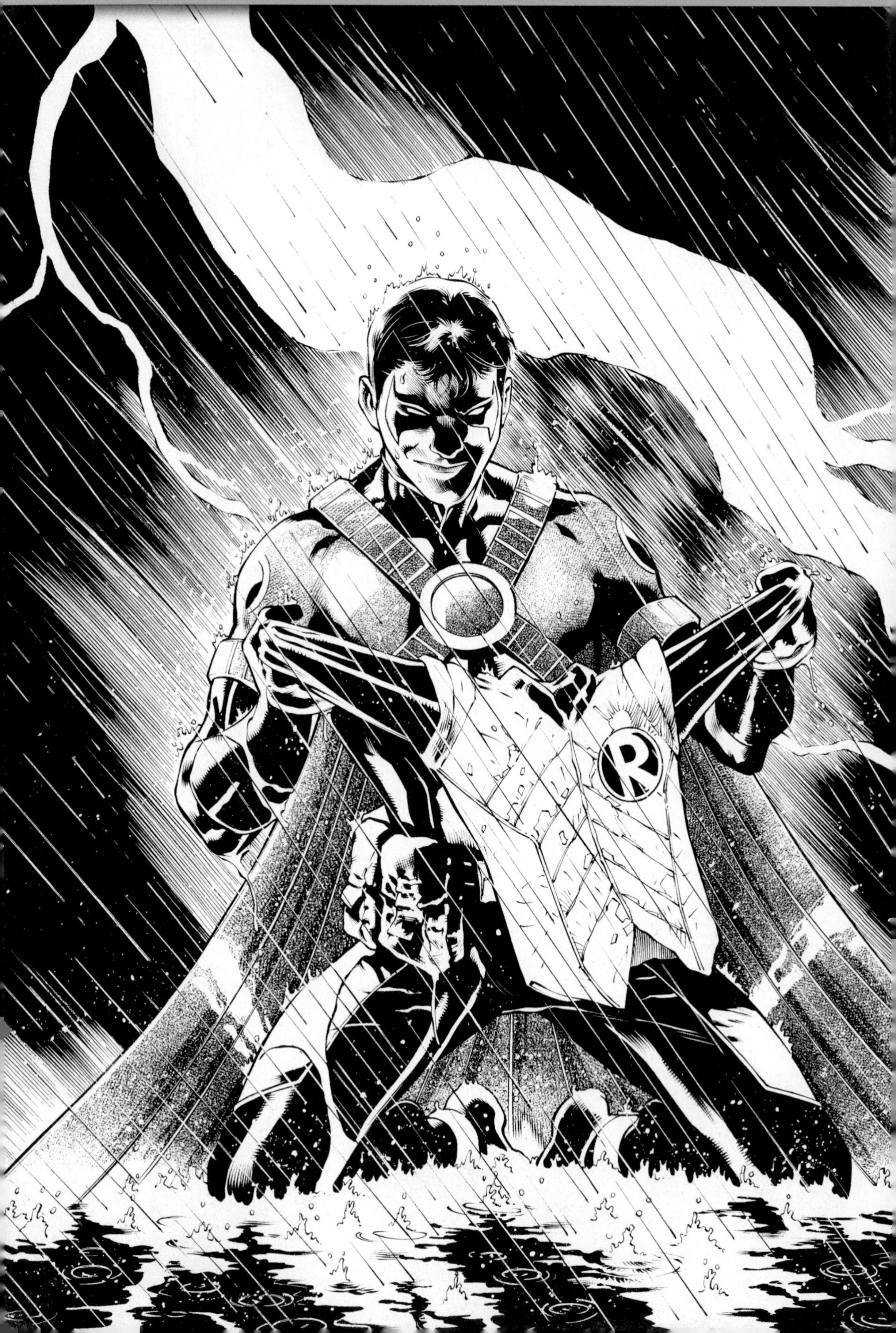
R

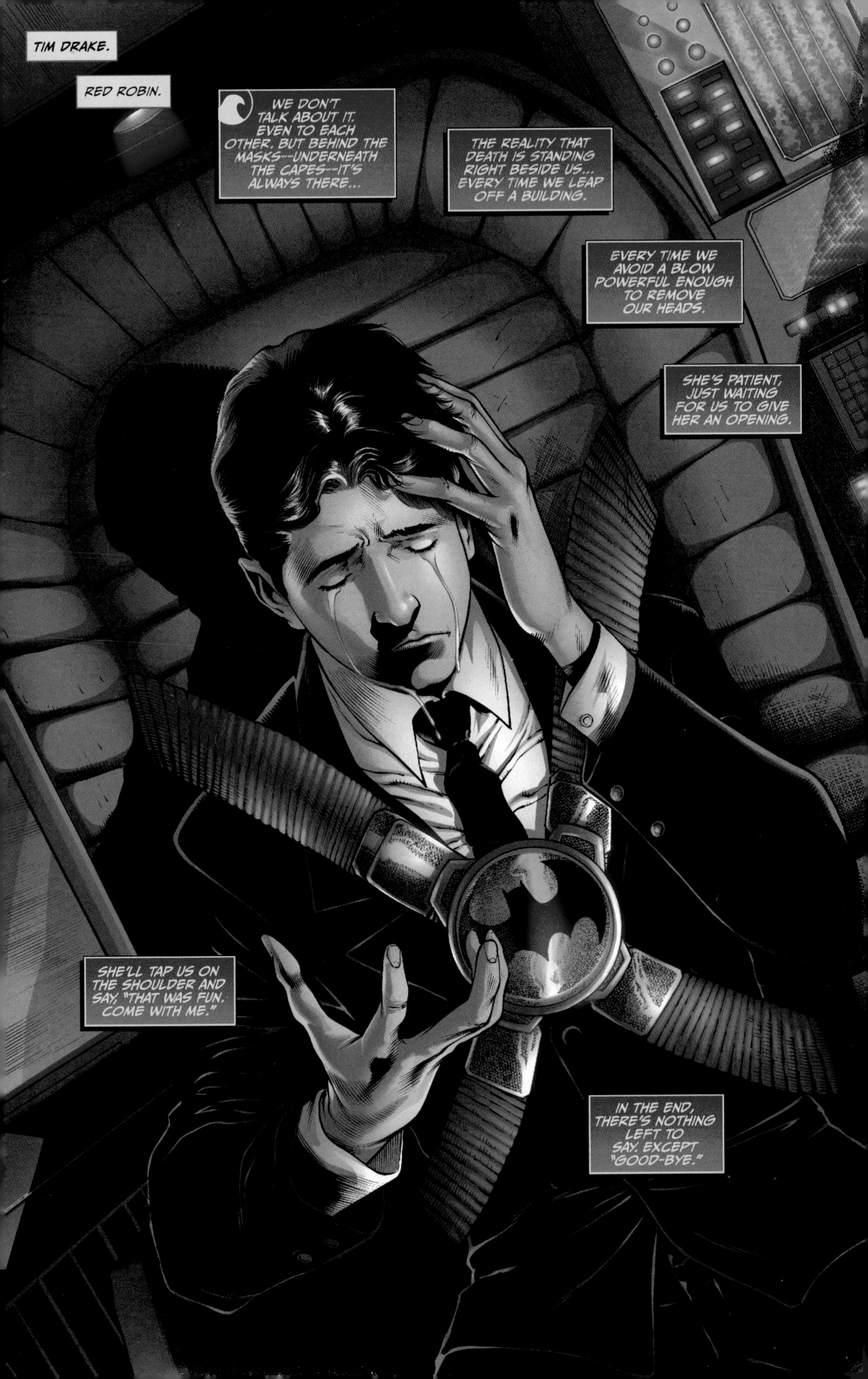
TIM DRAKE.
RED ROBIN.
WE DON'T TALK ABOUT IT, EVEN TO EACH OTHER. BUT BEHIND THE MASKS--UNDERNEATH THE CAPES--IT'S ALWAYS THERE...
THE REALITY THAT DEATH IS STANDING RIGHT BESIDE US... EVERY TIME WE LEAP OFF A BUILDING.
EVERY TIME WE AVOID A BLOW POWERFUL ENOUGH TO REMOVE OUR HEADS.
SHE'S PATIENT, JUST WAITING FOR US TO GIVE HER AN OPENING.
SHE'LL TAP US ON THE SHOULDER AND SAY, "THAT WAS FUN. COME WITH ME."
IN THE END, THERE'S NOTHING LEFT TO SAY. EXCEPT "GOOD-BYE."

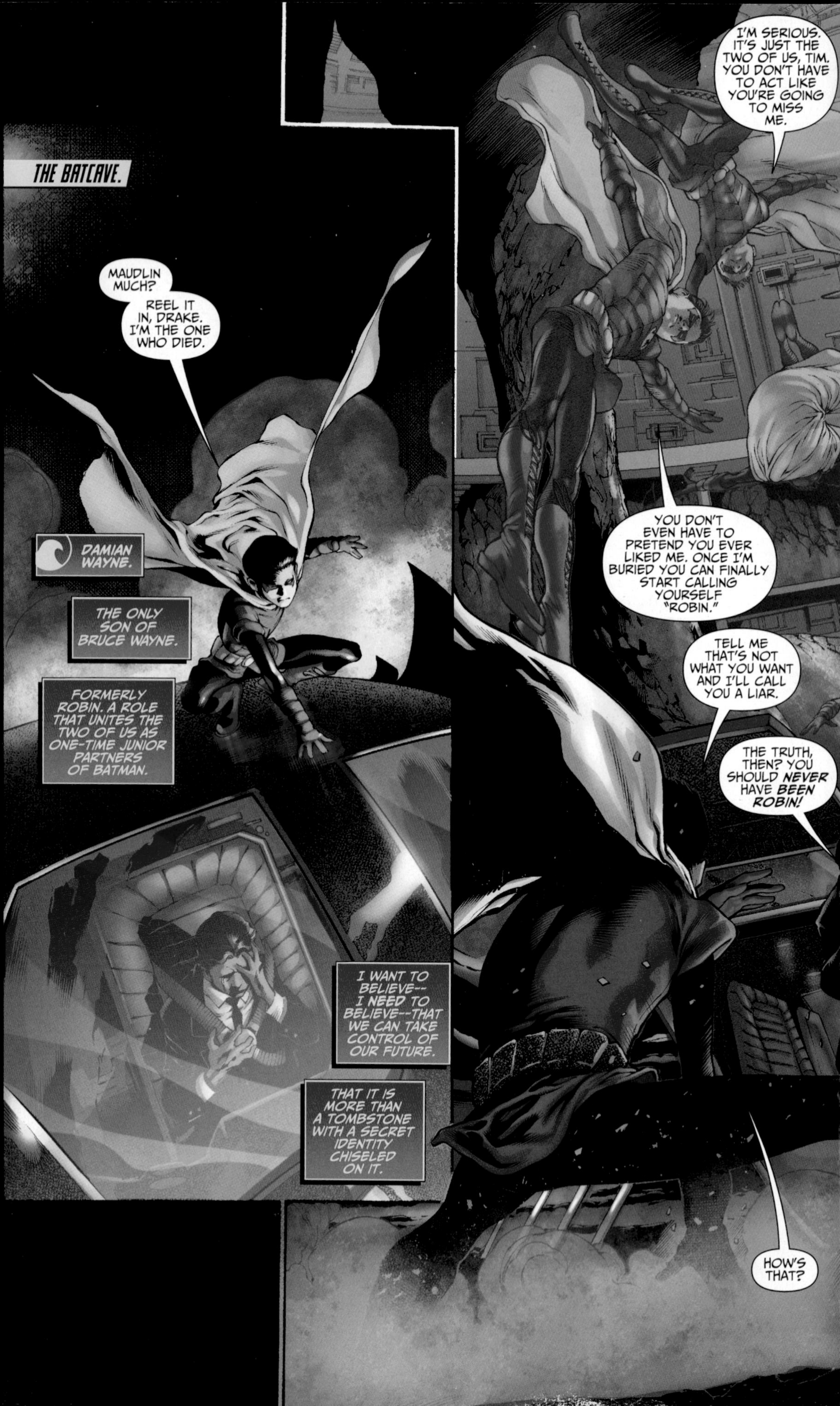
THE BATCAVE.
MAUDLIN MUCH?
REEL IT IN, DRAKE. I'M THE ONE WHO DIED.
DAMIAN WAYNE.
THE ONLY SON OF BRUCE WAYNE.
FORMERLY ROBIN. A ROLE THAT UNITES THE TWO OF US AS ONE-TIME JUNIOR PARTNERS OF BATMAN.
I WANT TO BELIEVE-- I NEED TO BELIEVE--THAT WE CAN TAKE CONTROL OF OUR FUTURE.
THAT IT IS MORE THAN A TOMBSTONE WITH A SECRET IDENTITY CHISELED ON IT.
I'M SERIOUS. IT'S JUST THE TWO OF US, TIM. YOU DON'T HAVE TO ACT LIKE YOU'RE GOING TO MISS ME.
YOU DON'T EVEN HAVE TO PRETEND YOU EVER LIKED ME. ONCE I'M BURIED YOU CAN FINALLY START CALLING YOURSELF "ROBIN."
TELL ME THAT'S NOT WHAT YOU WANT AND I'LL CALL YOU A LIAR.
THE TRUTH, THEN? YOU SHOULD NEVER HAVE BEEN ROBIN!
HOW'S THAT?

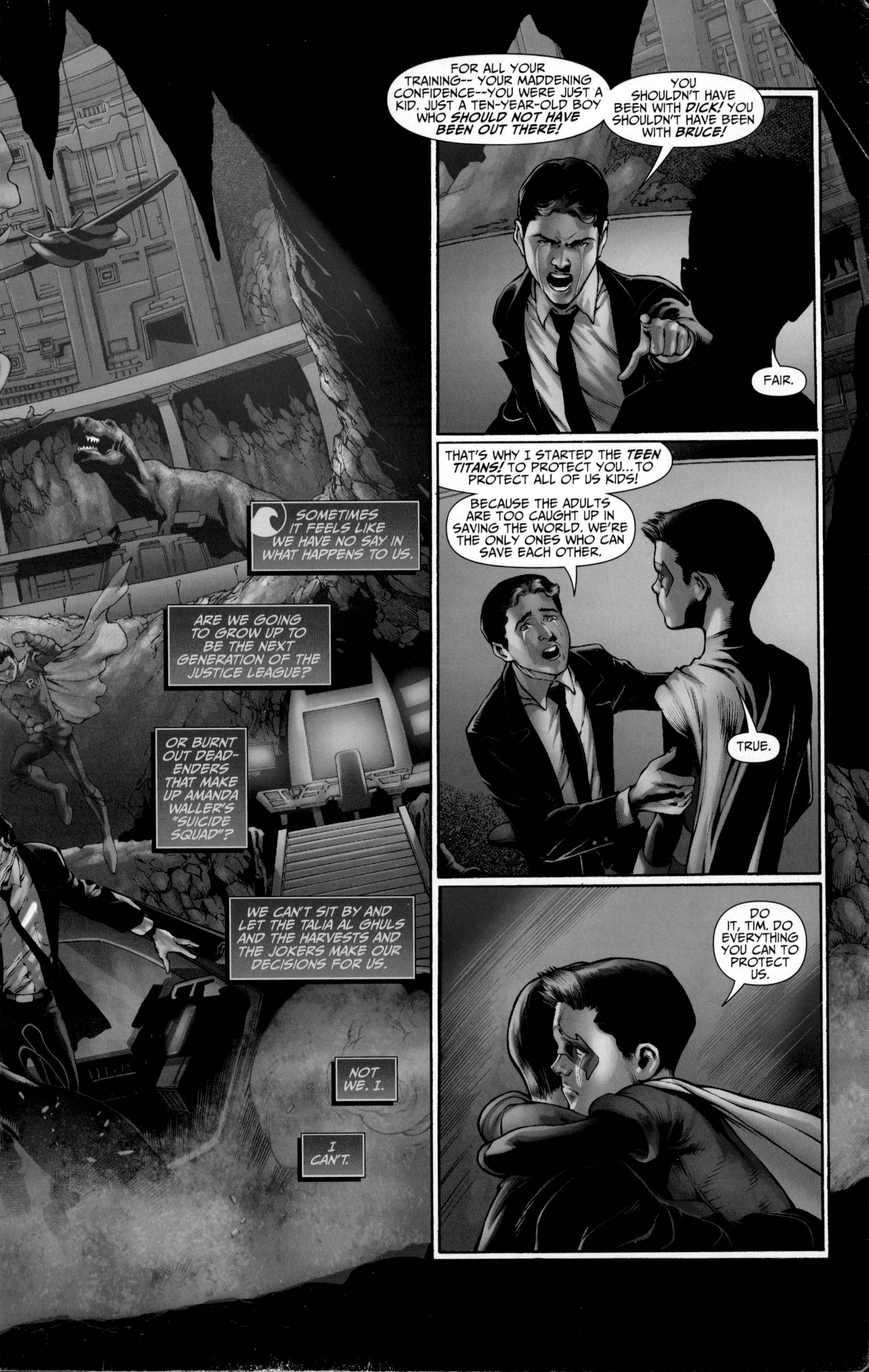

FOR ALL YOUR TRAINING-- YOUR MADDENING CONFIDENCE--YOU WERE JUST A KID. JUST A TEN-YEAR-OLD BOY WHO SHOULD NOT HAVE BEEN OUT THERE!
YOU SHOULDN'T HAVE BEEN WITH DICK! YOU SHOULDN'T HAVE BEEN WITH BRUCE!
FAIR.
THAT'S WHY I STARTED THE TEEN TITANS! TO PROTECT YOU...TO PROTECT ALL OF US KIDS!
BECAUSE THE ADULTS ARE TOO CAUGHT UP IN SAVING THE WORLD. WE'RE THE ONLY ONES WHO CAN SAVE EACH OTHER.
TRUE.
DO IT, TIM. DO EVERYTHING YOU CAN TO PROTECT US.
SOMETIMES IT FEELS LIKE WE HAVE NO SAY IN WHAT HAPPENS TO US.
ARE WE GOING TO GROW UP TO BE THE NEXT GENERATION OF THE JUSTICE LEAGUE?
OR BURNT OUT DEAD-ENDERS THAT MAKE UP AMANDA WALLER'S "SUICIDE SQUAD"?
WE CAN'T SIT BY AND LET THE TALIA AL GHULS AND THE HARVESTS AND THE JOKERS MAKE OUR DECISIONS FOR US.
NOT WE. I.
I CAN'T.

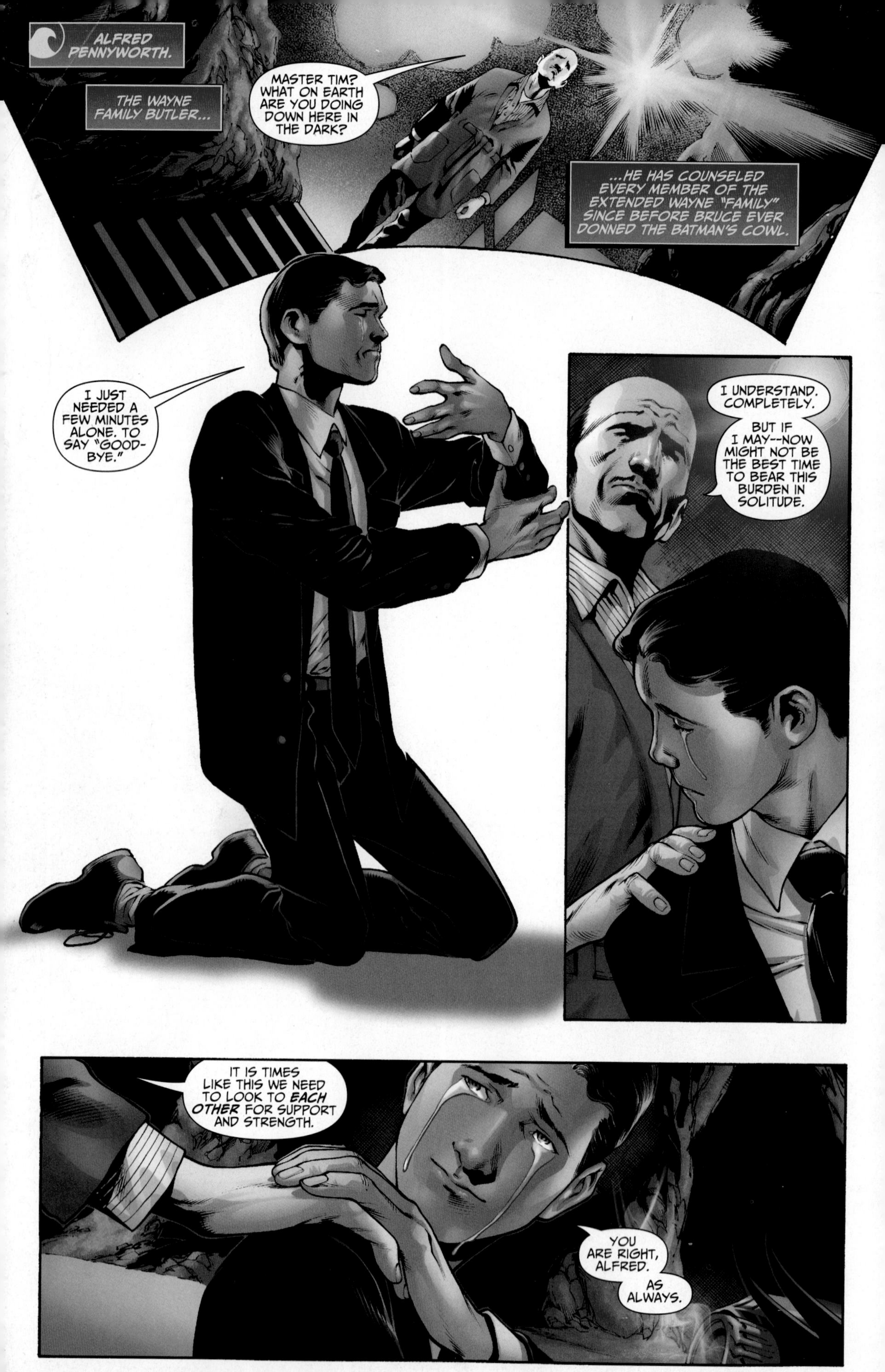
ALFRED PENNYWORTH.
THE WAYNE FAMILY BUTLER...
MASTER TIM? WHAT ON EARTH ARE YOU DOING DOWN HERE IN THE DARK?
...HE HAS COUNSELED EVERY MEMBER OF THE EXTENDED WAYNE "FAMILY" SINCE BEFORE BRUCE EVER DONNED THE BATMAN'S COWL.
I JUST NEEDED A FEW MINUTES ALONE. TO SAY "GOOD-BYE."
I UNDERSTAND. COMPLETELY.
BUT IF I MAY--NOW MIGHT NOT BE THE BEST TIME TO BEAR THIS BURDEN IN SOLITUDE.
IT IS TIMES LIKE THIS WE NEED TO LOOK TO *EACH OTHER* FOR SUPPORT AND STRENGTH.
YOU ARE RIGHT, ALFRED.
AS ALWAYS.

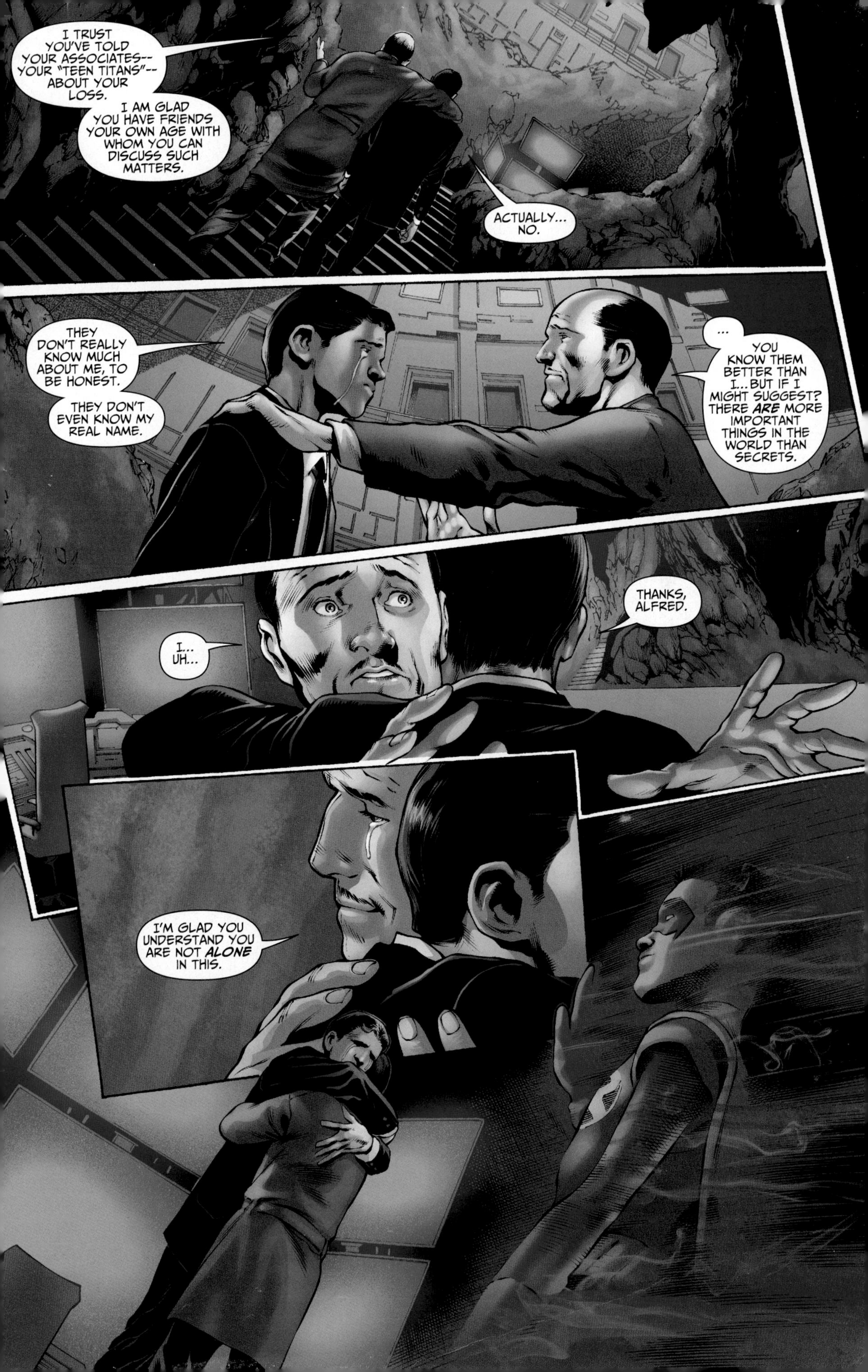
I TRUST YOU'VE TOLD YOUR ASSOCIATES-- YOUR "TEEN TITANS"-- ABOUT YOUR LOSS.
I AM GLAD YOU HAVE FRIENDS YOUR OWN AGE WITH WHOM YOU CAN DISCUSS SUCH MATTERS.
ACTUALLY... NO.
THEY DON'T REALLY KNOW MUCH ABOUT ME, TO BE HONEST.
THEY DON'T EVEN KNOW MY REAL NAME.
...
YOU KNOW THEM BETTER THAN I... BUT IF I MIGHT SUGGEST? THERE ARE MORE IMPORTANT THINGS IN THE WORLD THAN SECRETS.
THANKS, ALFRED.
I... UH...
I'M GLAD YOU UNDERSTAND YOU ARE NOT ALONE IN THIS.

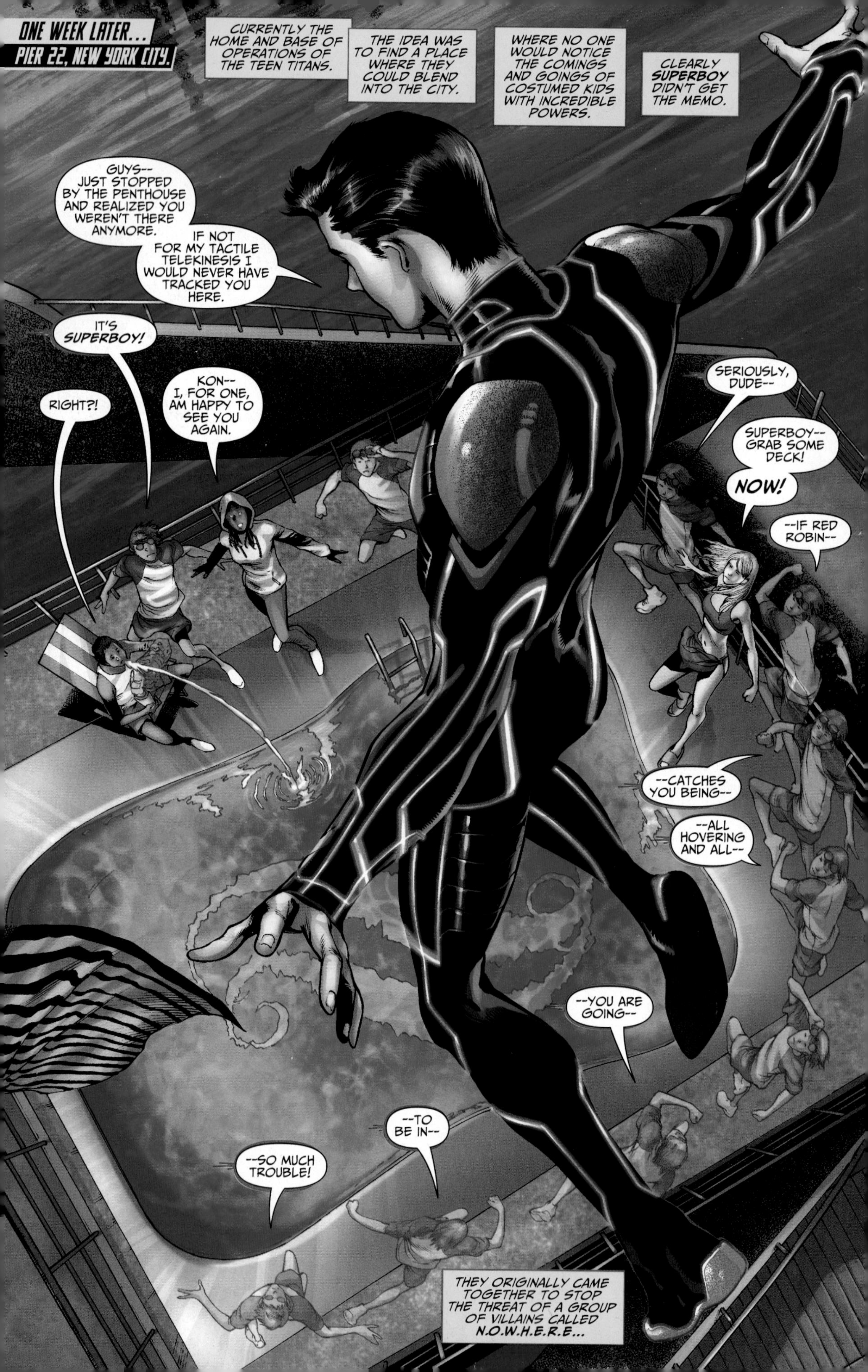
ONE WEEK LATER...
PIER 22, NEW YORK CITY.
CURRENTLY THE HOME AND BASE OF OPERATIONS OF THE TEEN TITANS.
THE IDEA WAS TO FIND A PLACE WHERE THEY COULD BLEND INTO THE CITY.
WHERE NO ONE WOULD NOTICE THE COMINGS AND GOINGS OF COSTUMED KIDS WITH INCREDIBLE POWERS.
CLEARLY SUPERBOY DIDN'T GET THE MEMO.
GUYS-- JUST STOPPED BY THE PENTHOUSE AND REALIZED YOU WEREN'T THERE ANYMORE.
IF NOT FOR MY TACTILE TELEKINESIS I WOULD NEVER HAVE TRACKED YOU HERE.
IT'S SUPERBOY!
RIGHT?!
KON-- I, FOR ONE, AM HAPPY TO SEE YOU AGAIN.
SERIOUSLY, DUDE--
SUPERBOY-- GRAB SOME DECK!
NOW!
--IF RED ROBIN--
--CATCHES YOU BEING--
--ALL HOVERING AND ALL--
--YOU ARE GOING--
--TO BE IN--
--SO MUCH TROUBLE!
THEY ORIGINALLY CAME TOGETHER TO STOP THE THREAT OF A GROUP OF VILLAINS CALLED N.O.W.H.E.R.E...

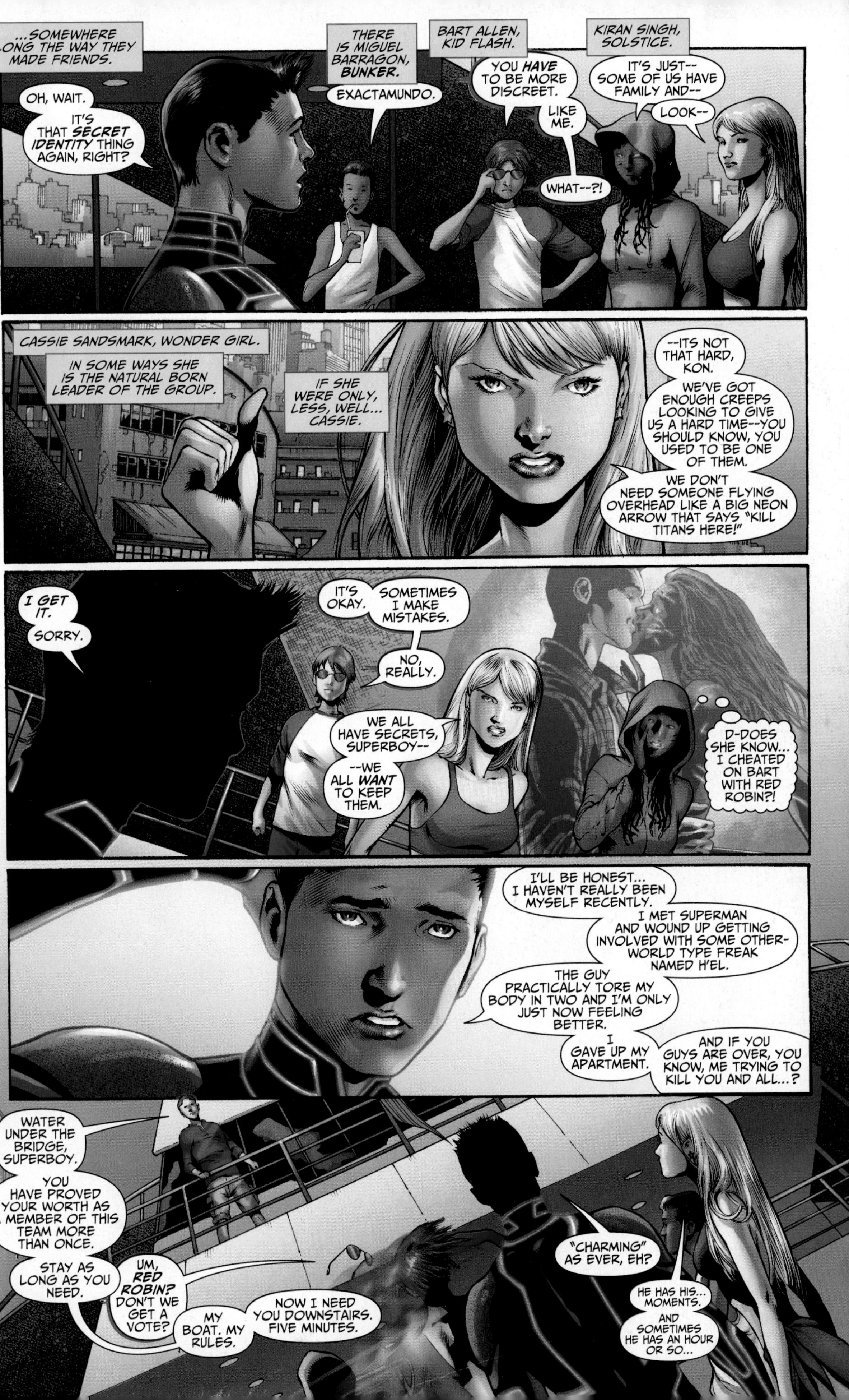
...SOMEWHERE ALONG THE WAY THEY MADE FRIENDS.
OH, WAIT.
IT'S THAT SECRET IDENTITY THING AGAIN, RIGHT?
THERE IS MIGUEL BARRAGON, BUNKER.
EXACTAMUNDO.
BART ALLEN, KID FLASH.
YOU HAVE TO BE MORE DISCREET.
LIKE ME.
WHAT--?!
KIRAN SINGH, SOLSTICE.
IT'S JUST-- SOME OF US HAVE FAMILY AND--
LOOK--
CASSIE SANDSMARK, WONDER GIRL.
IN SOME WAYS SHE IS THE NATURAL BORN LEADER OF THE GROUP.
IF SHE WERE ONLY, LESS, WELL... CASSIE.
--ITS NOT THAT HARD, KON.
WE'VE GOT ENOUGH CREEPS LOOKING TO GIVE US A HARD TIME--YOU SHOULD KNOW, YOU USED TO BE ONE OF THEM.
WE DON'T NEED SOMEONE FLYING OVERHEAD LIKE A BIG NEON ARROW THAT SAYS "KILL TITANS HERE!"
I GET IT.
SORRY.
IT'S OKAY.
SOMETIMES I MAKE MISTAKES.
NO, REALLY.
WE ALL HAVE SECRETS, SUPERBOY--
--WE ALL WANT TO KEEP THEM.
D-DOES SHE KNOW... I CHEATED ON BART WITH RED ROBIN?!
I'LL BE HONEST... I HAVEN'T REALLY BEEN MYSELF RECENTLY.
I MET SUPERMAN AND WOUND UP GETTING INVOLVED WITH SOME OTHER-WORLD TYPE FREAK NAMED H'EL.
THE GUY PRACTICALLY TORE MY BODY IN TWO AND I'M ONLY JUST NOW FEELING BETTER.
I GAVE UP MY APARTMENT.
AND IF YOU GUYS ARE OVER, YOU KNOW, ME TRYING TO KILL YOU AND ALL...?
WATER UNDER THE BRIDGE, SUPERBOY.
YOU HAVE PROVED YOUR WORTH AS A MEMBER OF THIS TEAM MORE THAN ONCE.
STAY AS LONG AS YOU NEED.
UM, RED ROBIN? DON'T WE GET A VOTE?
MY BOAT. MY RULES.
NOW I NEED YOU DOWNSTAIRS. FIVE MINUTES.
"CHARMING" AS EVER, EH?
HE HAS HIS... MOMENTS.
AND SOMETIMES HE HAS AN HOUR OR SO...

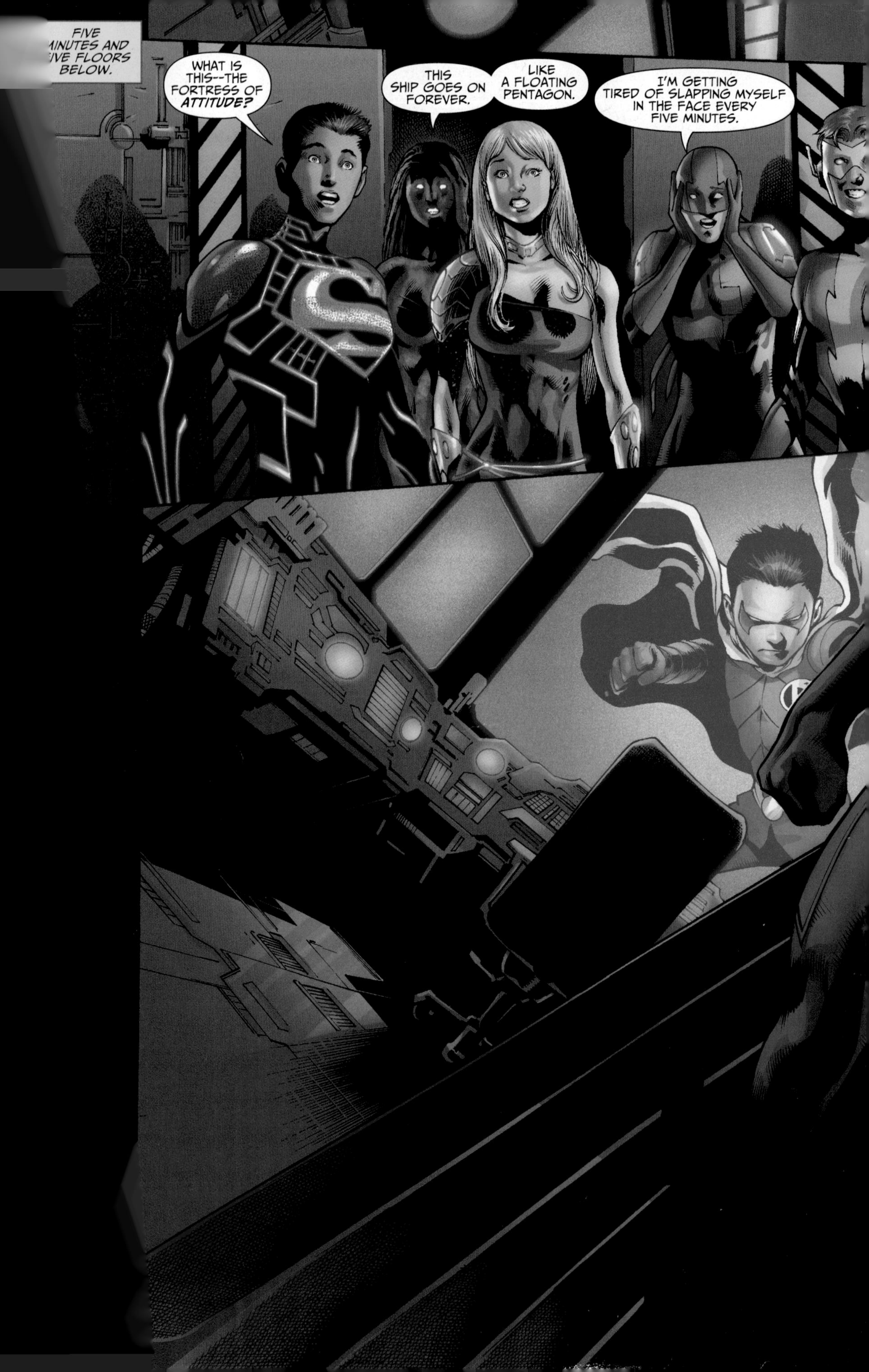
FIVE
INUTES AND
IVE FLOORS
BELOW.
WHAT IS THIS--THE FORTRESS OF ATTITUDE?
THIS SHIP GOES ON FOREVER.
LIKE A FLOATING PENTAGON.
I'M GETTING TIRED OF SLAPPING MYSELF IN THE FACE EVERY FIVE MINUTES.

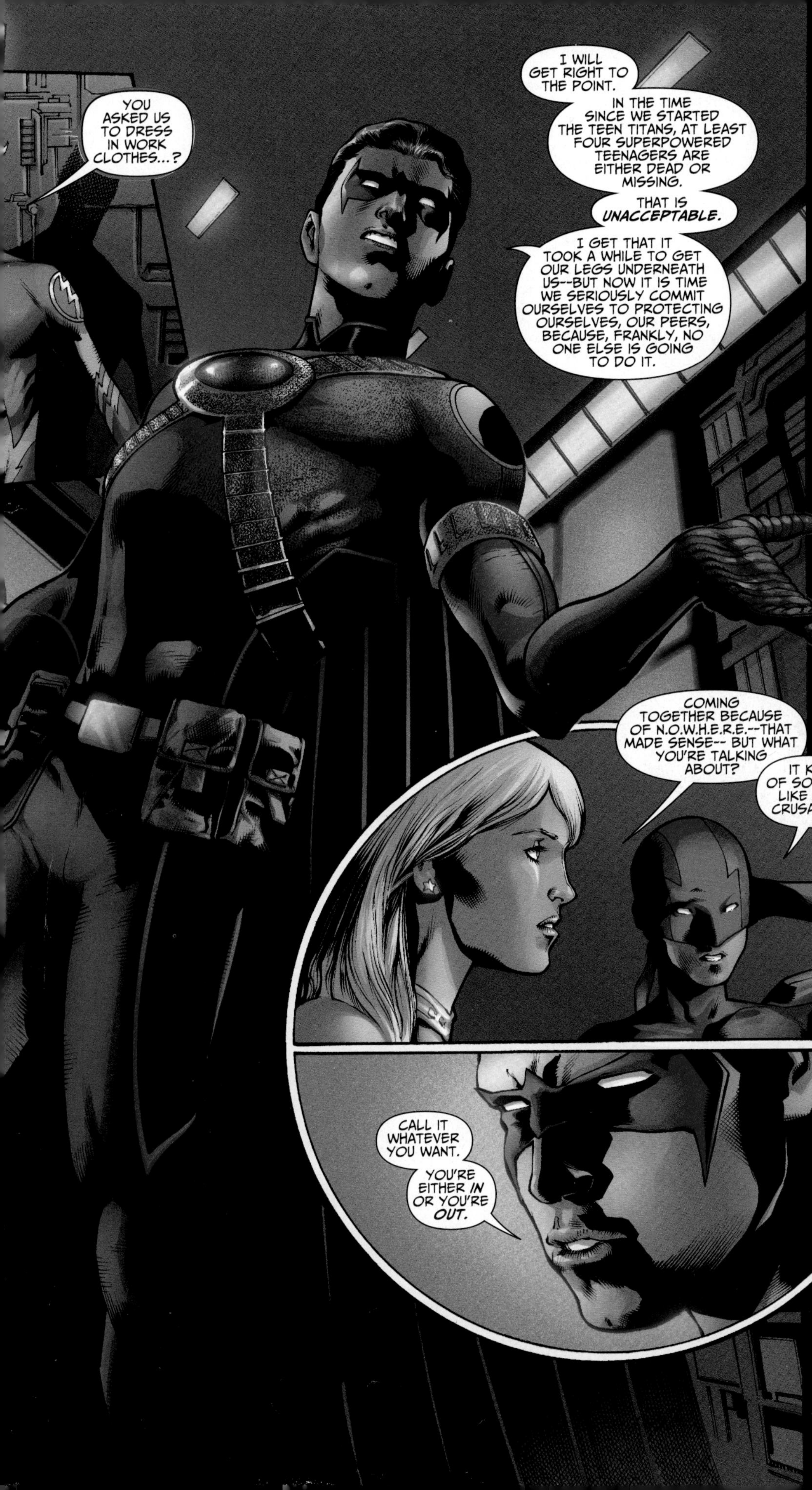
I WILL GET RIGHT TO THE POINT.
YOU ASKED US TO DRESS IN WORK CLOTHES...?
IN THE TIME SINCE WE STARTED THE TEEN TITANS, AT LEAST FOUR SUPERPOWERED TEENAGERS ARE EITHER DEAD OR MISSING.
THAT IS *UNACCEPTABLE.*
I GET THAT IT TOOK A WHILE TO GET OUR LEGS UNDERNEATH US--BUT NOW IT IS TIME WE SERIOUSLY COMMIT OURSELVES TO PROTECTING OURSELVES, OUR PEERS, BECAUSE, FRANKLY, NO ONE ELSE IS GOING TO DO IT.
COMING TOGETHER BECAUSE OF N.O.W.H.E.R.E.--THAT MADE SENSE-- BUT WHAT YOU'RE TALKING ABOUT?
IT KIND OF SOUNDS LIKE A... CRUSADE?
CALL IT WHATEVER YOU WANT.
YOU'RE EITHER *IN* OR YOU'RE *OUT.*

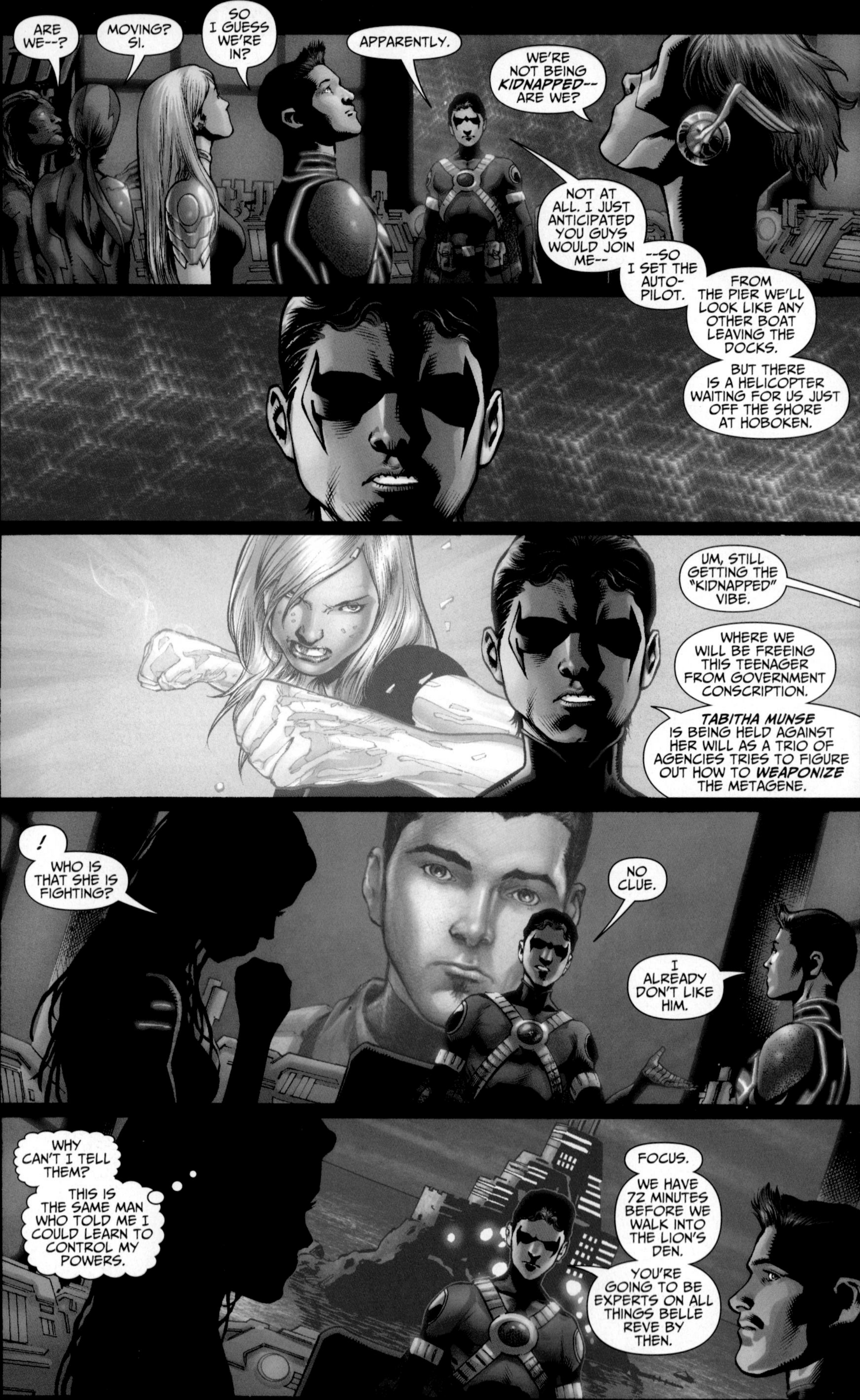
ARE WE--?
MOVING? SI.
SO I GUESS WE'RE IN?
APPARENTLY.
WE'RE NOT BEING KIDNAPPED-- ARE WE?
NOT AT ALL. I JUST ANTICIPATED YOU GUYS WOULD JOIN ME--
--SO I SET THE AUTO-PILOT.
FROM THE PIER WE'LL LOOK LIKE ANY OTHER BOAT LEAVING THE DOCKS.
BUT THERE IS A HELICOPTER WAITING FOR US JUST OFF THE SHORE AT HOBOKEN.
UM, STILL GETTING THE "KIDNAPPED" VIBE.
WHERE WE WILL BE FREEING THIS TEENAGER FROM GOVERNMENT CONSCRIPTION.
TABITHA MUNSE IS BEING HELD AGAINST HER WILL AS A TRIO OF AGENCIES TRIES TO FIGURE OUT HOW TO WEAPONIZE THE METAGENE.
!
WHO IS THAT SHE IS FIGHTING?
NO CLUE.
I ALREADY DON'T LIKE HIM.
WHY CAN'T I TELL THEM?
THIS IS THE SAME MAN WHO TOLD ME I COULD LEARN TO CONTROL MY POWERS.
FOCUS.
WE HAVE 72 MINUTES BEFORE WE WALK INTO THE LION'S DEN.
YOU'RE GOING TO BE EXPERTS ON ALL THINGS BELLE REVE BY THEN.

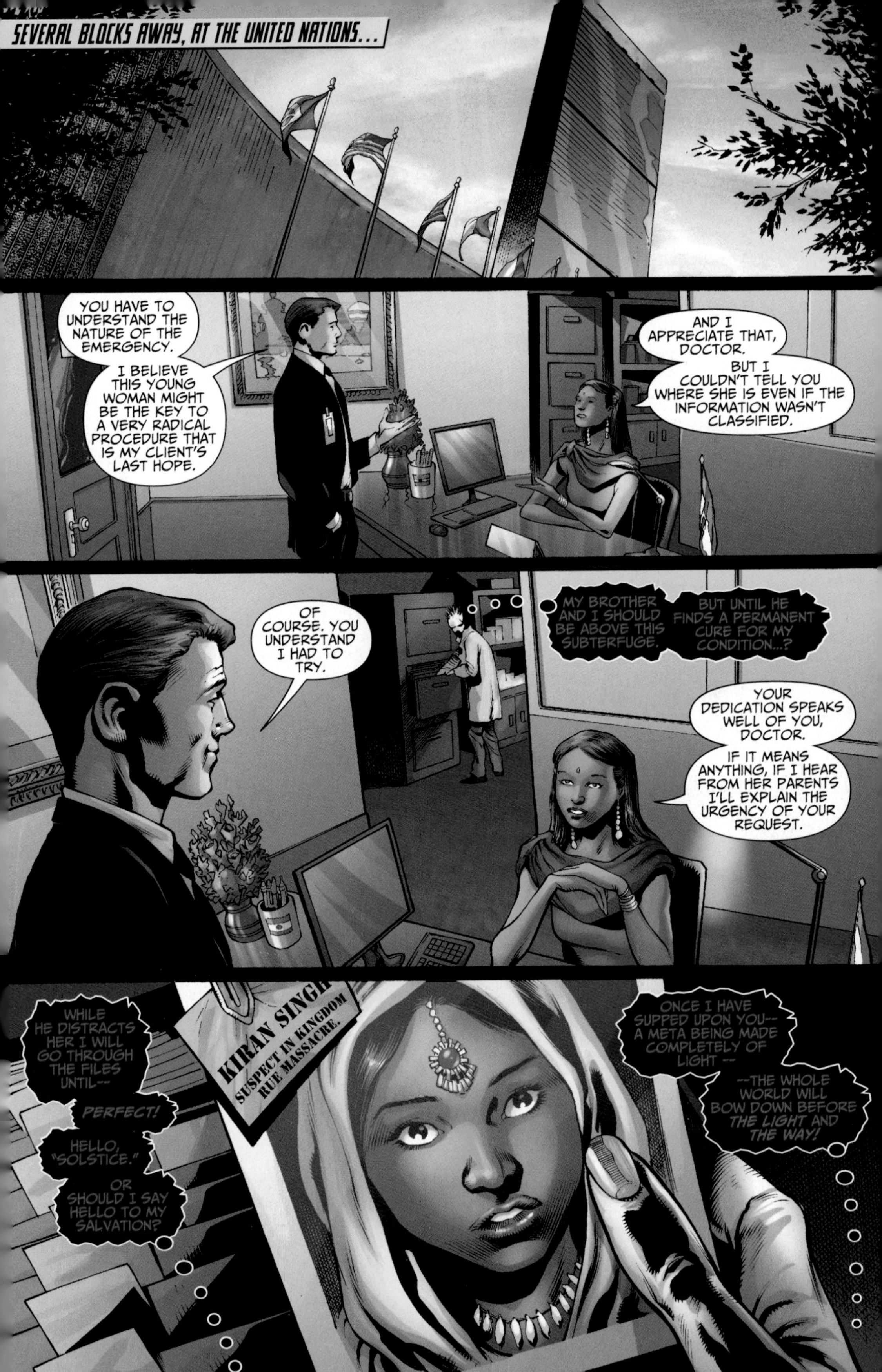

SEVERAL BLOCKS AWAY, AT THE UNITED NATIONS...
YOU HAVE TO UNDERSTAND THE NATURE OF THE EMERGENCY.
I BELIEVE THIS YOUNG WOMAN MIGHT BE THE KEY TO A VERY RADICAL PROCEDURE THAT IS MY CLIENT'S LAST HOPE.
AND I APPRECIATE THAT, DOCTOR.
BUT I COULDN'T TELL YOU WHERE SHE IS EVEN IF THE INFORMATION WASN'T CLASSIFIED.
OF COURSE. YOU UNDERSTAND I HAD TO TRY.
MY BROTHER AND I SHOULD BE ABOVE THIS SUBTERFUGE.
BUT UNTIL HE FINDS A PERMANENT CURE FOR MY CONDITION...?
YOUR DEDICATION SPEAKS WELL OF YOU, DOCTOR.
IF IT MEANS ANYTHING, IF I HEAR FROM HER PARENTS I'LL EXPLAIN THE URGENCY OF YOUR REQUEST.
WHILE HE DISTRACTS HER I WILL GO THROUGH THE FILES UNTIL--
PERFECT!
HELLO, "SOLSTICE."
OR SHOULD I SAY HELLO TO MY SALVATION?
KIRAN SINGH
SUSPECT IN KINGDOM RUE MASSACRE.
ONCE I HAVE SUPPED UPON YOU-- A META BEING MADE COMPLETELY OF LIGHT --
--THE WHOLE WORLD WILL BOW DOWN BEFORE THE LIGHT AND THE WAY!

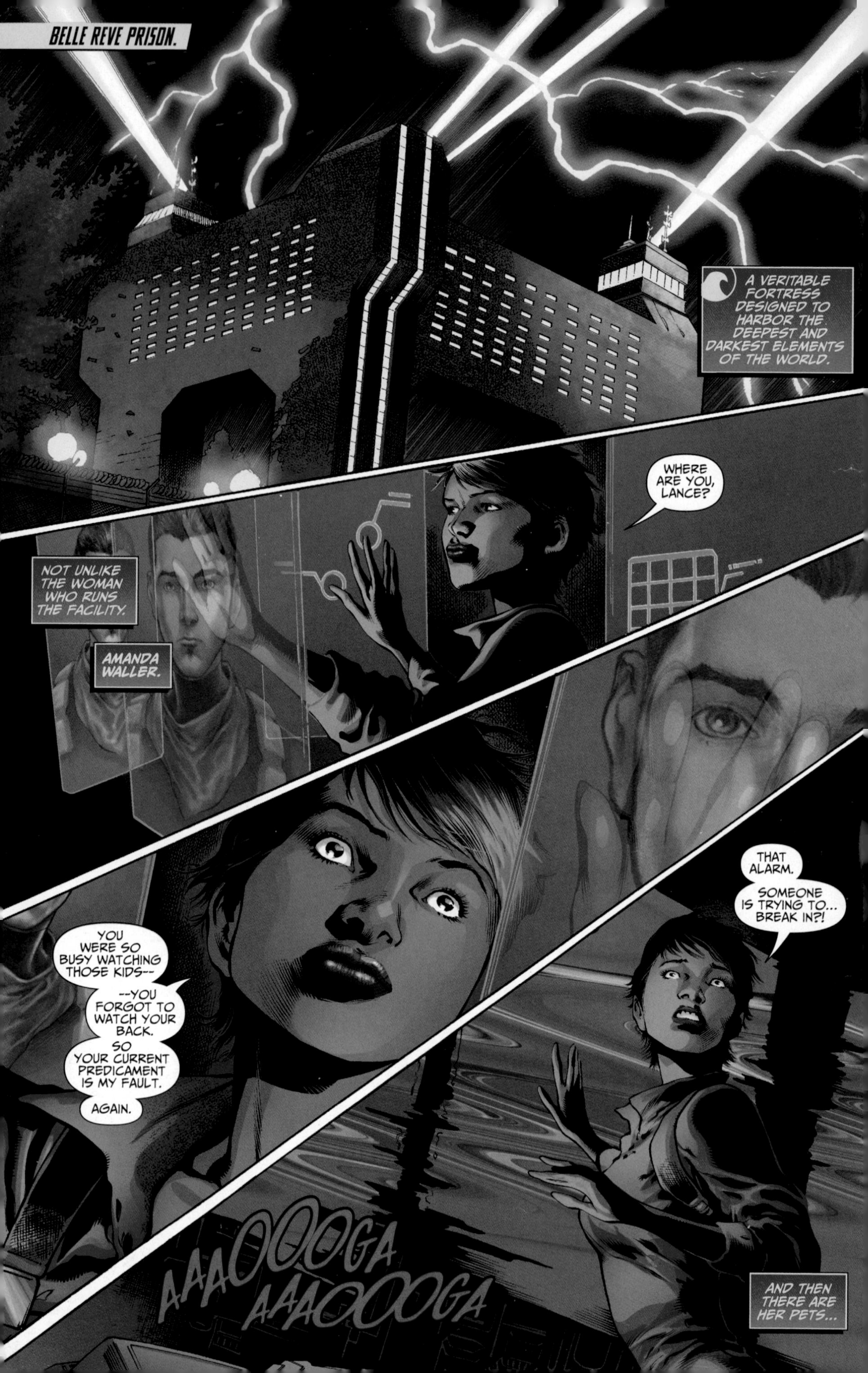
BELLE REVE PRISON.
A VERITABLE FORTRESS DESIGNED TO HARBOR THE DEEPEST AND DARKEST ELEMENTS OF THE WORLD.
WHERE ARE YOU, LANCE?
NOT UNLIKE THE WOMAN WHO RUNS THE FACILITY.
AMANDA WALLER.
YOU WERE SO BUSY WATCHING THOSE KIDS--
--YOU FORGOT TO WATCH YOUR BACK.
SO YOUR CURRENT PREDICAMENT IS MY FAULT.
AGAIN.
THAT ALARM.
SOMEONE IS TRYING TO... BREAK IN?!
AAAOOOGA
AAAOOOOGA
AND THEN THERE ARE HER PETS...

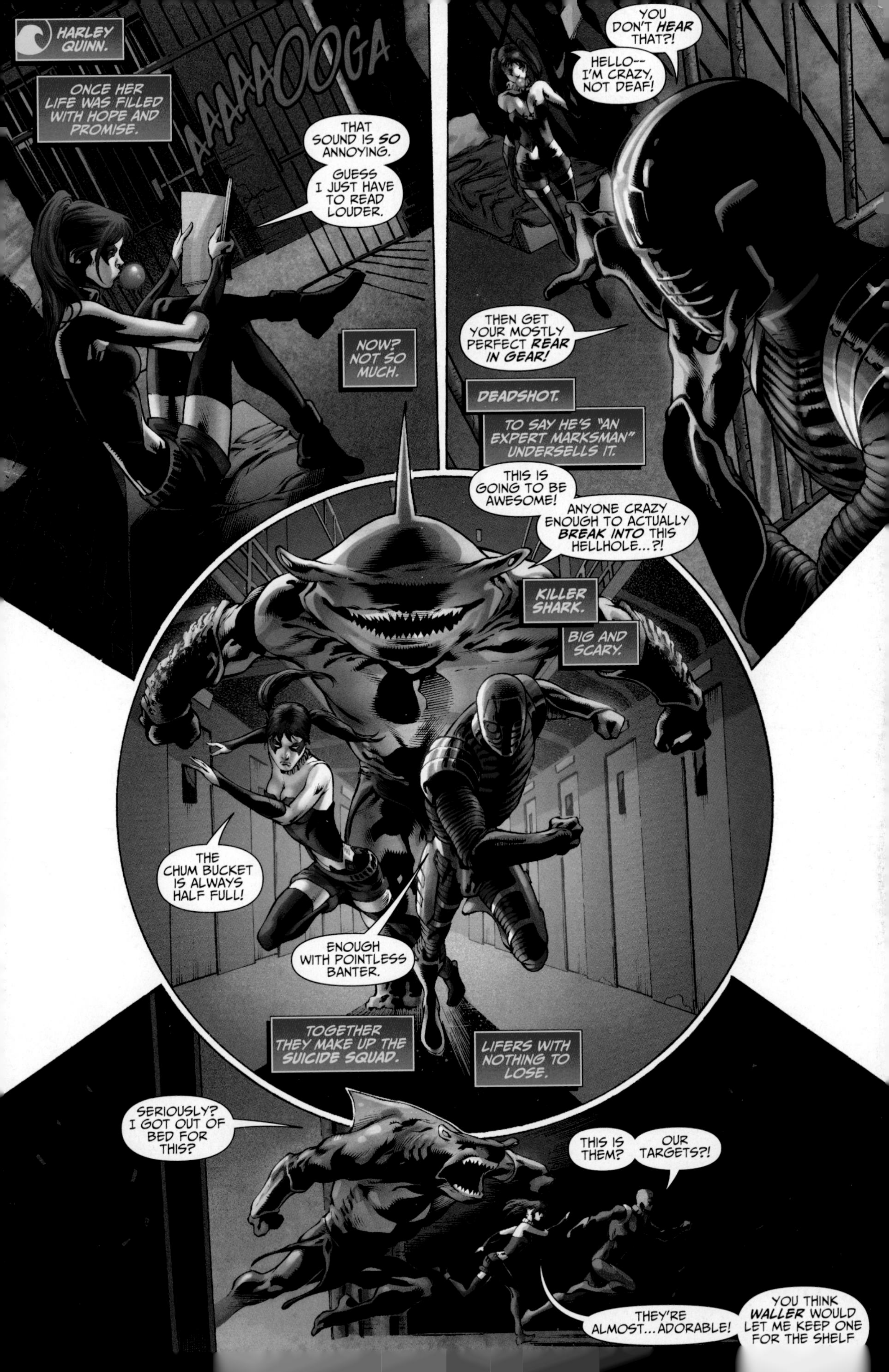
HARLEY QUINN.
ONCE HER LIFE WAS FILLED WITH HOPE AND PROMISE.
AAAAAOOGA
THAT SOUND IS SO ANNOYING.
GUESS I JUST HAVE TO READ LOUDER.
NOW? NOT SO MUCH.
YOU DON'T HEAR THAT?!
HELLO-- I'M CRAZY, NOT DEAF!
THEN GET YOUR MOSTLY PERFECT REAR IN GEAR!
DEADSHOT.
TO SAY HE'S "AN EXPERT MARKSMAN" UNDERSELLS IT.
THIS IS GOING TO BE AWESOME!
ANYONE CRAZY ENOUGH TO ACTUALLY BREAK INTO THIS HELLHOLE...?!
KILLER SHARK.
BIG AND SCARY.
THE CHUM BUCKET IS ALWAYS HALF FULL!
ENOUGH WITH POINTLESS BANTER.
TOGETHER THEY MAKE UP THE SUICIDE SQUAD.
LIFERS WITH NOTHING TO LOSE.
SERIOUSLY? I GOT OUT OF BED FOR THIS?
THIS IS THEM?
OUR TARGETS?!
THEY'RE ALMOST...ADORABLE!
YOU THINK WALLER WOULD LET ME KEEP ONE FOR THE SHELF

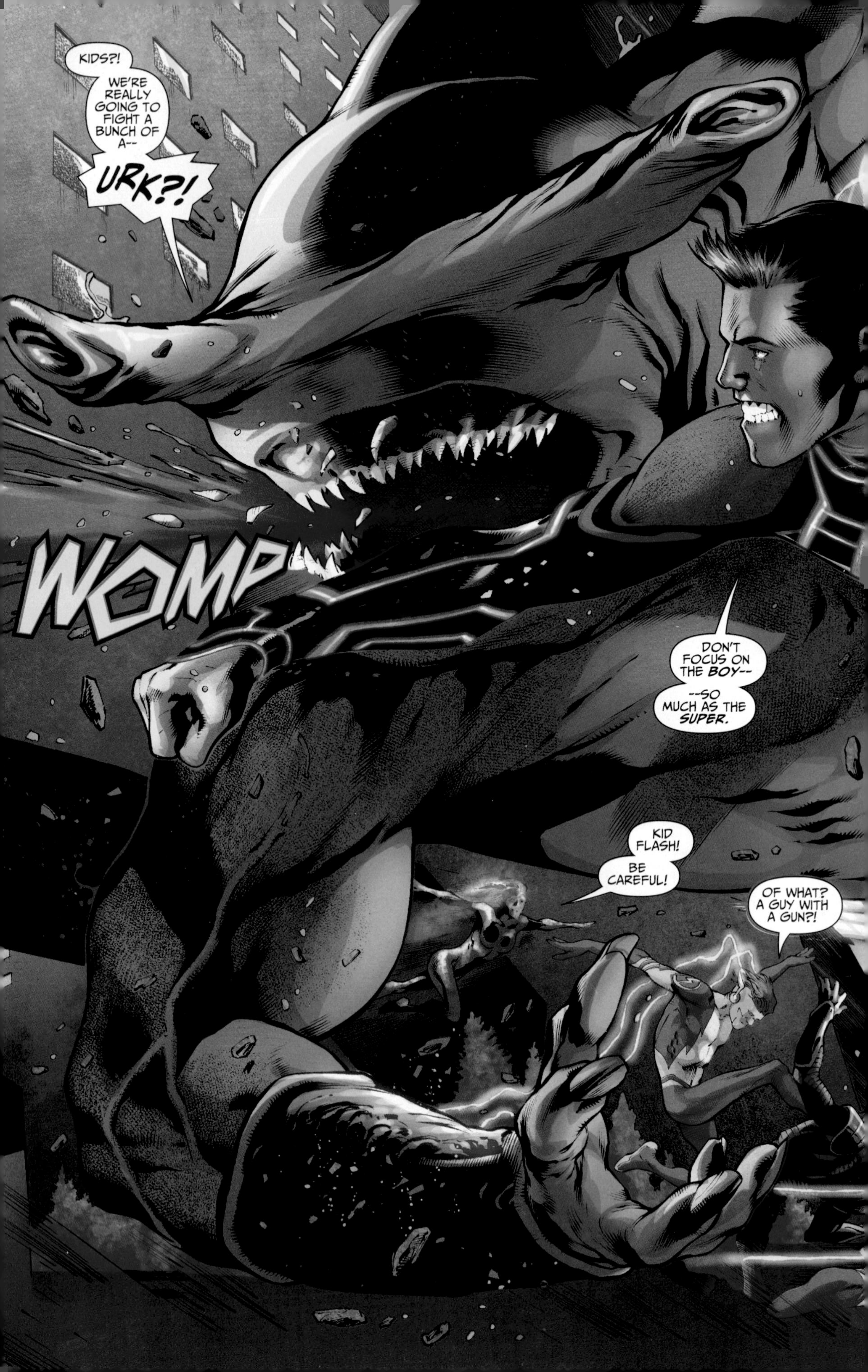
KIDS?!
WE'RE REALLY GOING TO FIGHT A BUNCH OF A--
URK?!
WOMP
DON'T FOCUS ON THE BOY--
--SO MUCH AS THE SUPER.
KID FLASH!
BE CAREFUL!
OF WHAT? A GUY WITH A GUN?!

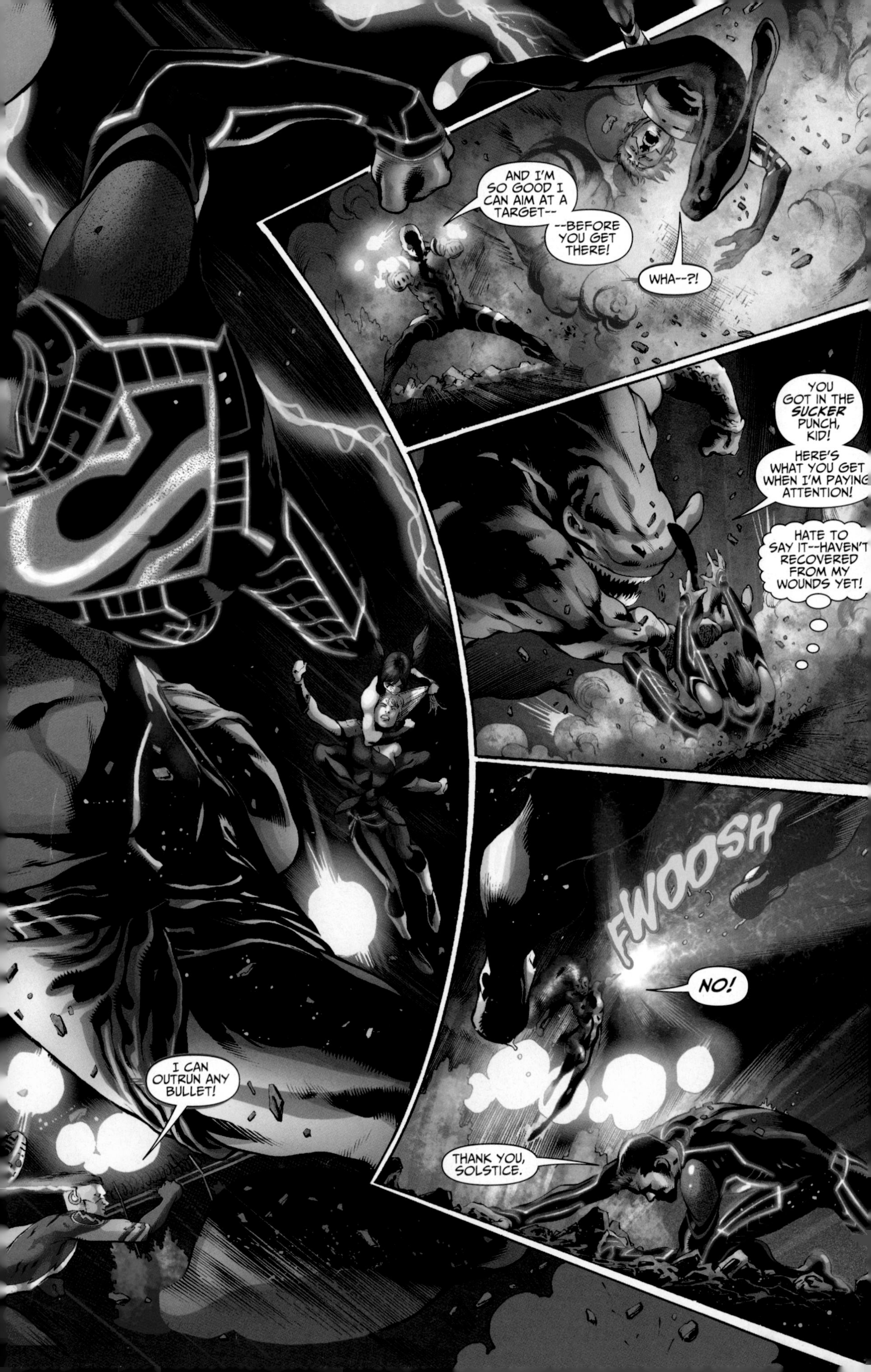
AND I'M SO GOOD I CAN AIM AT A TARGET--
--BEFORE YOU GET THERE!
WHA--?!
YOU GOT IN THE SUCKER PUNCH, KID!
HERE'S WHAT YOU GET WHEN I'M PAYING ATTENTION!
HATE TO SAY IT--HAVEN'T RECOVERED FROM MY WOUNDS YET!
I CAN OUTRUN ANY BULLET!
FWOOSH
NO!
THANK YOU, SOLSTICE.

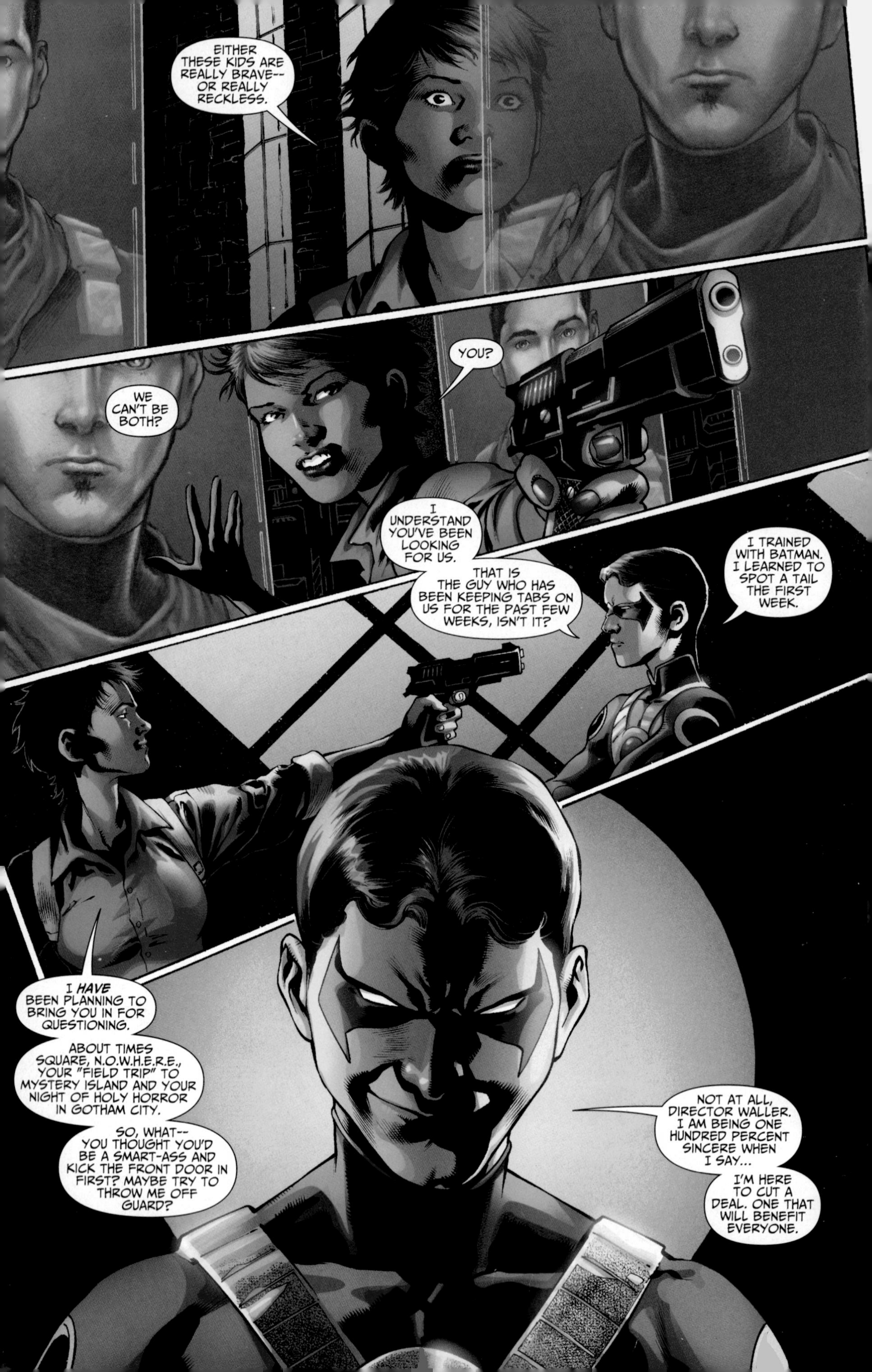
EITHER THESE KIDS ARE REALLY BRAVE-- OR REALLY RECKLESS.
WE CAN'T BE BOTH?
YOU?
I UNDERSTAND YOU'VE BEEN LOOKING FOR US.
THAT IS THE GUY WHO HAS BEEN KEEPING TABS ON US FOR THE PAST FEW WEEKS, ISN'T IT?
I TRAINED WITH BATMAN. I LEARNED TO SPOT A TAIL THE FIRST WEEK.
I HAVE BEEN PLANNING TO BRING YOU IN FOR QUESTIONING.
ABOUT TIMES SQUARE, N.O.W.H.E.R.E., YOUR "FIELD TRIP" TO MYSTERY ISLAND AND YOUR NIGHT OF HOLY HORROR IN GOTHAM CITY.
SO, WHAT-- YOU THOUGHT YOU'D BE A SMART-ASS AND KICK THE FRONT DOOR IN FIRST? MAYBE TRY TO THROW ME OFF GUARD?
NOT AT ALL, DIRECTOR WALLER. I AM BEING ONE HUNDRED PERCENT SINCERE WHEN I SAY...
I'M HERE TO CUT A DEAL. ONE THAT WILL BENEFIT EVERYONE.

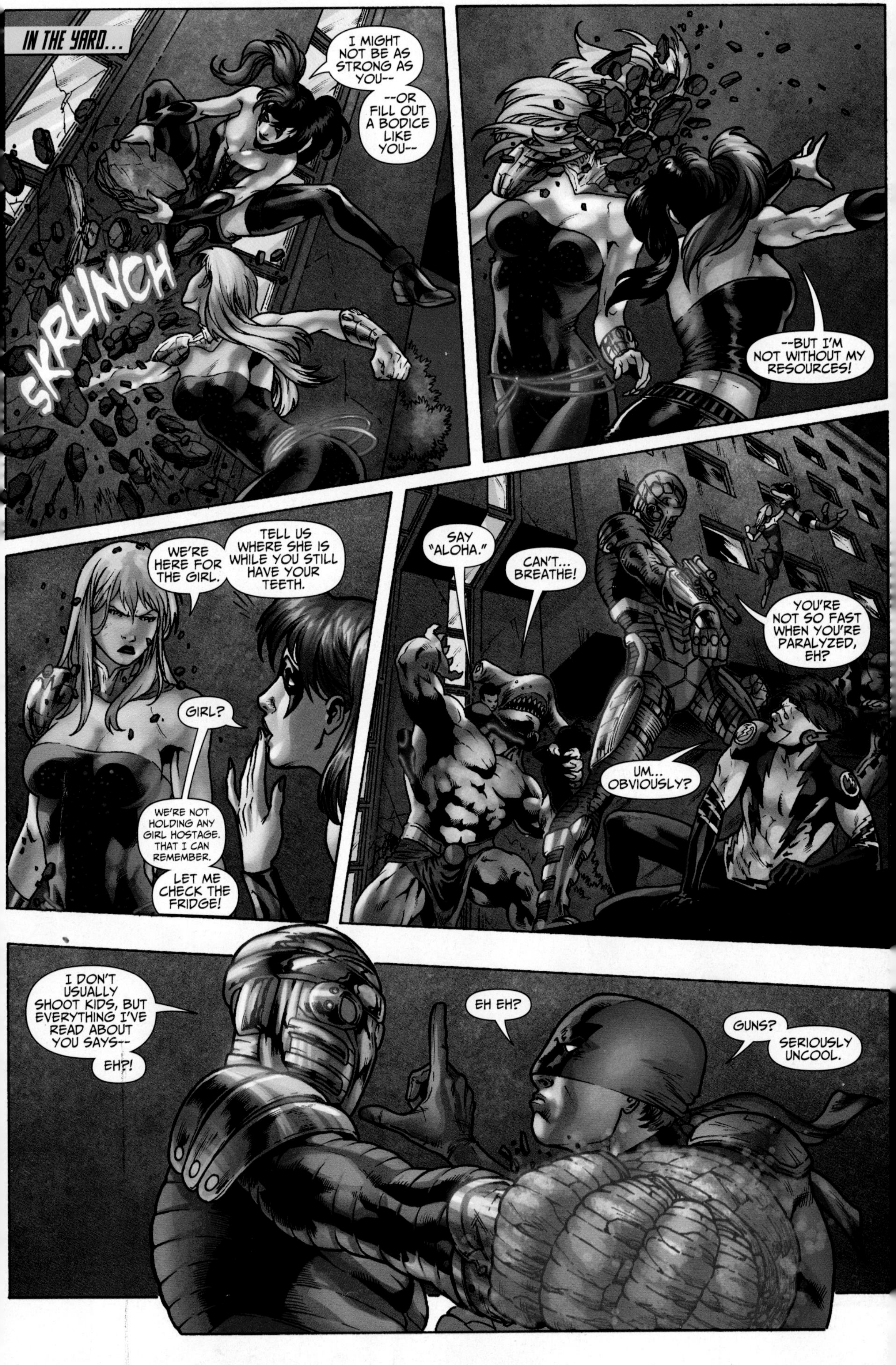
IN THE YARD...
I MIGHT NOT BE AS STRONG AS YOU--
--OR FILL OUT A BODICE LIKE YOU--
SKRUNCH
--BUT I'M NOT WITHOUT MY RESOURCES!
WE'RE HERE FOR THE GIRL.
TELL US WHERE SHE IS WHILE YOU STILL HAVE YOUR TEETH.
GIRL?
WE'RE NOT HOLDING ANY GIRL HOSTAGE. THAT I CAN REMEMBER.
LET ME CHECK THE FRIDGE!
SAY "ALOHA."
CAN'T... BREATHE!
YOU'RE NOT SO FAST WHEN YOU'RE PARALYZED, EH?
UM... OBVIOUSLY?
I DON'T USUALLY SHOOT KIDS, BUT EVERYTHING I'VE READ ABOUT YOU SAYS--
EH?!
EH EH?
GUNS? SERIOUSLY UNCOOL.

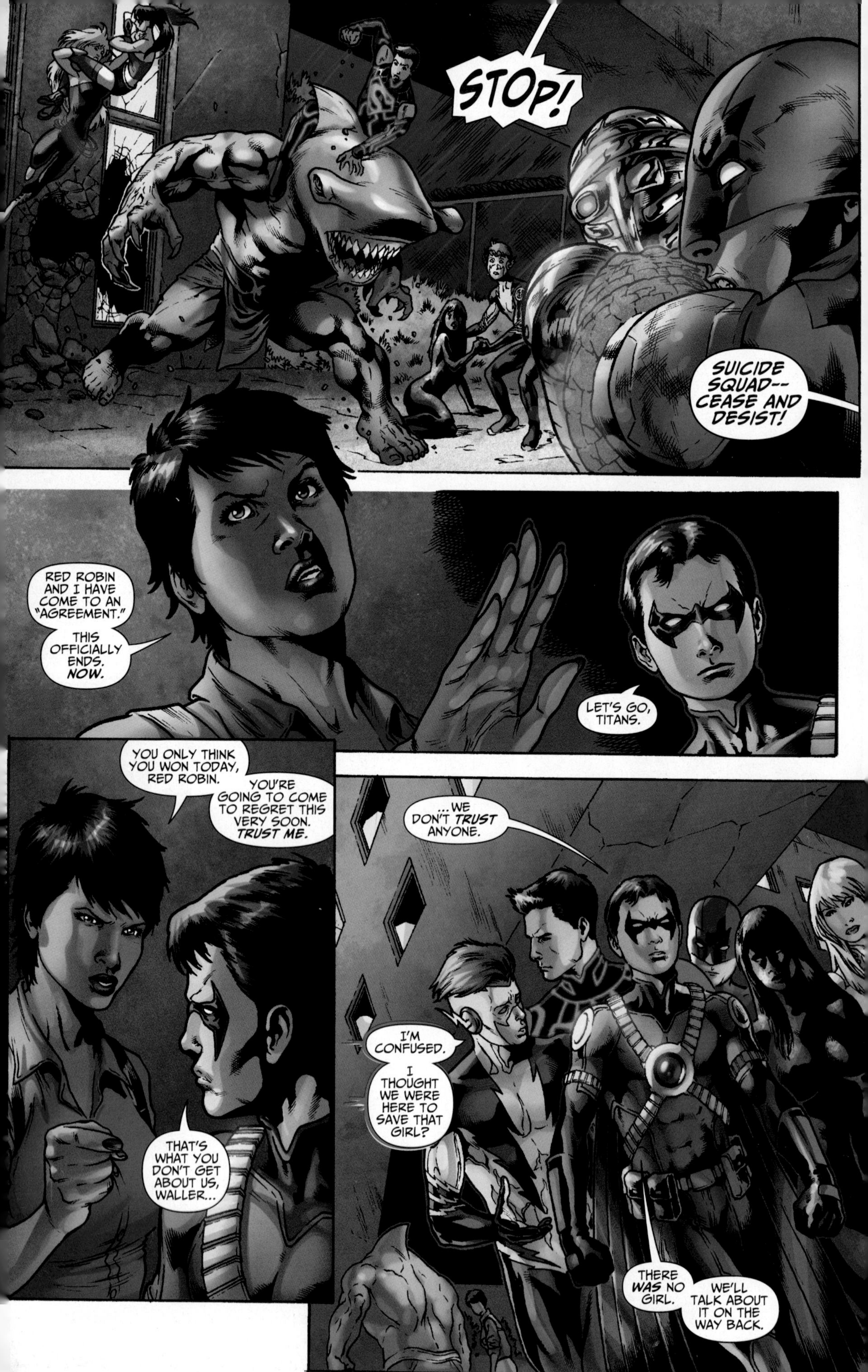
STOP!
SUICIDE SQUAD-- CEASE AND DESIST!
RED ROBIN AND I HAVE COME TO AN "AGREEMENT."
THIS OFFICIALLY ENDS. NOW.
LET'S GO, TITANS.
YOU ONLY THINK YOU WON TODAY, RED ROBIN.
YOU'RE GOING TO COME TO REGRET THIS VERY SOON. TRUST ME.
THAT'S WHAT YOU DON'T GET ABOUT US, WALLER...
...WE DON'T TRUST ANYONE.
I'M CONFUSED.
I THOUGHT WE WERE HERE TO SAVE THAT GIRL?
THERE WAS NO GIRL.
WE'LL TALK ABOUT IT ON THE WAY BACK.

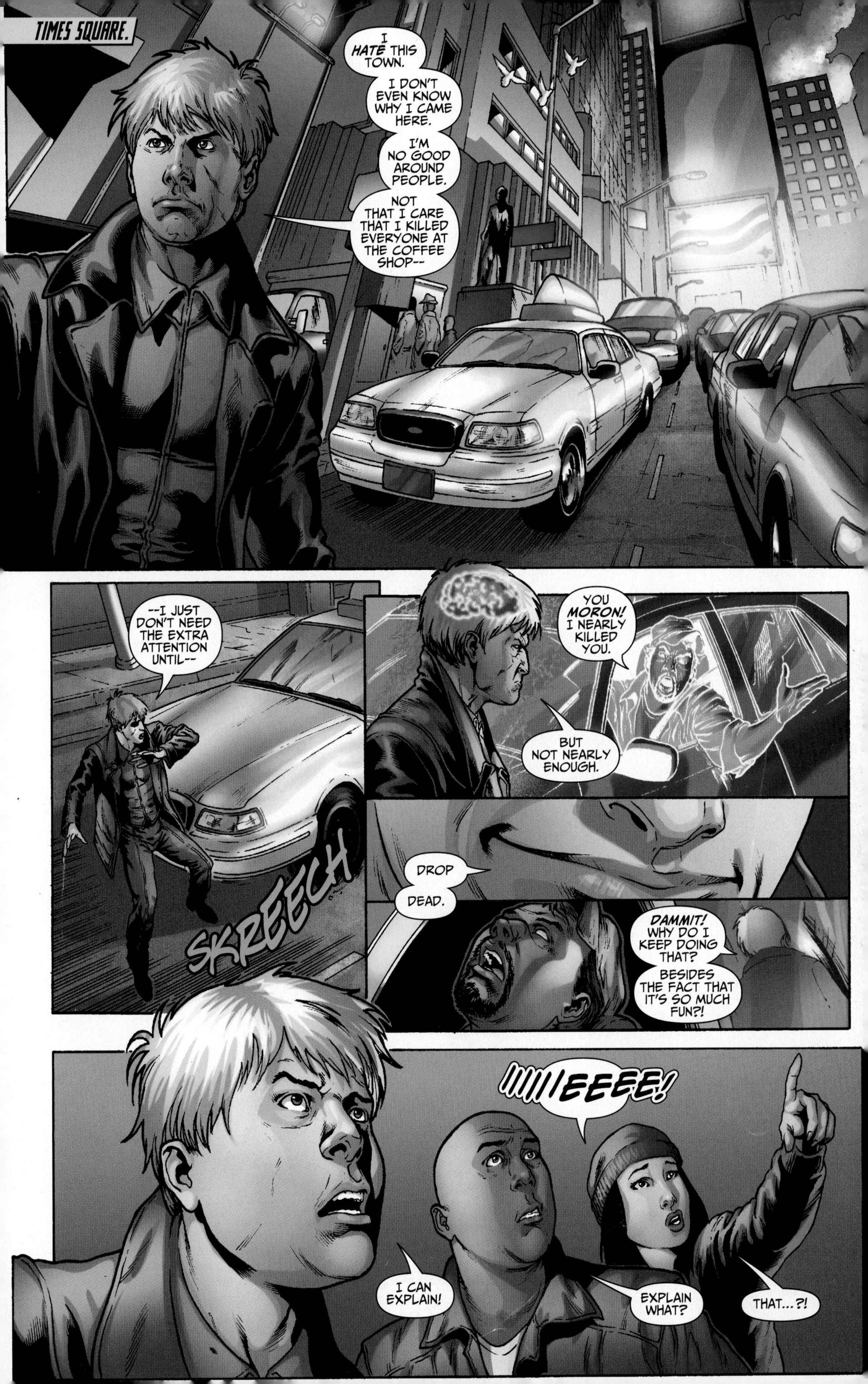
TIMES SQUARE.
I *HATE* THIS TOWN.
I DON'T EVEN KNOW WHY I CAME HERE.
I'M NO GOOD AROUND PEOPLE.
NOT THAT I CARE THAT I KILLED EVERYONE AT THE COFFEE SHOP--
--I JUST DON'T NEED THE EXTRA ATTENTION UNTIL--
SKREECH
YOU *MORON!* I NEARLY KILLED YOU.
BUT NOT NEARLY ENOUGH.
DROP
DEAD.
DAMMIT! WHY DO I KEEP DOING THAT?
BESIDES THE FACT THAT IT'S SO MUCH FUN?!
IIIIIIEEEEE!
I CAN EXPLAIN!
EXPLAIN WHAT?
THAT...?!

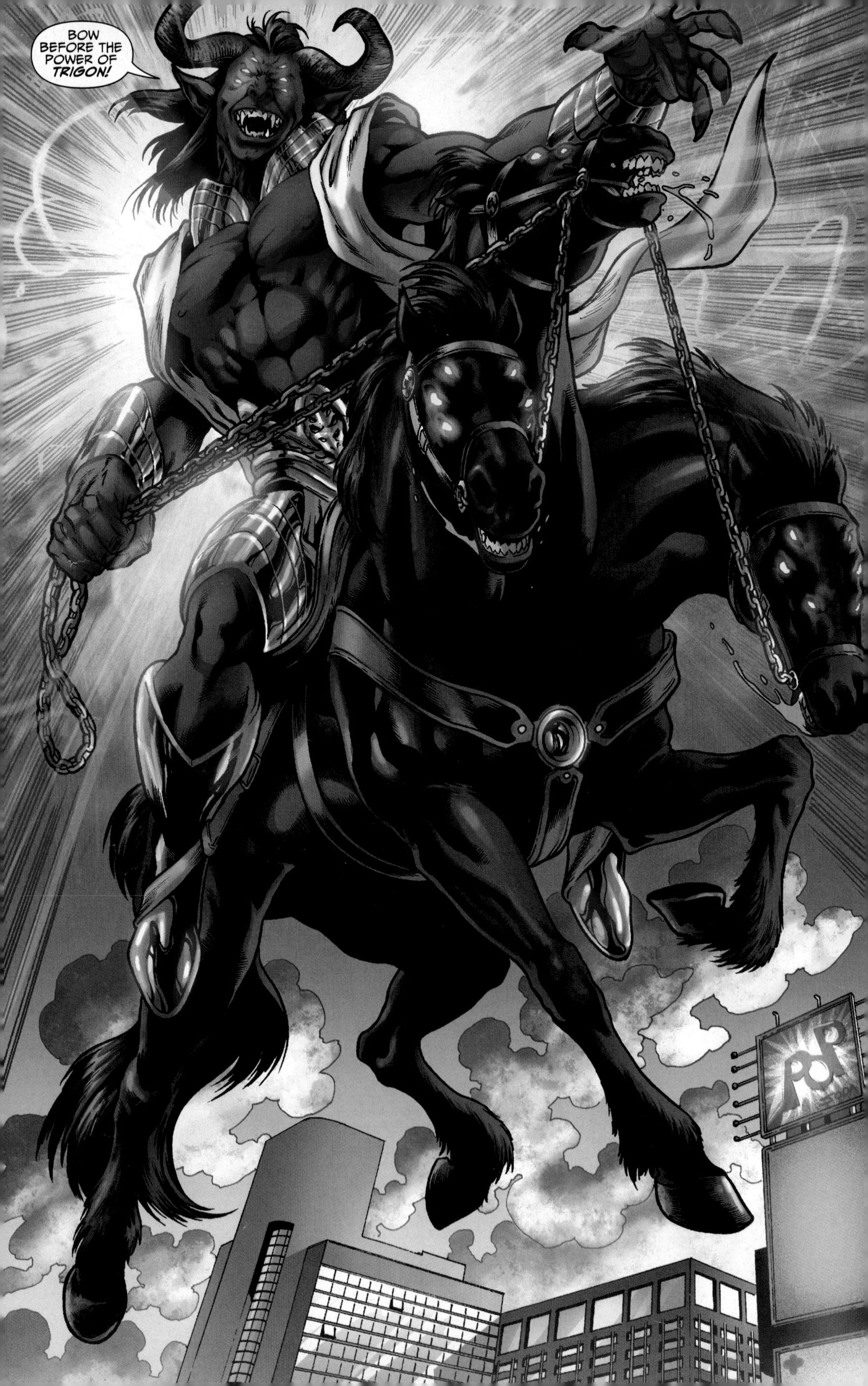
BOW BEFORE THE POWER OF TRIGON!

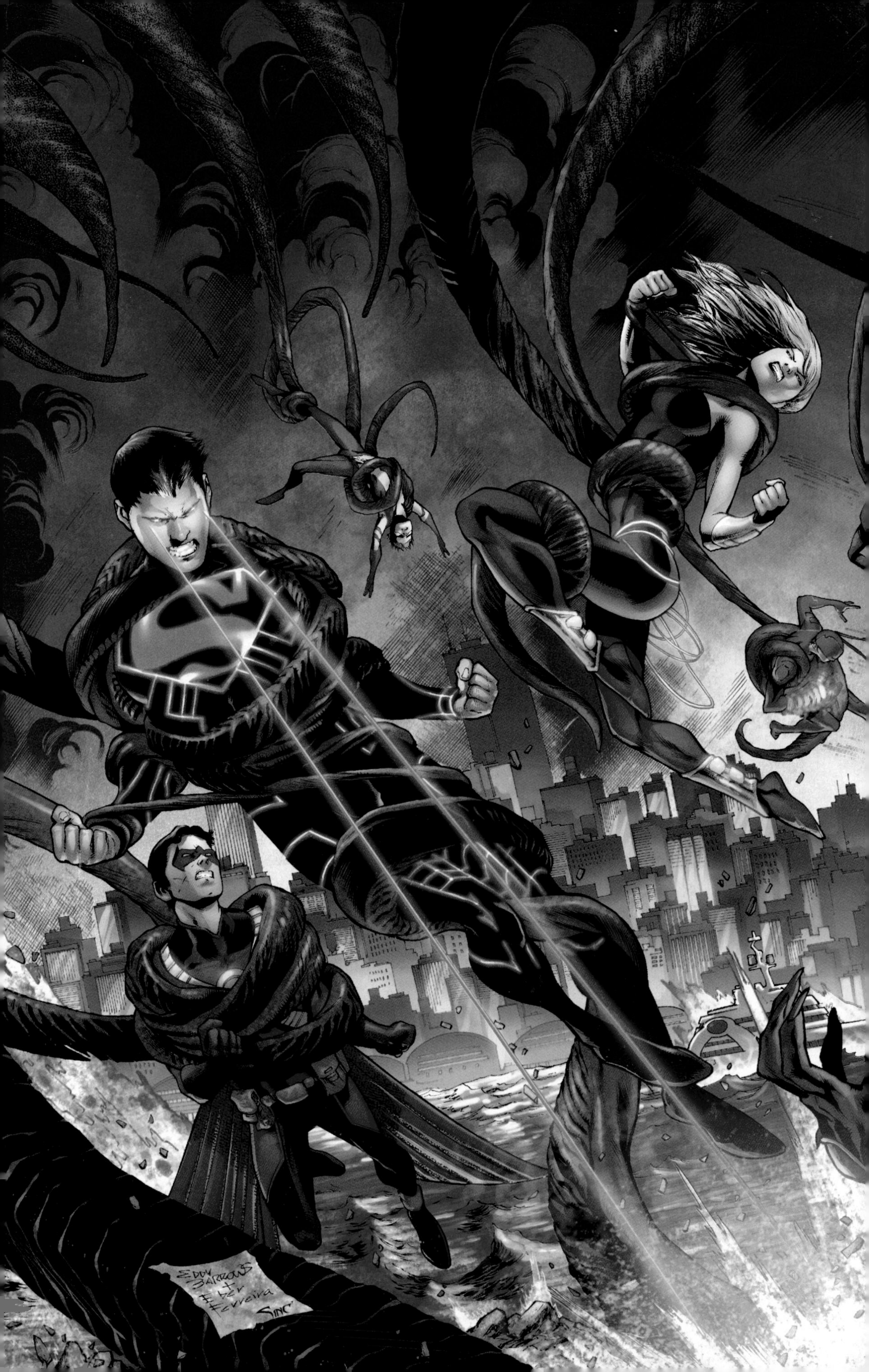
EDDY BARROWS + Eber Ferreira
SINC'

TRIGON-OMETRY

SCOTT LOBDELL & TONY BEDARD writers EDDY BARROWS penciller EBER FERREIRA inker
cover art by EDDY BARROWS, EBER FERRIERA & ALEX SINCLAIR

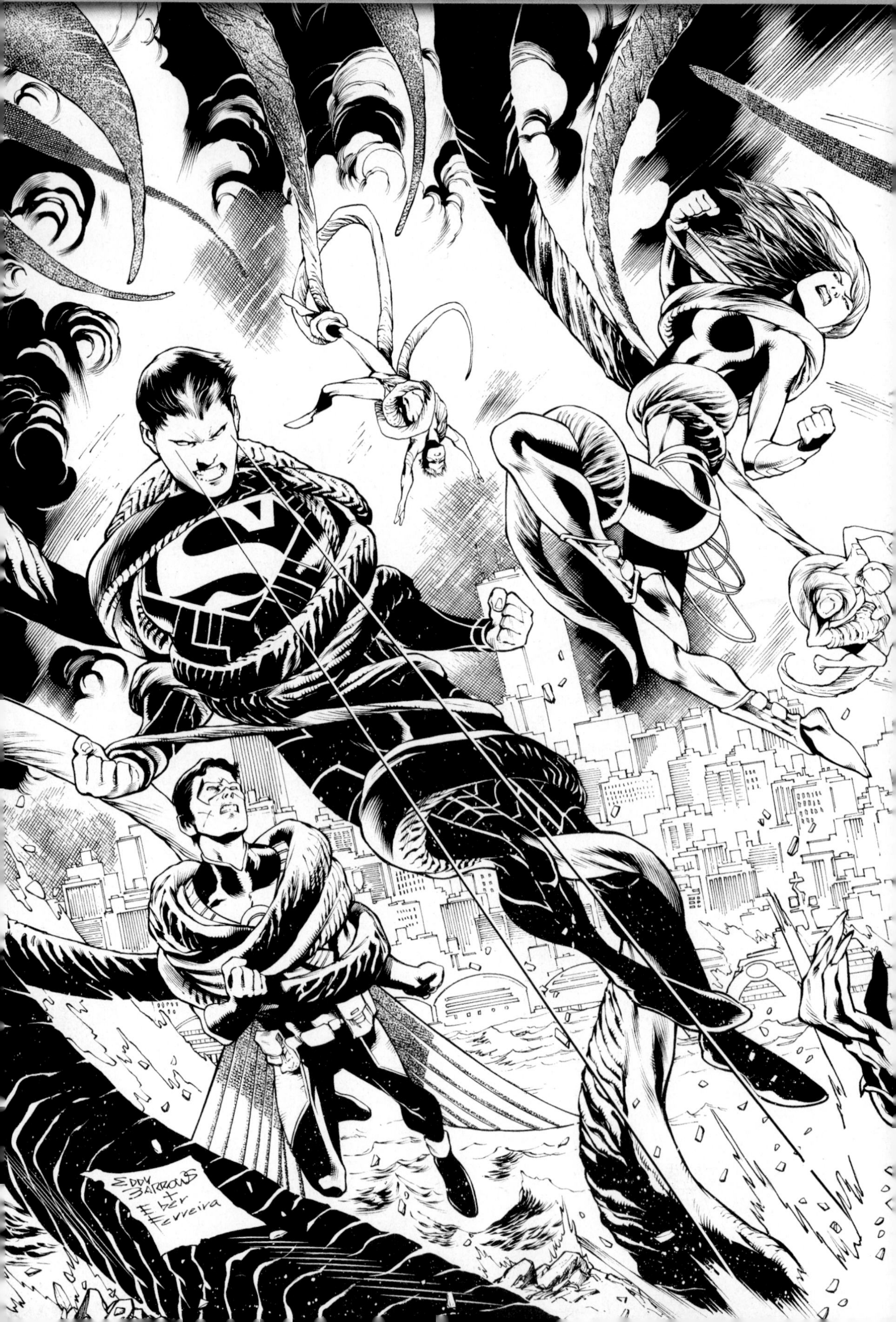
EDDY BARROWS + Eber Ferreira

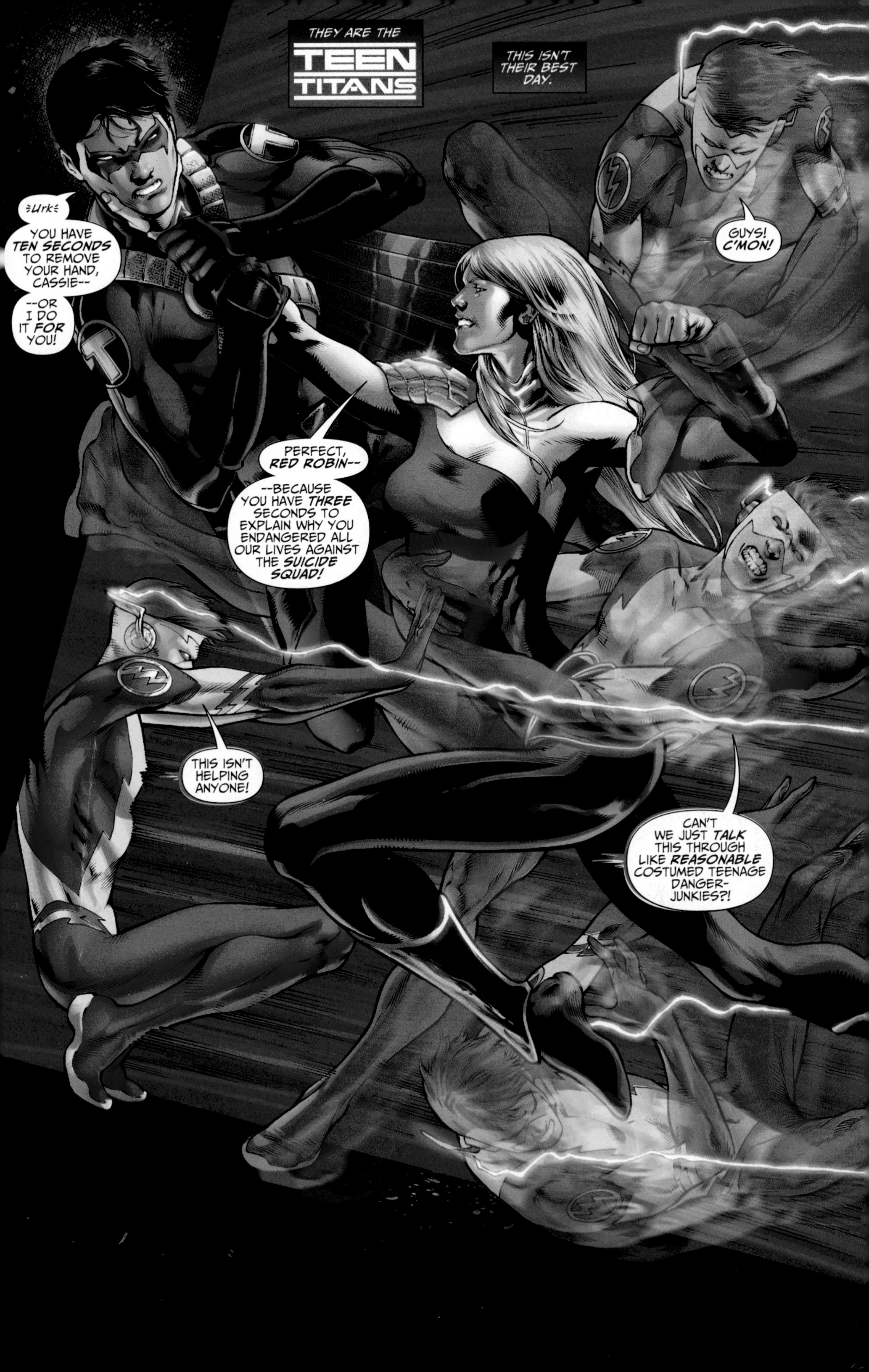
THEY ARE THE
TEEN TITANS
THIS ISN'T THEIR BEST DAY.
Urk
YOU HAVE TEN SECONDS TO REMOVE YOUR HAND, CASSIE--
--OR I DO IT FOR YOU!
GUYS! C'MON!
PERFECT, RED ROBIN--
--BECAUSE YOU HAVE THREE SECONDS TO EXPLAIN WHY YOU ENDANGERED ALL OUR LIVES AGAINST THE SUICIDE SQUAD!
THIS ISN'T HELPING ANYONE!
CAN'T WE JUST TALK THIS THROUGH LIKE REASONABLE COSTUMED TEENAGE DANGER-JUNKIES?!

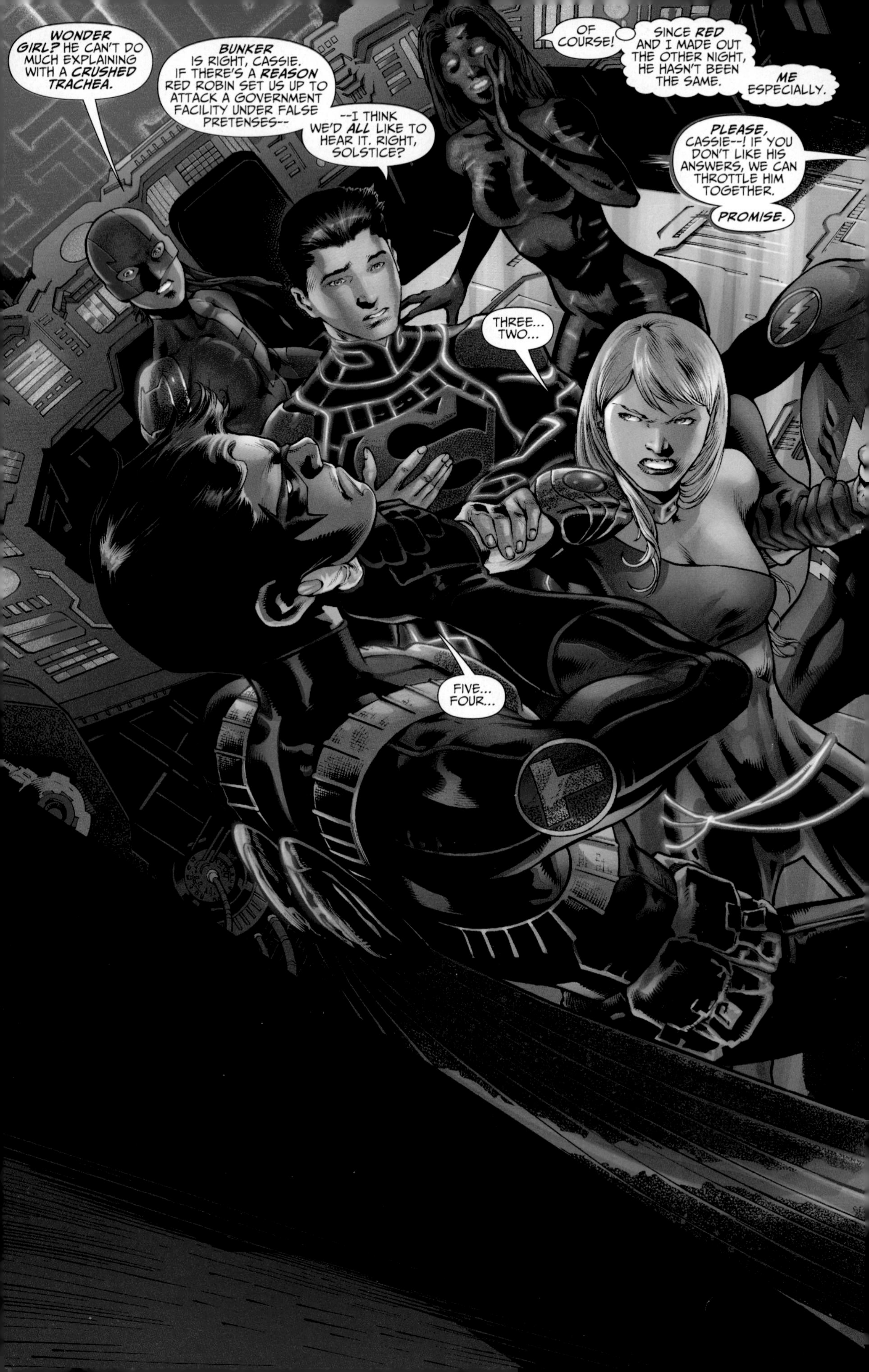
WONDER GIRL? HE CAN'T DO MUCH EXPLAINING WITH A CRUSHED TRACHEA.
BUNKER IS RIGHT, CASSIE. IF THERE'S A REASON RED ROBIN SET US UP TO ATTACK A GOVERNMENT FACILITY UNDER FALSE PRETENSES--
--I THINK WE'D ALL LIKE TO HEAR IT. RIGHT, SOLSTICE?
OF COURSE!
SINCE RED AND I MADE OUT THE OTHER NIGHT, HE HASN'T BEEN THE SAME.
ME ESPECIALLY.
PLEASE, CASSIE--! IF YOU DON'T LIKE HIS ANSWERS, WE CAN THROTTLE HIM TOGETHER.
PROMISE.
THREE... TWO...
FIVE... FOUR...

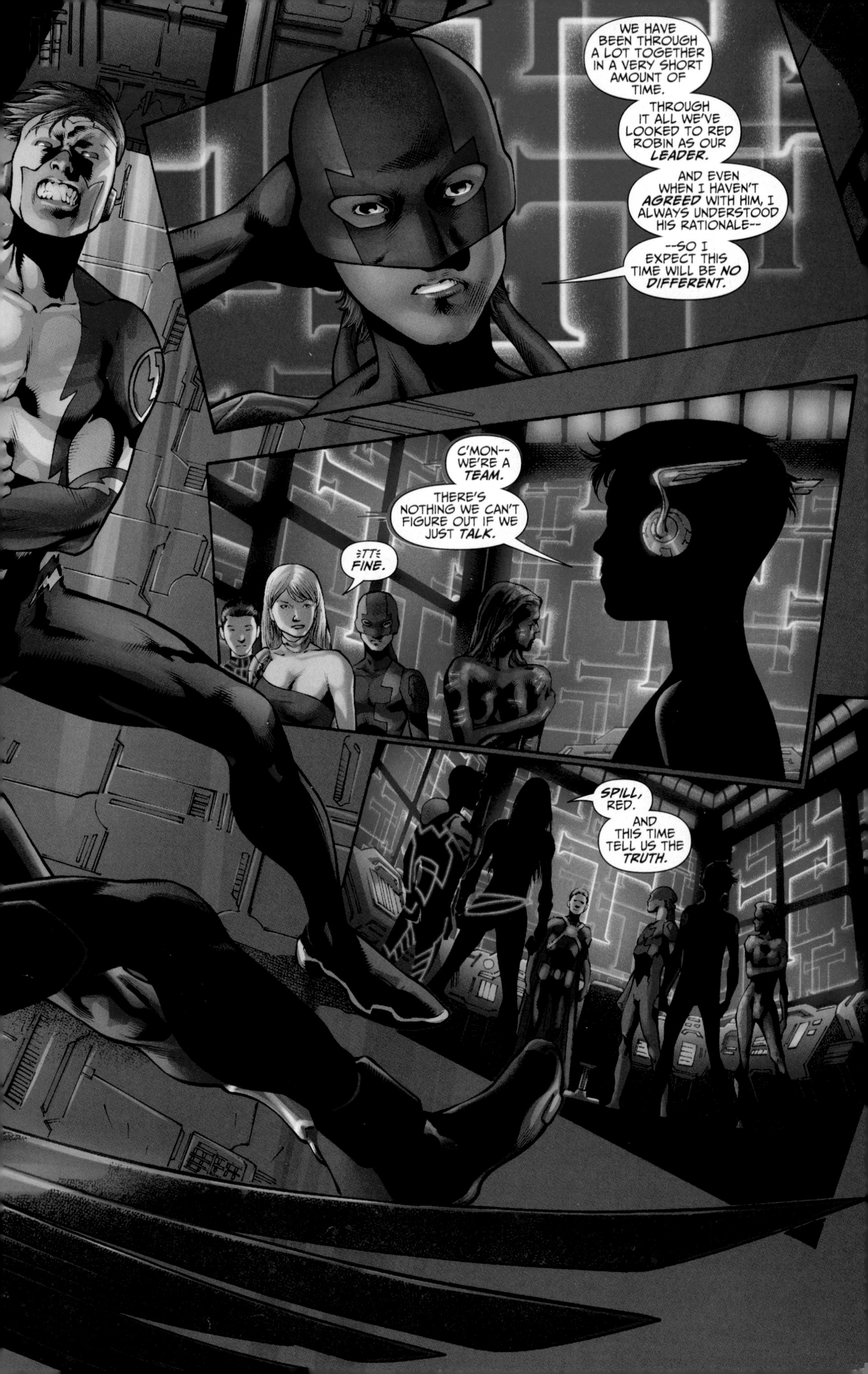
WE HAVE BEEN THROUGH A LOT TOGETHER IN A VERY SHORT AMOUNT OF TIME.
THROUGH IT ALL WE'VE LOOKED TO RED ROBIN AS OUR LEADER.
AND EVEN WHEN I HAVEN'T AGREED WITH HIM, I ALWAYS UNDERSTOOD HIS RATIONALE--
--SO I EXPECT THIS TIME WILL BE NO DIFFERENT.
C'MON-- WE'RE A TEAM.
THERE'S NOTHING WE CAN'T FIGURE OUT IF WE JUST TALK.
TT FINE.
SPILL, RED.
AND THIS TIME TELL US THE TRUTH.

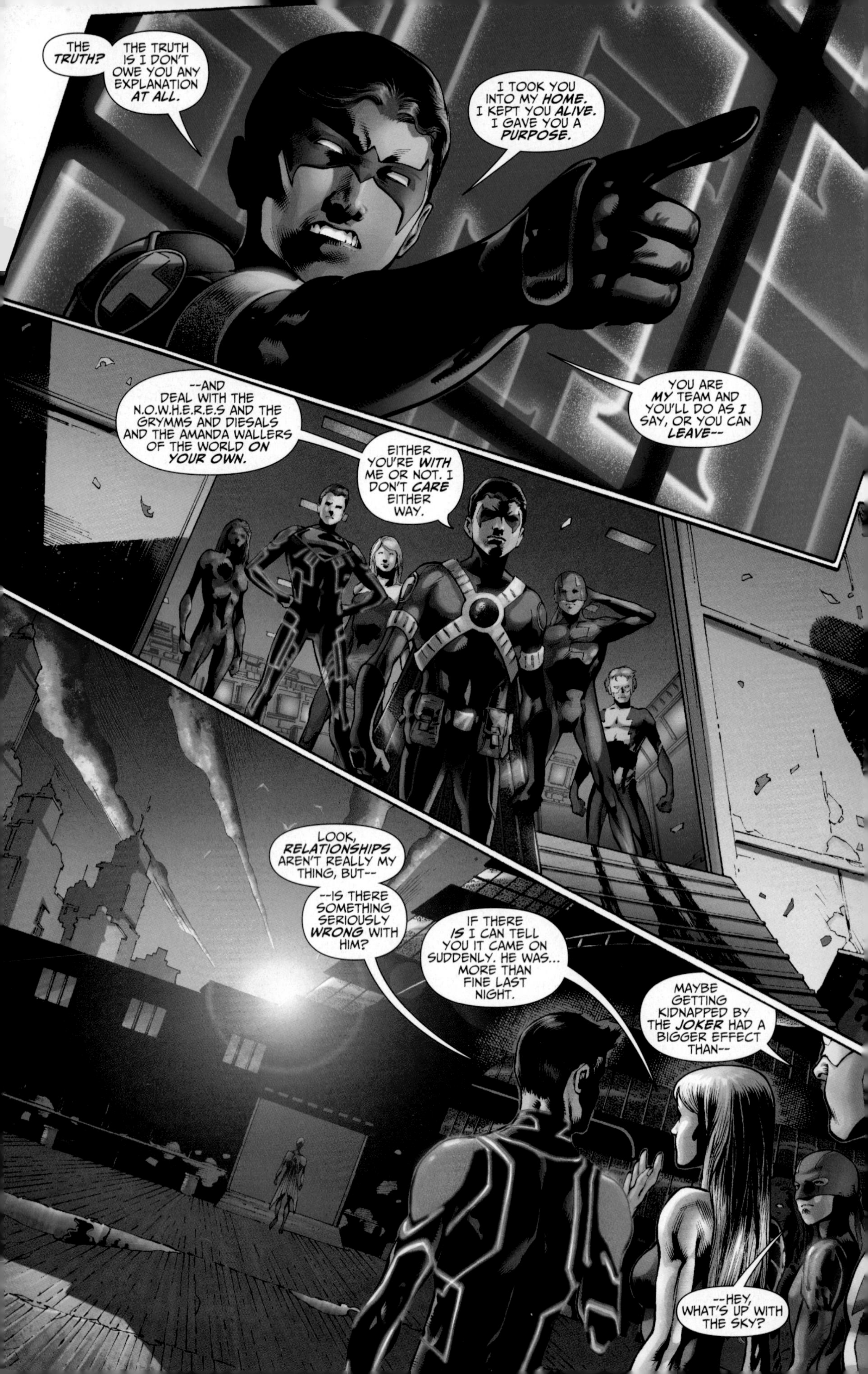
THE TRUTH?
THE TRUTH IS I DON'T OWE YOU ANY EXPLANATION AT ALL.
I TOOK YOU INTO MY HOME. I KEPT YOU ALIVE. I GAVE YOU A PURPOSE.
YOU ARE MY TEAM AND YOU'LL DO AS I SAY, OR YOU CAN LEAVE--
--AND DEAL WITH THE N.O.W.H.E.R.E.S AND THE GRYMMS AND DIESALS AND THE AMANDA WALLERS OF THE WORLD ON YOUR OWN.
EITHER YOU'RE WITH ME OR NOT. I DON'T CARE EITHER WAY.
LOOK, RELATIONSHIPS AREN'T REALLY MY THING, BUT--
--IS THERE SOMETHING SERIOUSLY WRONG WITH HIM?
IF THERE IS I CAN TELL YOU IT CAME ON SUDDENLY. HE WAS... MORE THAN FINE LAST NIGHT.
MAYBE GETTING KIDNAPPED BY THE JOKER HAD A BIGGER EFFECT THAN--
--HEY, WHAT'S UP WITH THE SKY?

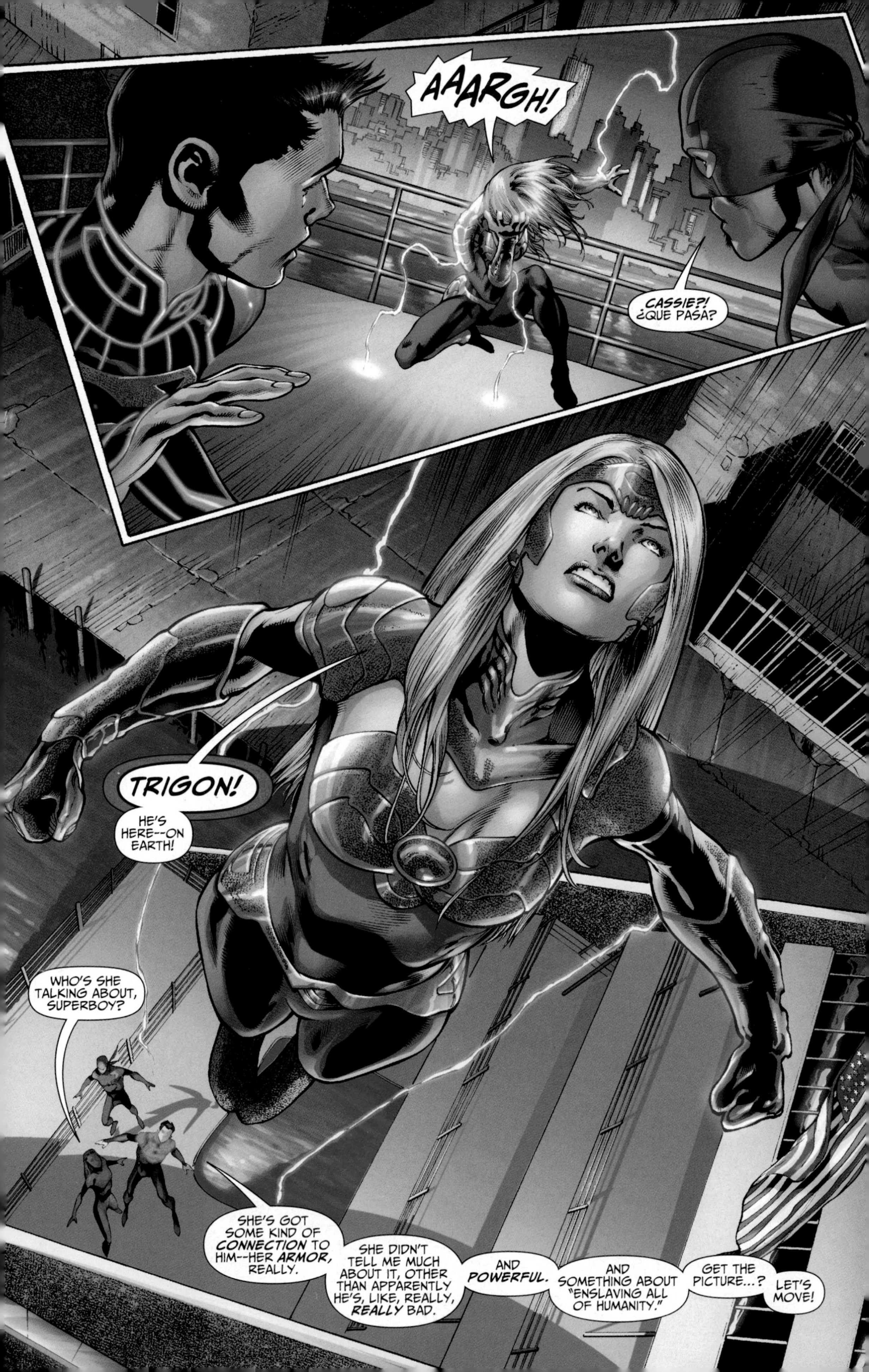
AAARGH!
CASSIE?! ¿QUE PASA?
TRIGON!
HE'S HERE--ON EARTH!
WHO'S SHE TALKING ABOUT, SUPERBOY?
SHE'S GOT SOME KIND OF CONNECTION TO HIM--HER ARMOR, REALLY.
SHE DIDN'T TELL ME MUCH ABOUT IT, OTHER THAN APPARENTLY HE'S, LIKE, REALLY, REALLY BAD.
AND POWERFUL.
AND SOMETHING ABOUT "ENSLAVING ALL OF HUMANITY."
GET THE PICTURE...?
LET'S MOVE!

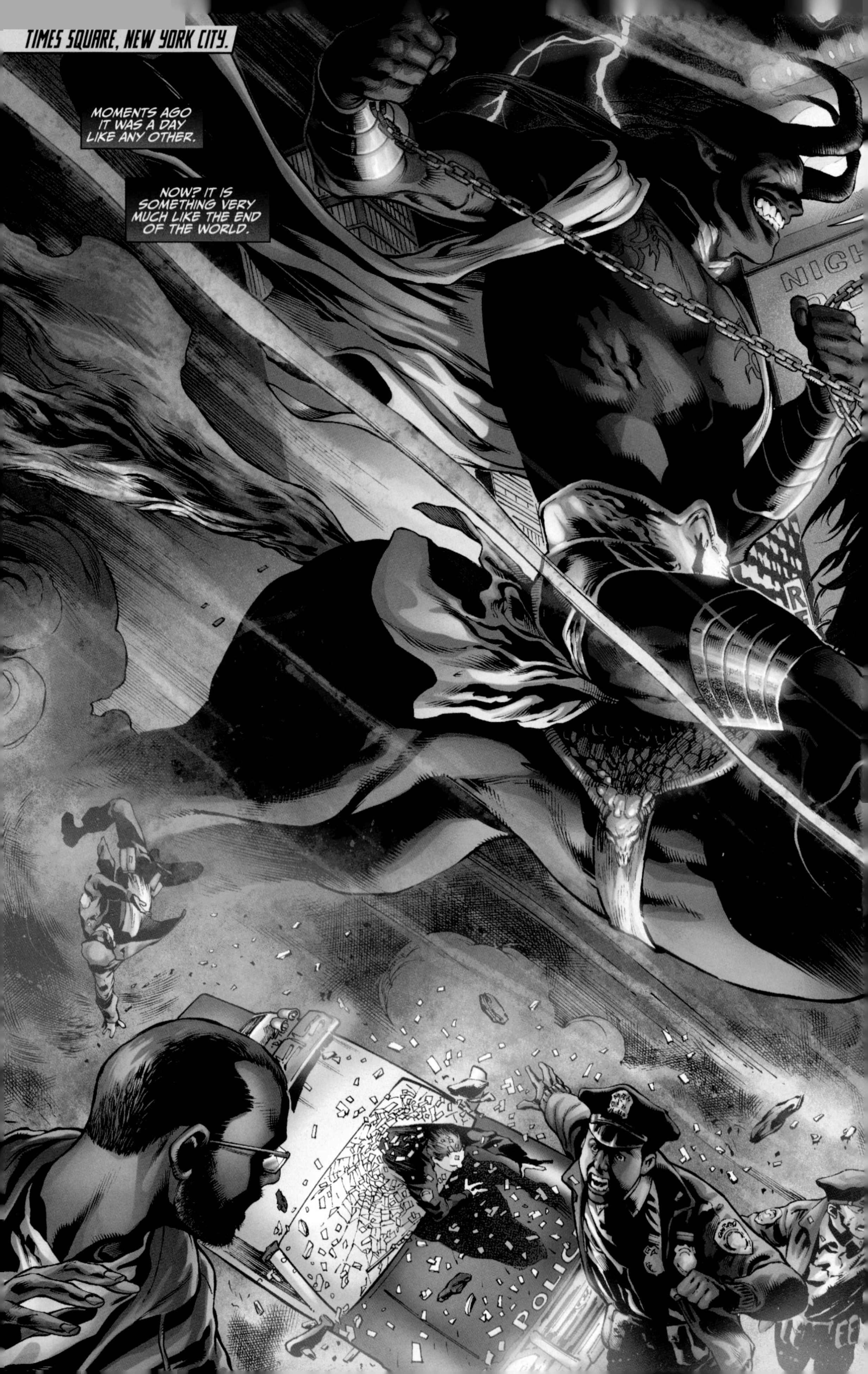
TIMES SQUARE, NEW YORK CITY.
MOMENTS AGO IT WAS A DAY LIKE ANY OTHER.
NOW? IT IS SOMETHING VERY MUCH LIKE THE END OF THE WORLD.
POLICE

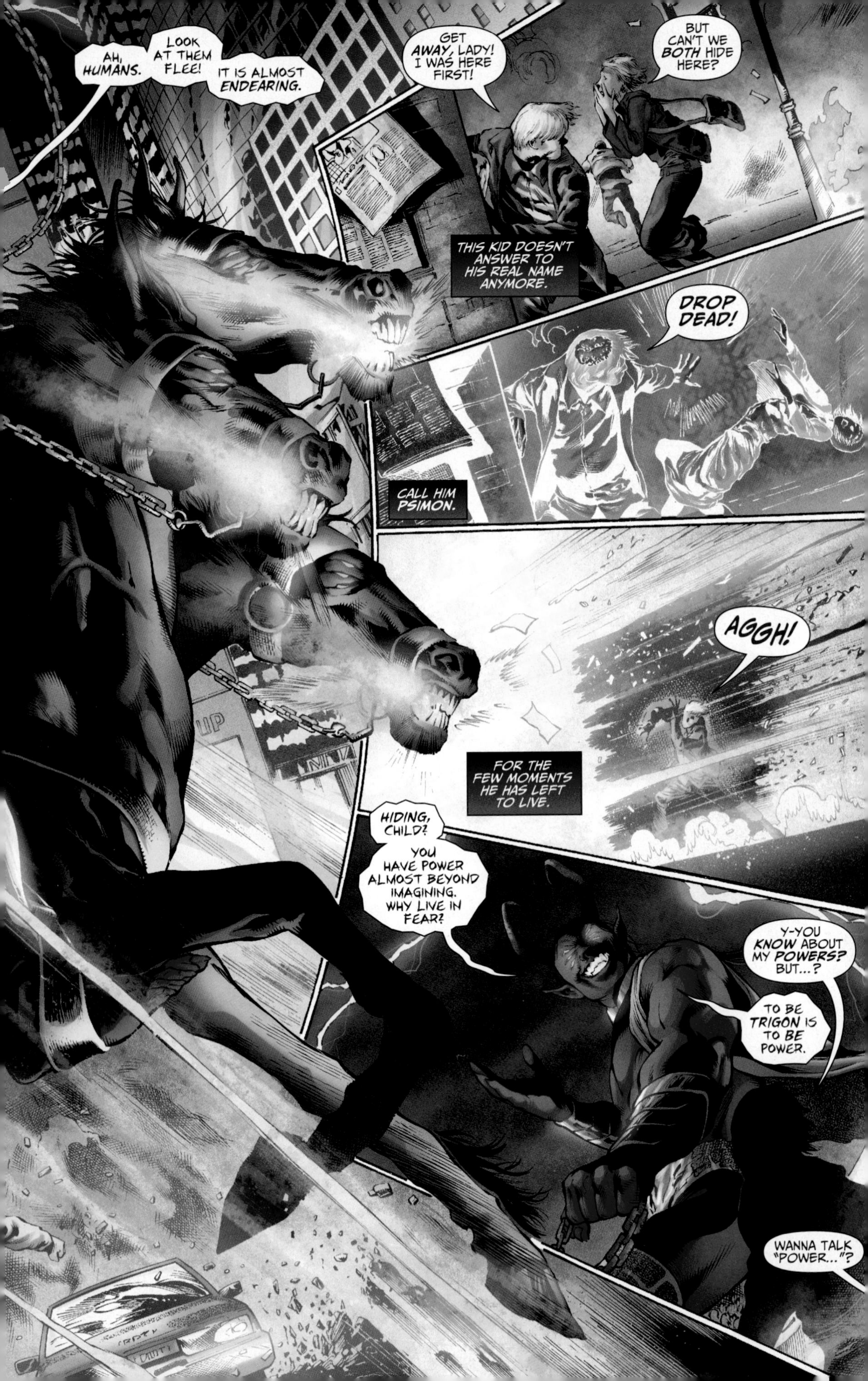
AH, HUMANS.
LOOK AT THEM FLEE!
IT IS ALMOST ENDEARING.
GET AWAY, LADY! I WAS HERE FIRST!
BUT CAN'T WE BOTH HIDE HERE?
THIS KID DOESN'T ANSWER TO HIS REAL NAME ANYMORE.
DROP DEAD!
CALL HIM PSIMON.
AGGH!
FOR THE FEW MOMENTS HE HAS LEFT TO LIVE.
HIDING, CHILD?
YOU HAVE POWER ALMOST BEYOND IMAGINING. WHY LIVE IN FEAR?
Y-YOU KNOW ABOUT MY POWERS? BUT...?
TO BE TRIGON IS TO BE POWER.
WANNA TALK "POWER..."?

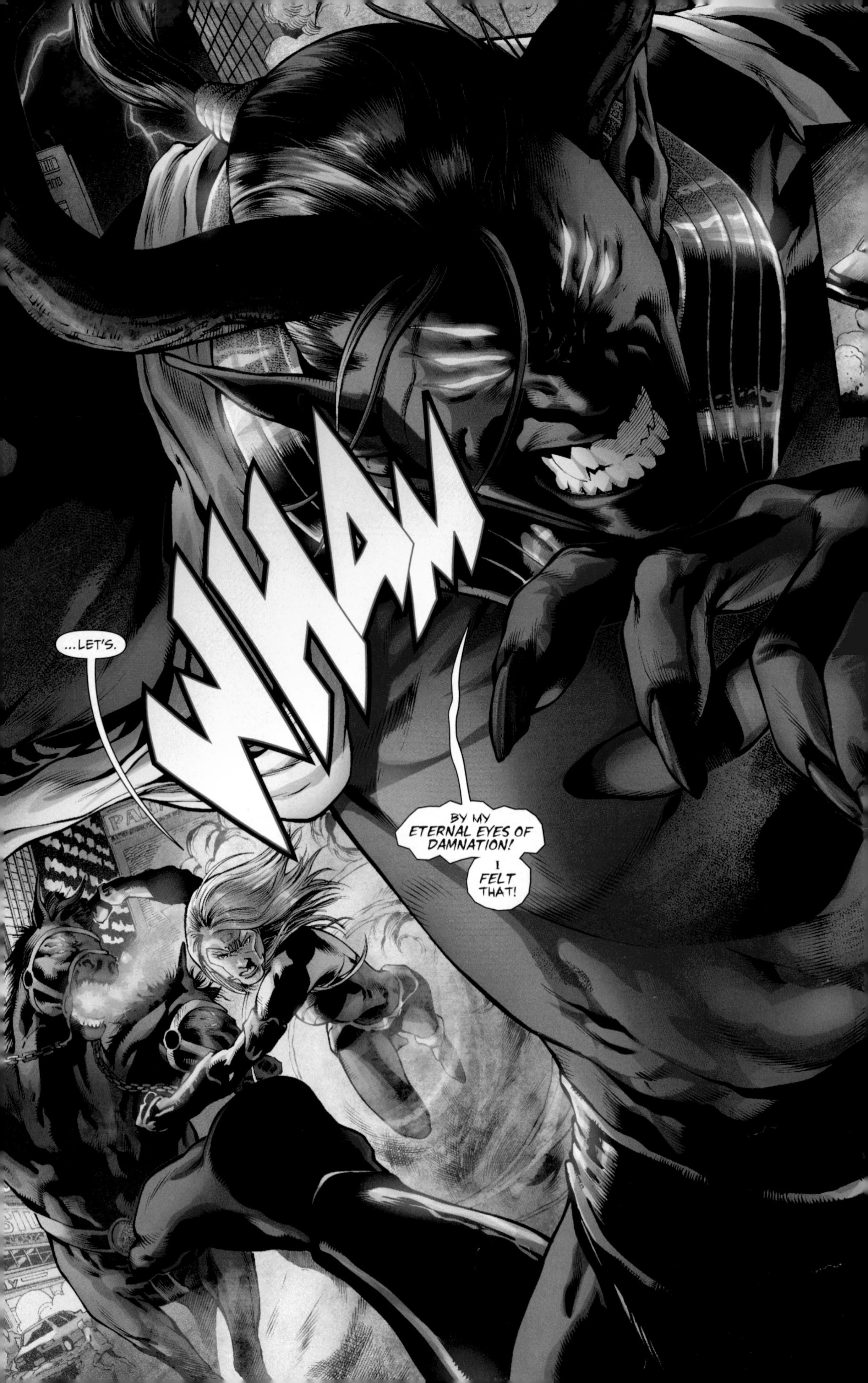

...LET'S.
WHAM
BY MY ETERNAL EYES OF DAMNATION!
I FELT THAT!

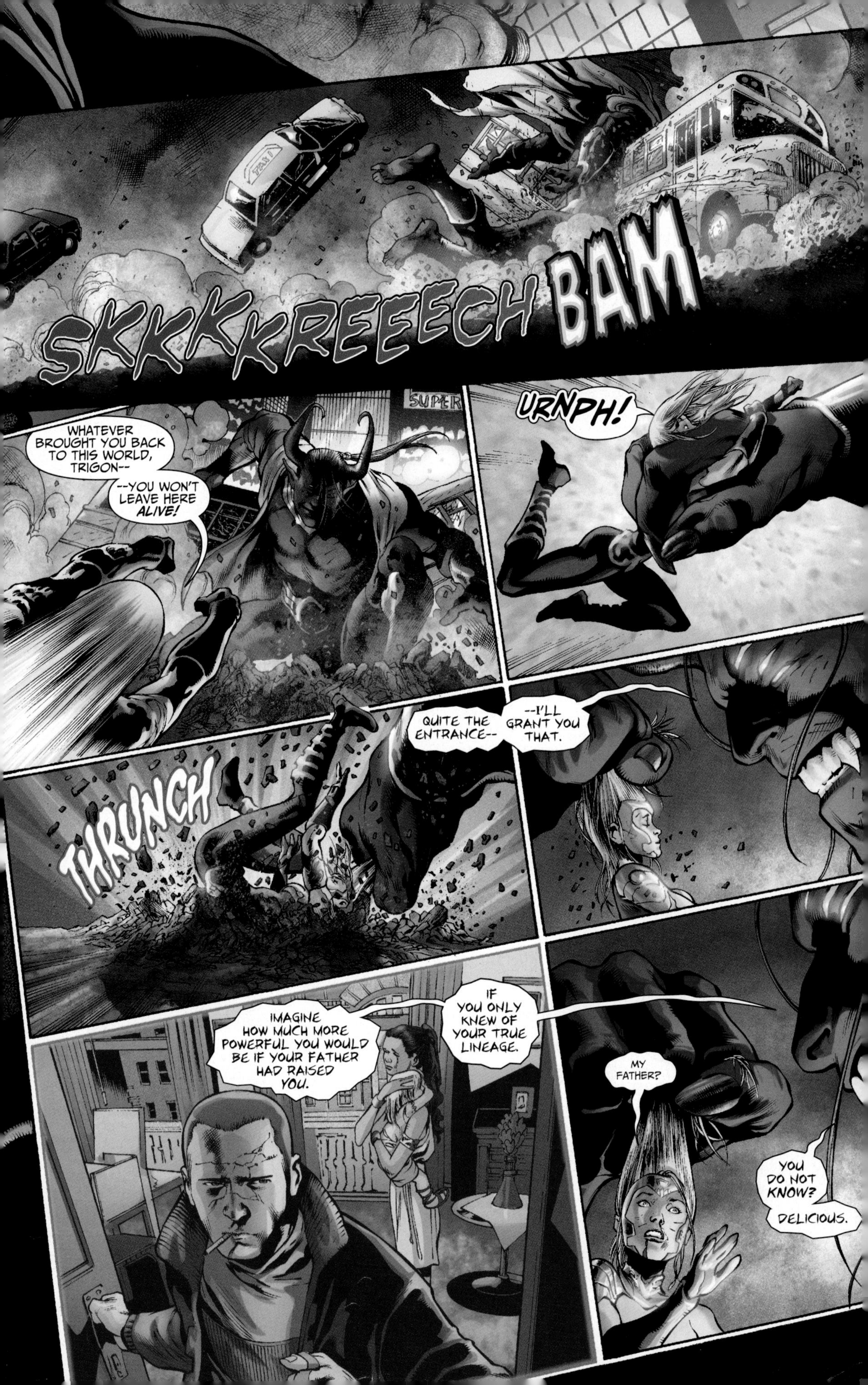
SKKKKREEEECH
BAM
SUPER
WHATEVER BROUGHT YOU BACK TO THIS WORLD, TRIGON--
--YOU WON'T LEAVE HERE ALIVE!
URNPH!
THRUNCH
QUITE THE ENTRANCE--
--I'LL GRANT YOU THAT.
IMAGINE HOW MUCH MORE POWERFUL YOU WOULD BE IF YOUR FATHER HAD RAISED YOU.
IF YOU ONLY KNEW OF YOUR TRUE LINEAGE.
MY FATHER?
YOU DO NOT KNOW?
DELICIOUS.

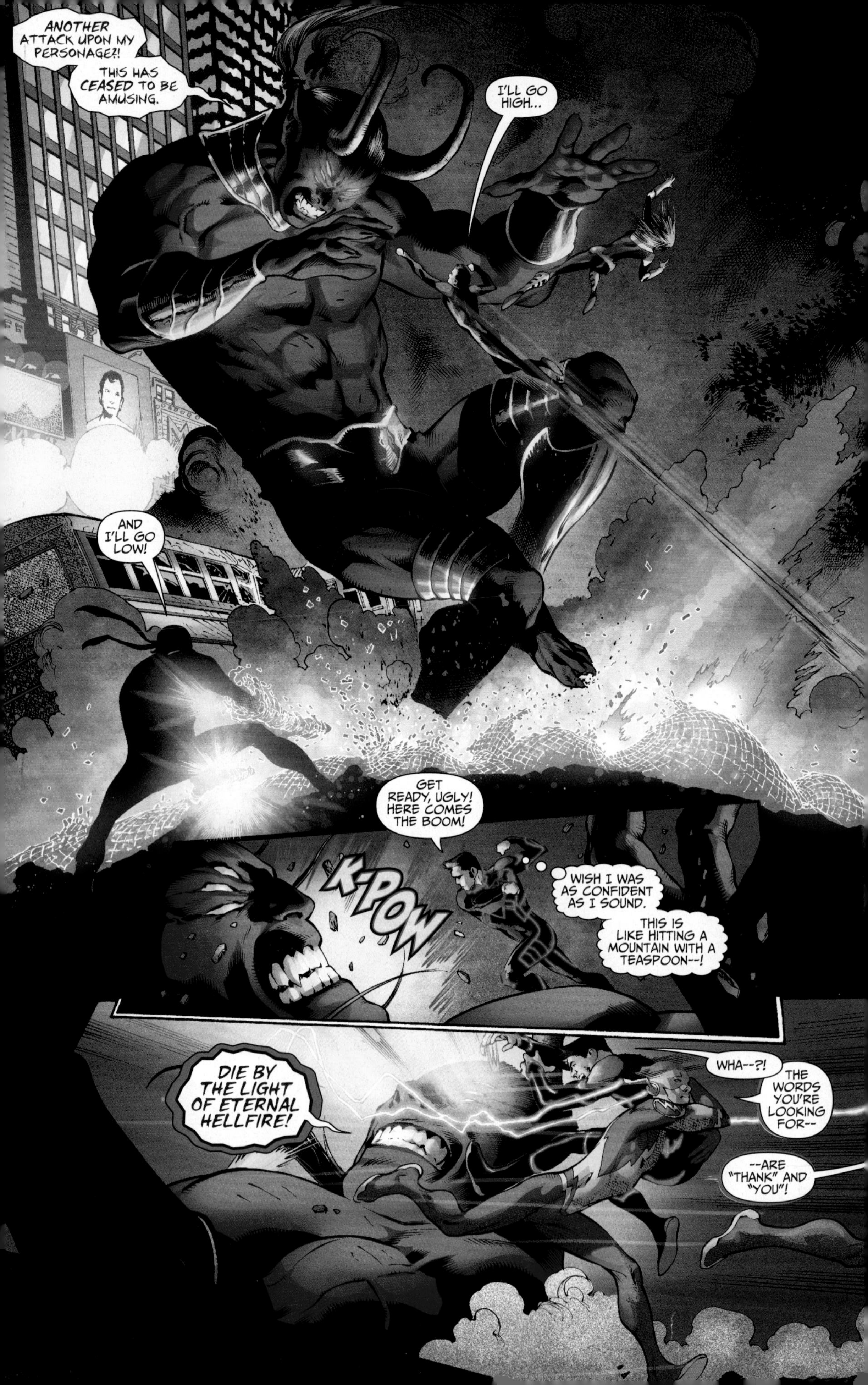
ANOTHER ATTACK UPON MY PERSONAGE?!
THIS HAS CEASED TO BE AMUSING.
I'LL GO HIGH...
AND I'LL GO LOW!
GET READY, UGLY! HERE COMES THE BOOM!
K-POW
WISH I WAS AS CONFIDENT AS I SOUND.
THIS IS LIKE HITTING A MOUNTAIN WITH A TEASPOON--!
DIE BY THE LIGHT OF ETERNAL HELLFIRE!
WHA--?!
THE WORDS YOU'RE LOOKING FOR--
--ARE "THANK" AND "YOU"!

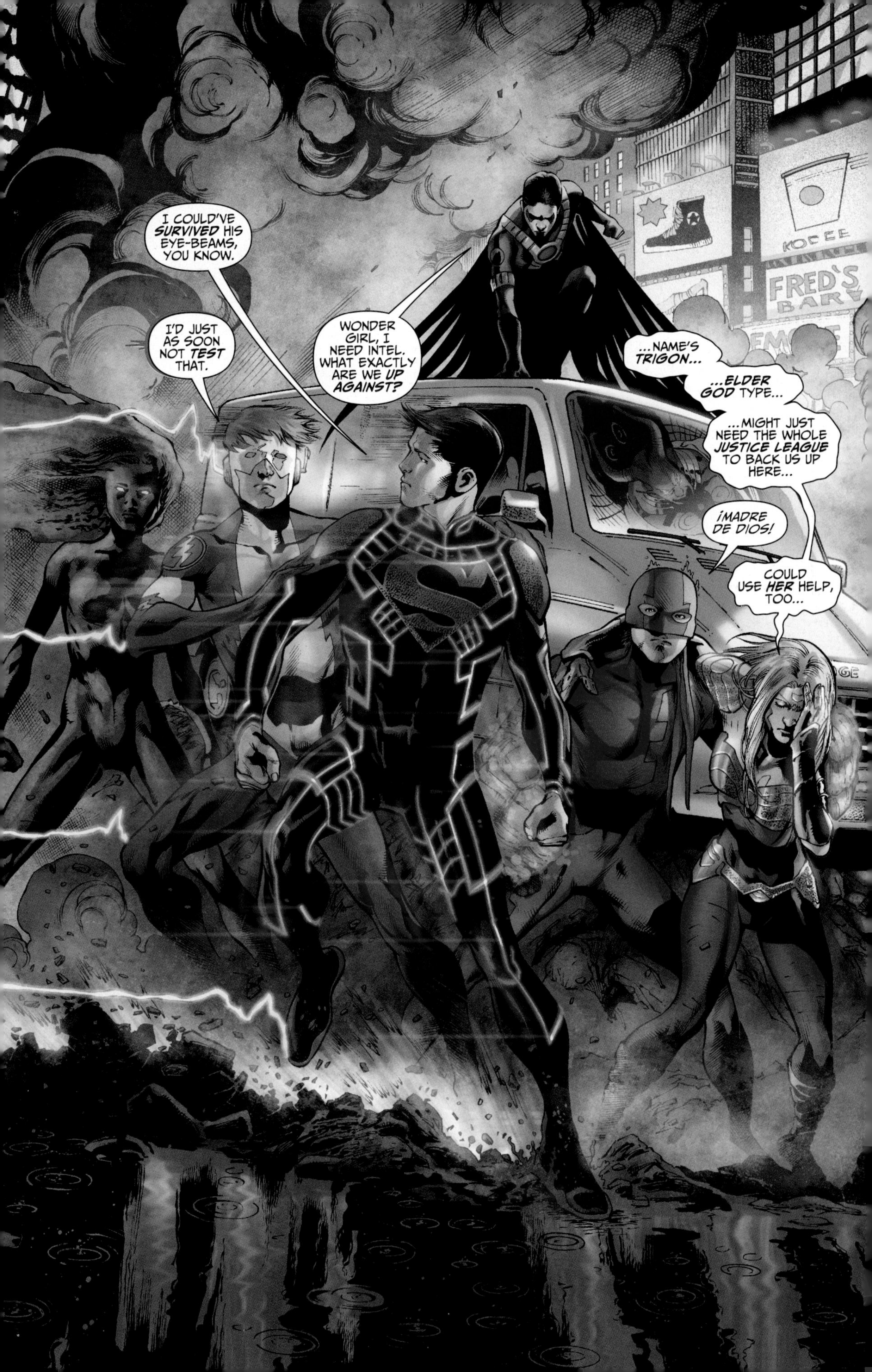
I'D JUST AS SOON NOT TEST THAT.
I COULD'VE SURVIVED HIS EYE-BEAMS, YOU KNOW.
WONDER GIRL, I NEED INTEL. WHAT EXACTLY ARE WE UP AGAINST?
...NAME'S TRIGON...
...ELDER GOD TYPE...
...MIGHT JUST NEED THE WHOLE JUSTICE LEAGUE TO BACK US UP HERE...
¡MADRE DE DIOS!
COULD USE HER HELP, TOO...
KOFEE
FRED'S BAR

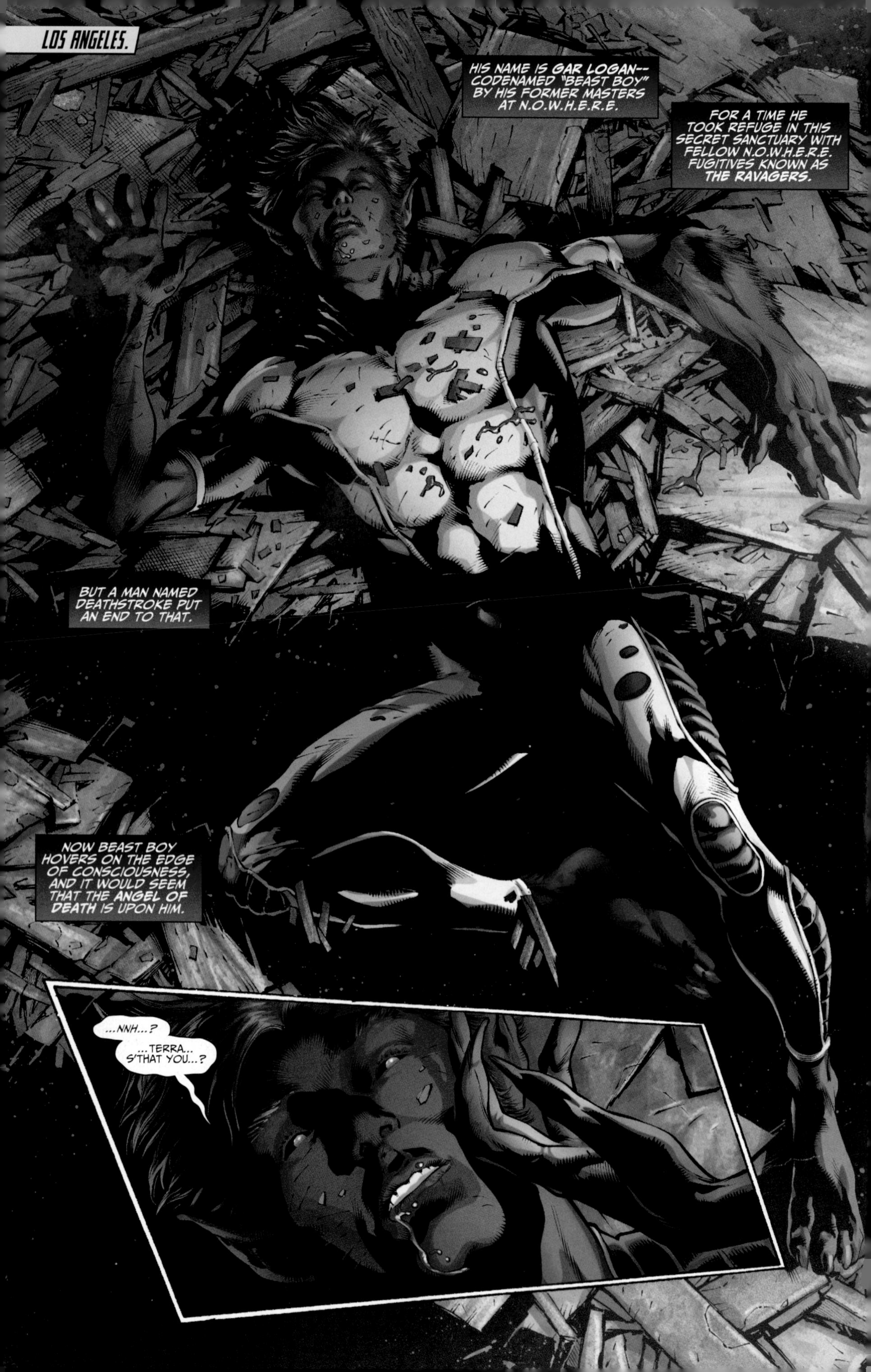
LOS ANGELES.
HIS NAME IS GAR LOGAN--CODENAMED "BEAST BOY" BY HIS FORMER MASTERS AT N.O.W.H.E.R.E.
FOR A TIME HE TOOK REFUGE IN THIS SECRET SANCTUARY WITH FELLOW N.O.W.H.E.R.E. FUGITIVES KNOWN AS THE RAVAGERS.
BUT A MAN NAMED DEATHSTROKE PUT AN END TO THAT.
NOW BEAST BOY HOVERS ON THE EDGE OF CONSCIOUSNESS, AND IT WOULD SEEM THAT THE ANGEL OF DEATH IS UPON HIM.
...NNH...?
...TERRA... S'THAT YOU...?

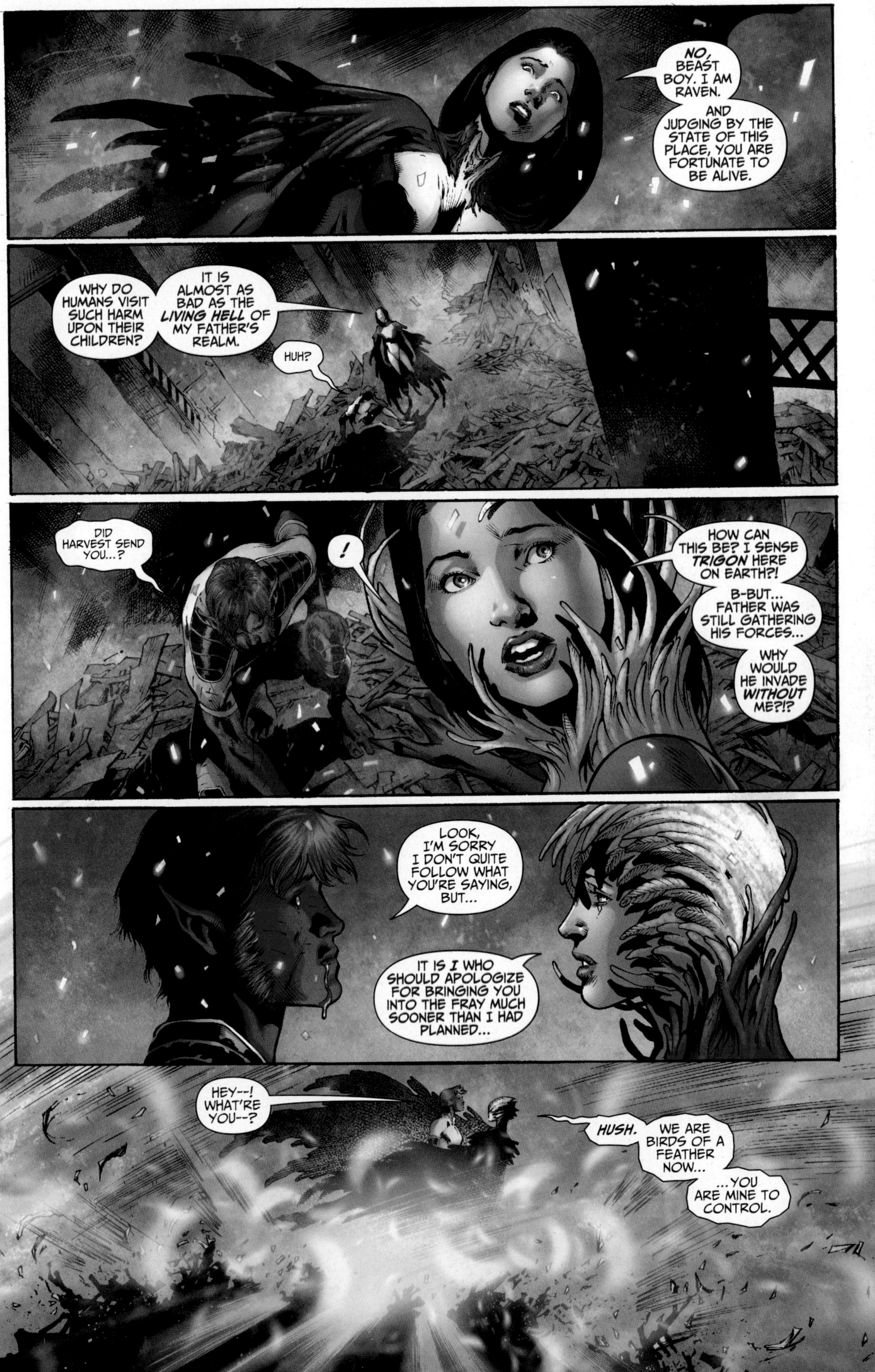
NO, BEAST BOY. I AM RAVEN.
AND JUDGING BY THE STATE OF THIS PLACE, YOU ARE FORTUNATE TO BE ALIVE.
WHY DO HUMANS VISIT SUCH HARM UPON THEIR CHILDREN?
IT IS ALMOST AS BAD AS THE LIVING HELL OF MY FATHER'S REALM.
HUH?
DID HARVEST SEND YOU...?
!
HOW CAN THIS BE? I SENSE TRIGON HERE ON EARTH?!
B-BUT... FATHER WAS STILL GATHERING HIS FORCES...
WHY WOULD HE INVADE WITHOUT ME?!?
LOOK, I'M SORRY I DON'T QUITE FOLLOW WHAT YOU'RE SAYING, BUT...
IT IS I WHO SHOULD APOLOGIZE FOR BRINGING YOU INTO THE FRAY MUCH SOONER THAN I HAD PLANNED...
HEY--! WHAT'RE YOU--?
HUSH.
WE ARE BIRDS OF A FEATHER NOW...
...YOU ARE MINE TO CONTROL.

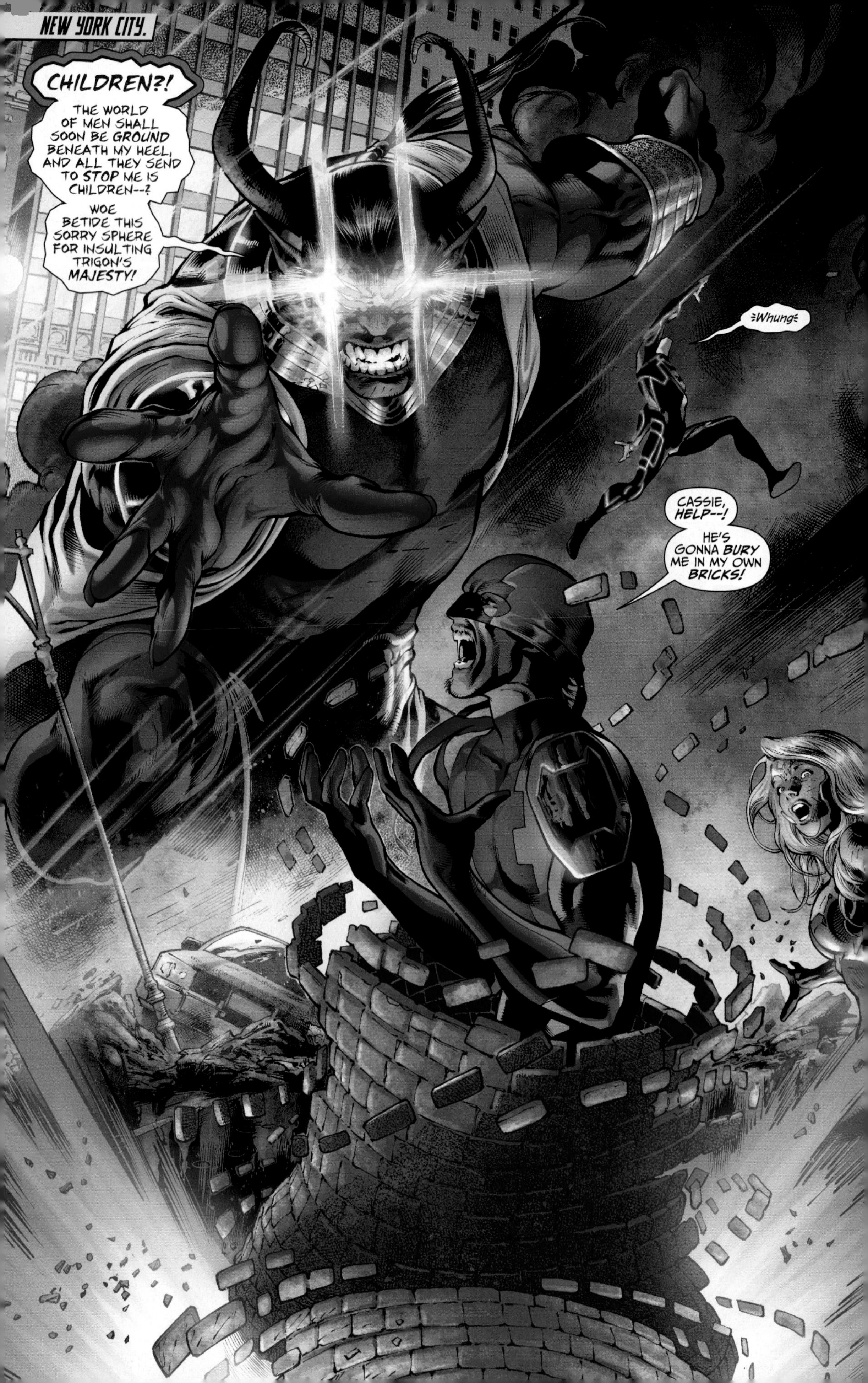
NEW YORK CITY.
CHILDREN?!
THE WORLD OF MEN SHALL SOON BE GROUND BENEATH MY HEEL, AND ALL THEY SEND TO STOP ME IS CHILDREN--?
WOE BETIDE THIS SORRY SPHERE FOR INSULTING TRIGON'S MAJESTY!
Whung
CASSIE, HELP--!
HE'S GONNA BURY ME IN MY OWN BRICKS!

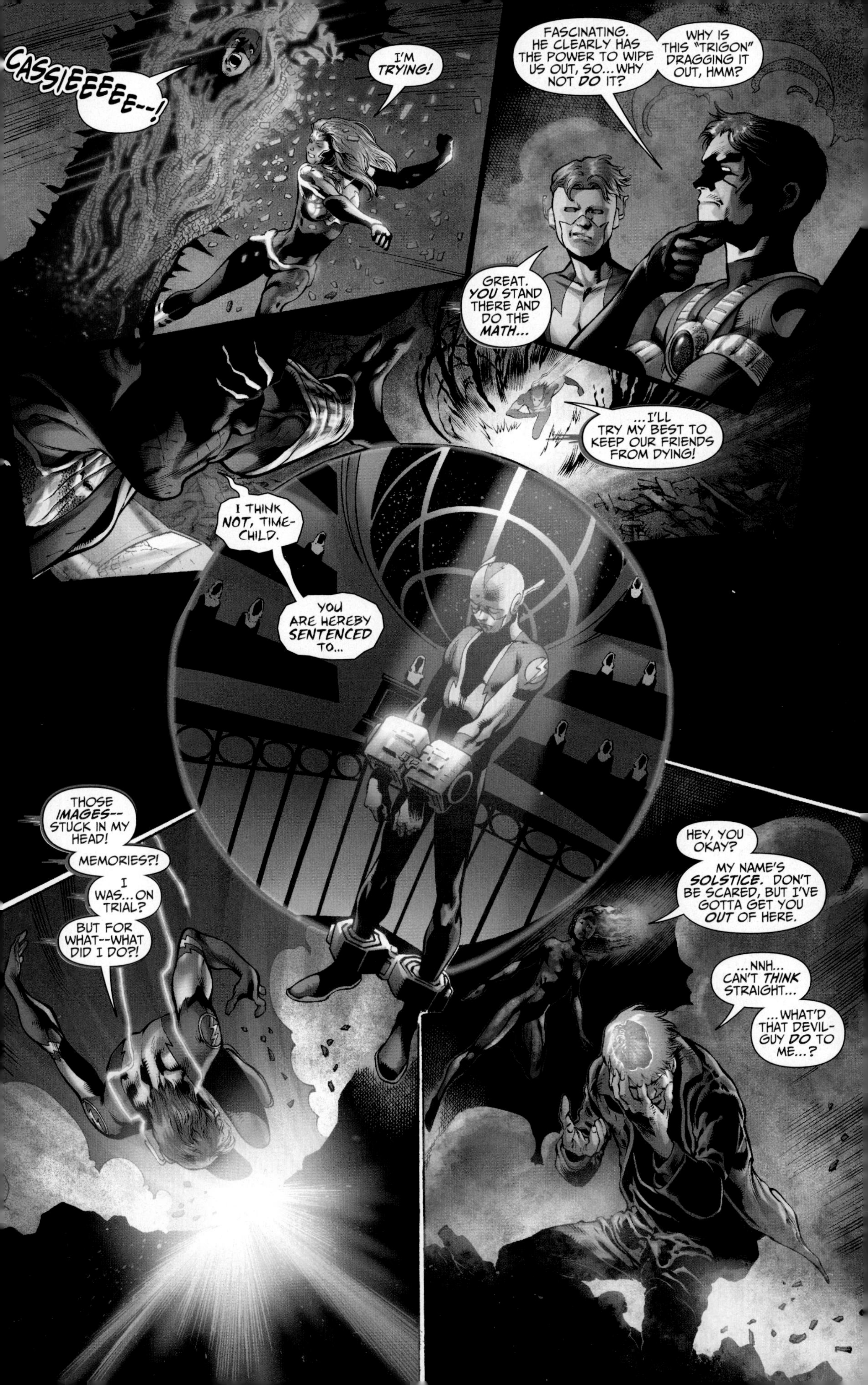
CASSIEEEEEE--!
I'M TRYING!
FASCINATING. HE CLEARLY HAS THE POWER TO WIPE US OUT, SO... WHY NOT DO IT?
WHY IS THIS "TRIGON" DRAGGING IT OUT, HMM?
GREAT. YOU STAND THERE AND DO THE MATH...
...I'LL TRY MY BEST TO KEEP OUR FRIENDS FROM DYING!
I THINK NOT, TIME-CHILD.
YOU ARE HEREBY SENTENCED TO...
THOSE IMAGES-- STUCK IN MY HEAD!
MEMORIES?!
I WAS...ON TRIAL?
BUT FOR WHAT--WHAT DID I DO?!
HEY, YOU OKAY?
MY NAME'S SOLSTICE. DON'T BE SCARED, BUT I'VE GOTTA GET YOU OUT OF HERE.
...NNH... CAN'T THINK STRAIGHT...
...WHAT'D THAT DEVIL-GUY DO TO ME...?

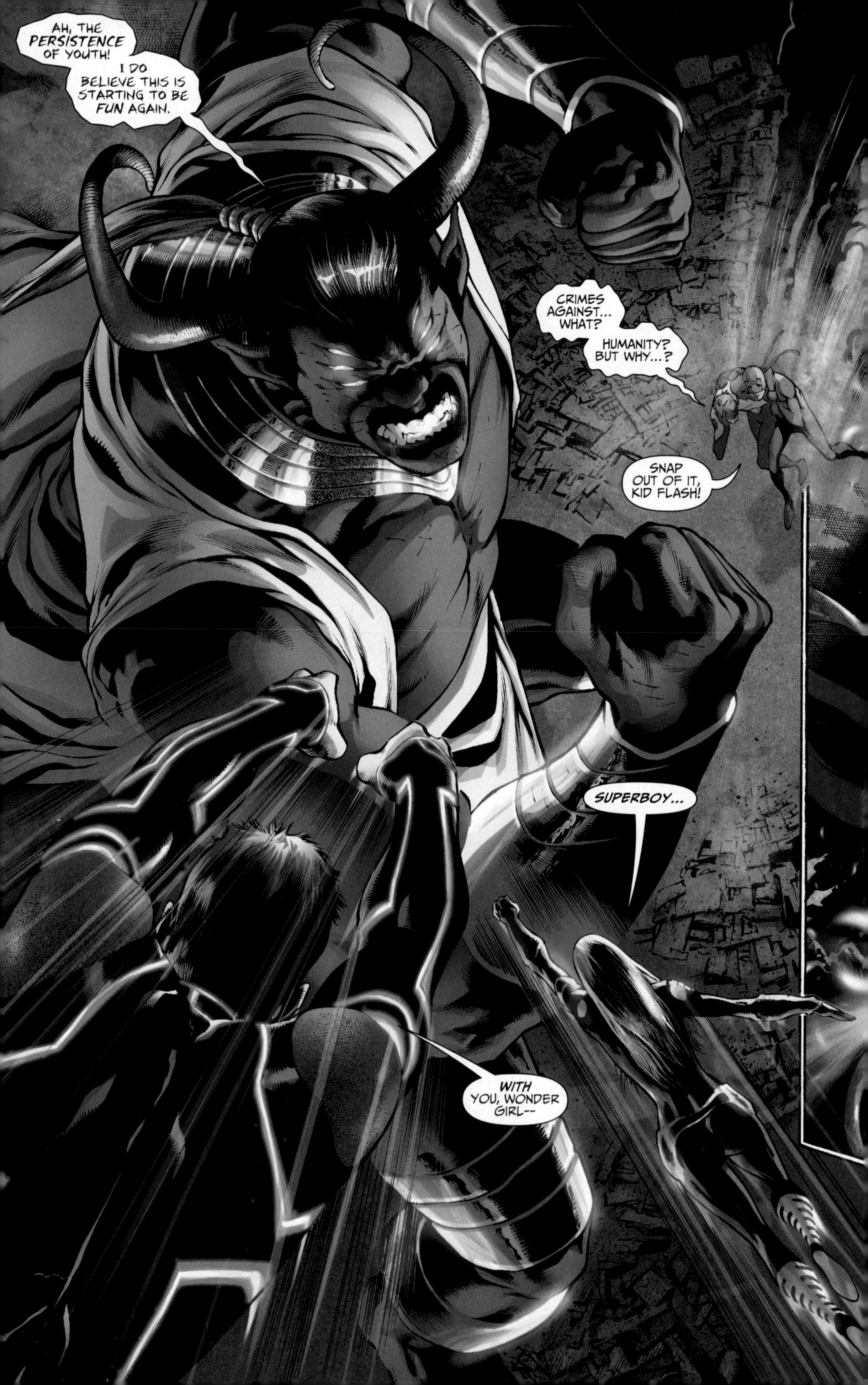
AH, THE PERSISTENCE OF YOUTH!
I DO BELIEVE THIS IS STARTING TO BE FUN AGAIN.
CRIMES AGAINST... WHAT?
HUMANITY? BUT WHY...?
SNAP OUT OF IT, KID FLASH!
SUPERBOY...
WITH YOU, WONDER GIRL--

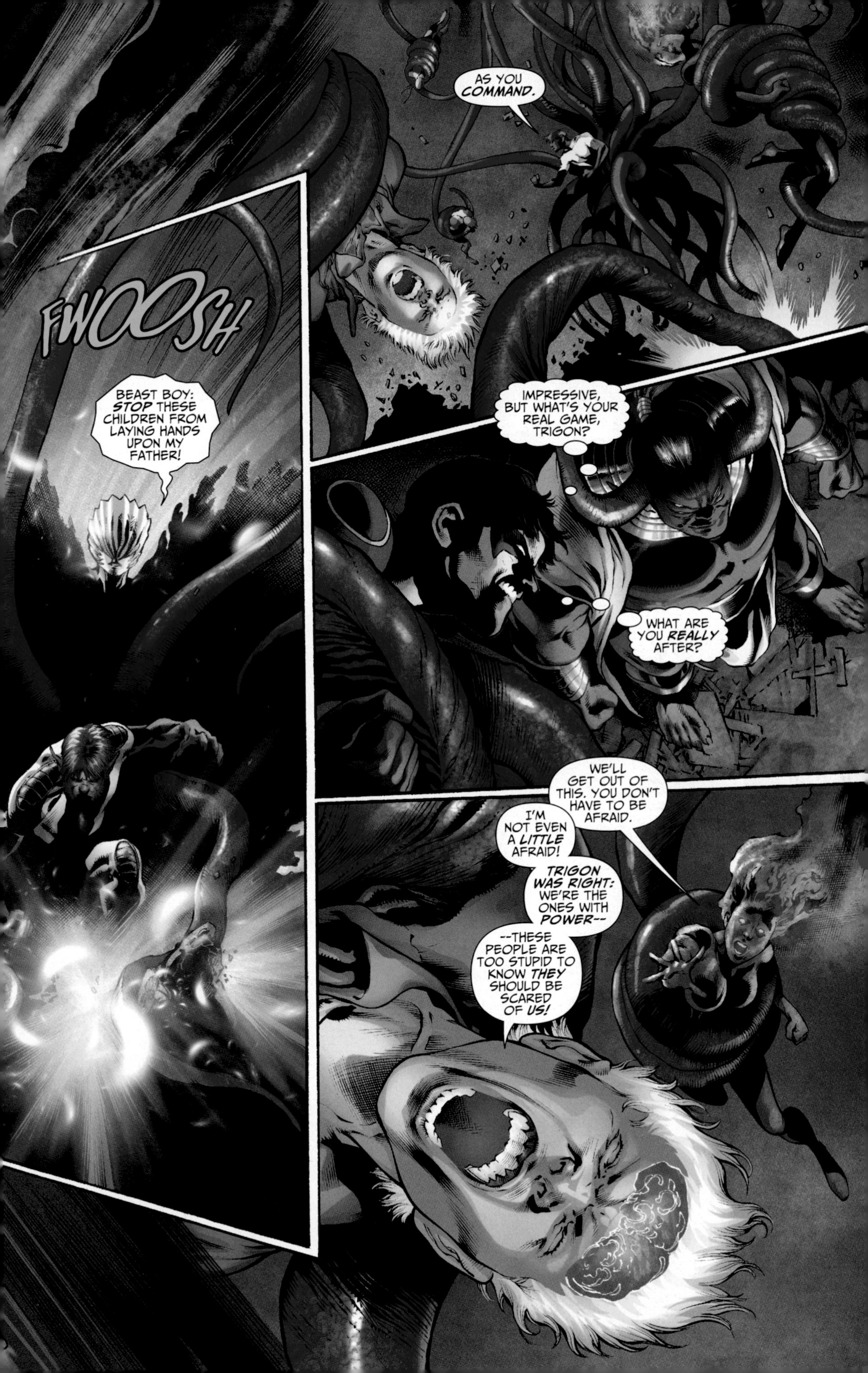
AS YOU COMMAND.
FWOOSH
BEAST BOY: STOP THESE CHILDREN FROM LAYING HANDS UPON MY FATHER!
IMPRESSIVE, BUT WHAT'S YOUR REAL GAME, TRIGON?
WHAT ARE YOU REALLY AFTER?
WE'LL GET OUT OF THIS. YOU DON'T HAVE TO BE AFRAID.
I'M NOT EVEN A LITTLE AFRAID!
TRIGON WAS RIGHT: WE'RE THE ONES WITH POWER--
--THESE PEOPLE ARE TOO STUPID TO KNOW THEY SHOULD BE SCARED OF US!

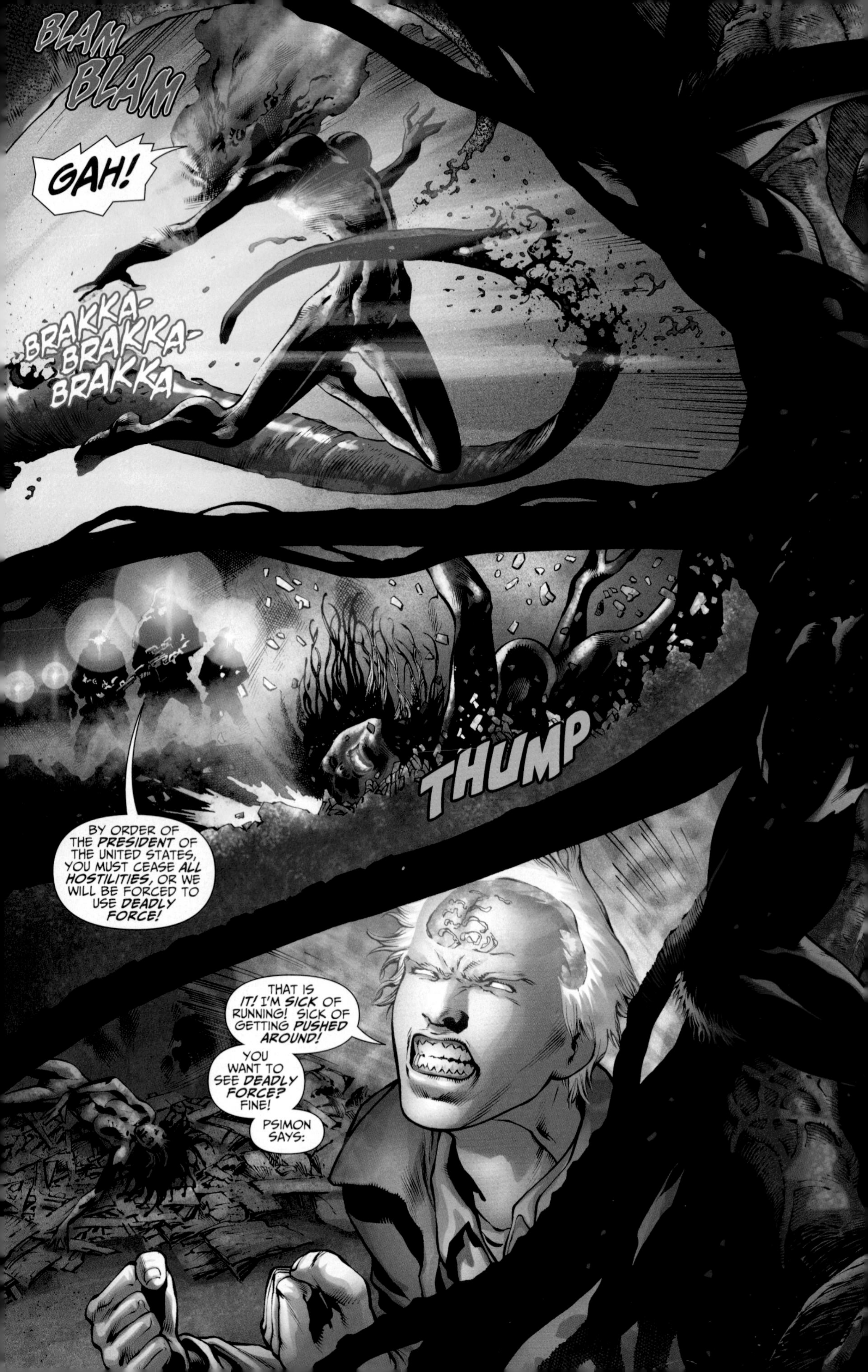
BLAM
BLAM
GAH!
BRAKKA-BRAKKA-BRAKKA-BRAKKA
THUMP
BY ORDER OF THE PRESIDENT OF THE UNITED STATES, YOU MUST CEASE ALL HOSTILITIES, OR WE WILL BE FORCED TO USE DEADLY FORCE!
THAT IS IT! I'M SICK OF RUNNING! SICK OF GETTING PUSHED AROUND!
YOU WANT TO SEE DEADLY FORCE? FINE!
PSIMON SAYS:

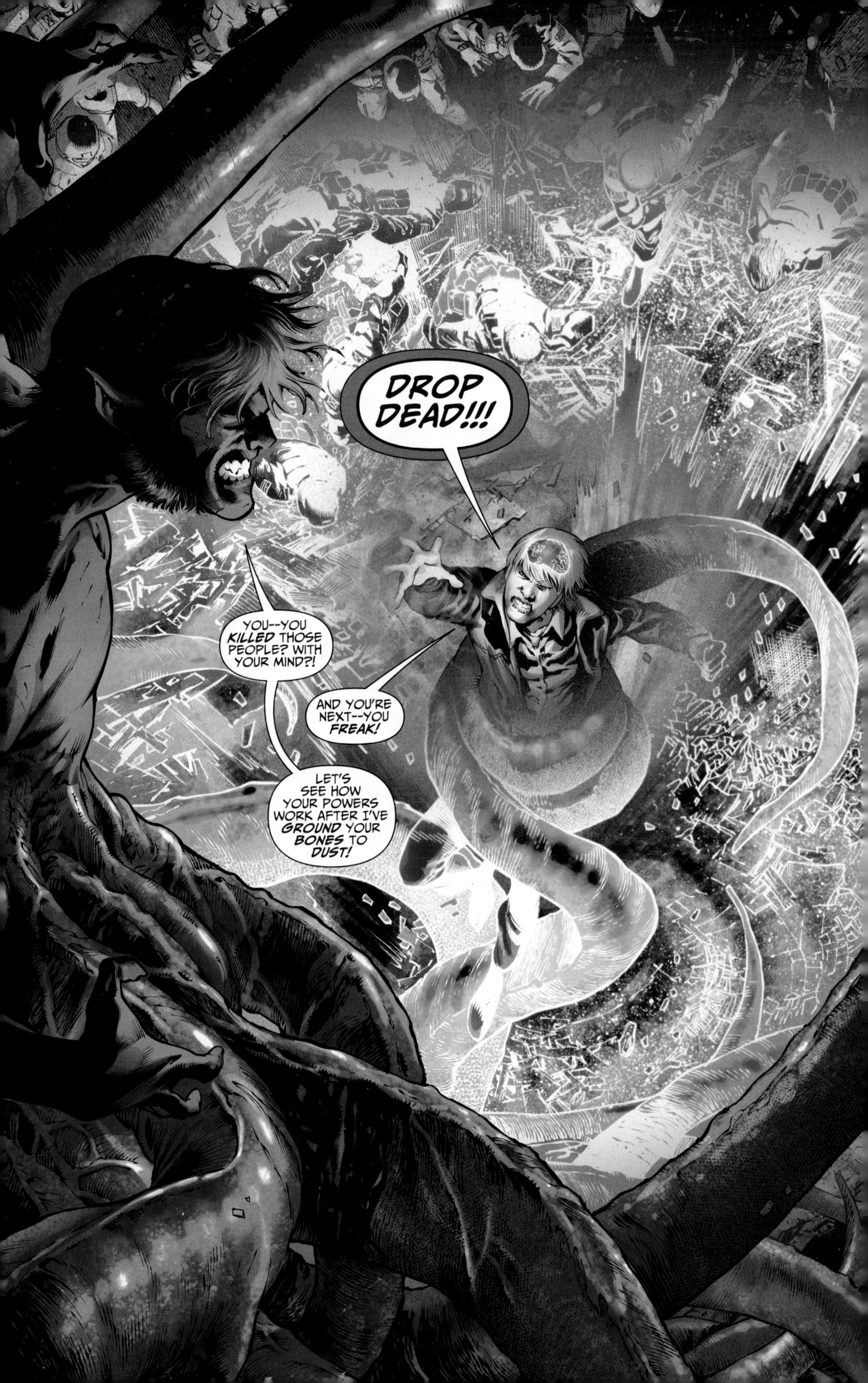
DROP DEAD!!!
YOU--YOU KILLED THOSE PEOPLE? WITH YOUR MIND?!
AND YOU'RE NEXT--YOU FREAK!
LET'S SEE HOW YOUR POWERS WORK AFTER I'VE GROUND YOUR BONES TO DUST!

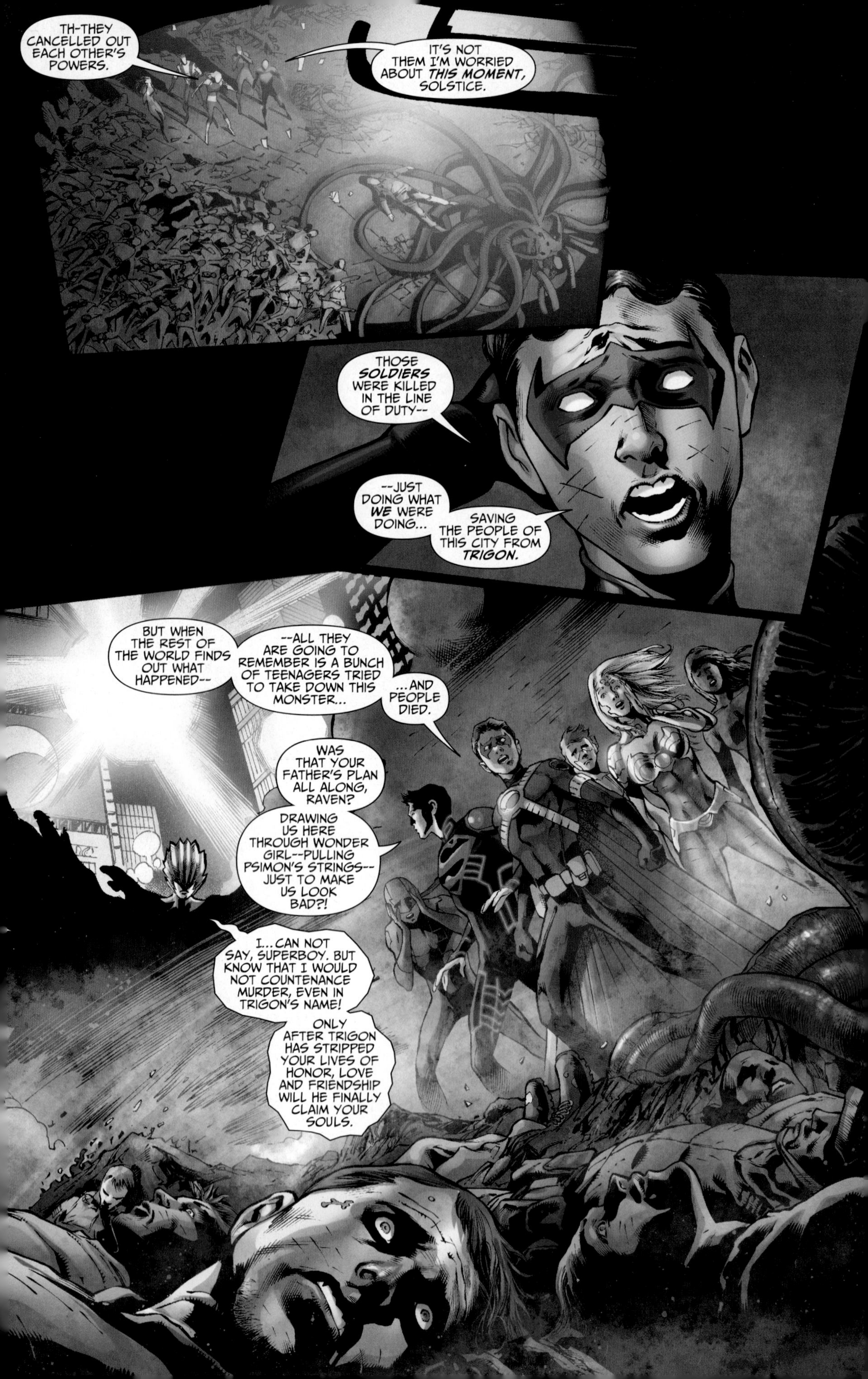
TH-THEY CANCELLED OUT EACH OTHER'S POWERS.
IT'S NOT THEM I'M WORRIED ABOUT THIS MOMENT, SOLSTICE.
THOSE SOLDIERS WERE KILLED IN THE LINE OF DUTY--
--JUST DOING WHAT WE WERE DOING...
SAVING THE PEOPLE OF THIS CITY FROM TRIGON.
BUT WHEN THE REST OF THE WORLD FINDS OUT WHAT HAPPENED--
--ALL THEY ARE GOING TO REMEMBER IS A BUNCH OF TEENAGERS TRIED TO TAKE DOWN THIS MONSTER...
...AND PEOPLE DIED.
WAS THAT YOUR FATHER'S PLAN ALL ALONG, RAVEN?
DRAWING US HERE THROUGH WONDER GIRL--PULLING PSIMON'S STRINGS--JUST TO MAKE US LOOK BAD?!
I...CAN NOT SAY, SUPERBOY. BUT KNOW THAT I WOULD NOT COUNTENANCE MURDER, EVEN IN TRIGON'S NAME!
ONLY AFTER TRIGON HAS STRIPPED YOUR LIVES OF HONOR, LOVE AND FRIENDSHIP WILL HE FINALLY CLAIM YOUR SOULS.

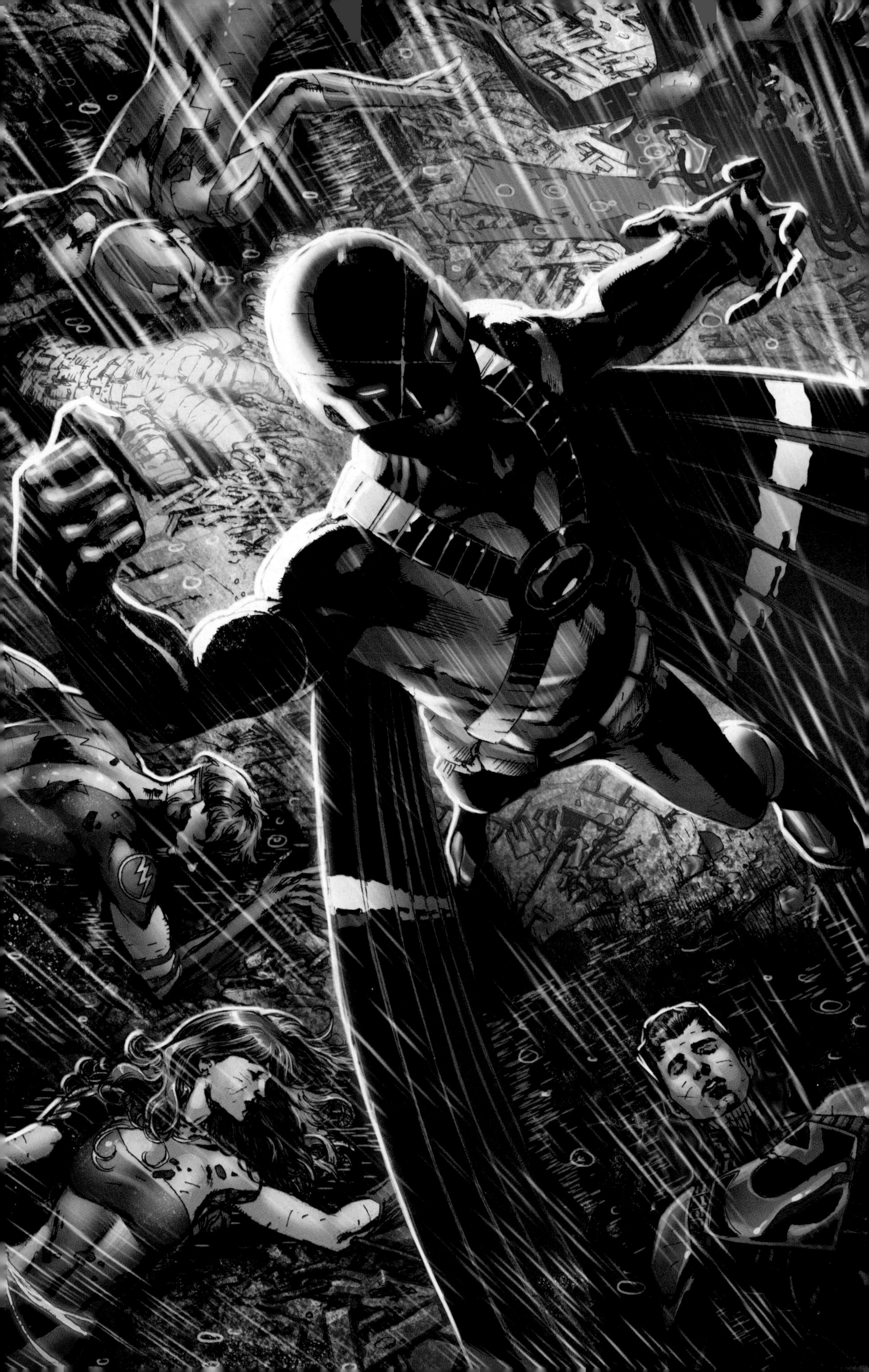

ONLY BEGOTTEN

SCOTT LOBDELL writer EDDY BARROWS & PATRICK ZIRCHER pencillers EBER FERREIRA & PATRICK ZIRCHER inkers
cover art by EDDY BARROWS, EBER FERREIRA & ALEX SINCLAIR

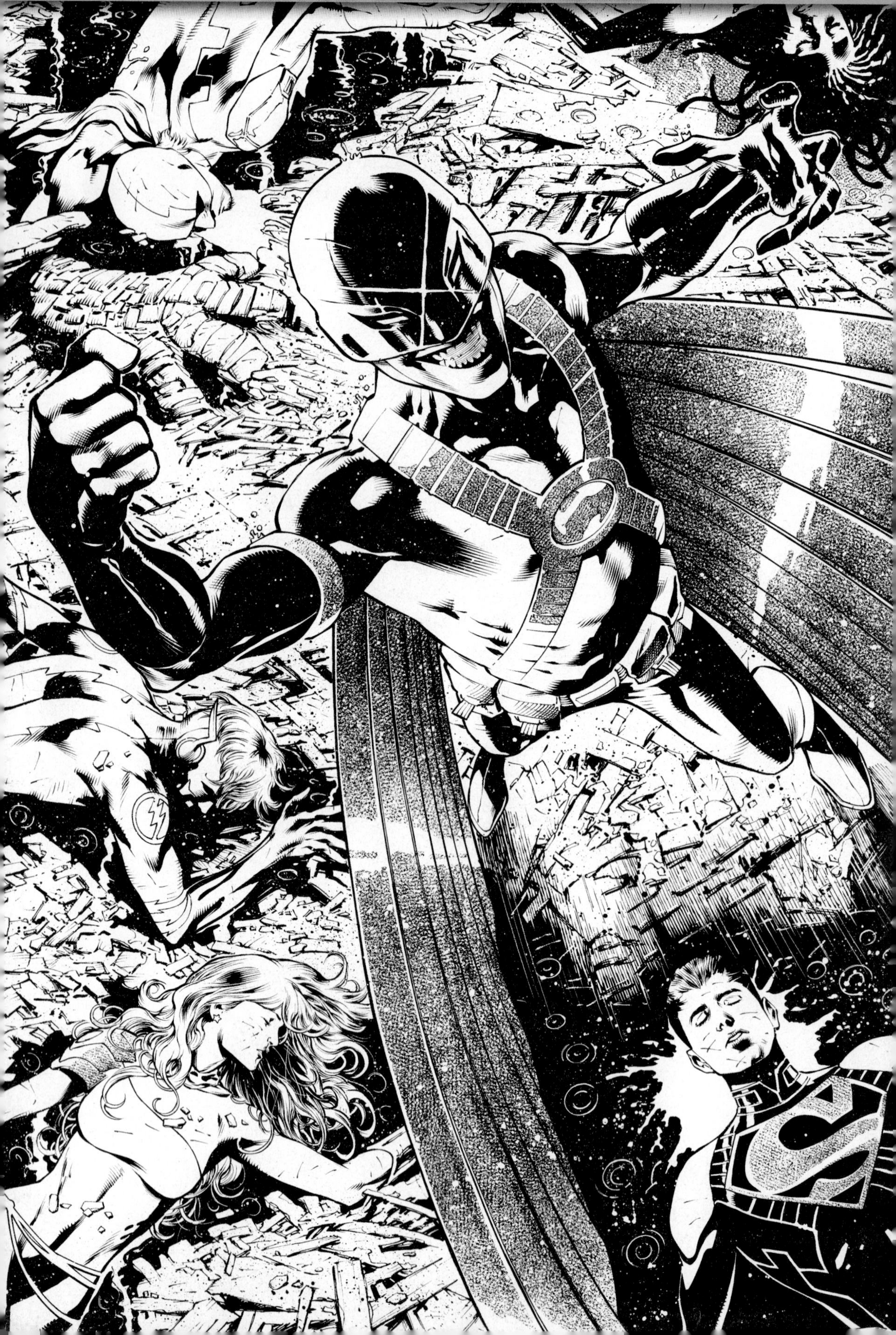

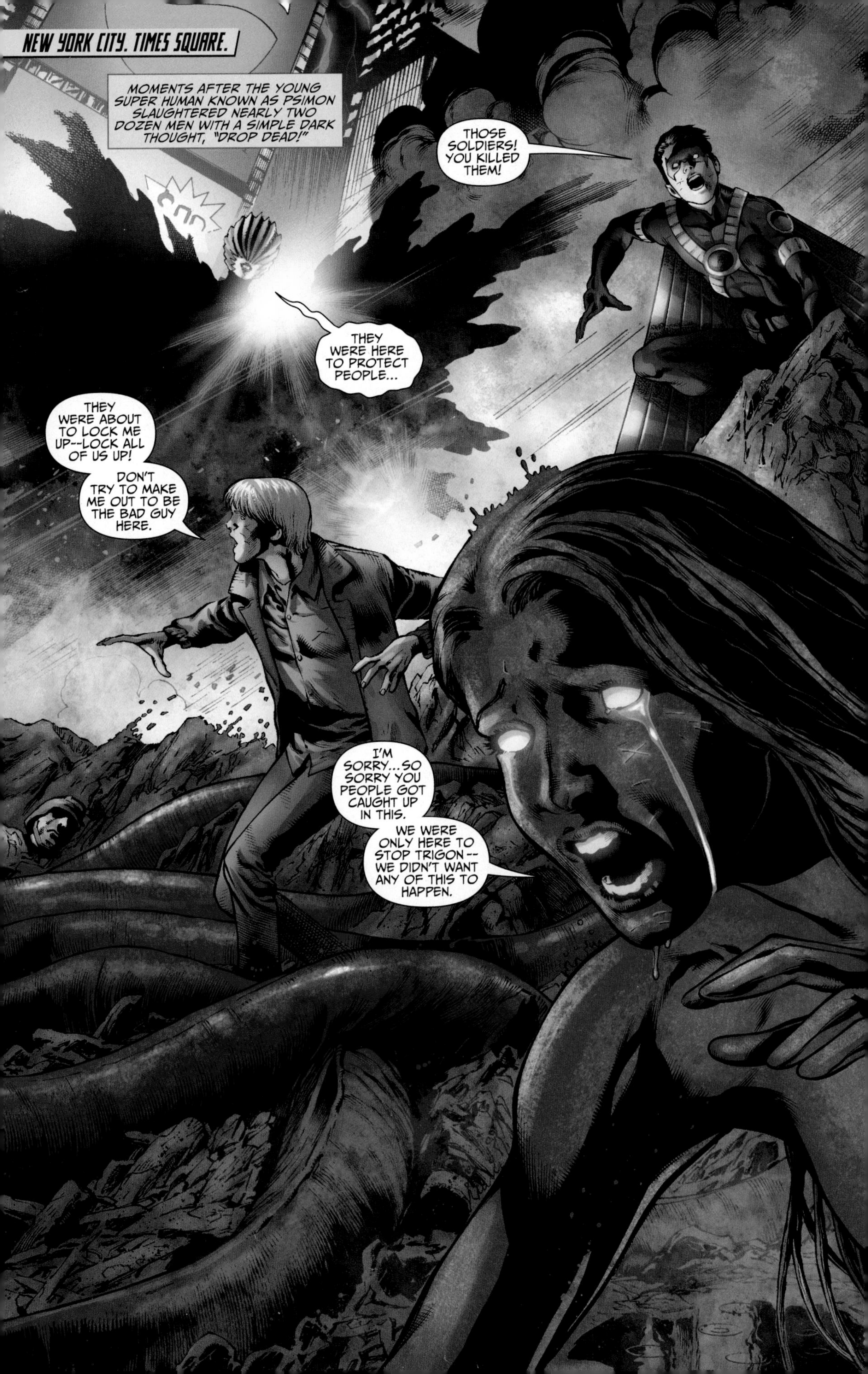
NEW YORK CITY. TIMES SQUARE.
MOMENTS AFTER THE YOUNG SUPER HUMAN KNOWN AS PSIMON SLAUGHTERED NEARLY TWO DOZEN MEN WITH A SIMPLE DARK THOUGHT, "DROP DEAD!"
THOSE SOLDIERS! YOU KILLED THEM!
THEY WERE HERE TO PROTECT PEOPLE...
THEY WERE ABOUT TO LOCK ME UP--LOCK ALL OF US UP!
DON'T TRY TO MAKE ME OUT TO BE THE BAD GUY HERE.
I'M SORRY...SO SORRY YOU PEOPLE GOT CAUGHT UP IN THIS.
WE WERE ONLY HERE TO STOP TRIGON-- WE DIDN'T WANT ANY OF THIS TO HAPPEN.

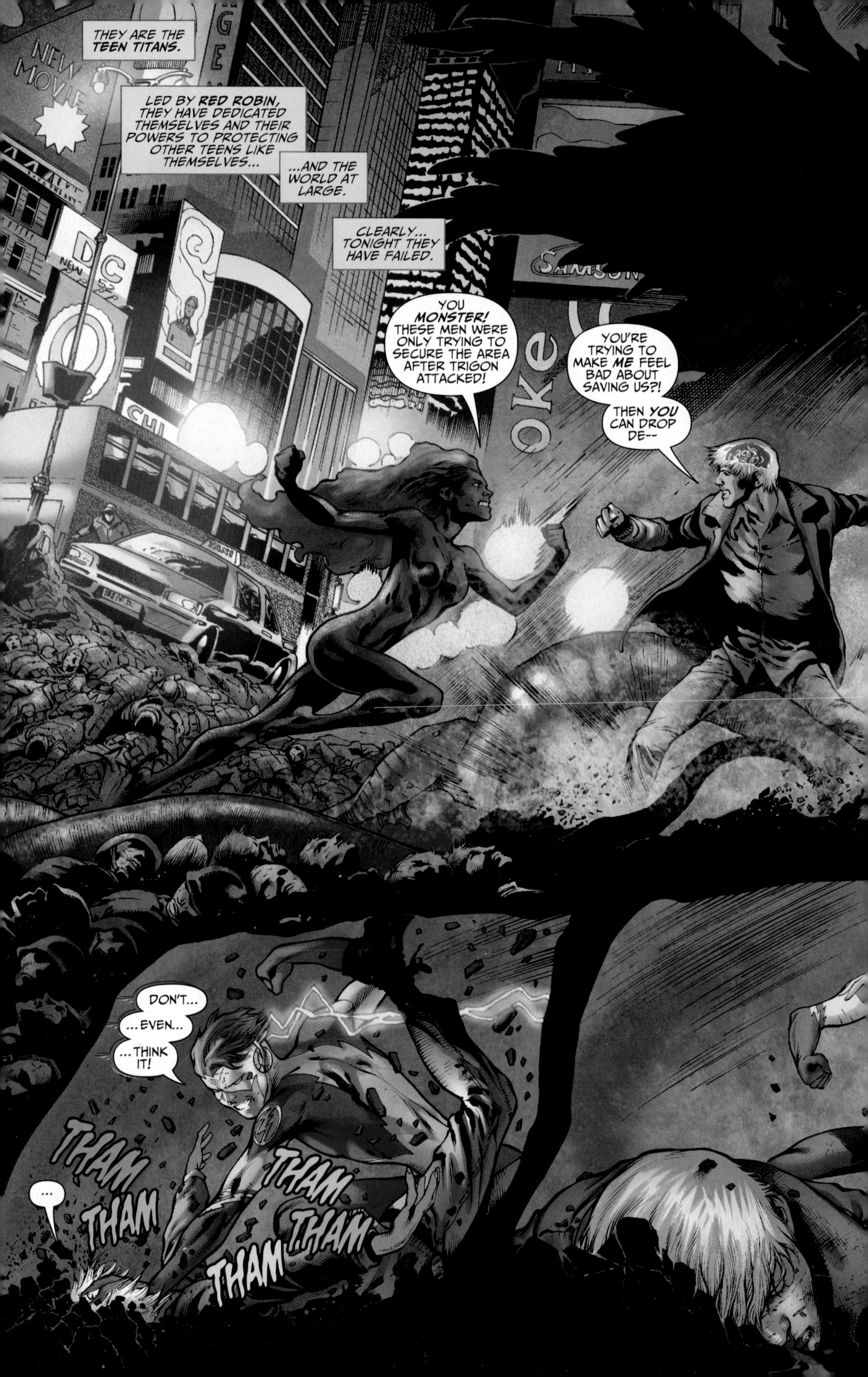

THEY ARE THE TEEN TITANS.
LED BY RED ROBIN, THEY HAVE DEDICATED THEMSELVES AND THEIR POWERS TO PROTECTING OTHER TEENS LIKE THEMSELVES...
...AND THE WORLD AT LARGE.
CLEARLY... TONIGHT THEY HAVE FAILED.
YOU MONSTER! THESE MEN WERE ONLY TRYING TO SECURE THE AREA AFTER TRIGON ATTACKED!
YOU'RE TRYING TO MAKE ME FEEL BAD ABOUT SAVING US?!
THEN YOU CAN DROP DE--
DON'T...
...EVEN...
...THINK IT!
THAM
THAM
THAM
THAM
THAM
THAM
...

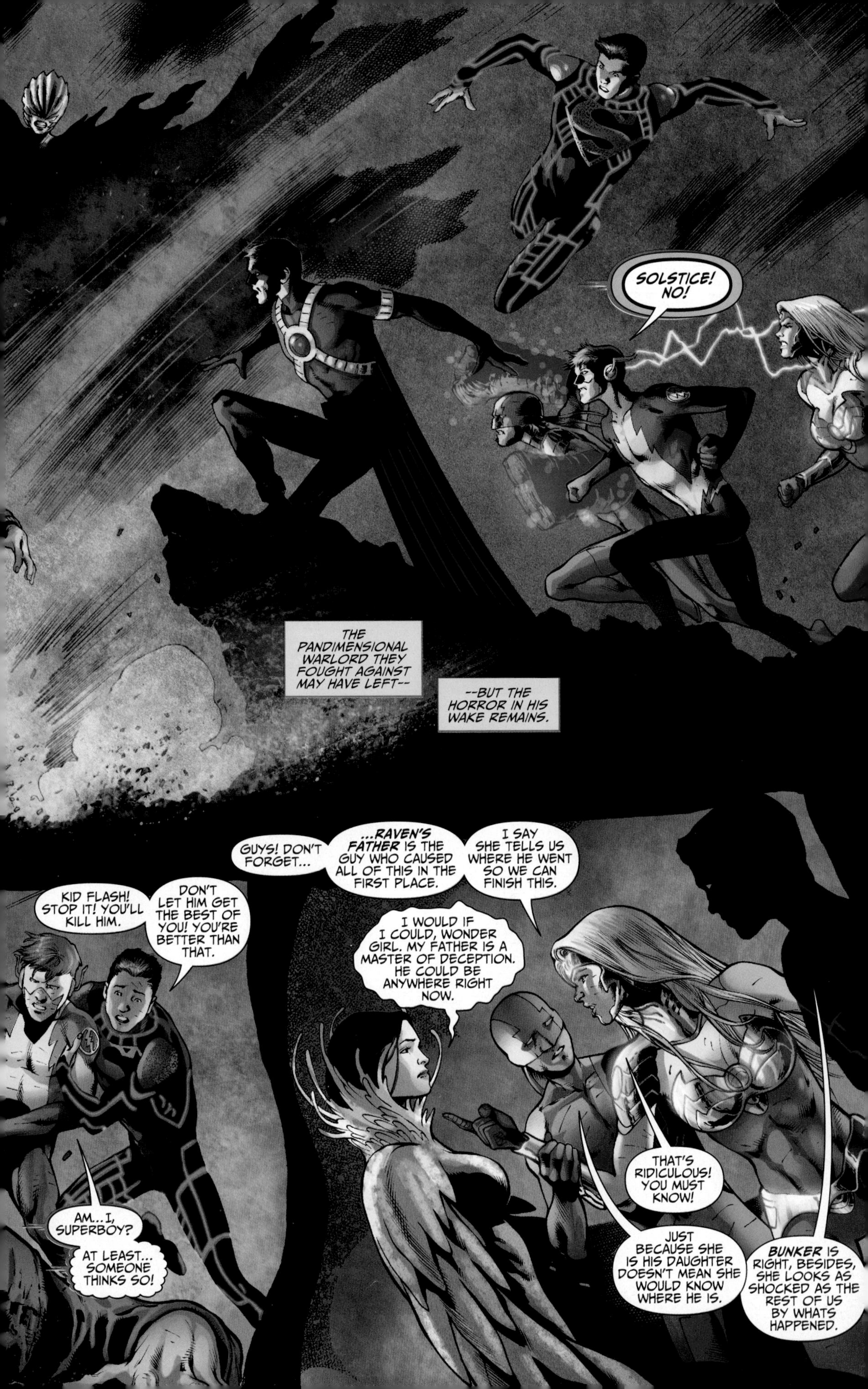
SOLSTICE! NO!
THE PANDIMENSIONAL WARLORD THEY FOUGHT AGAINST MAY HAVE LEFT--
--BUT THE HORROR IN HIS WAKE REMAINS.
GUYS! DON'T FORGET...
...RAVEN'S FATHER IS THE GUY WHO CAUSED ALL OF THIS IN THE FIRST PLACE.
I SAY SHE TELLS US WHERE HE WENT SO WE CAN FINISH THIS.
KID FLASH! STOP IT! YOU'LL KILL HIM.
DON'T LET HIM GET THE BEST OF YOU! YOU'RE BETTER THAN THAT.
I WOULD IF I COULD, WONDER GIRL. MY FATHER IS A MASTER OF DECEPTION. HE COULD BE ANYWHERE RIGHT NOW.
AM...I, SUPERBOY?
AT LEAST... SOMEONE THINKS SO!
THAT'S RIDICULOUS! YOU MUST KNOW!
JUST BECAUSE SHE IS HIS DAUGHTER DOESN'T MEAN SHE WOULD KNOW WHERE HE IS.
BUNKER IS RIGHT, BESIDES, SHE LOOKS AS SHOCKED AS THE REST OF US BY WHATS HAPPENED.

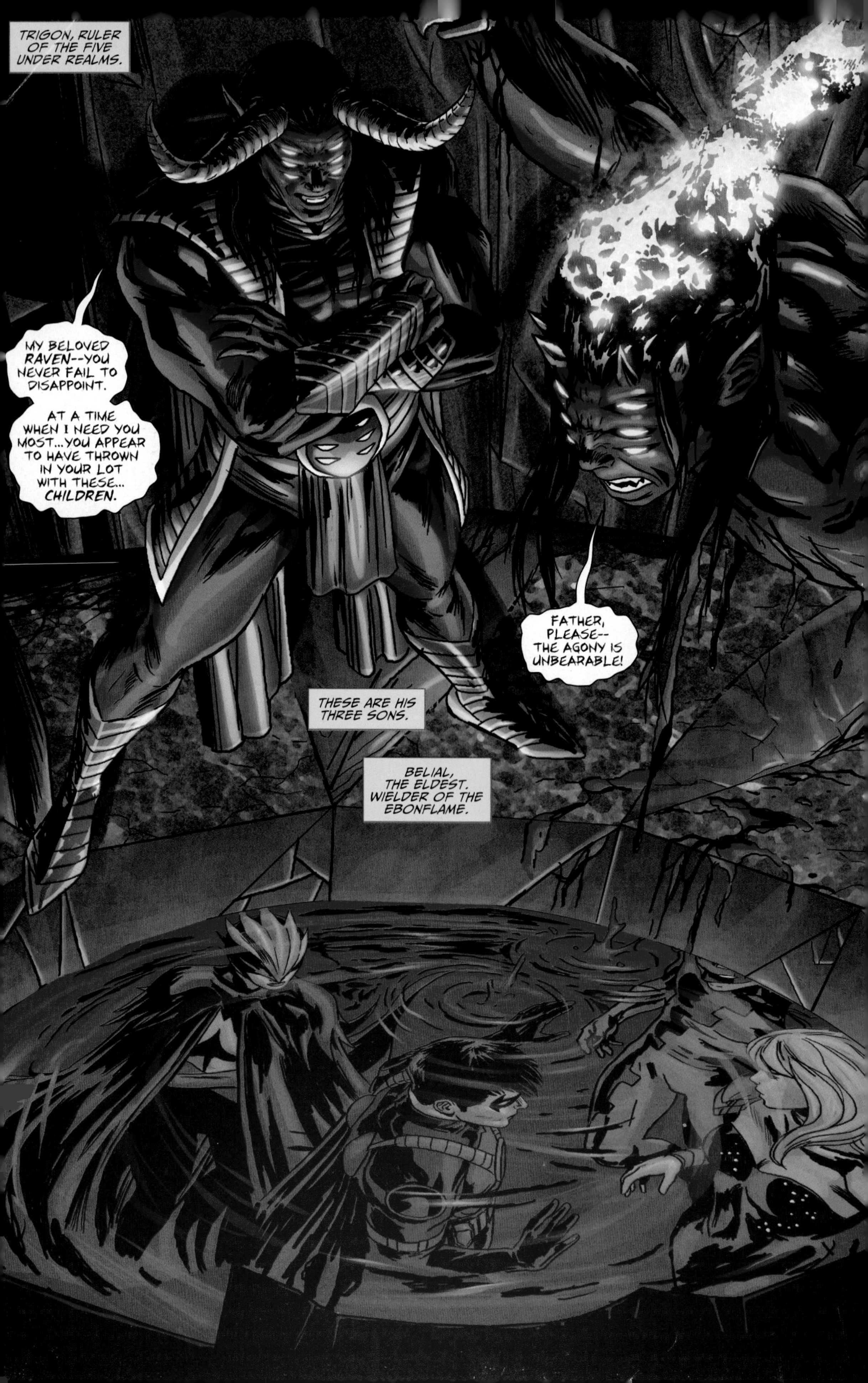
TRIGON, RULER OF THE FIVE UNDER REALMS.
MY BELOVED RAVEN--YOU NEVER FAIL TO DISAPPOINT.
AT A TIME WHEN I NEED YOU MOST...YOU APPEAR TO HAVE THROWN IN YOUR LOT WITH THESE... CHILDREN.
FATHER, PLEASE-- THE AGONY IS UNBEARABLE!
THESE ARE HIS THREE SONS.
BELIAL, THE ELDEST. WIELDER OF THE EBONFLAME.

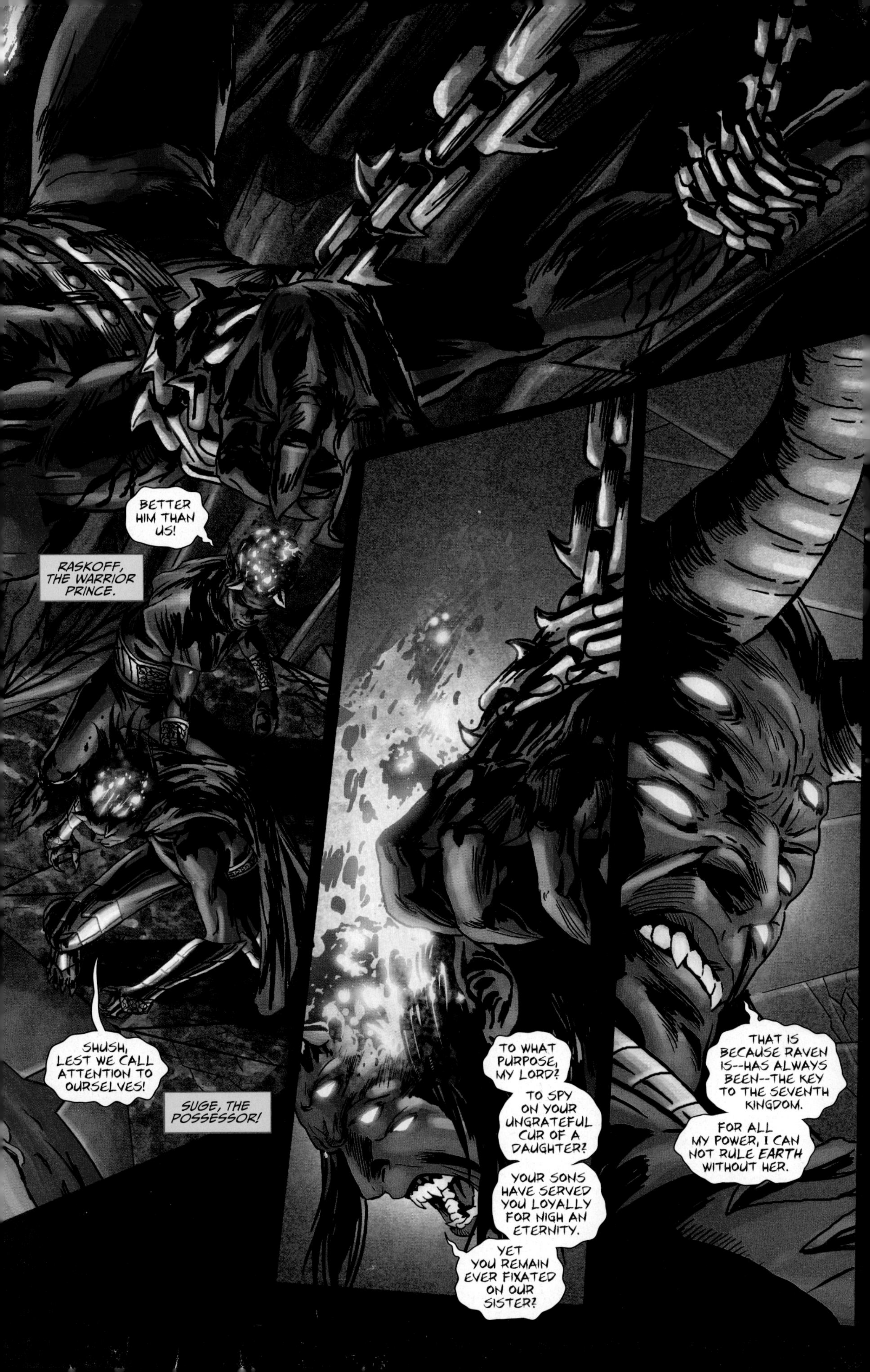
BETTER HIM THAN US!
RASKOFF, THE WARRIOR PRINCE.
SHUSH, LEST WE CALL ATTENTION TO OURSELVES!
SUGE, THE POSSESSOR!
TO WHAT PURPOSE, MY LORD?
TO SPY ON YOUR UNGRATEFUL CUR OF A DAUGHTER?
YOUR SONS HAVE SERVED YOU LOYALLY FOR NIGH AN ETERNITY.
YET YOU REMAIN EVER FIXATED ON OUR SISTER?
THAT IS BECAUSE RAVEN IS--HAS ALWAYS BEEN--THE KEY TO THE SEVENTH KINGDOM.
FOR ALL MY POWER, I CAN NOT RULE EARTH WITHOUT HER.

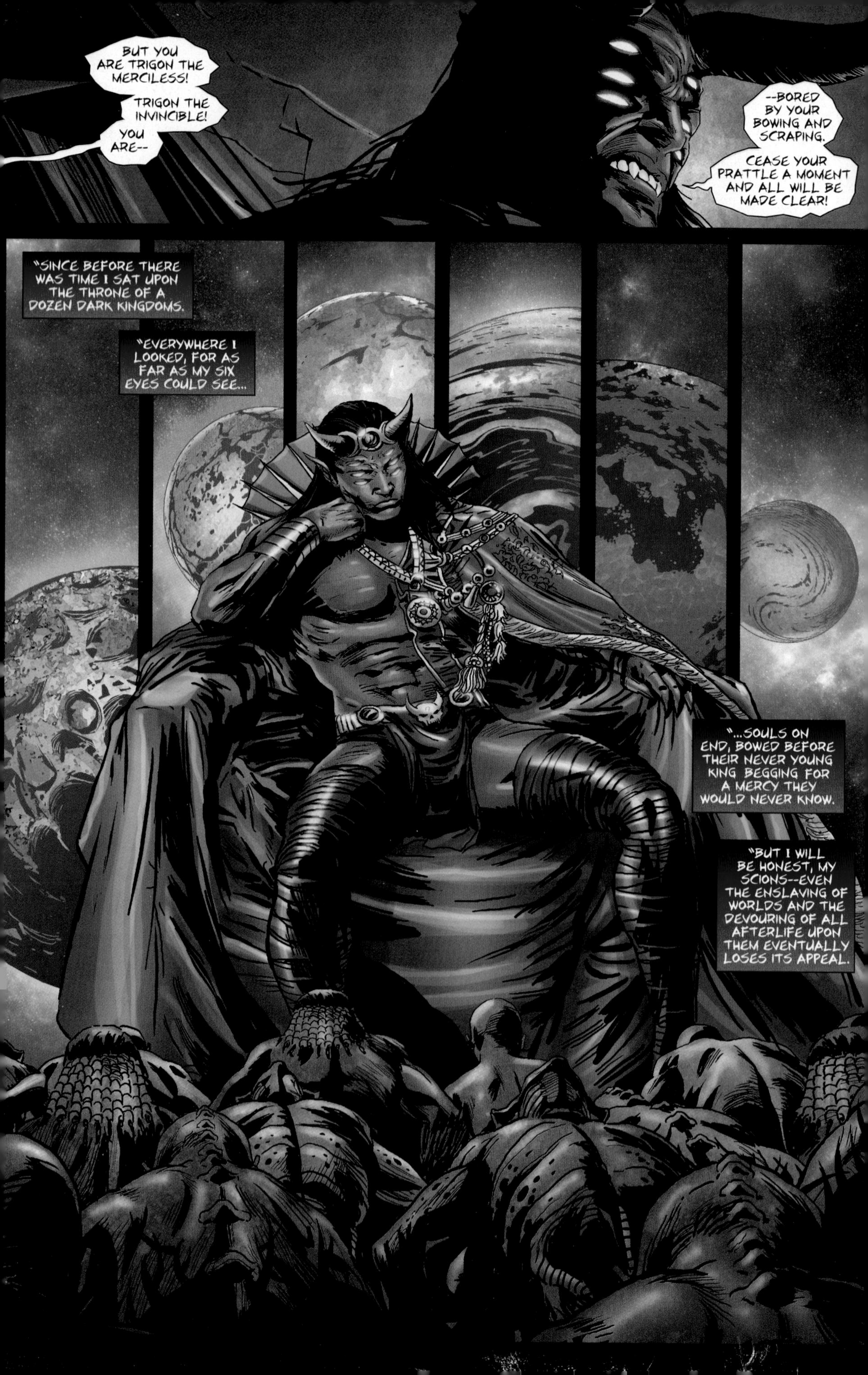

BUT YOU ARE TRIGON THE MERCILESS!
TRIGON THE INVINCIBLE!
YOU ARE--
--BORED BY YOUR BOWING AND SCRAPING.
CEASE YOUR PRATTLE A MOMENT AND ALL WILL BE MADE CLEAR!
"SINCE BEFORE THERE WAS TIME I SAT UPON THE THRONE OF A DOZEN DARK KINGDOMS.
"EVERYWHERE I LOOKED, FOR AS FAR AS MY SIX EYES COULD SEE...
"...SOULS ON END, BOWED BEFORE THEIR NEVER YOUNG KING BEGGING FOR A MERCY THEY WOULD NEVER KNOW.
"BUT I WILL BE HONEST, MY SCIONS--EVEN THE ENSLAVING OF WORLDS AND THE DEVOURING OF ALL AFTERLIFE UPON THEM EVENTUALLY LOSES ITS APPEAL.

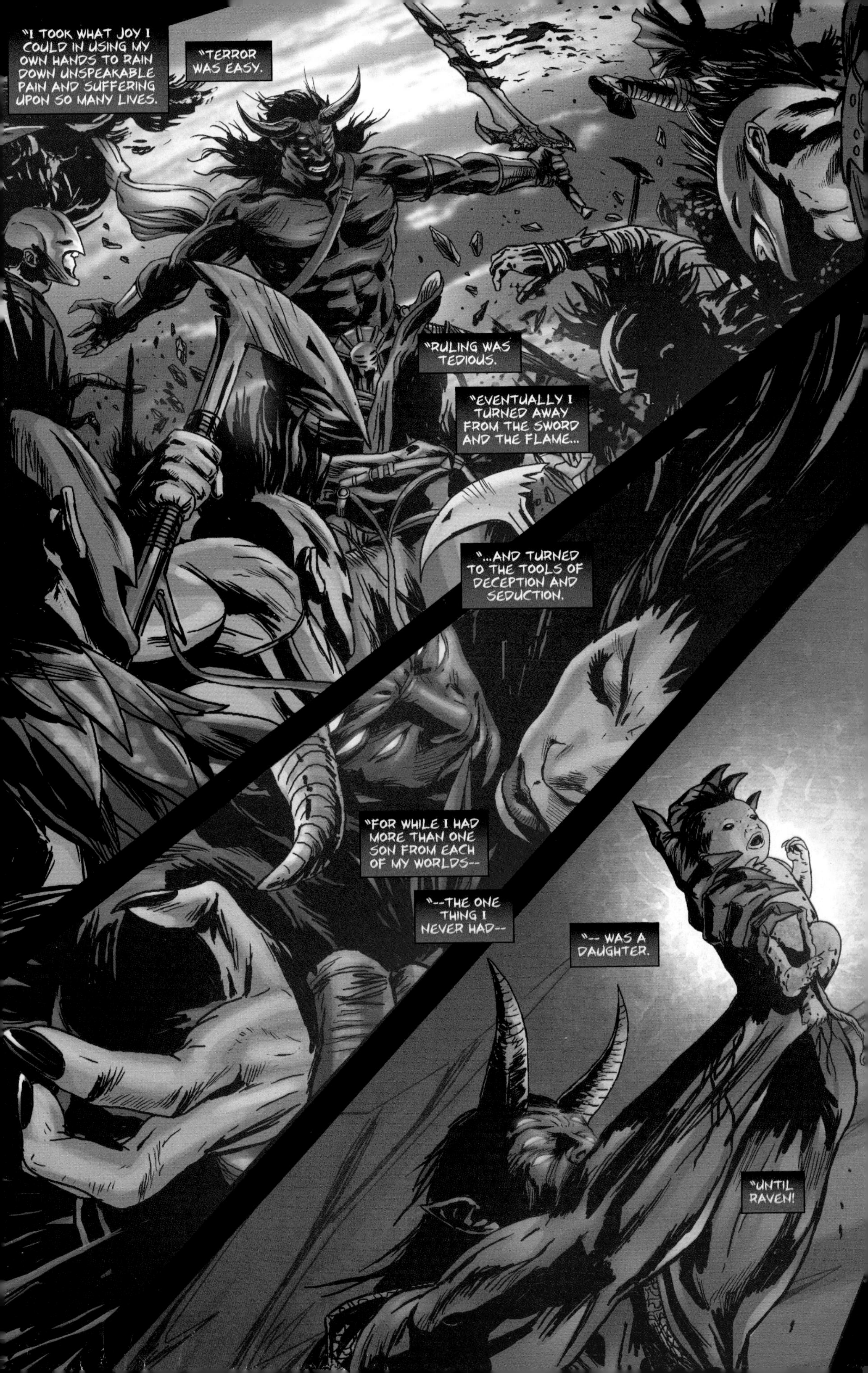
"I TOOK WHAT JOY I COULD IN USING MY OWN HANDS TO RAIN DOWN UNSPEAKABLE PAIN AND SUFFERING UPON SO MANY LIVES.
"TERROR WAS EASY.
"RULING WAS TEDIOUS.
"EVENTUALLY I TURNED AWAY FROM THE SWORD AND THE FLAME...
"...AND TURNED TO THE TOOLS OF DECEPTION AND SEDUCTION.
"FOR WHILE I HAD MORE THAN ONE SON FROM EACH OF MY WORLDS--
"--THE ONE THING I NEVER HAD--
"-- WAS A DAUGHTER.
"UNTIL RAVEN!

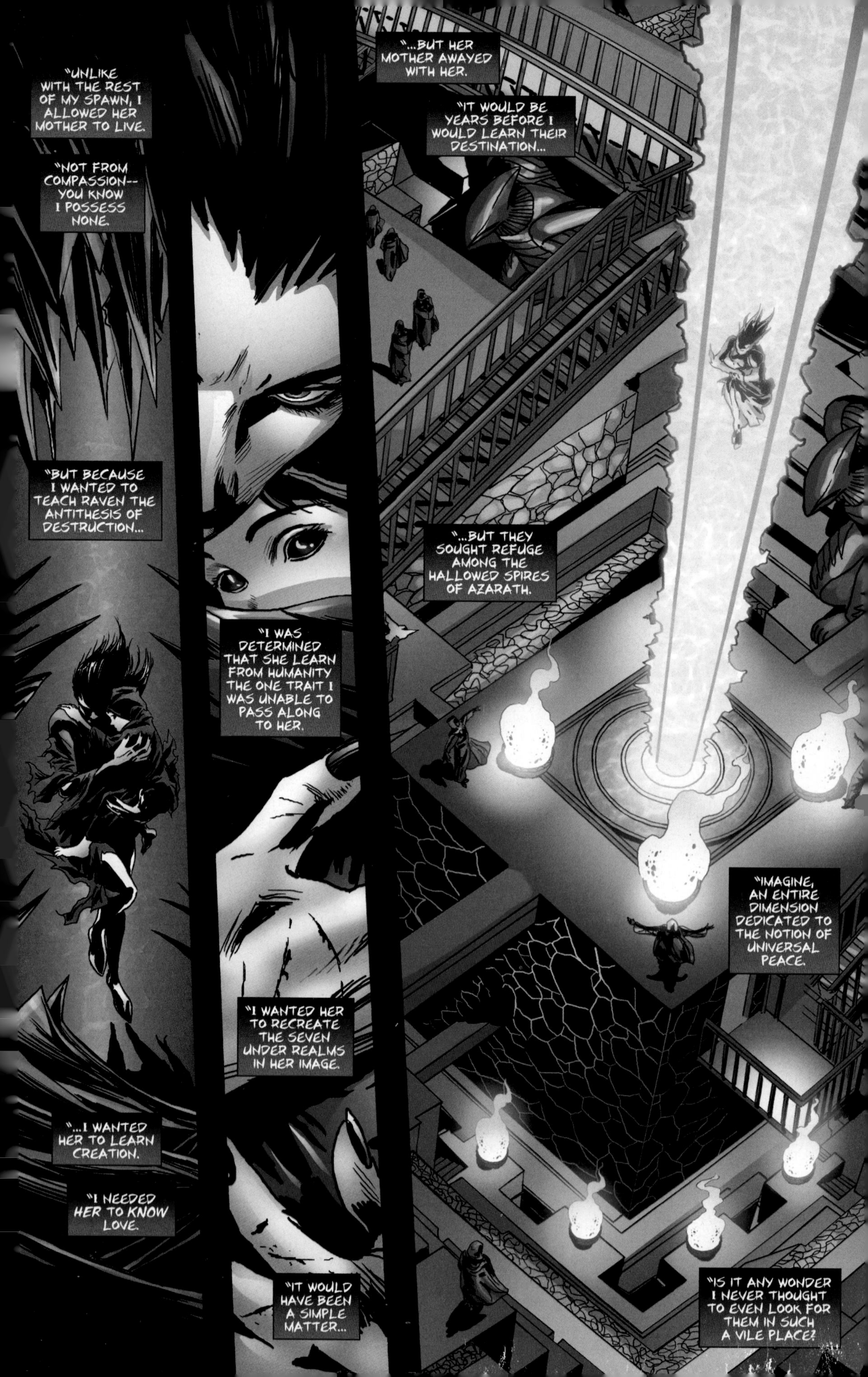
"UNLIKE WITH THE REST OF MY SPAWN, I ALLOWED HER MOTHER TO LIVE.
"NOT FROM COMPASSION--YOU KNOW I POSSESS NONE.
"BUT BECAUSE I WANTED TO TEACH RAVEN THE ANTITHESIS OF DESTRUCTION...
"I WAS DETERMINED THAT SHE LEARN FROM HUMANITY THE ONE TRAIT I WAS UNABLE TO PASS ALONG TO HER.
"I WANTED HER TO RECREATE THE SEVEN UNDER REALMS IN HER IMAGE.
"...I WANTED HER TO LEARN CREATION.
"I NEEDED HER TO KNOW LOVE.
"IT WOULD HAVE BEEN A SIMPLE MATTER...
"...BUT HER MOTHER AWAYED WITH HER.
"IT WOULD BE YEARS BEFORE I WOULD LEARN THEIR DESTINATION...
"...BUT THEY SOUGHT REFUGE AMONG THE HALLOWED SPIRES OF AZARATH.
"IMAGINE, AN ENTIRE DIMENSION DEDICATED TO THE NOTION OF UNIVERSAL PEACE.
"IS IT ANY WONDER I NEVER THOUGHT TO EVEN LOOK FOR THEM IN SUCH A VILE PLACE?

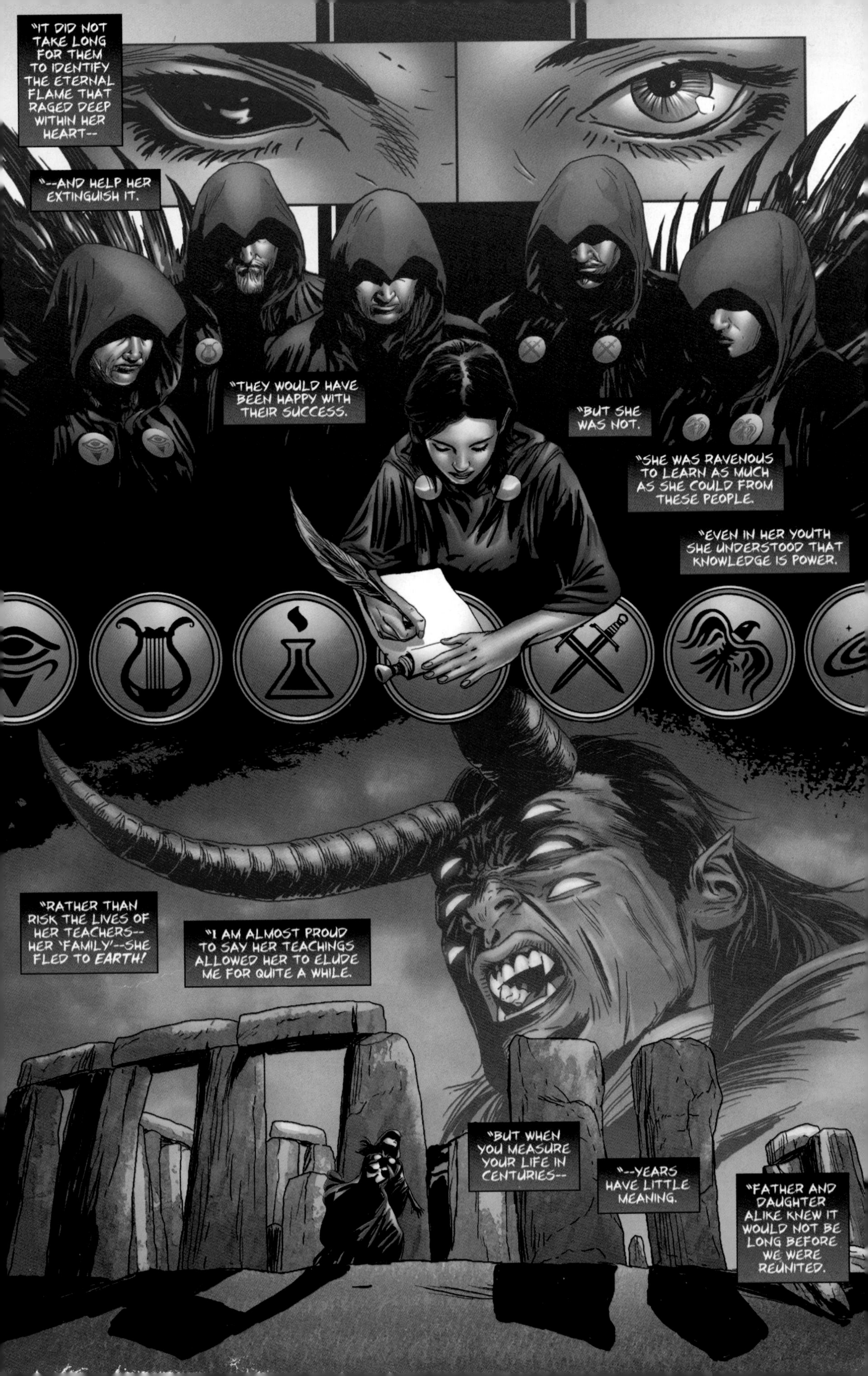
"IT DID NOT TAKE LONG FOR THEM TO IDENTIFY THE ETERNAL FLAME THAT RAGED DEEP WITHIN HER HEART--
"--AND HELP HER EXTINGUISH IT.
"THEY WOULD HAVE BEEN HAPPY WITH THEIR SUCCESS.
"BUT SHE WAS NOT.
"SHE WAS RAVENOUS TO LEARN AS MUCH AS SHE COULD FROM THESE PEOPLE.
"EVEN IN HER YOUTH SHE UNDERSTOOD THAT KNOWLEDGE IS POWER.
"RATHER THAN RISK THE LIVES OF HER TEACHERS-- HER 'FAMILY'--SHE FLED TO EARTH!
"I AM ALMOST PROUD TO SAY HER TEACHINGS ALLOWED HER TO ELUDE ME FOR QUITE A WHILE.
"BUT WHEN YOU MEASURE YOUR LIFE IN CENTURIES--
"--YEARS HAVE LITTLE MEANING.
"FATHER AND DAUGHTER ALIKE KNEW IT WOULD NOT BE LONG BEFORE WE WERE REUNITED.

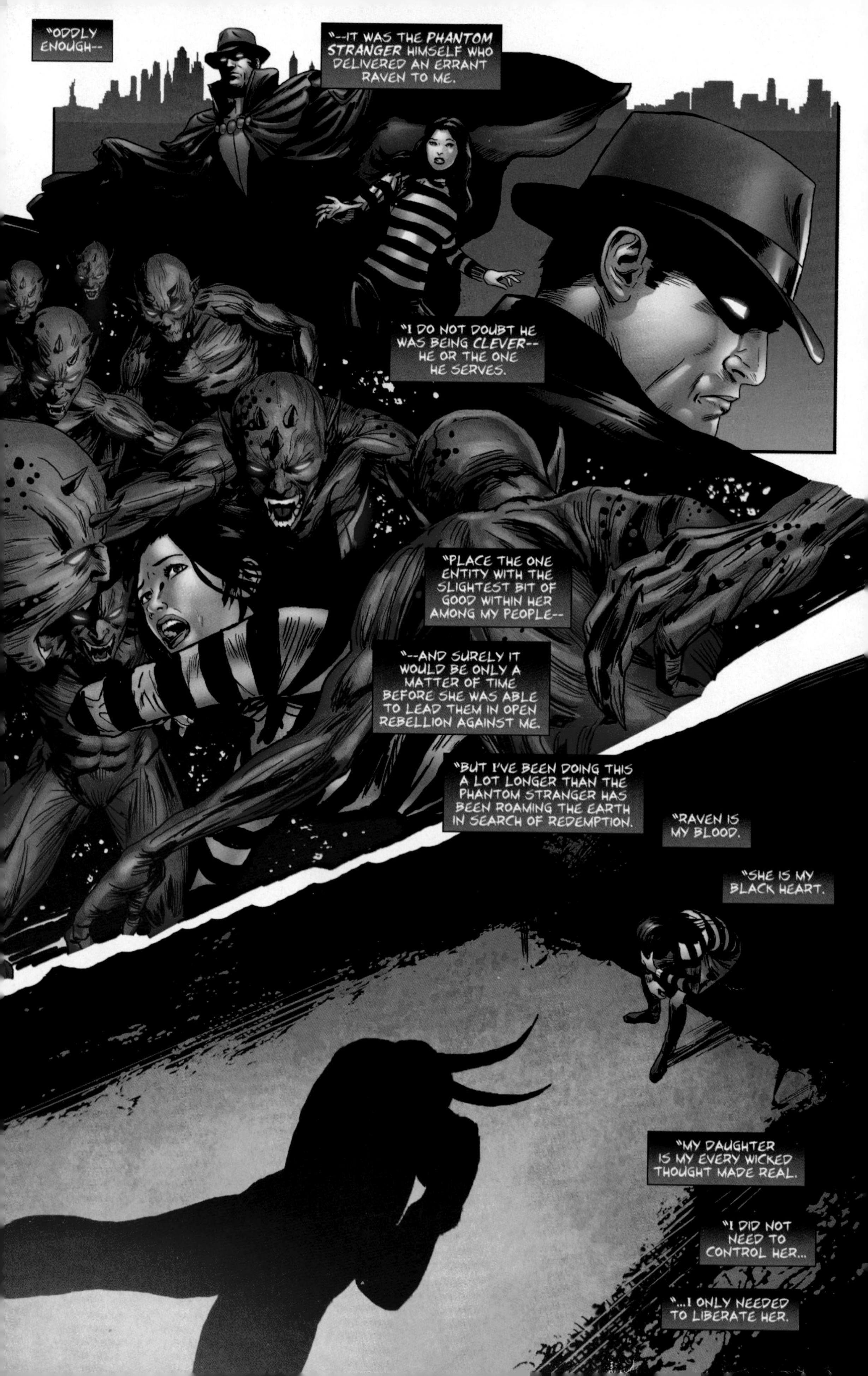
"ODDLY ENOUGH--
"--IT WAS THE PHANTOM STRANGER HIMSELF WHO DELIVERED AN ERRANT RAVEN TO ME.
"I DO NOT DOUBT HE WAS BEING CLEVER-- HE OR THE ONE HE SERVES.
"PLACE THE ONE ENTITY WITH THE SLIGHTEST BIT OF GOOD WITHIN HER AMONG MY PEOPLE--
"--AND SURELY IT WOULD BE ONLY A MATTER OF TIME BEFORE SHE WAS ABLE TO LEAD THEM IN OPEN REBELLION AGAINST ME.
"BUT I'VE BEEN DOING THIS A LOT LONGER THAN THE PHANTOM STRANGER HAS BEEN ROAMING THE EARTH IN SEARCH OF REDEMPTION.
"RAVEN IS MY BLOOD.
"SHE IS MY BLACK HEART.
"MY DAUGHTER IS MY EVERY WICKED THOUGHT MADE REAL.
"I DID NOT NEED TO CONTROL HER...
"...I ONLY NEEDED TO LIBERATE HER.

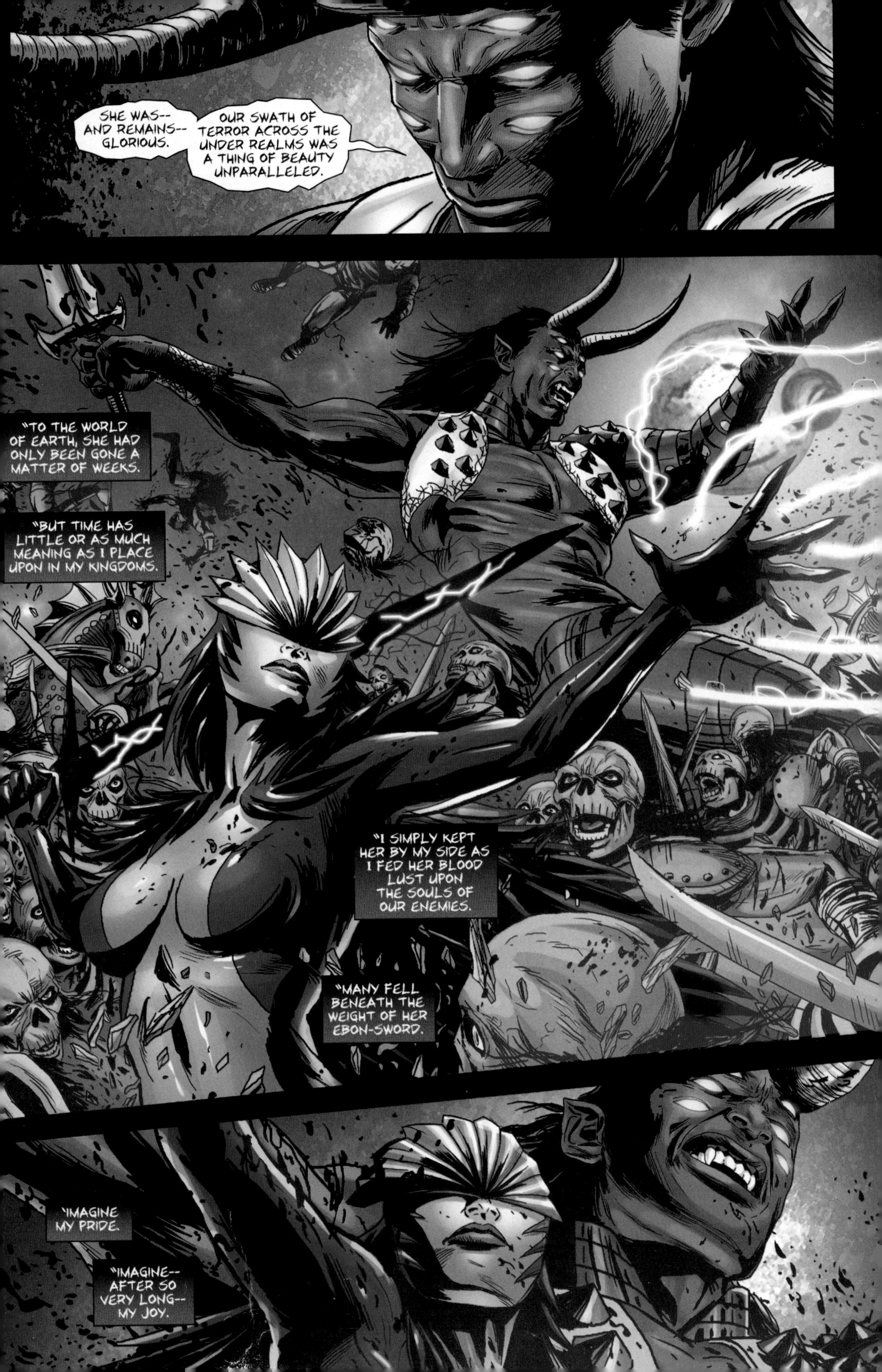
SHE WAS--
AND REMAINS--
GLORIOUS.
OUR SWATH OF TERROR ACROSS THE UNDER REALMS WAS A THING OF BEAUTY UNPARALLELED.
"TO THE WORLD OF EARTH, SHE HAD ONLY BEEN GONE A MATTER OF WEEKS.
"BUT TIME HAS LITTLE OR AS MUCH MEANING AS I PLACE UPON IN MY KINGDOMS.
"I SIMPLY KEPT HER BY MY SIDE AS I FED HER BLOOD LUST UPON THE SOULS OF OUR ENEMIES.
"MANY FELL BENEATH THE WEIGHT OF HER EBON-SWORD.
"IMAGINE MY PRIDE.
"IMAGINE-- AFTER SO VERY LONG-- MY JOY.

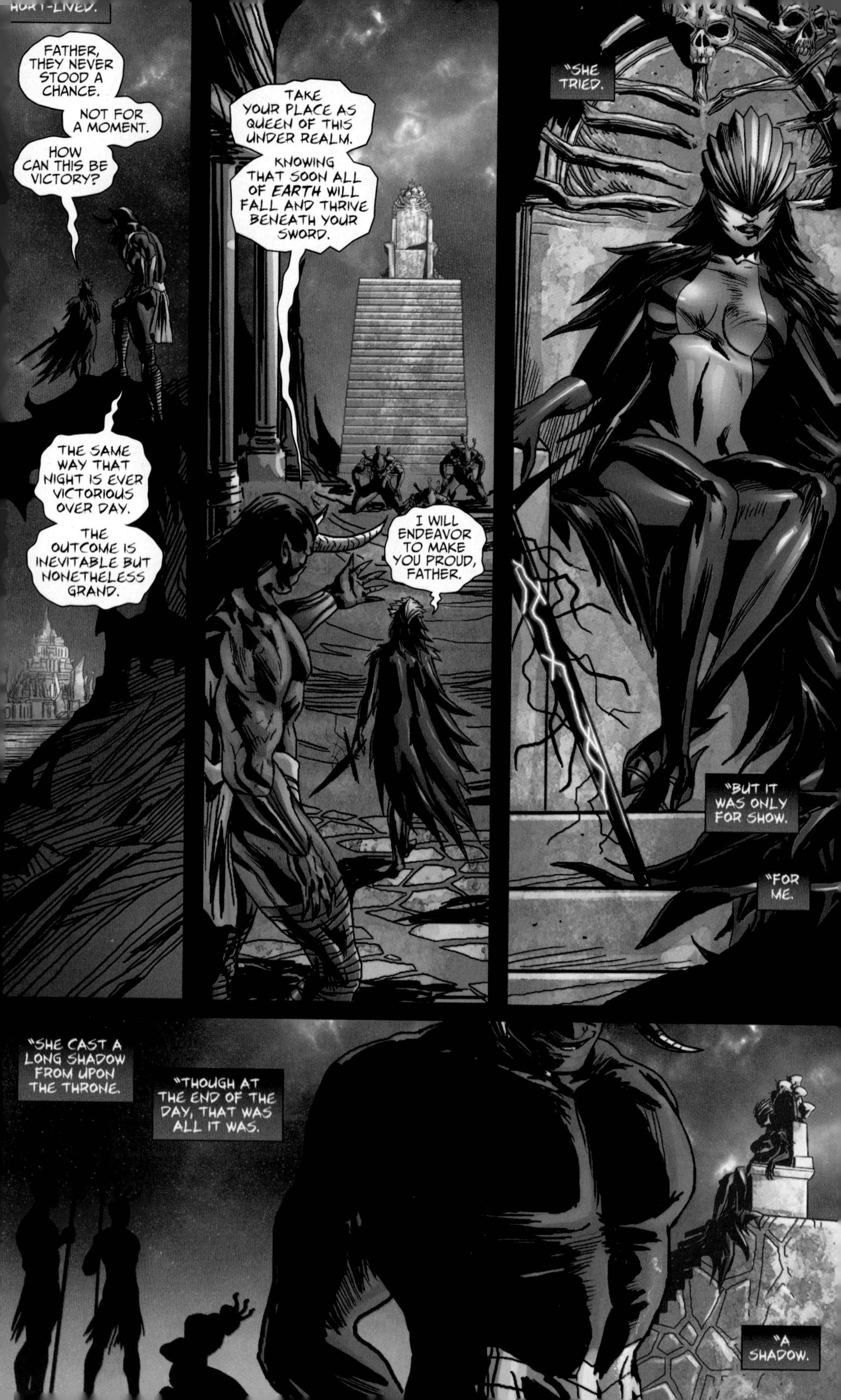

HORT-LIVED.
FATHER, THEY NEVER STOOD A CHANCE.
NOT FOR A MOMENT.
HOW CAN THIS BE VICTORY?
THE SAME WAY THAT NIGHT IS EVER VICTORIOUS OVER DAY.
THE OUTCOME IS INEVITABLE BUT NONETHELESS GRAND.
TAKE YOUR PLACE AS QUEEN OF THIS UNDER REALM.
KNOWING THAT SOON ALL OF EARTH WILL FALL AND THRIVE BENEATH YOUR SWORD.
I WILL ENDEAVOR TO MAKE YOU PROUD, FATHER.
"SHE TRIED.
"BUT IT WAS ONLY FOR SHOW.
"FOR ME.
"SHE CAST A LONG SHADOW FROM UPON THE THRONE.
"THOUGH AT THE END OF THE DAY, THAT WAS ALL IT WAS.
"A SHADOW.

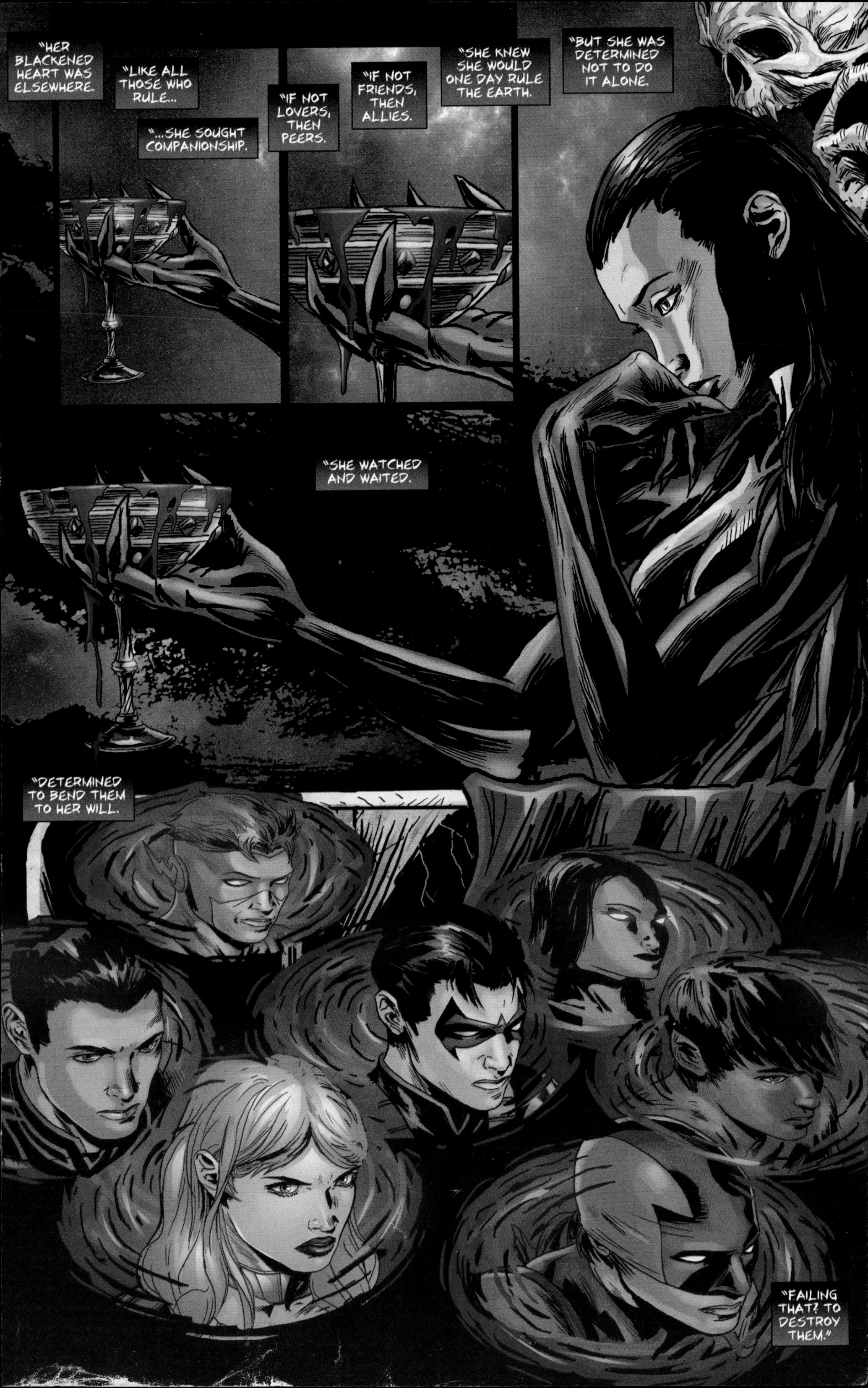
"HER BLACKENED HEART WAS ELSEWHERE.
"LIKE ALL THOSE WHO RULE...
"...SHE SOUGHT COMPANIONSHIP.
"IF NOT LOVERS, THEN PEERS.
"IF NOT FRIENDS, THEN ALLIES.
"SHE KNEW SHE WOULD ONE DAY RULE THE EARTH.
"BUT SHE WAS DETERMINED NOT TO DO IT ALONE.
"SHE WATCHED AND WAITED.
"DETERMINED TO BEND THEM TO HER WILL.
"FAILING THAT? TO DESTROY THEM."

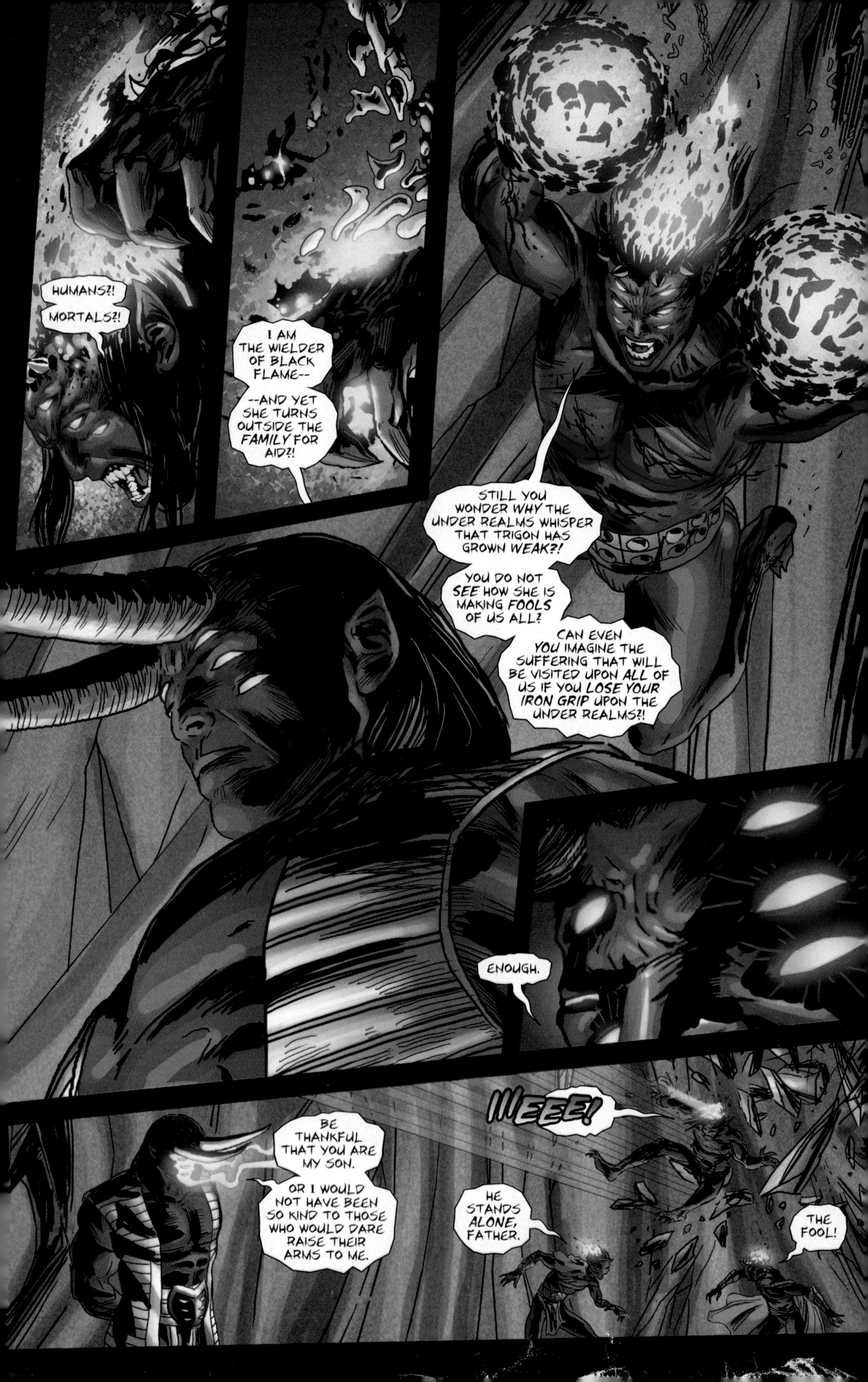
HUMANS?!
MORTALS?!
I AM THE WIELDER OF BLACK FLAME--
--AND YET SHE TURNS OUTSIDE THE FAMILY FOR AID?!
STILL YOU WONDER WHY THE UNDER REALMS WHISPER THAT TRIGON HAS GROWN WEAK?!
YOU DO NOT SEE HOW SHE IS MAKING FOOLS OF US ALL?
CAN EVEN YOU IMAGINE THE SUFFERING THAT WILL BE VISITED UPON ALL OF US IF YOU LOSE YOUR IRON GRIP UPON THE UNDER REALMS?!
ENOUGH.
IIIEEEE!
BE THANKFUL THAT YOU ARE MY SON.
OR I WOULD NOT HAVE BEEN SO KIND TO THOSE WHO WOULD DARE RAISE THEIR ARMS TO ME.
HE STANDS ALONE, FATHER.
THE FOOL!

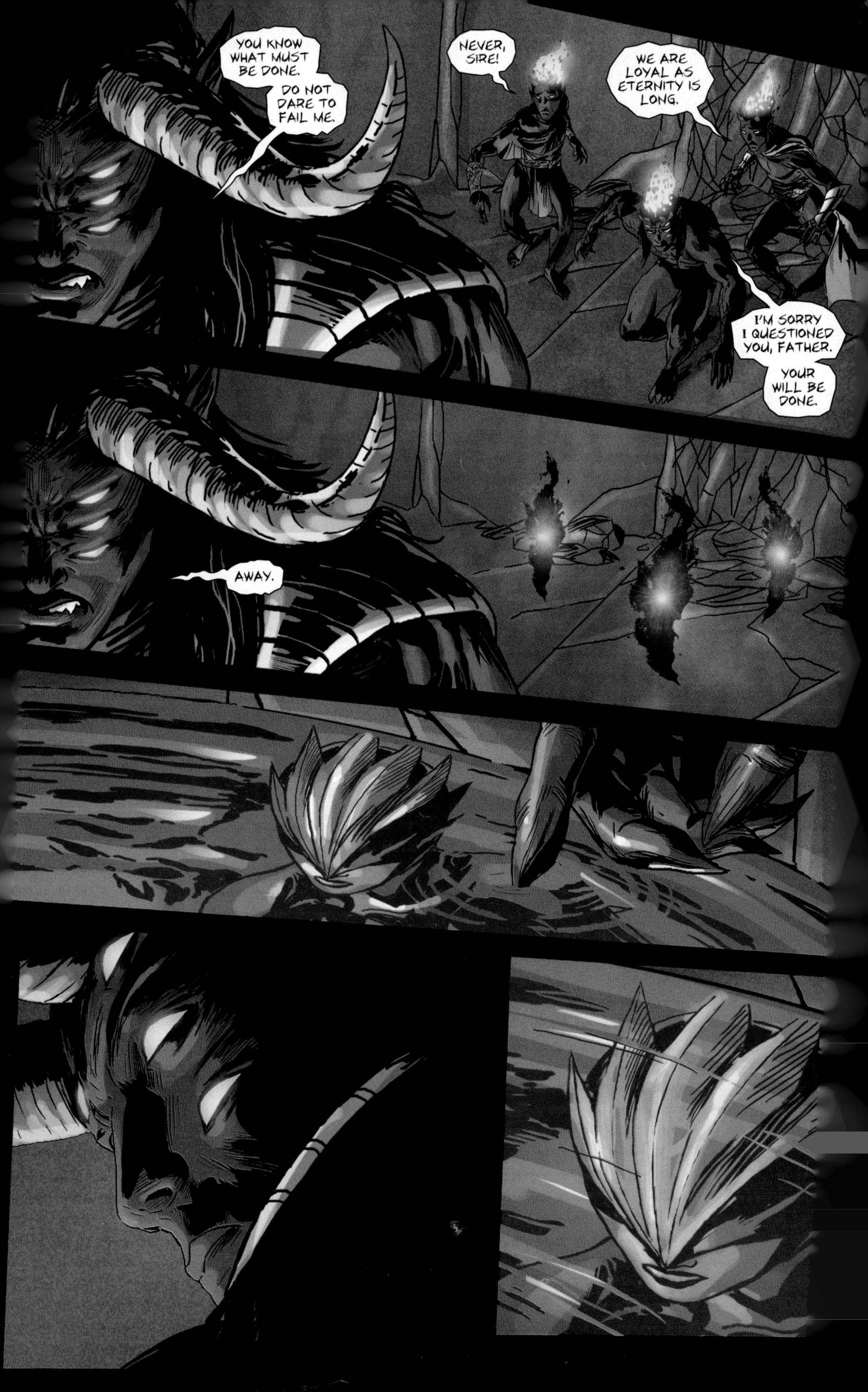
YOU KNOW WHAT MUST BE DONE.
DO NOT DARE TO FAIL ME.
NEVER, SIRE!
WE ARE LOYAL AS ETERNITY IS LONG.
I'M SORRY I QUESTIONED YOU, FATHER.
YOUR WILL BE DONE.
AWAY.

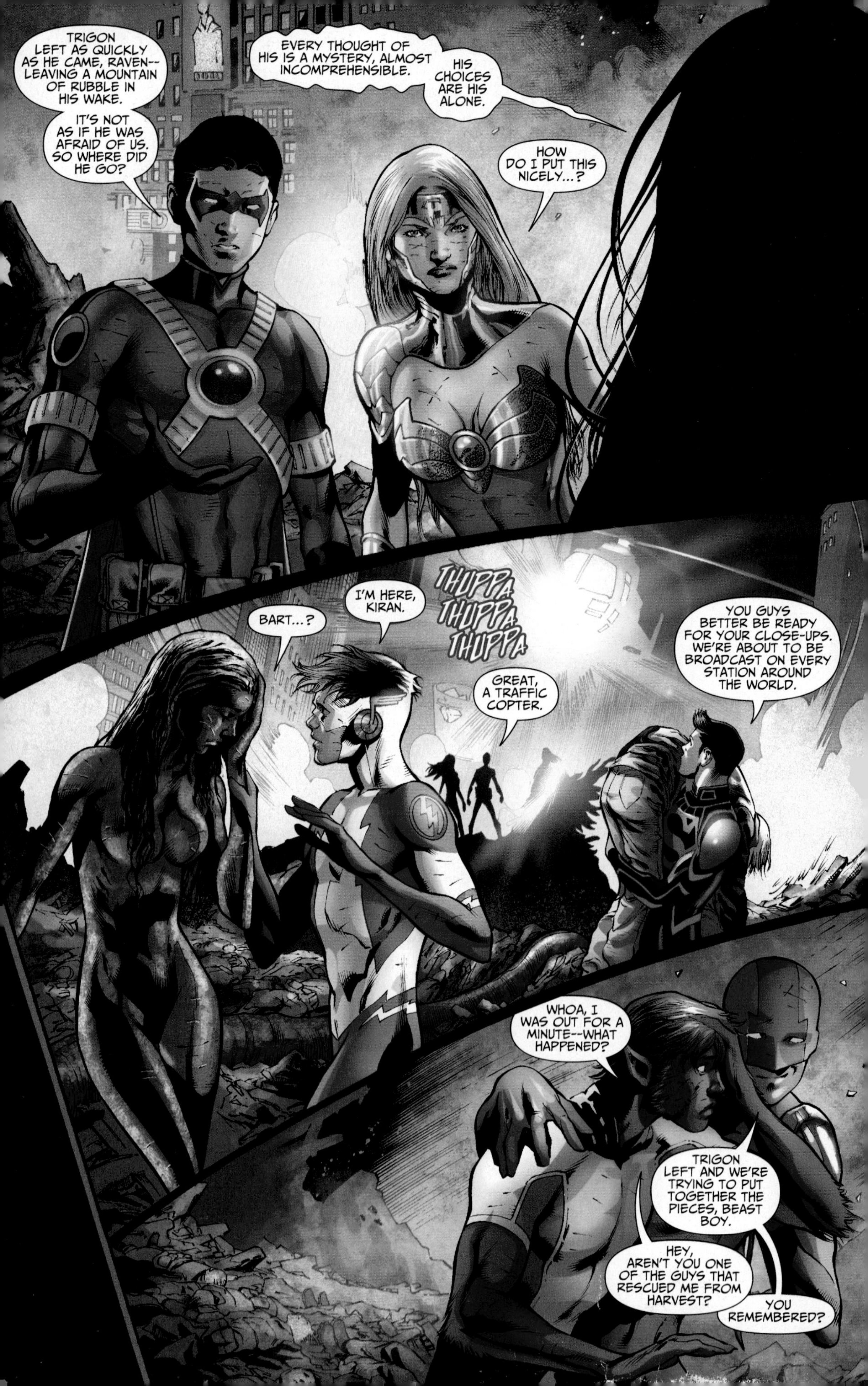
TRIGON LEFT AS QUICKLY AS HE CAME, RAVEN-- LEAVING A MOUNTAIN OF RUBBLE IN HIS WAKE.
IT'S NOT AS IF HE WAS AFRAID OF US. SO WHERE DID HE GO?
EVERY THOUGHT OF HIS IS A MYSTERY, ALMOST INCOMPREHENSIBLE.
HIS CHOICES ARE HIS ALONE.
HOW DO I PUT THIS NICELY...?
THUPPA THUPPA THUPPA
BART...?
I'M HERE, KIRAN.
GREAT, A TRAFFIC COPTER.
YOU GUYS BETTER BE READY FOR YOUR CLOSE-UPS. WE'RE ABOUT TO BE BROADCAST ON EVERY STATION AROUND THE WORLD.
WHOA, I WAS OUT FOR A MINUTE--WHAT HAPPENED?
TRIGON LEFT AND WE'RE TRYING TO PUT TOGETHER THE PIECES, BEAST BOY.
HEY, AREN'T YOU ONE OF THE GUYS THAT RESCUED ME FROM HARVEST?
YOU REMEMBERED?

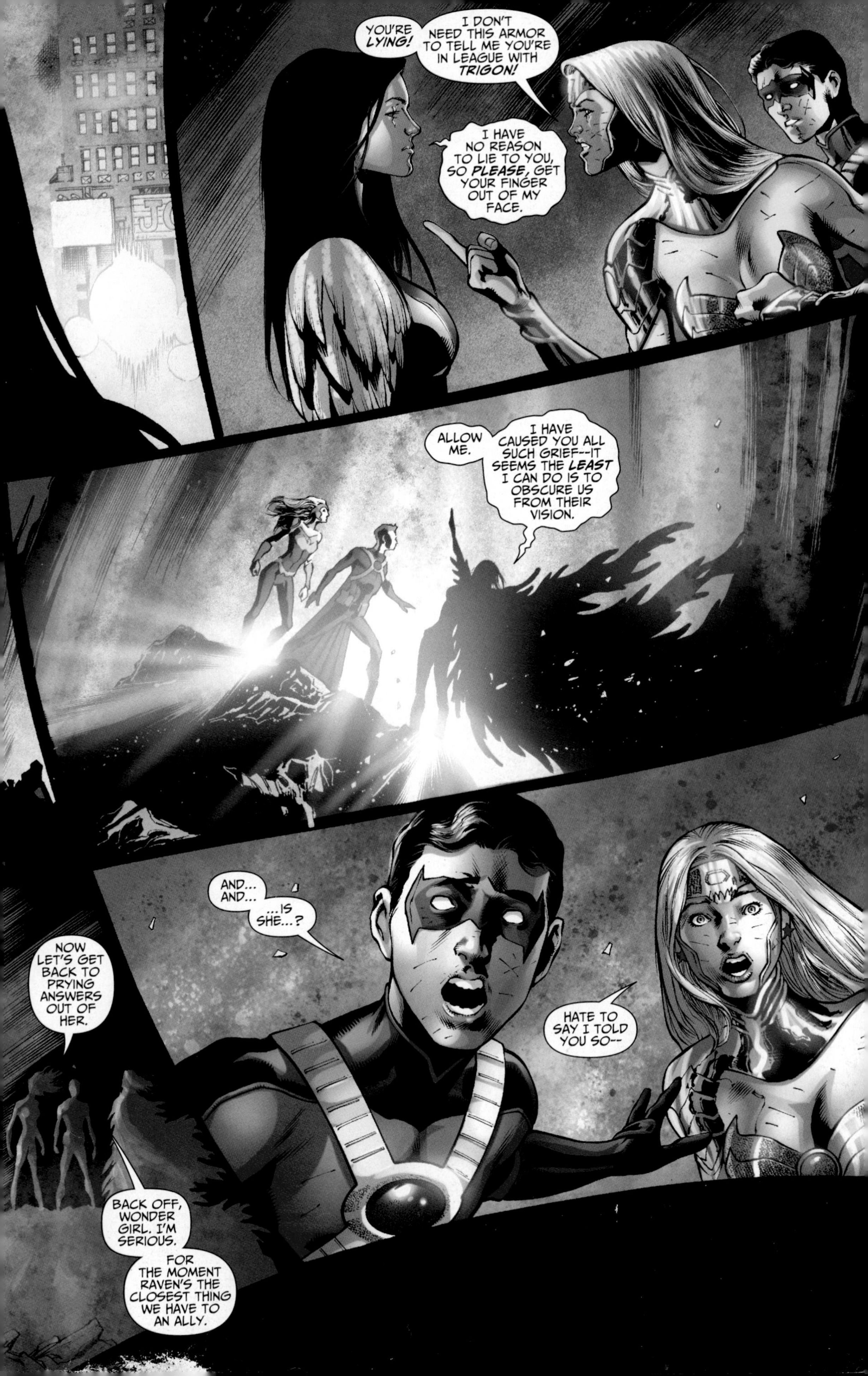
YOU'RE LYING!
I DON'T NEED THIS ARMOR TO TELL ME YOU'RE IN LEAGUE WITH TRIGON!
I HAVE NO REASON TO LIE TO YOU, SO PLEASE, GET YOUR FINGER OUT OF MY FACE.
ALLOW ME.
I HAVE CAUSED YOU ALL SUCH GRIEF--IT SEEMS THE LEAST I CAN DO IS TO OBSCURE US FROM THEIR VISION.
AND... AND...
...IS SHE...?
HATE TO SAY I TOLD YOU SO--
NOW LET'S GET BACK TO PRYING ANSWERS OUT OF HER.
BACK OFF, WONDER GIRL. I'M SERIOUS.
FOR THE MOMENT RAVEN'S THE CLOSEST THING WE HAVE TO AN ALLY.

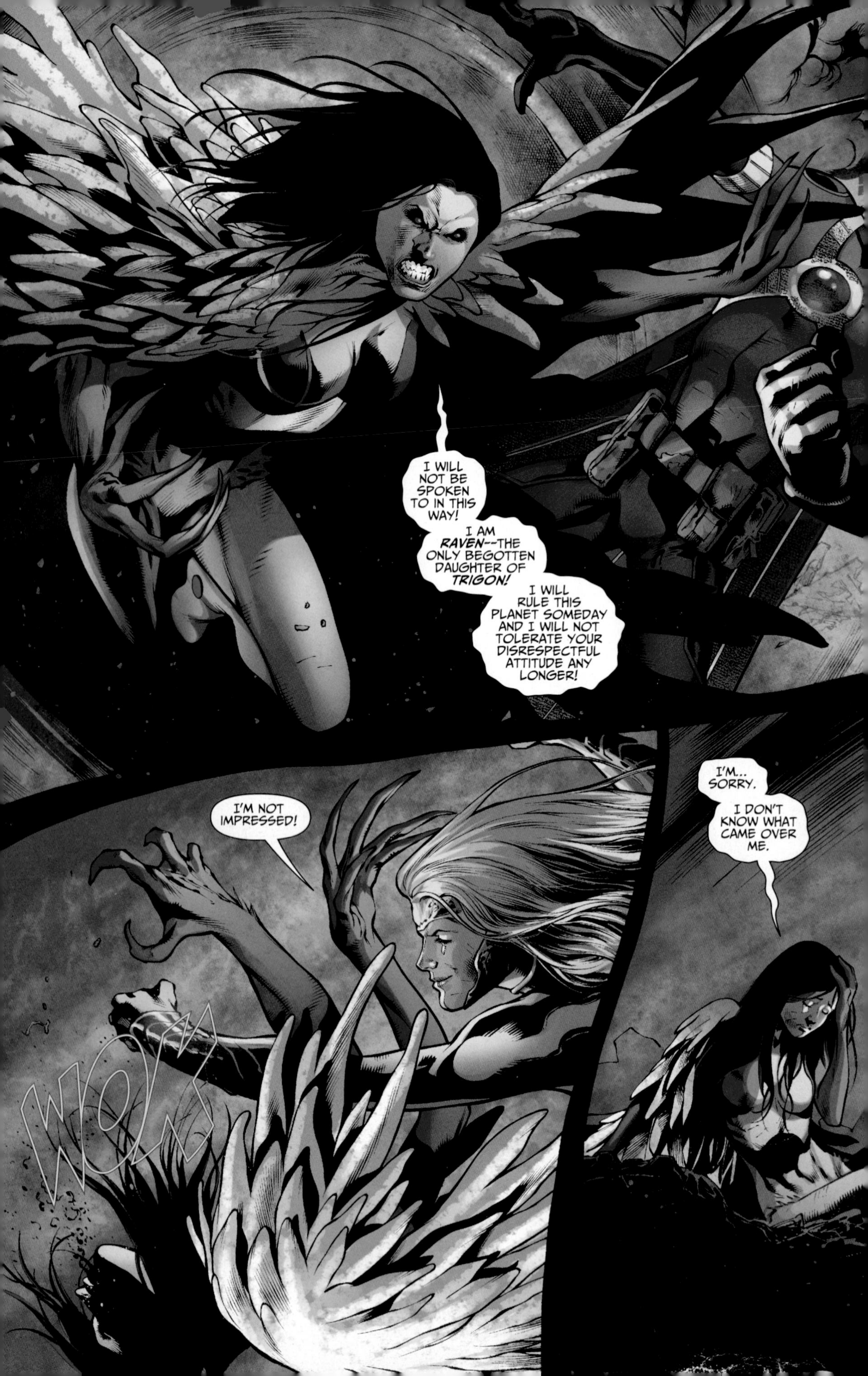
I WILL NOT BE SPOKEN TO IN THIS WAY!
I AM *RAVEN*--THE ONLY BEGOTTEN DAUGHTER OF *TRIGON!*
I WILL RULE THIS PLANET SOMEDAY AND I WILL NOT TOLERATE YOUR DISRESPECTFUL ATTITUDE ANY LONGER!
I'M NOT IMPRESSED!
WOM
I'M... SORRY.
I DON'T KNOW WHAT CAME OVER ME.

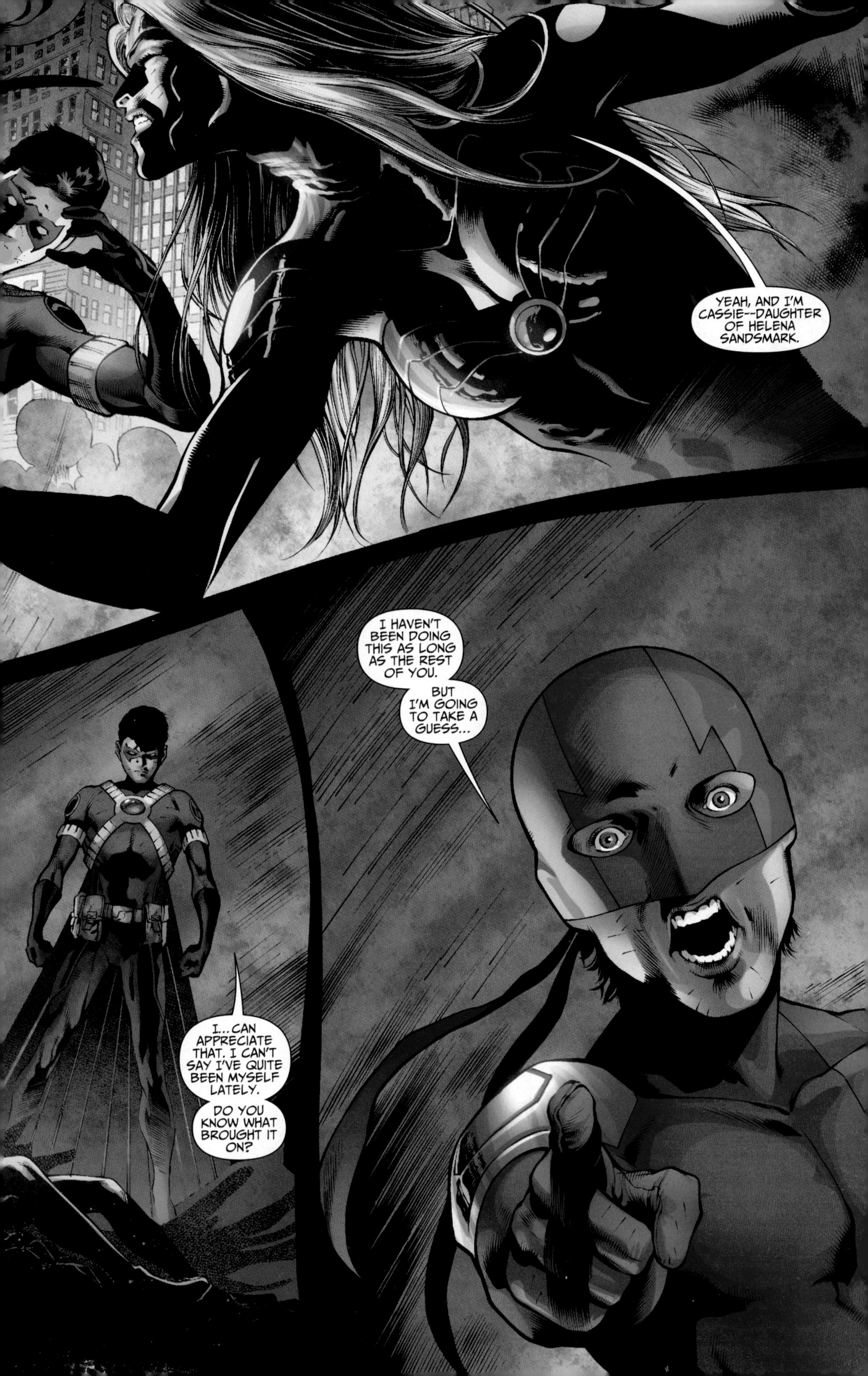
YEAH, AND I'M CASSIE--DAUGHTER OF HELENA SANDSMARK.
I HAVEN'T BEEN DOING THIS AS LONG AS THE REST OF YOU.
BUT I'M GOING TO TAKE A GUESS...
I...CAN APPRECIATE THAT. I CAN'T SAY I'VE QUITE BEEN MYSELF LATELY.
DO YOU KNOW WHAT BROUGHT IT ON?

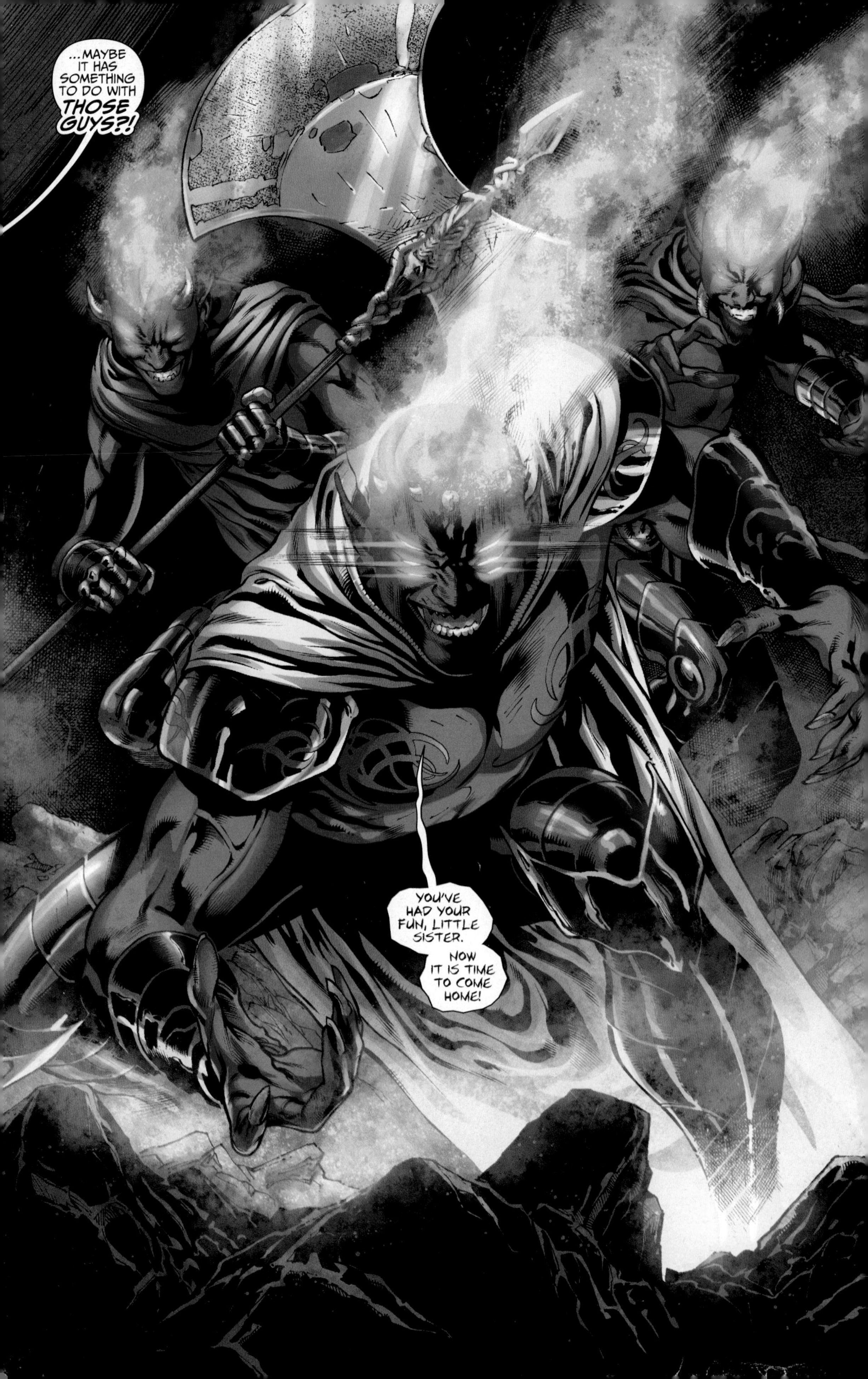
...MAYBE IT HAS SOMETHING TO DO WITH THOSE GUYS?!
YOU'VE HAD YOUR FUN, LITTLE SISTER.
NOW IT IS TIME TO COME HOME!

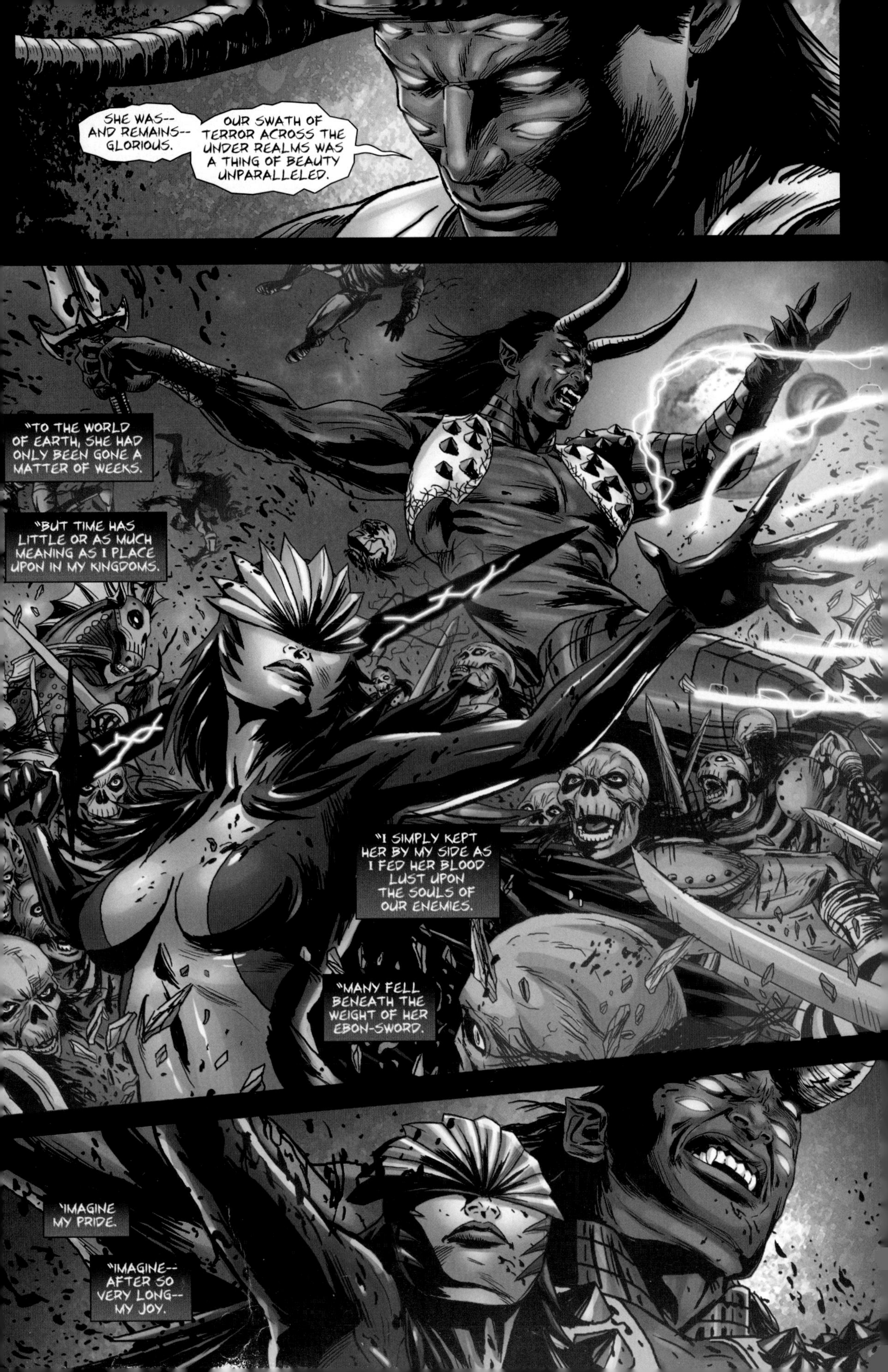
SHE WAS-- AND REMAINS-- GLORIOUS.
OUR SWATH OF TERROR ACROSS THE UNDER REALMS WAS A THING OF BEAUTY UNPARALLELED.
"TO THE WORLD OF EARTH, SHE HAD ONLY BEEN GONE A MATTER OF WEEKS.
"BUT TIME HAS LITTLE OR AS MUCH MEANING AS I PLACE UPON IN MY KINGDOMS.
"I SIMPLY KEPT HER BY MY SIDE AS I FED HER BLOOD LUST UPON THE SOULS OF OUR ENEMIES.
"MANY FELL BENEATH THE WEIGHT OF HER EBON-SWORD.
"IMAGINE MY PRIDE.
"IMAGINE-- AFTER SO VERY LONG-- MY JOY.

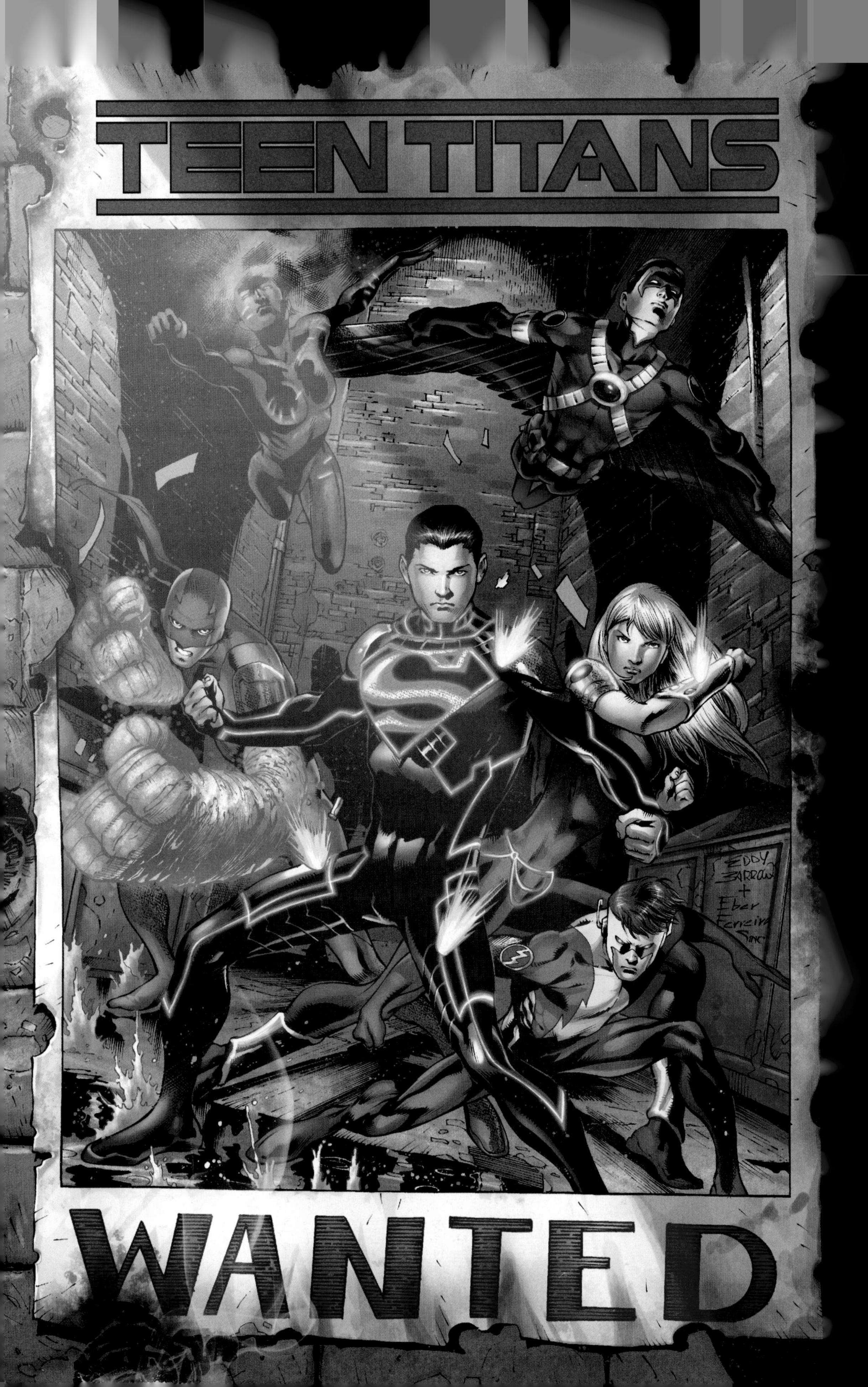
TEEN TITANS
WANTED

THE BROTHERS TRIGON

SCOTT LOBDELL & TONY BEDARD writers EDDY BARROWS layouts JESUS MERINO finishes
cover art by EDDY BARROWS, EBER FERREIRA & ALEX SINCLAIR

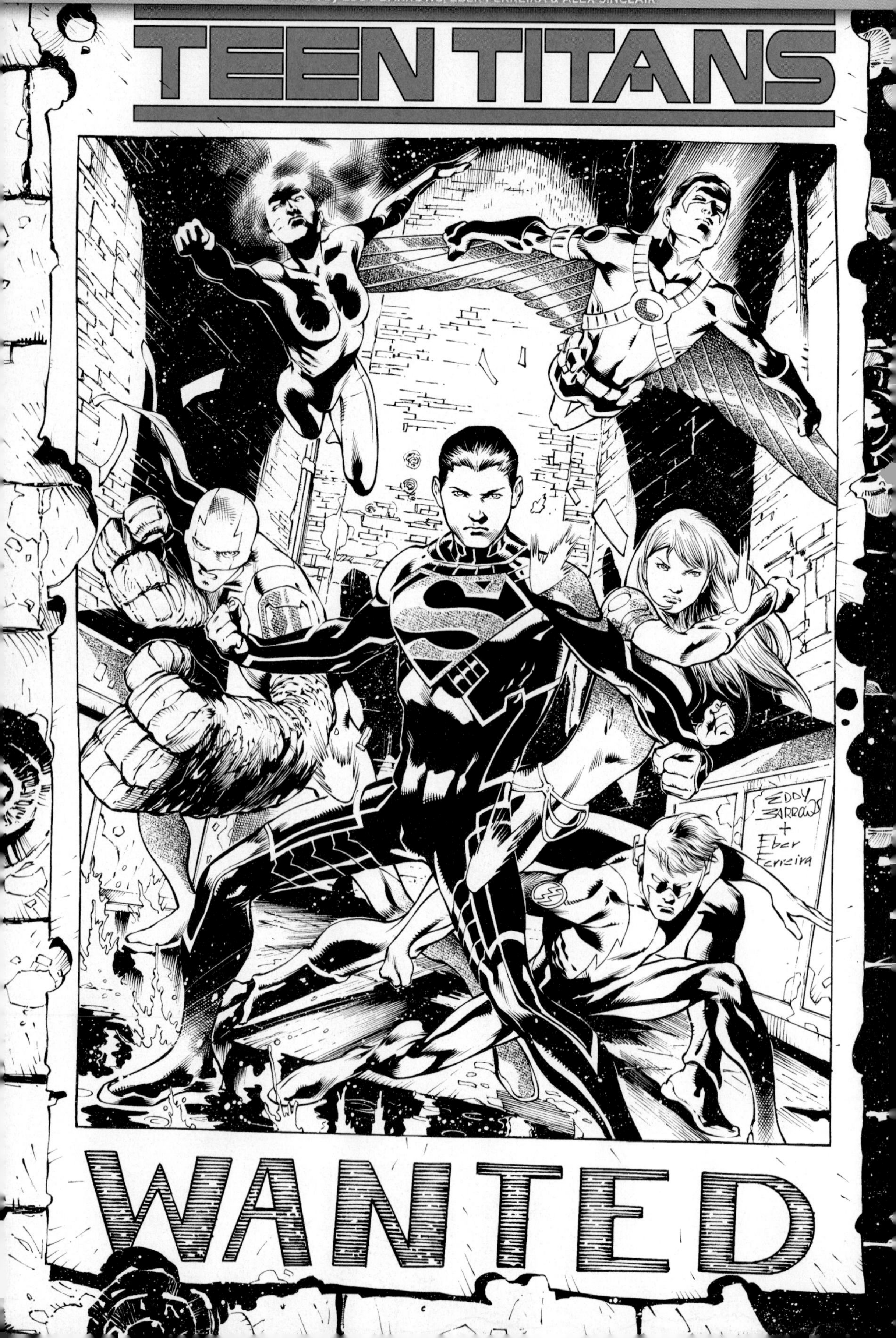
TEEN TITANS
EDDY BARROWS + Eber Ferreira
WANTED

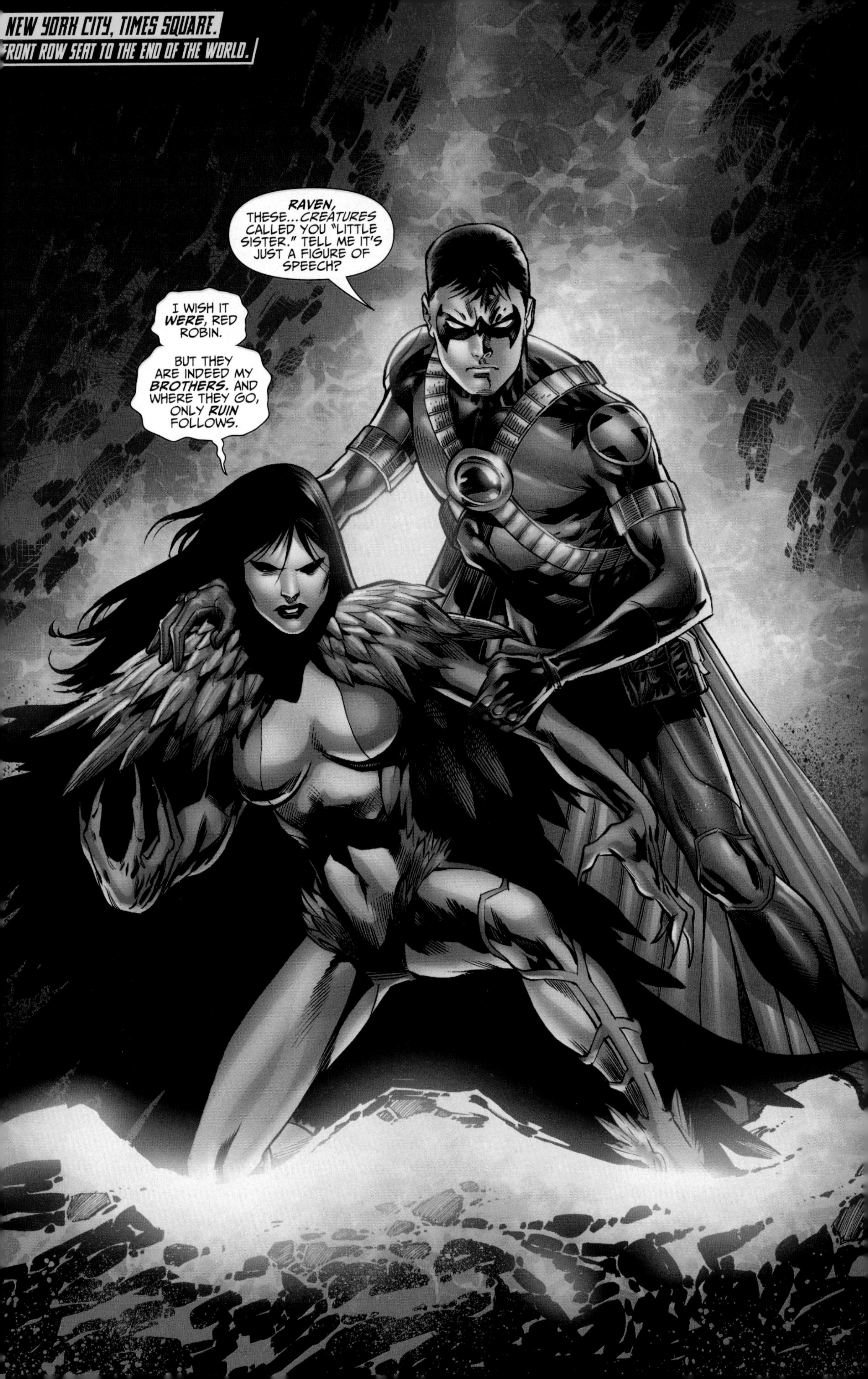
NEW YORK CITY, TIMES SQUARE.
FRONT ROW SEAT TO THE END OF THE WORLD.
RAVEN, THESE...CREATURES CALLED YOU "LITTLE SISTER." TELL ME IT'S JUST A FIGURE OF SPEECH?
I WISH IT WERE, RED ROBIN.
BUT THEY ARE INDEED MY BROTHERS. AND WHERE THEY GO, ONLY RUIN FOLLOWS.

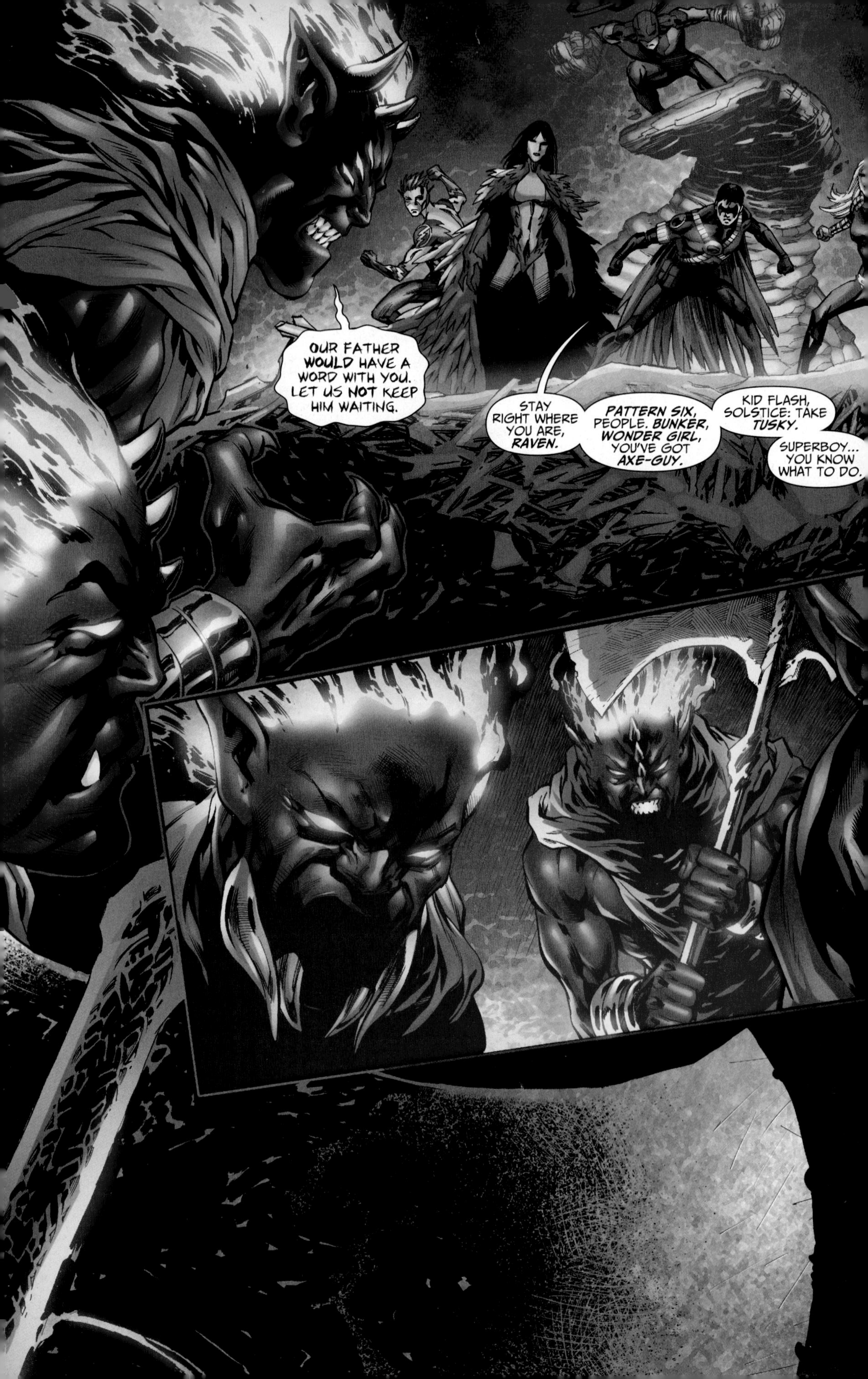
OUR FATHER WOULD HAVE A WORD WITH YOU. LET US NOT KEEP HIM WAITING.
STAY RIGHT WHERE YOU ARE, RAVEN.
PATTERN SIX, PEOPLE. BUNKER, WONDER GIRL, YOU'VE GOT AXE-GUY.
KID FLASH, SOLSTICE: TAKE TUSKY.
SUPERBOY... YOU KNOW WHAT TO DO.

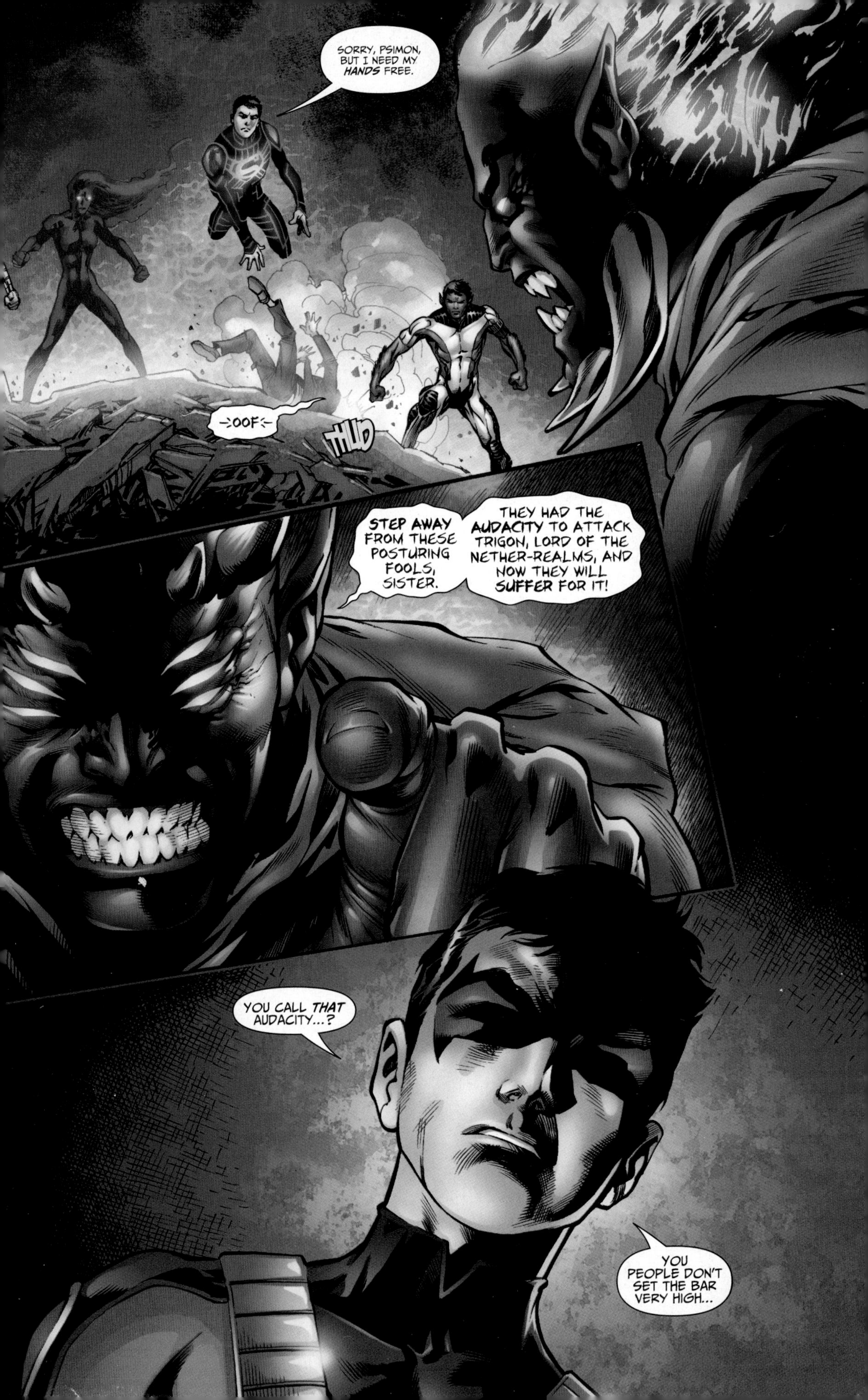
SORRY, PSIMON, BUT I NEED MY HANDS FREE.
-OOF-
THUD
STEP AWAY FROM THESE POSTURING FOOLS, SISTER.
THEY HAD THE AUDACITY TO ATTACK TRIGON, LORD OF THE NETHER-REALMS, AND NOW THEY WILL SUFFER FOR IT!
YOU CALL THAT AUDACITY...?
YOU PEOPLE DON'T SET THE BAR VERY HIGH...

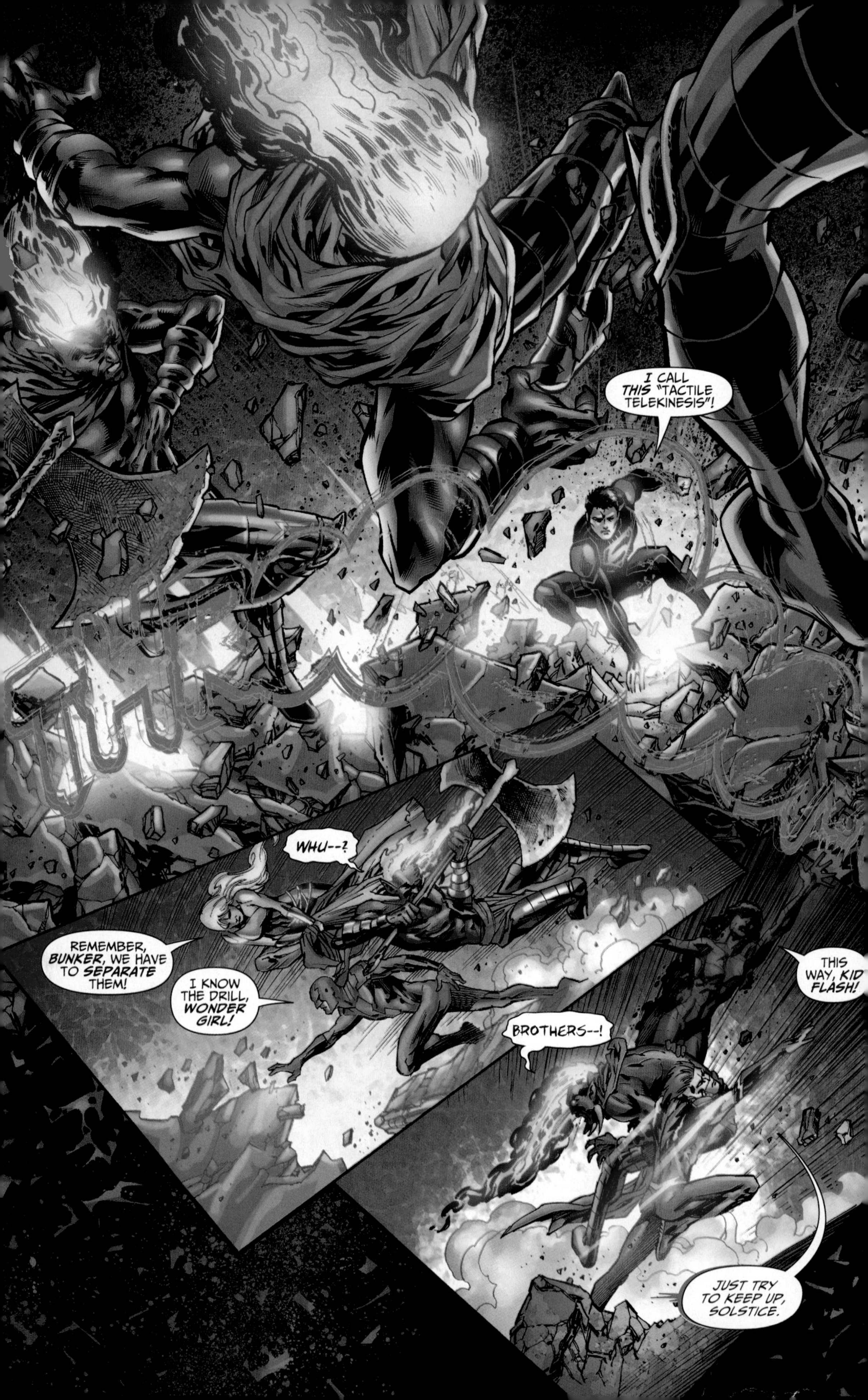
I CALL THIS "TACTILE TELEKINESIS"!
WHU--?
REMEMBER, BUNKER, WE HAVE TO SEPARATE THEM!
I KNOW THE DRILL, WONDER GIRL!
THIS WAY, KID FLASH!
BROTHERS--!
JUST TRY TO KEEP UP, SOLSTICE.

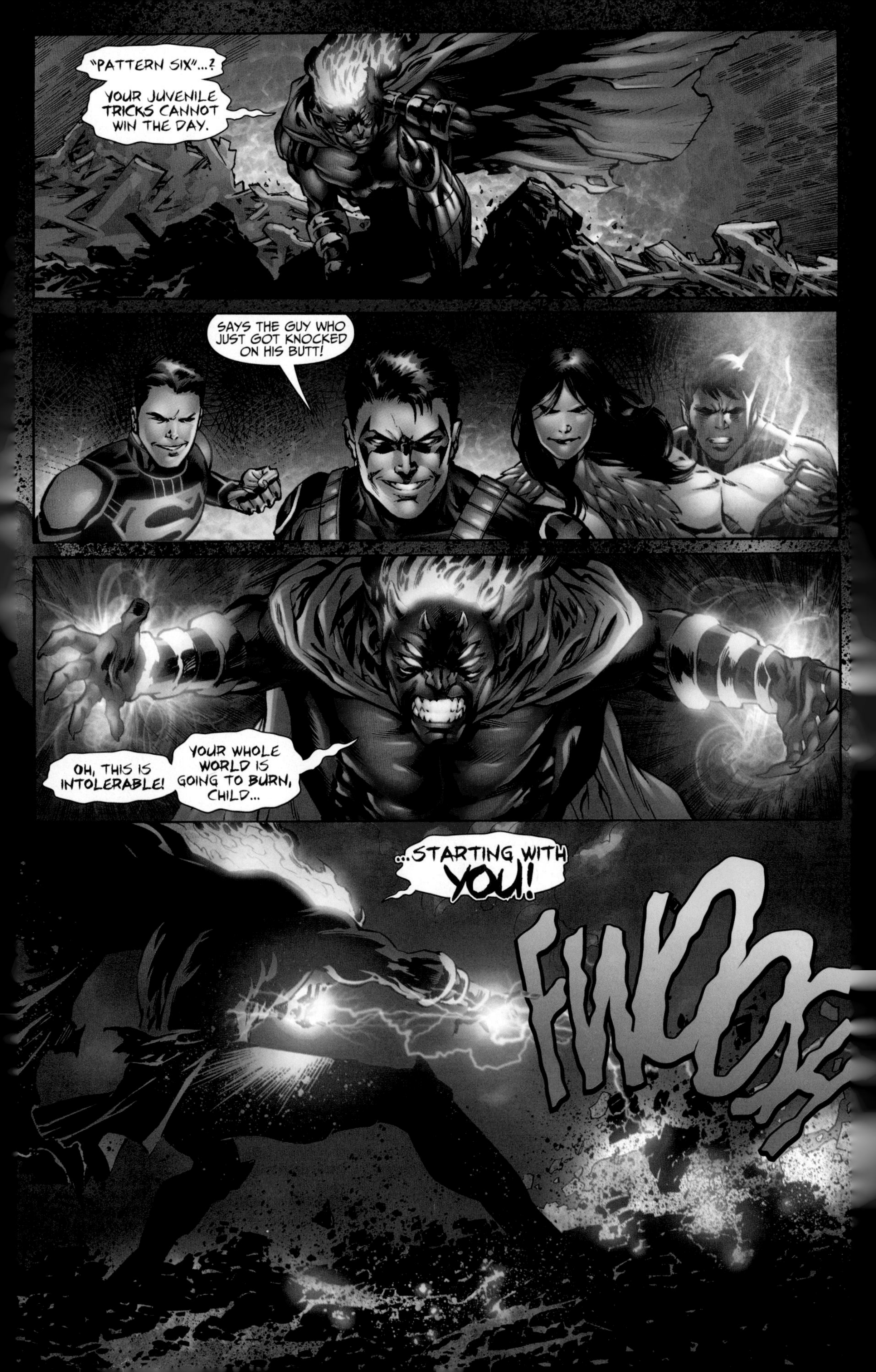
"PATTERN SIX"...?
YOUR JUVENILE TRICKS CANNOT WIN THE DAY.
SAYS THE GUY WHO JUST GOT KNOCKED ON HIS BUTT!
OH, THIS IS INTOLERABLE!
YOUR WHOLE WORLD IS GOING TO BURN, CHILD...
...STARTING WITH YOU!
FWOOS

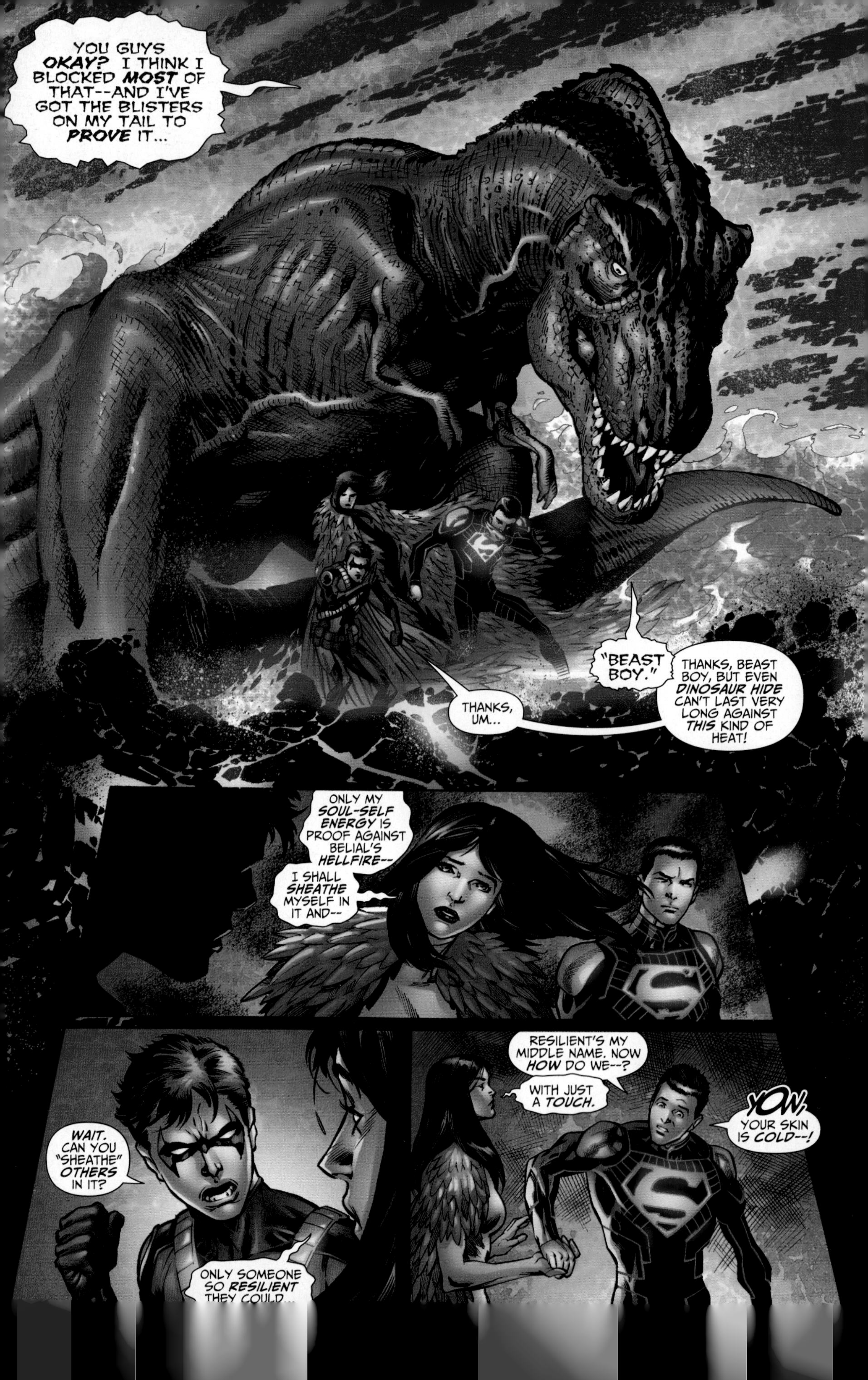
YOU GUYS OKAY? I THINK I BLOCKED MOST OF THAT--AND I'VE GOT THE BLISTERS ON MY TAIL TO PROVE IT...
THANKS, UM...
"BEAST BOY."
THANKS, BEAST BOY, BUT EVEN DINOSAUR HIDE CAN'T LAST VERY LONG AGAINST THIS KIND OF HEAT!
ONLY MY SOUL-SELF ENERGY IS PROOF AGAINST BELIAL'S HELLFIRE--
I SHALL SHEATHE MYSELF IN IT AND--
WAIT. CAN YOU "SHEATHE" OTHERS IN IT?
ONLY SOMEONE SO RESILIENT THEY COULD...
RESILIENT'S MY MIDDLE NAME. NOW HOW DO WE--?
WITH JUST A TOUCH.
YOW, YOUR SKIN IS COLD--!

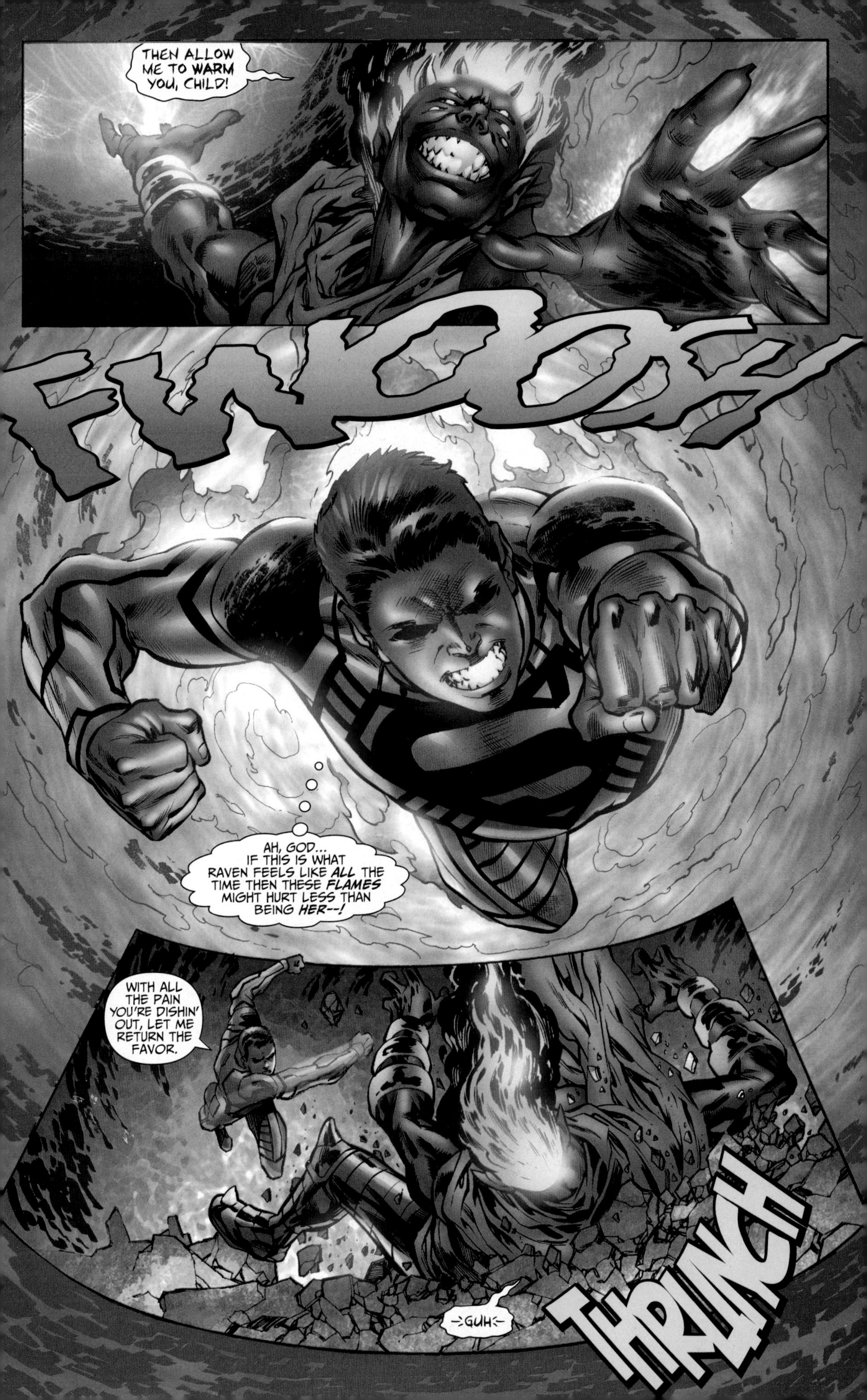
THEN ALLOW ME TO WARM YOU, CHILD!
FWOOSH
AH, GOD... IF THIS IS WHAT RAVEN FEELS LIKE ALL THE TIME THEN THESE FLAMES MIGHT HURT LESS THAN BEING HER--!
WITH ALL THE PAIN YOU'RE DISHIN' OUT, LET ME RETURN THE FAVOR.
THRUNCH
GUH

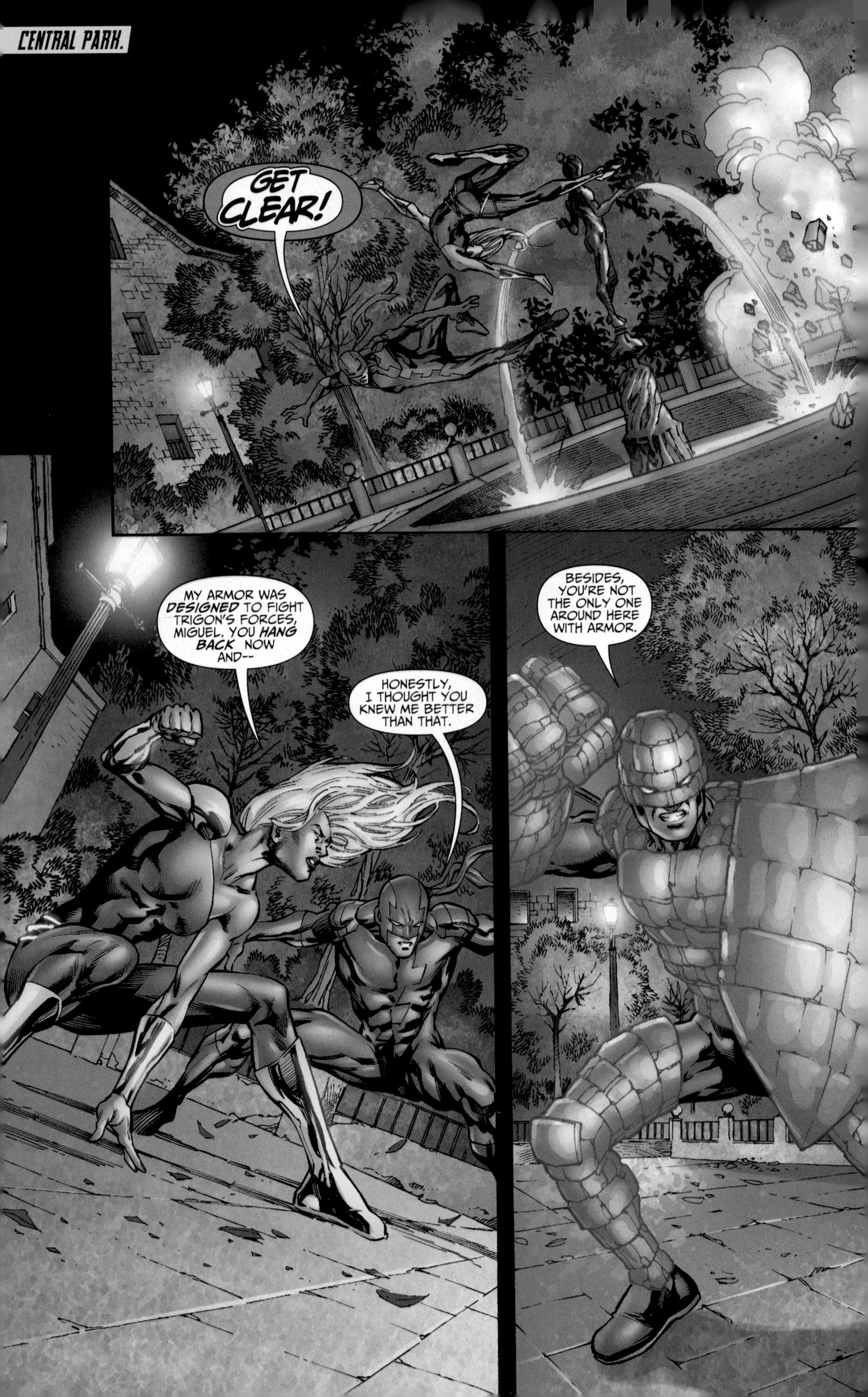
CENTRAL PARK.
GET CLEAR!
MY ARMOR WAS DESIGNED TO FIGHT TRIGON'S FORCES, MIGUEL. YOU HANG BACK NOW AND--
HONESTLY, I THOUGHT YOU KNEW ME BETTER THAN THAT.
BESIDES, YOU'RE NOT THE ONLY ONE AROUND HERE WITH ARMOR.

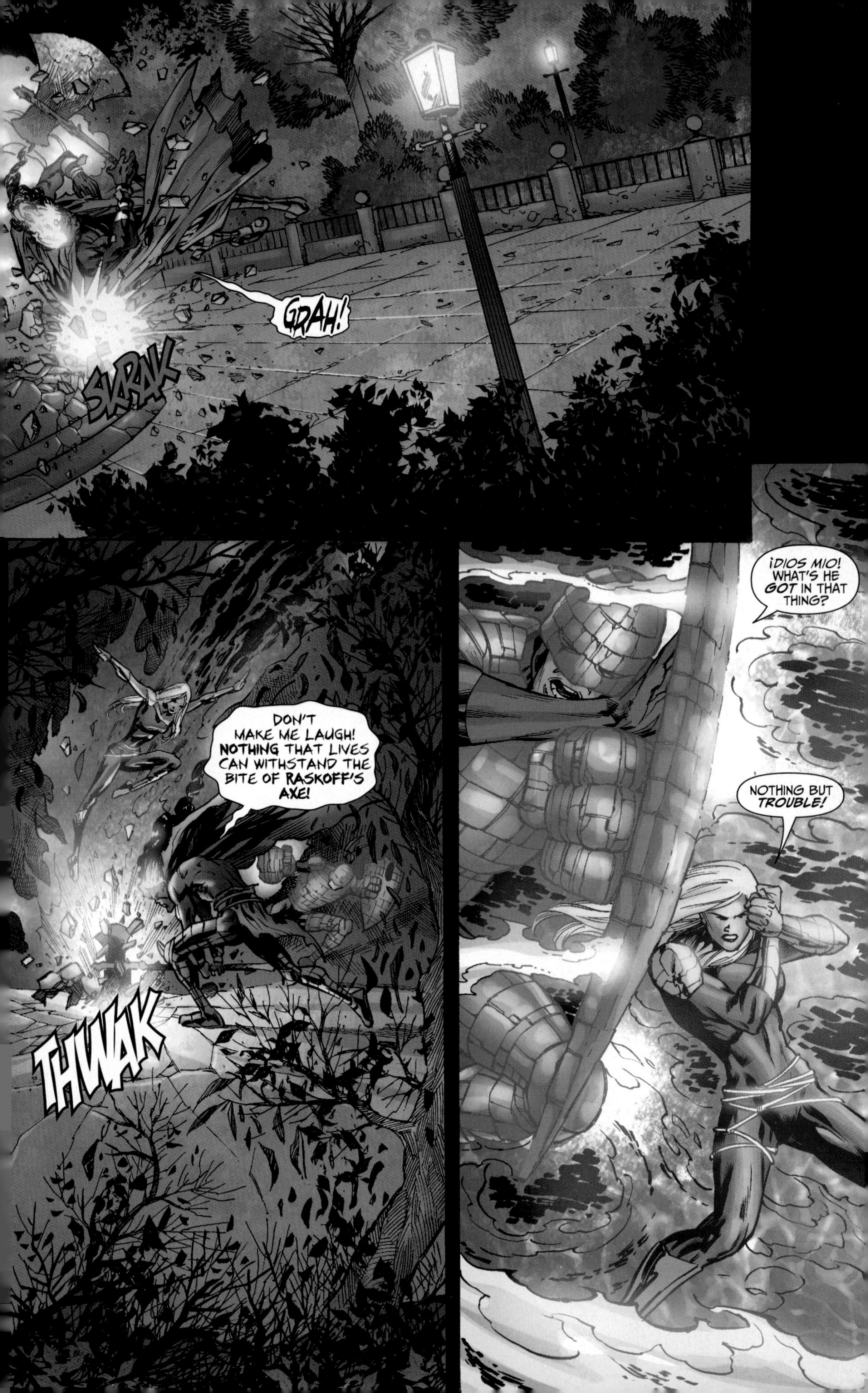
GRAH!
SKRAK
DON'T MAKE ME LAUGH! NOTHING THAT LIVES CAN WITHSTAND THE BITE OF RASKOFF'S AXE!
THWAK
¡DIOS MIO! WHAT'S HE GOT IN THAT THING?
NOTHING BUT TROUBLE!

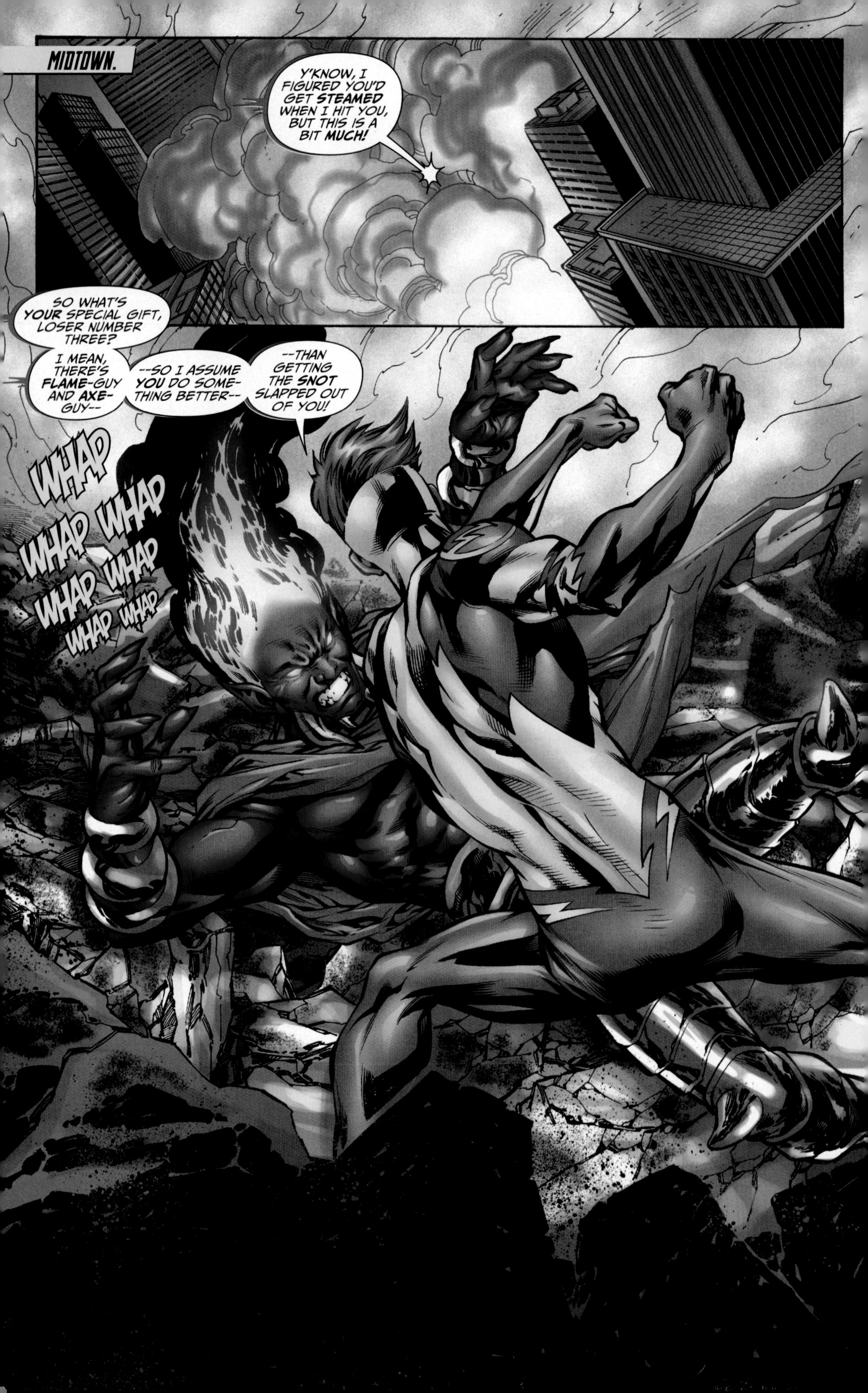
MIDTOWN.
Y'KNOW, I FIGURED YOU'D GET STEAMED WHEN I HIT YOU, BUT THIS IS A BIT MUCH!
SO WHAT'S YOUR SPECIAL GIFT, LOSER NUMBER THREE?
I MEAN, THERE'S FLAME-GUY AND AXE-GUY--
--SO I ASSUME YOU DO SOMETHING BETTER--
--THAN GETTING THE SNOT SLAPPED OUT OF YOU!
WHAP
WHAP WHAP
WHAP WHAP
WHAP WHAP

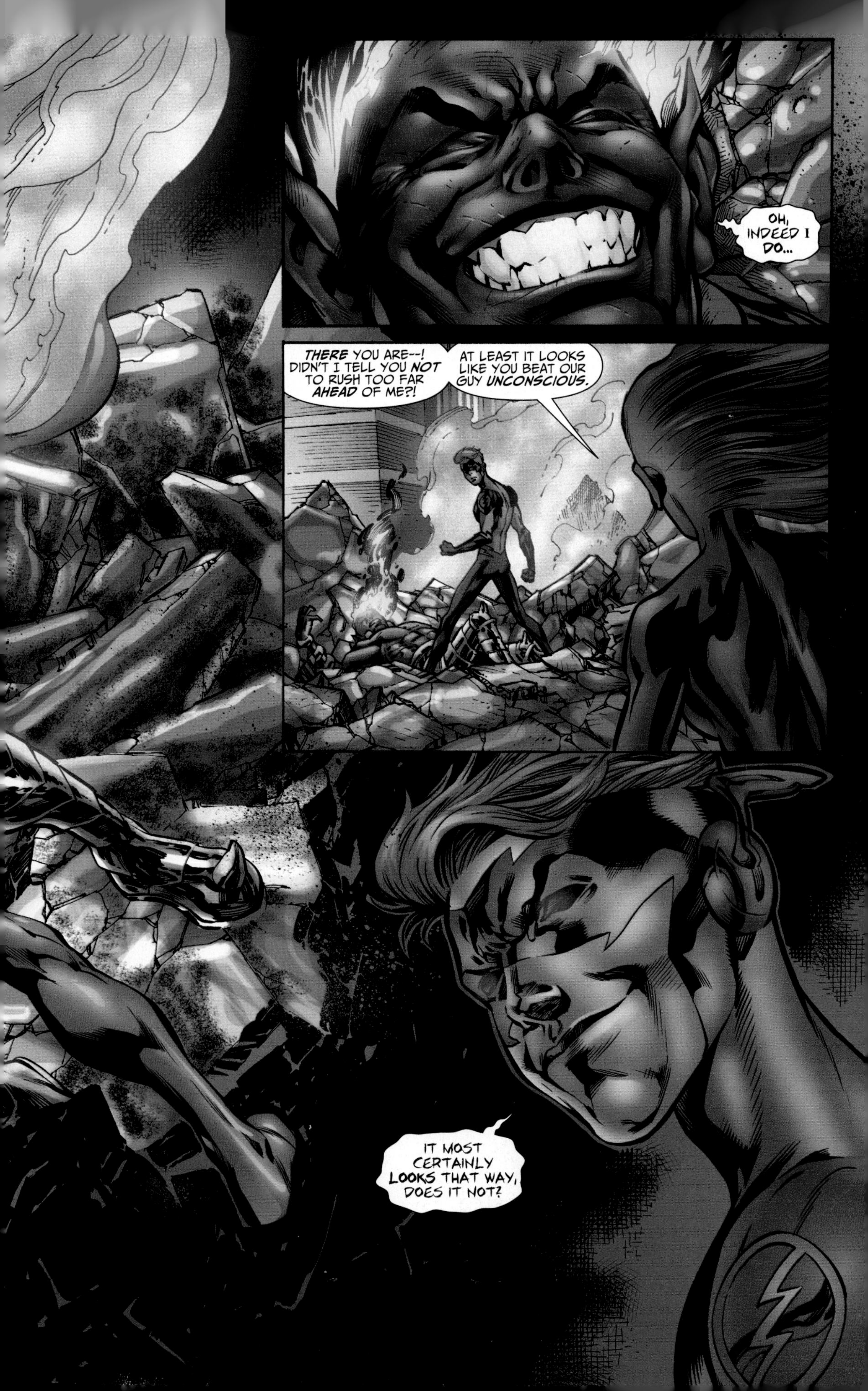
OH, INDEED I DO...
THERE YOU ARE--! DIDN'T I TELL YOU NOT TO RUSH TOO FAR AHEAD OF ME?!
AT LEAST IT LOOKS LIKE YOU BEAT OUR GUY UNCONSCIOUS.
IT MOST CERTAINLY LOOKS THAT WAY, DOES IT NOT?

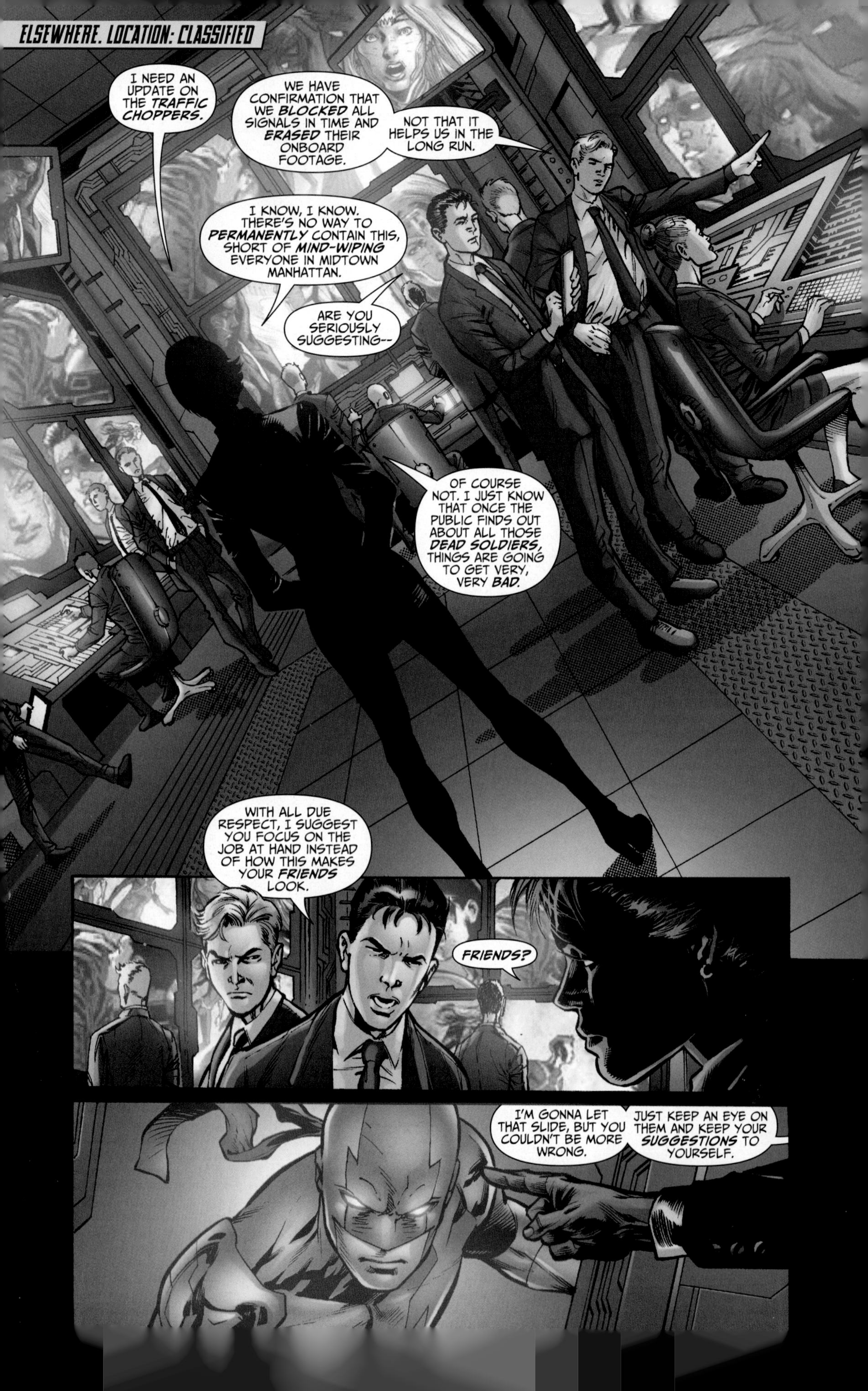
ELSEWHERE. LOCATION: CLASSIFIED
I NEED AN UPDATE ON THE TRAFFIC CHOPPERS.
WE HAVE CONFIRMATION THAT WE BLOCKED ALL SIGNALS IN TIME AND ERASED THEIR ONBOARD FOOTAGE.
NOT THAT IT HELPS US IN THE LONG RUN.
I KNOW, I KNOW. THERE'S NO WAY TO PERMANENTLY CONTAIN THIS, SHORT OF MIND-WIPING EVERYONE IN MIDTOWN MANHATTAN.
ARE YOU SERIOUSLY SUGGESTING--
OF COURSE NOT. I JUST KNOW THAT ONCE THE PUBLIC FINDS OUT ABOUT ALL THOSE DEAD SOLDIERS, THINGS ARE GOING TO GET VERY, VERY BAD.
WITH ALL DUE RESPECT, I SUGGEST YOU FOCUS ON THE JOB AT HAND INSTEAD OF HOW THIS MAKES YOUR FRIENDS LOOK.
FRIENDS?
I'M GONNA LET THAT SLIDE, BUT YOU COULDN'T BE MORE WRONG.
JUST KEEP AN EYE ON THEM AND KEEP YOUR SUGGESTIONS TO YOURSELF.

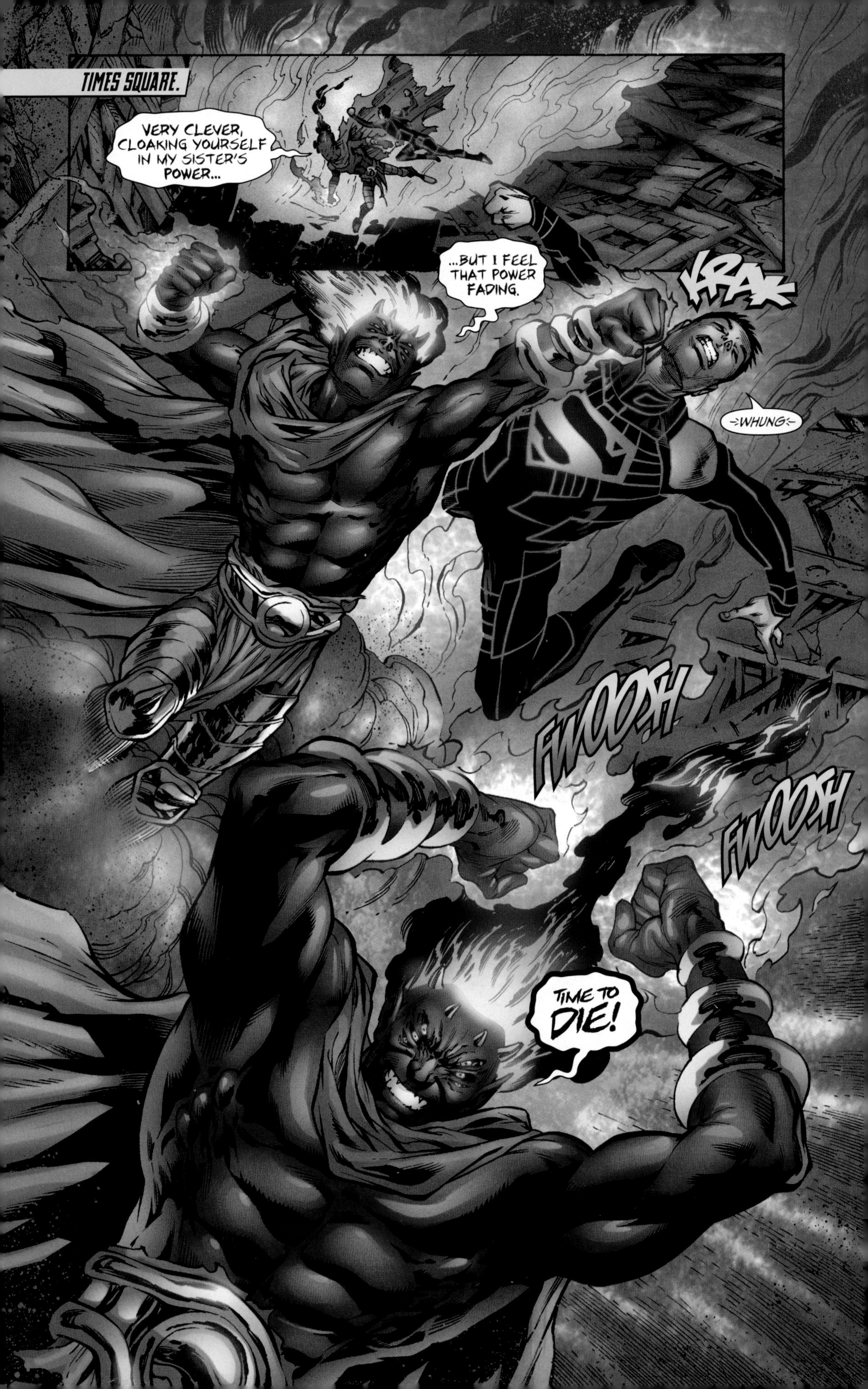
TIMES SQUARE.
VERY CLEVER, CLOAKING YOURSELF IN MY SISTER'S POWER...
...BUT I FEEL THAT POWER FADING.
KRAK
WHUNG
FWOOSH
FWOOSH
TIME TO DIE!

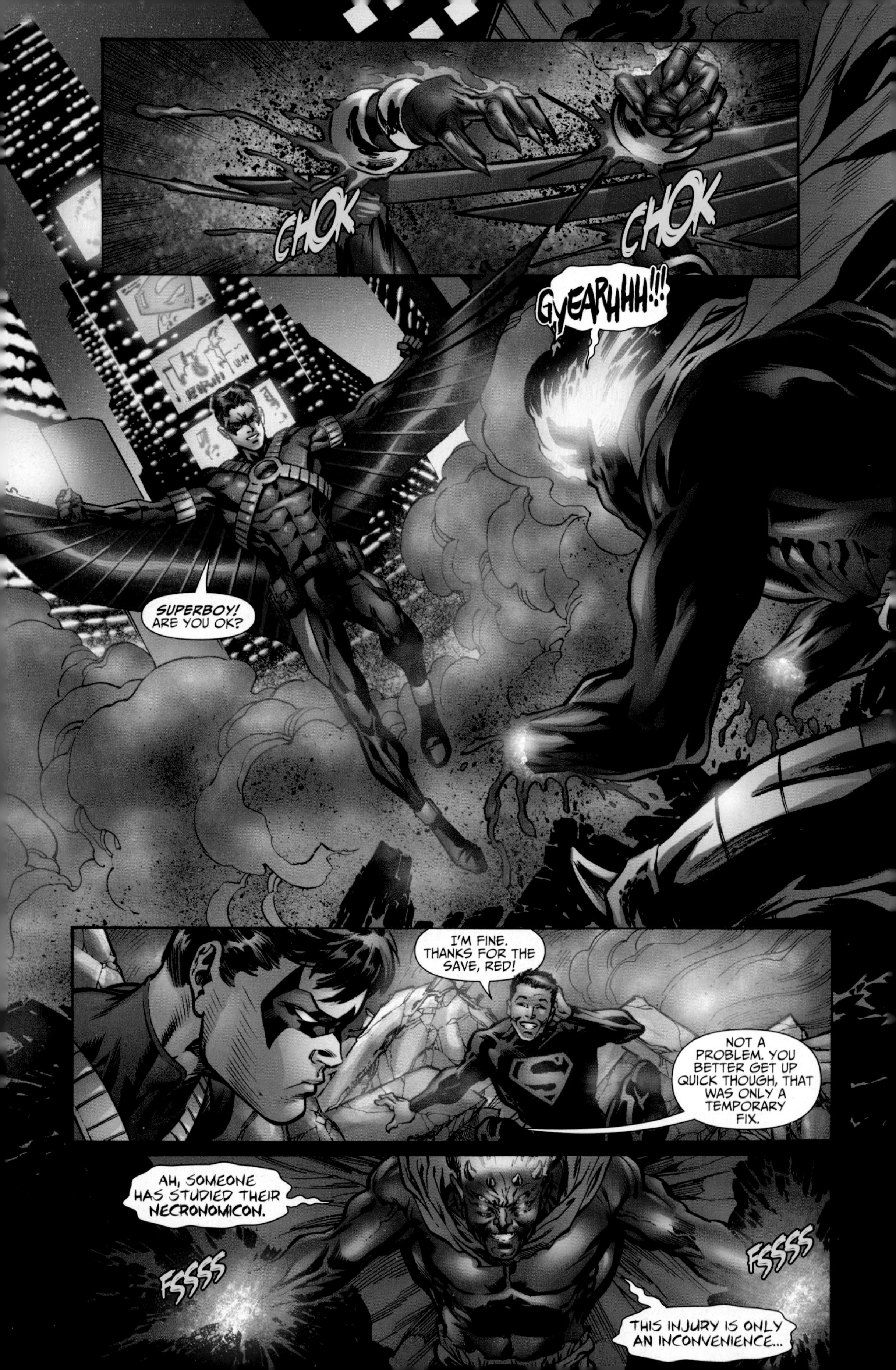
CHOK
CHOK
GYEARHHH!!!
SUPERBOY! ARE YOU OK?
I'M FINE. THANKS FOR THE SAVE, RED!
NOT A PROBLEM. YOU BETTER GET UP QUICK THOUGH, THAT WAS ONLY A TEMPORARY FIX.
AH, SOMEONE HAS STUDIED THEIR NECRONOMICON.
FSSSS
FSSSS
THIS INJURY IS ONLY AN INCONVENIENCE...

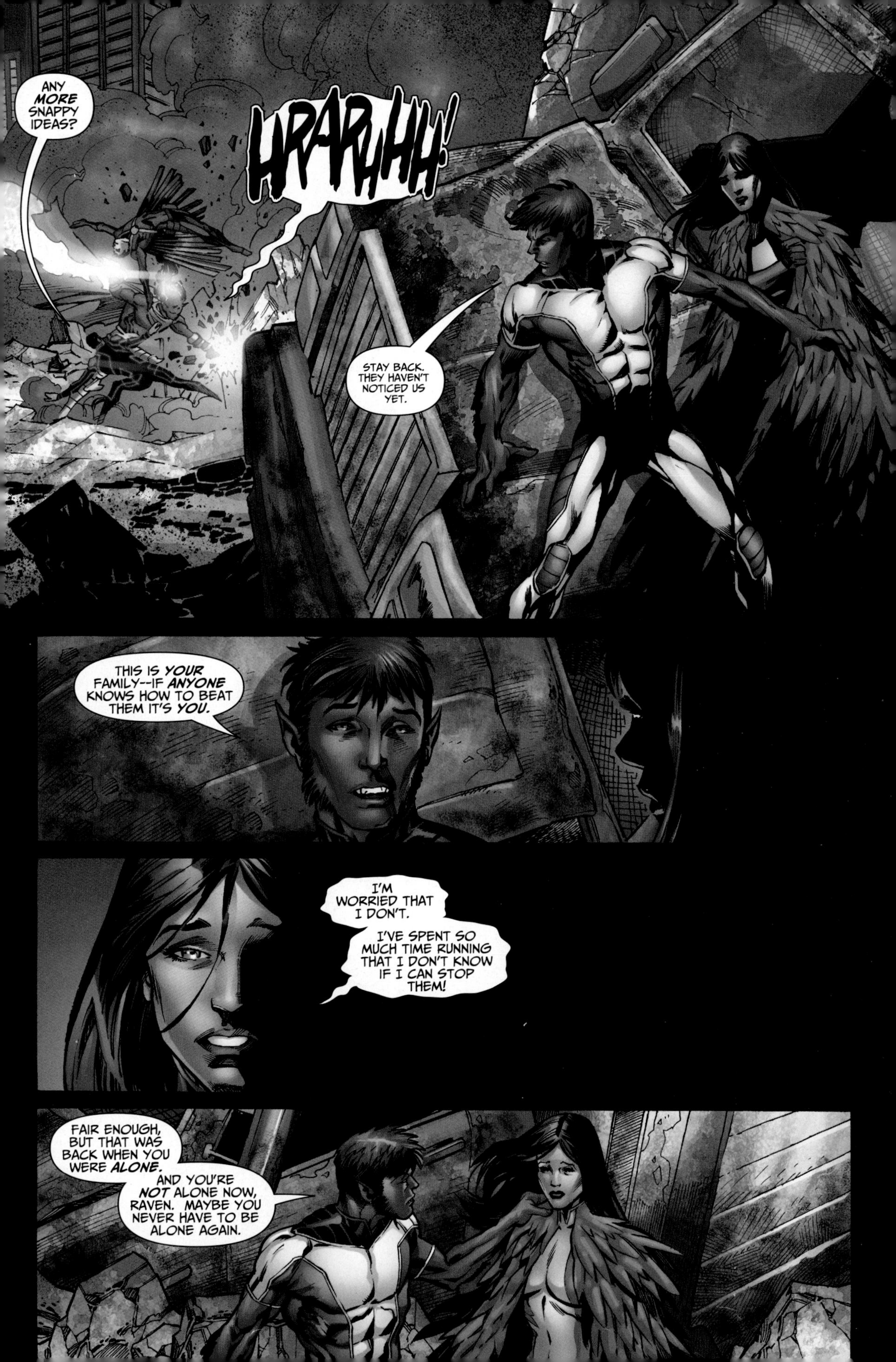
ANY MORE SNAPPY IDEAS?
URARHHH!
STAY BACK. THEY HAVEN'T NOTICED US YET.
THIS IS YOUR FAMILY--IF ANYONE KNOWS HOW TO BEAT THEM IT'S YOU.
I'M WORRIED THAT I DON'T.
I'VE SPENT SO MUCH TIME RUNNING THAT I DON'T KNOW IF I CAN STOP THEM!
FAIR ENOUGH, BUT THAT WAS BACK WHEN YOU WERE ALONE.
AND YOU'RE NOT ALONE NOW, RAVEN. MAYBE YOU NEVER HAVE TO BE ALONE AGAIN.

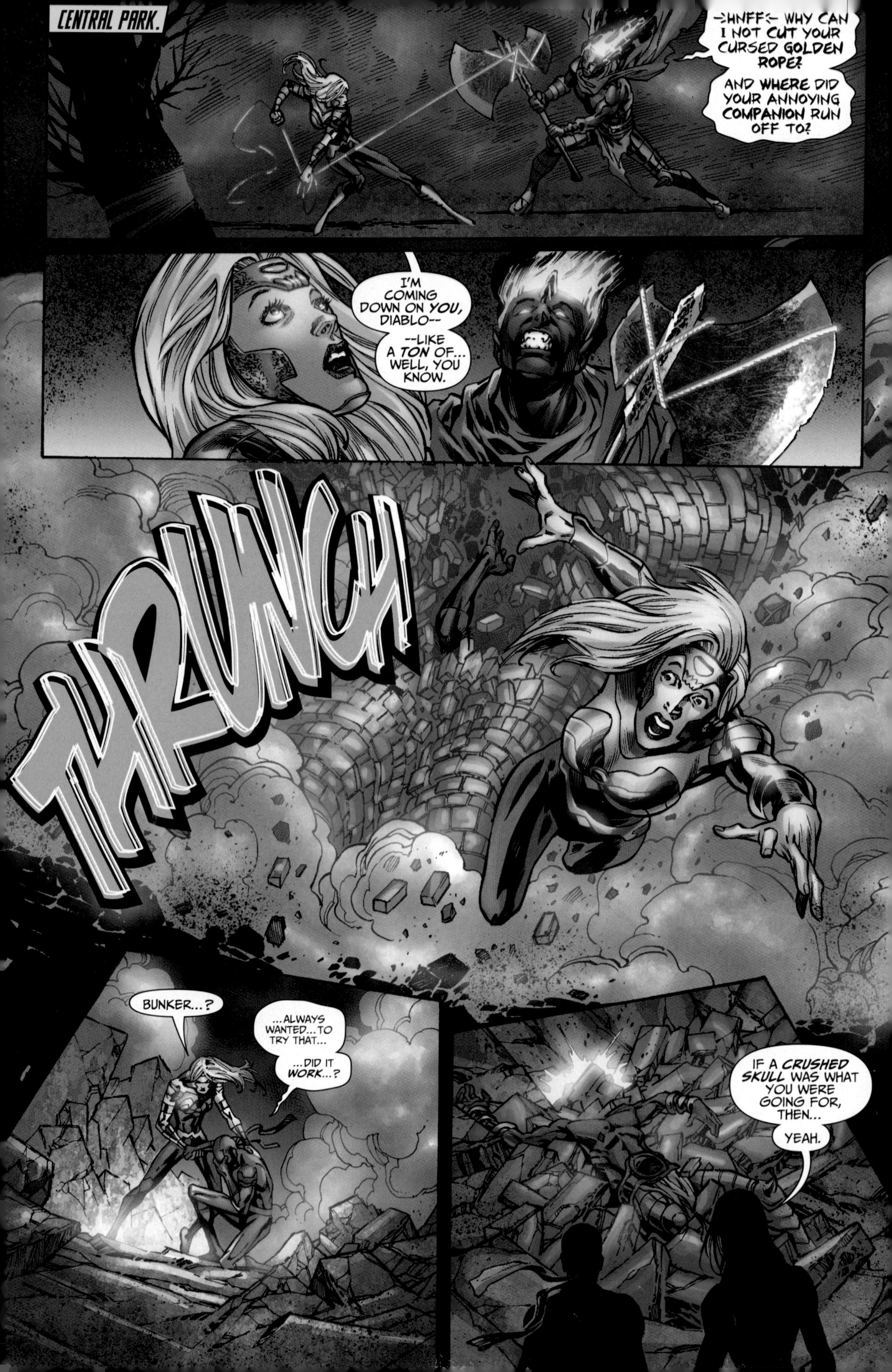
CENTRAL PARK.
-SHNFF- WHY CAN I NOT CUT YOUR CURSED GOLDEN ROPE?
AND WHERE DID YOUR ANNOYING COMPANION RUN OFF TO?
I'M COMING DOWN ON YOU, DIABLO--
--LIKE A TON OF... WELL, YOU KNOW.
THRUNCH
BUNKER...?
...ALWAYS WANTED...TO TRY THAT...
...DID IT WORK...?
IF A CRUSHED SKULL WAS WHAT YOU WERE GOING FOR, THEN...
YEAH.

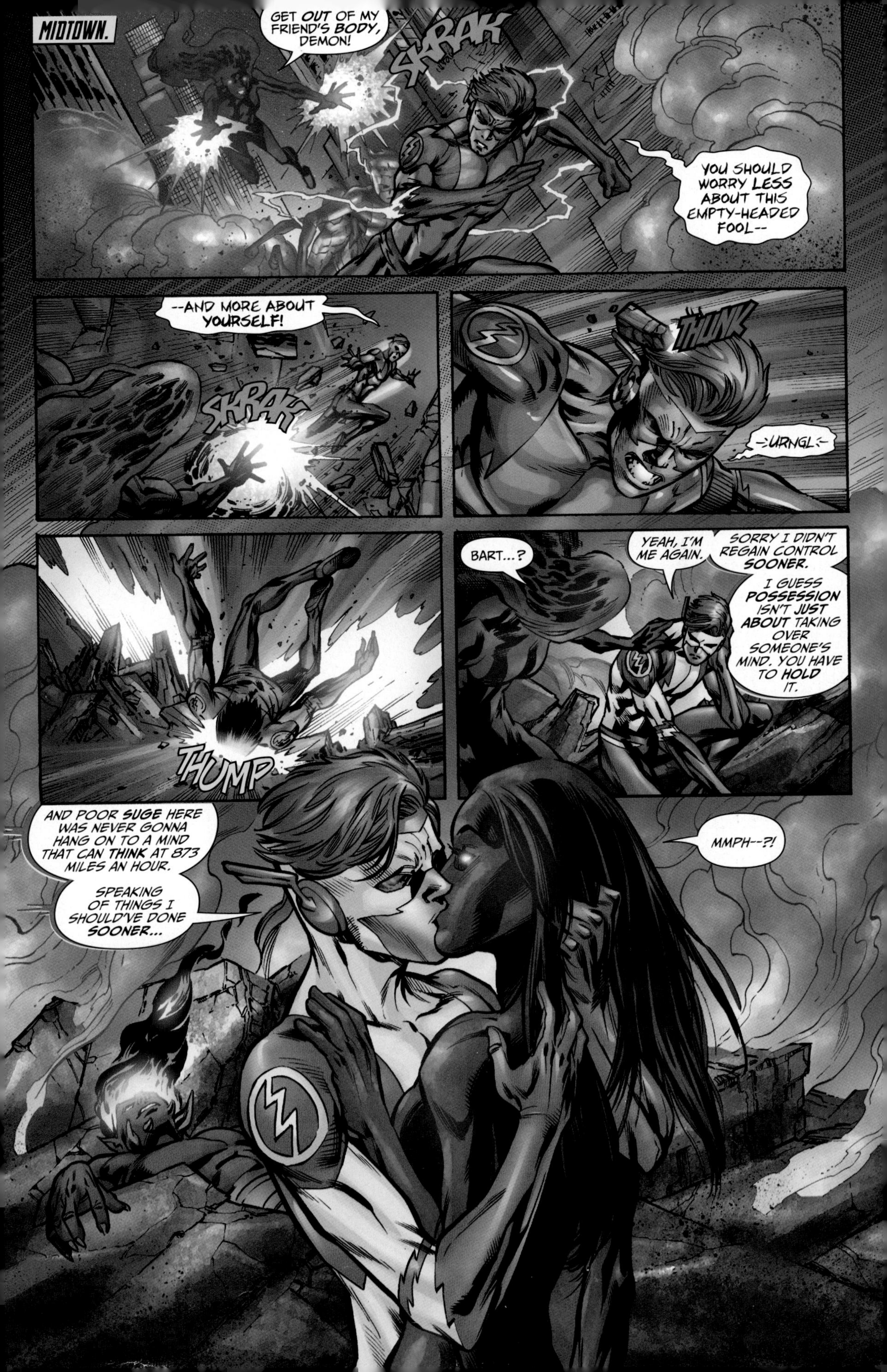
MIDTOWN.
GET OUT OF MY FRIEND'S BODY, DEMON!
SKRAK
YOU SHOULD WORRY LESS ABOUT THIS EMPTY-HEADED FOOL--
--AND MORE ABOUT YOURSELF!
SKRAK
THUNK
URNGL
THUMP
BART...?
YEAH, I'M ME AGAIN.
SORRY I DIDN'T REGAIN CONTROL SOONER.
I GUESS POSSESSION ISN'T JUST ABOUT TAKING OVER SOMEONE'S MIND. YOU HAVE TO HOLD IT.
AND POOR SUGE HERE WAS NEVER GONNA HANG ON TO A MIND THAT CAN THINK AT 873 MILES AN HOUR.
SPEAKING OF THINGS I SHOULD'VE DONE SOONER...
MMPH--?!

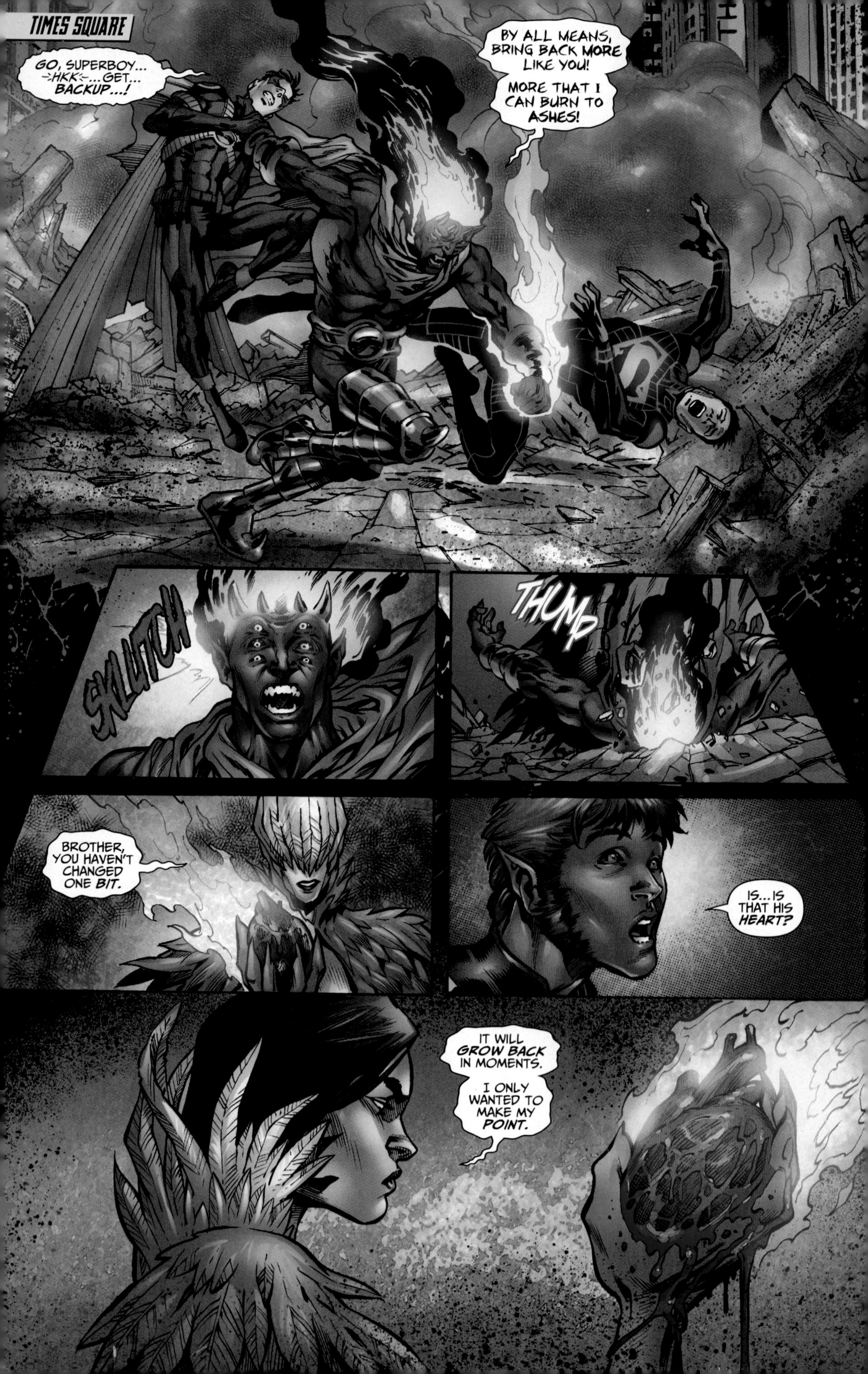
TIMES SQUARE
GO, SUPERBOY... HKK... GET... BACKUP...!
BY ALL MEANS, BRING BACK MORE LIKE YOU!
MORE THAT I CAN BURN TO ASHES!
SKLUTCH
THUMP
BROTHER, YOU HAVEN'T CHANGED ONE BIT.
IS...IS THAT HIS HEART?
IT WILL GROW BACK IN MOMENTS.
I ONLY WANTED TO MAKE MY POINT.

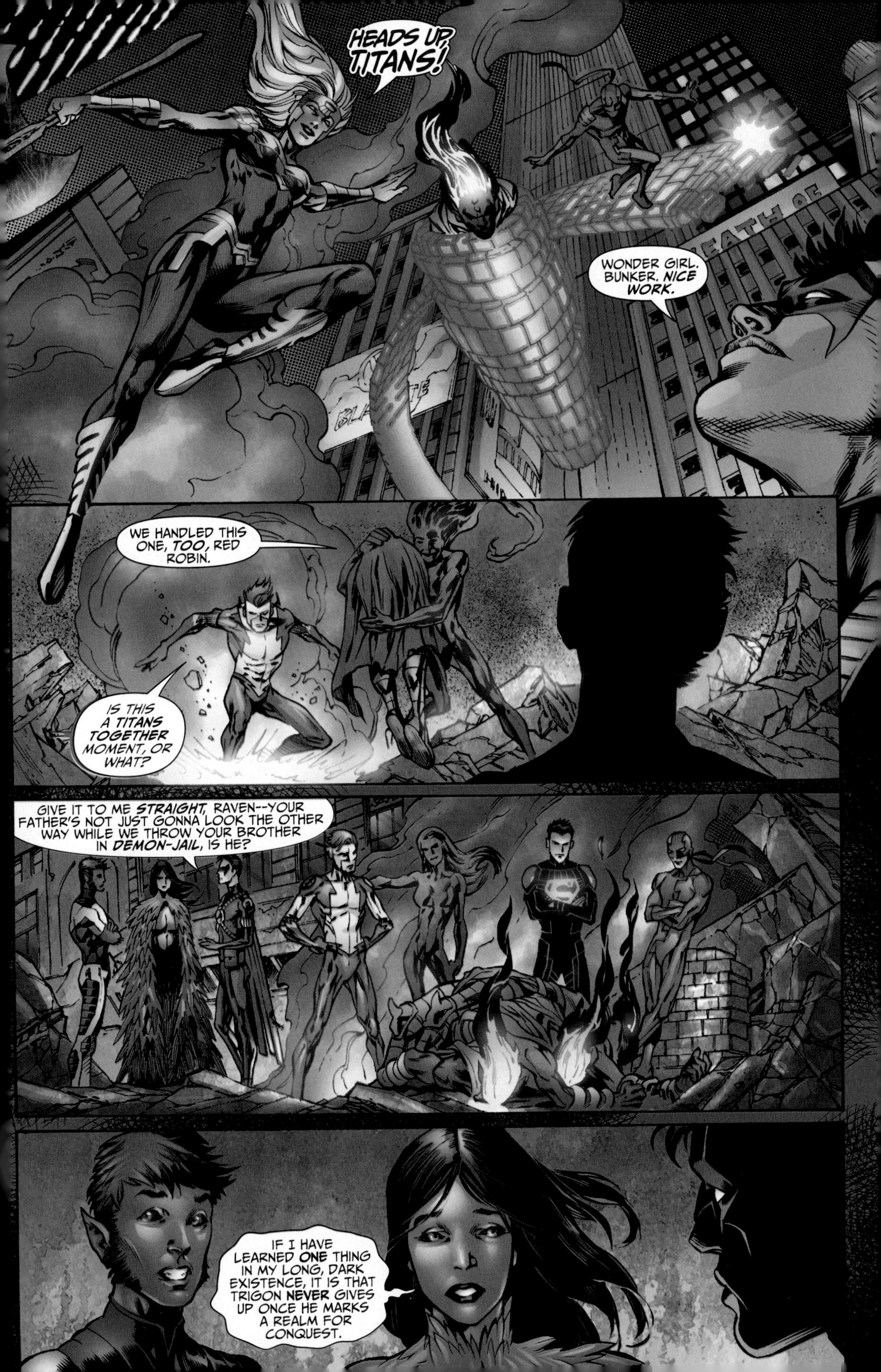

HEADS UP, TITANS!
WONDER GIRL. BUNKER. NICE WORK.
WE HANDLED THIS ONE, TOO, RED ROBIN.
IS THIS A TITANS TOGETHER MOMENT, OR WHAT?
GIVE IT TO ME STRAIGHT, RAVEN--YOUR FATHER'S NOT JUST GONNA LOOK THE OTHER WAY WHILE WE THROW YOUR BROTHER IN DEMON-JAIL, IS HE?
IF I HAVE LEARNED ONE THING IN MY LONG, DARK EXISTENCE, IT IS THAT TRIGON NEVER GIVES UP ONCE HE MARKS A REALM FOR CONQUEST.

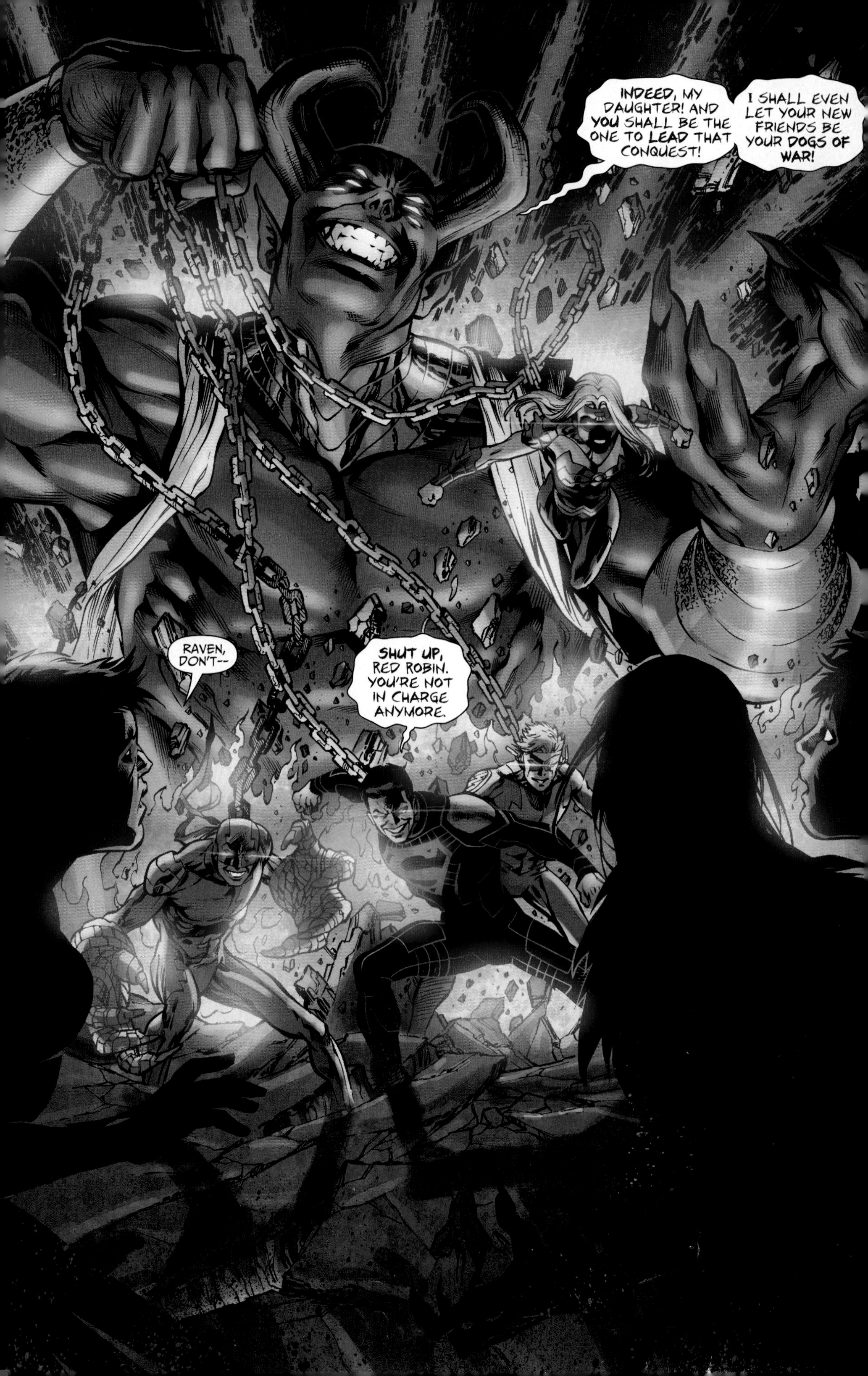
INDEED, MY DAUGHTER! AND YOU SHALL BE THE ONE TO LEAD THAT CONQUEST!
I SHALL EVEN LET YOUR NEW FRIENDS BE YOUR DOGS OF WAR!
RAVEN, DON'T--
SHUT UP, RED ROBIN. YOU'RE NOT IN CHARGE ANYMORE.

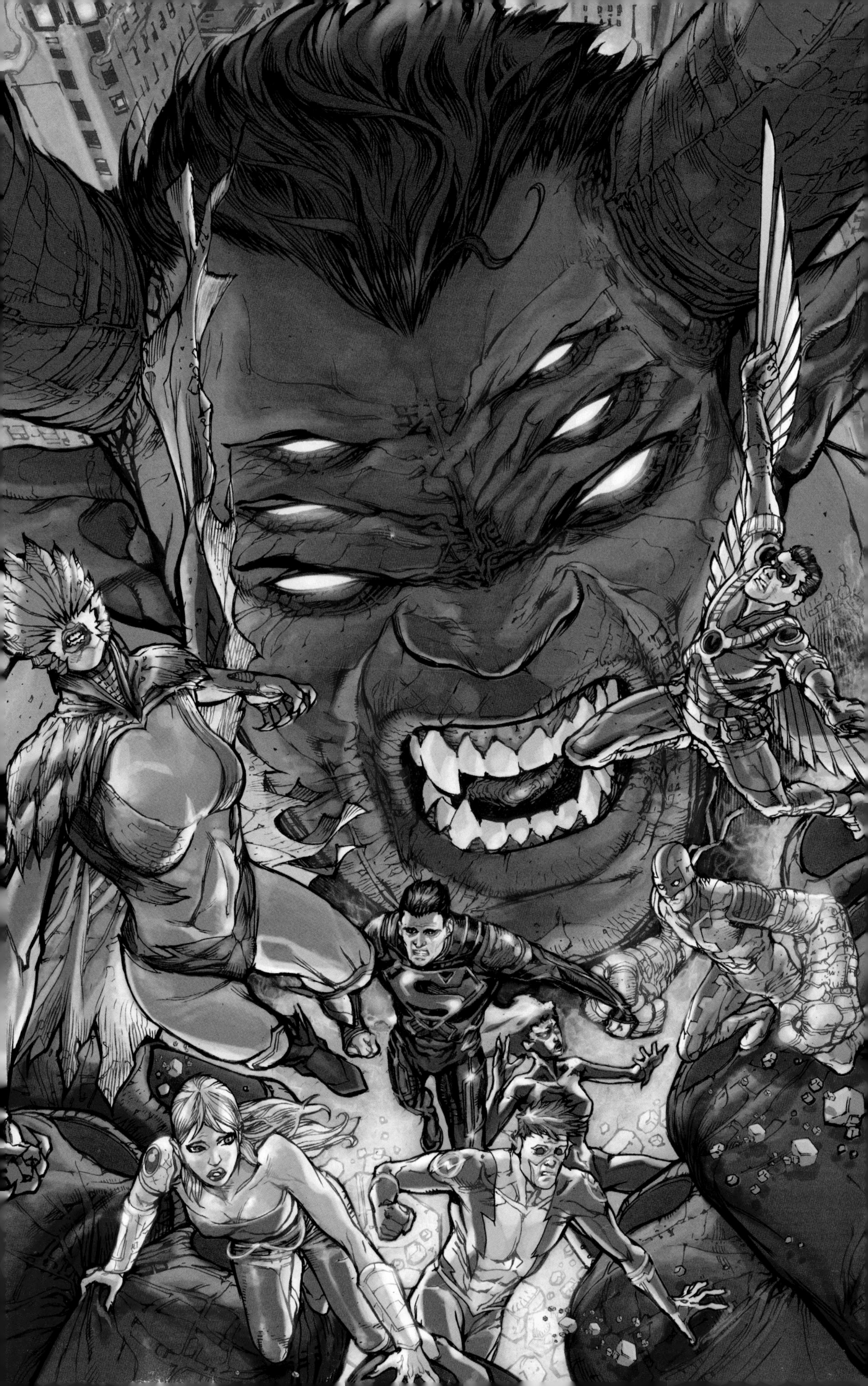

DARK TITANS

SCOTT LOBDELL writer JESUS MERINO finishes EDDY BARROWS layouts cover art by HOWARD PORTER

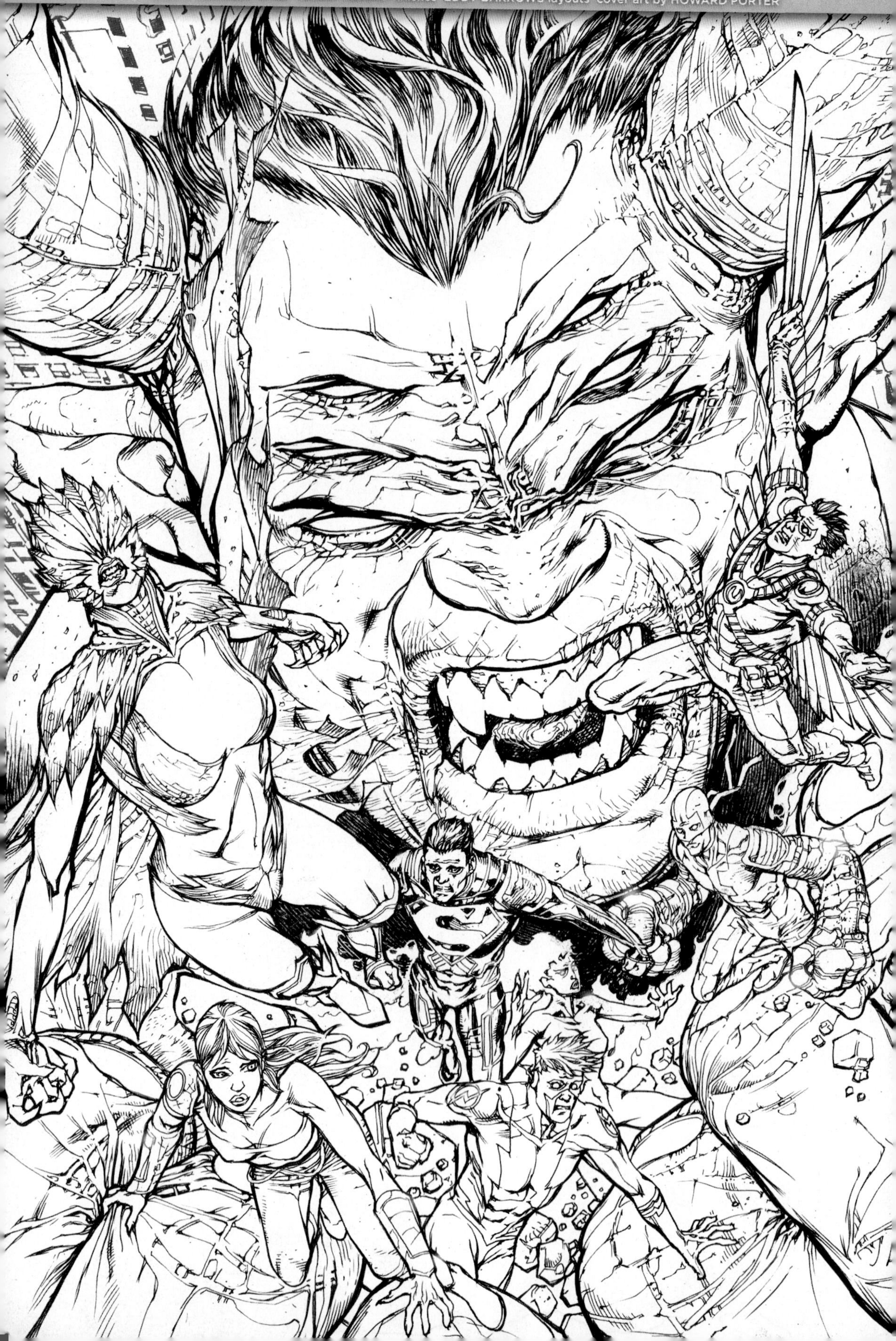

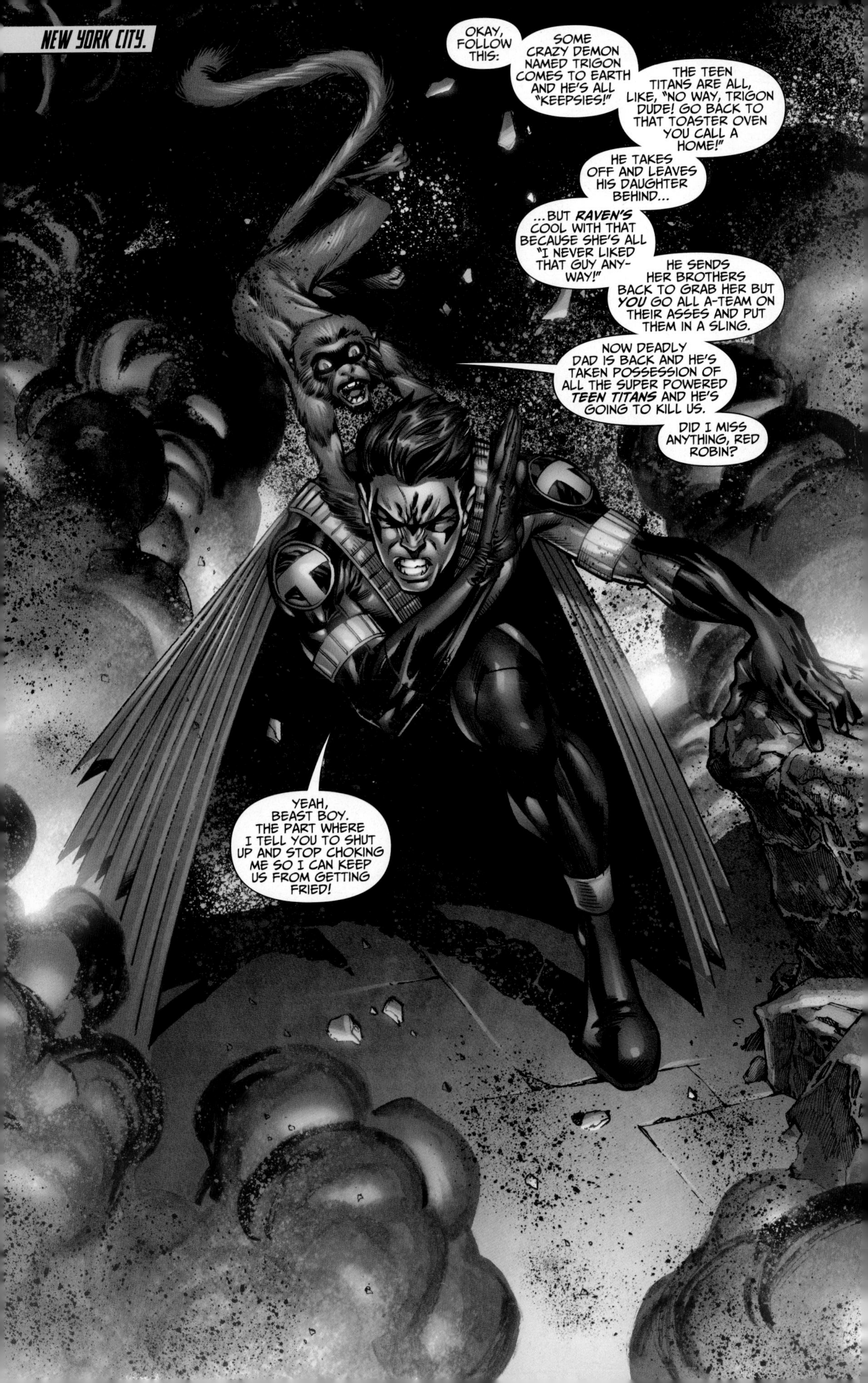
NEW YORK CITY.
OKAY, FOLLOW THIS:
SOME CRAZY DEMON NAMED TRIGON COMES TO EARTH AND HE'S ALL "KEEPSIES!"
THE TEEN TITANS ARE ALL, LIKE, "NO WAY, TRIGON DUDE! GO BACK TO THAT TOASTER OVEN YOU CALL A HOME!"
HE TAKES OFF AND LEAVES HIS DAUGHTER BEHIND...
...BUT RAVEN'S COOL WITH THAT BECAUSE SHE'S ALL "I NEVER LIKED THAT GUY ANY-WAY!"
HE SENDS HER BROTHERS BACK TO GRAB HER BUT YOU GO ALL A-TEAM ON THEIR ASSES AND PUT THEM IN A SLING.
NOW DEADLY DAD IS BACK AND HE'S TAKEN POSSESSION OF ALL THE SUPER POWERED TEEN TITANS AND HE'S GOING TO KILL US.
DID I MISS ANYTHING, RED ROBIN?
YEAH, BEAST BOY. THE PART WHERE I TELL YOU TO SHUT UP AND STOP CHOKING ME SO I CAN KEEP US FROM GETTING FRIED!

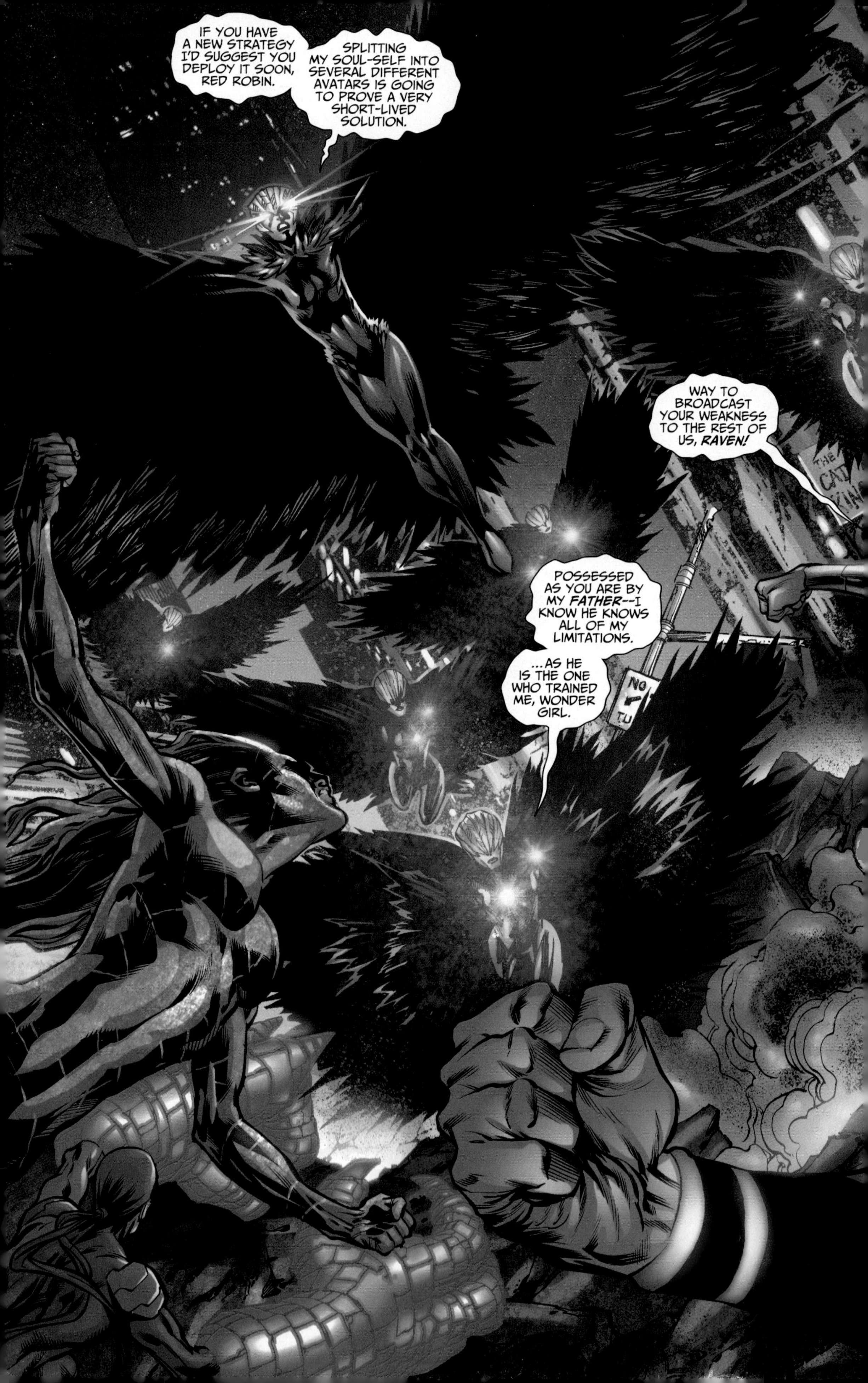
IF YOU HAVE A NEW STRATEGY I'D SUGGEST YOU DEPLOY IT SOON, RED ROBIN.
SPLITTING MY SOUL-SELF INTO SEVERAL DIFFERENT AVATARS IS GOING TO PROVE A VERY SHORT-LIVED SOLUTION.
WAY TO BROADCAST YOUR WEAKNESS TO THE REST OF US, RAVEN!
POSSESSED AS YOU ARE BY MY FATHER--I KNOW HE KNOWS ALL OF MY LIMITATIONS.
...AS HE IS THE ONE WHO TRAINED ME, WONDER GIRL.

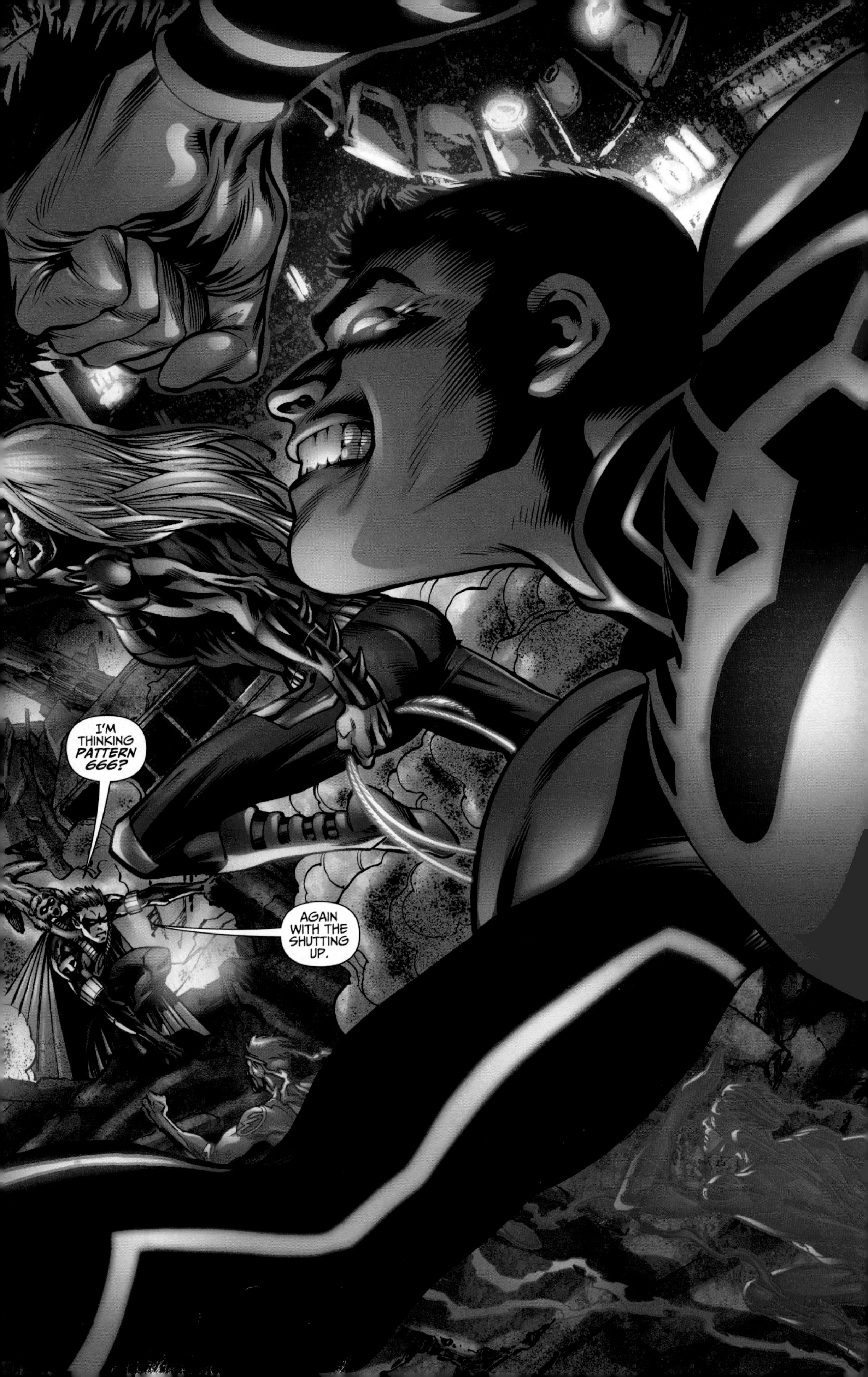
I'M THINKING *PATTERN 666?*
AGAIN WITH THE SHUTTING UP.

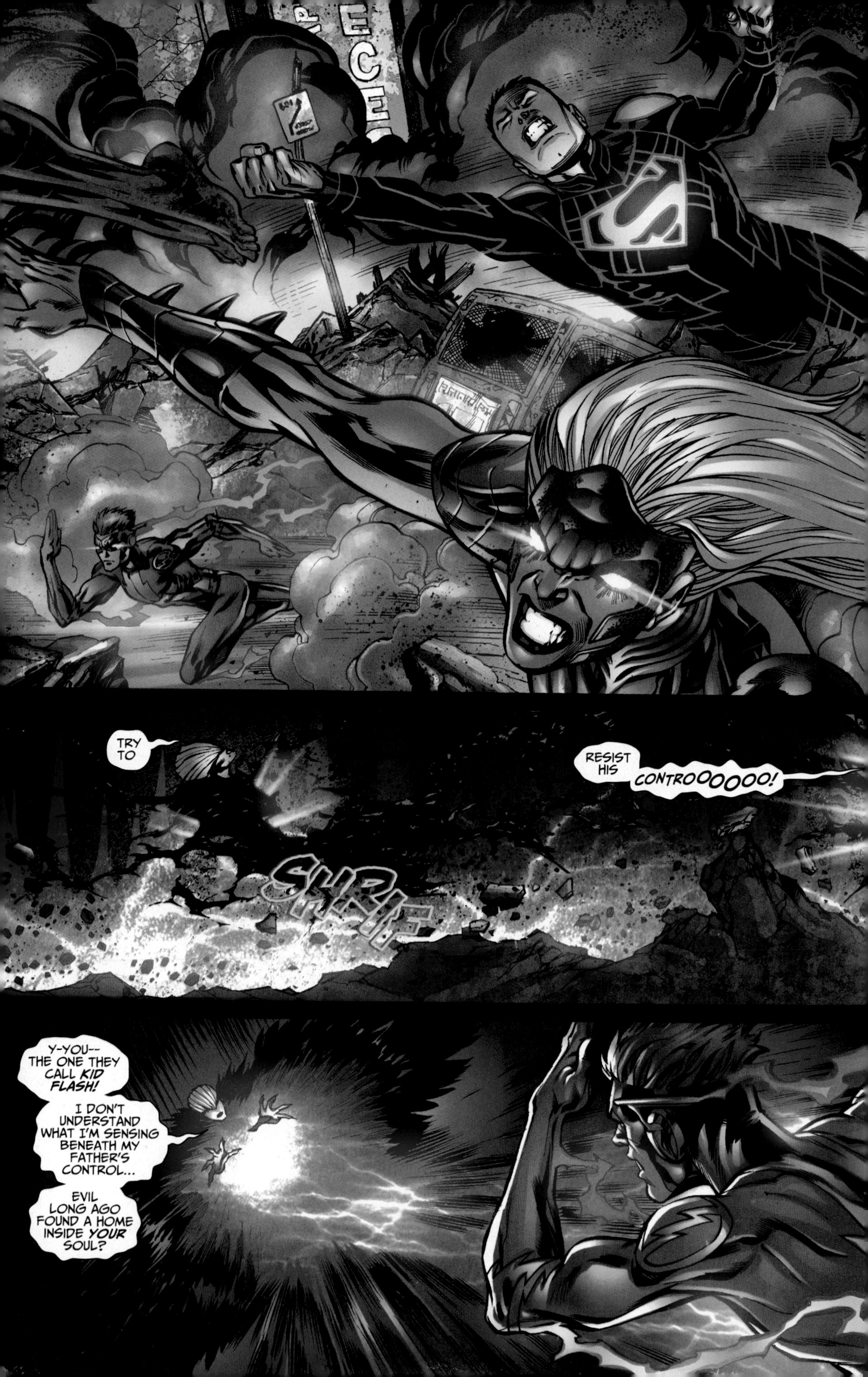
TRY TO
RESIST HIS CONTROOOOOO!
SHRIP
Y-YOU-- THE ONE THEY CALL KID FLASH!
I DON'T UNDERSTAND WHAT I'M SENSING BENEATH MY FATHER'S CONTROL...
EVIL LONG AGO FOUND A HOME INSIDE YOUR SOUL?

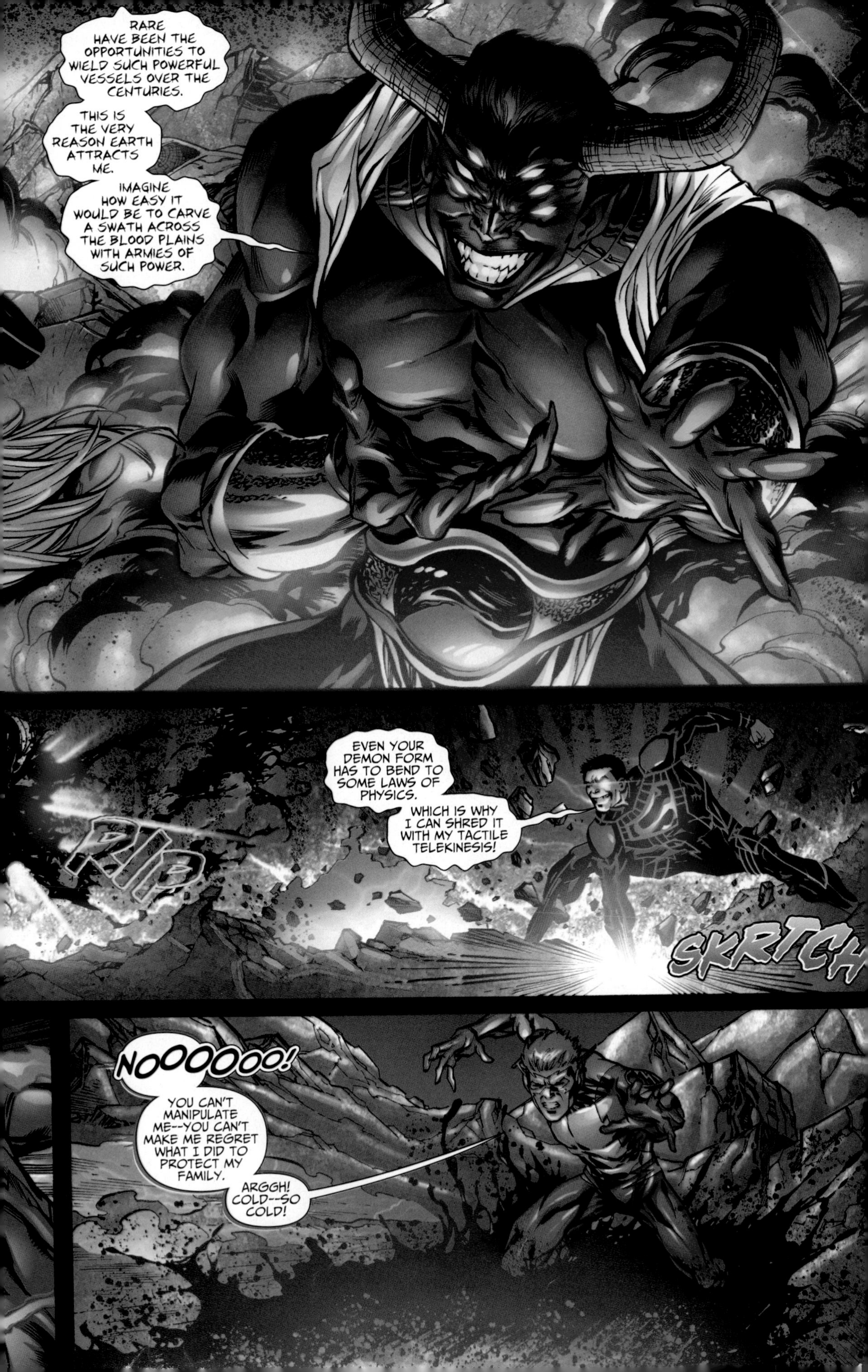
RARE HAVE BEEN THE OPPORTUNITIES TO WIELD SUCH POWERFUL VESSELS OVER THE CENTURIES.
THIS IS THE VERY REASON EARTH ATTRACTS ME.
IMAGINE HOW EASY IT WOULD BE TO CARVE A SWATH ACROSS THE BLOOD PLAINS WITH ARMIES OF SUCH POWER.
EVEN YOUR DEMON FORM HAS TO BEND TO SOME LAWS OF PHYSICS.
WHICH IS WHY I CAN SHRED IT WITH MY TACTILE TELEKINESIS!
RIP
SKRTCH
NOOOOOO!
YOU CAN'T MANIPULATE ME--YOU CAN'T MAKE ME REGRET WHAT I DID TO PROTECT MY FAMILY.
ARGGH! COLD--SO COLD!

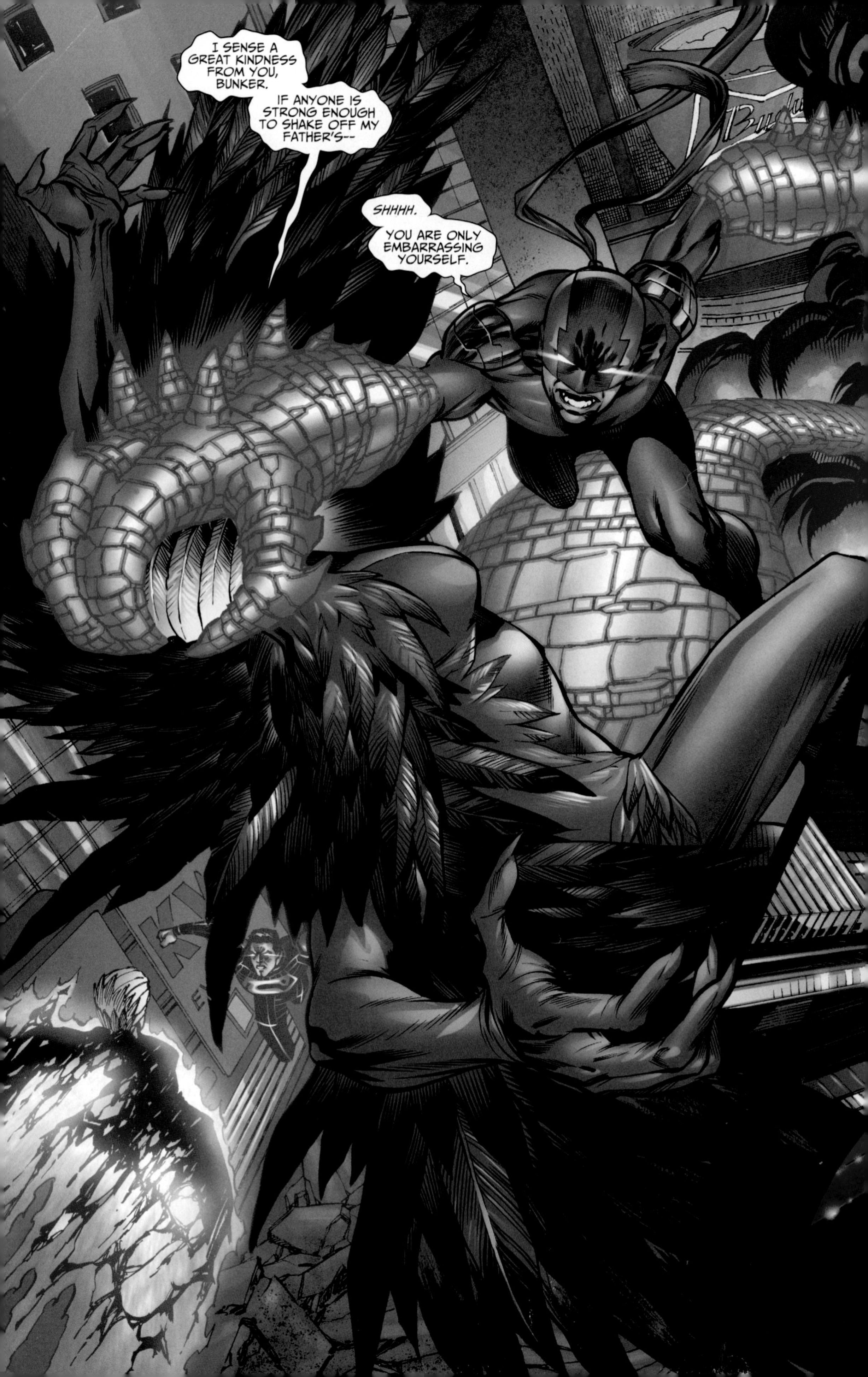
I SENSE A GREAT KINDNESS FROM YOU, BUNKER.
IF ANYONE IS STRONG ENOUGH TO SHAKE OFF MY FATHER'S--
SHHHH.
YOU ARE ONLY EMBARRASSING YOURSELF.

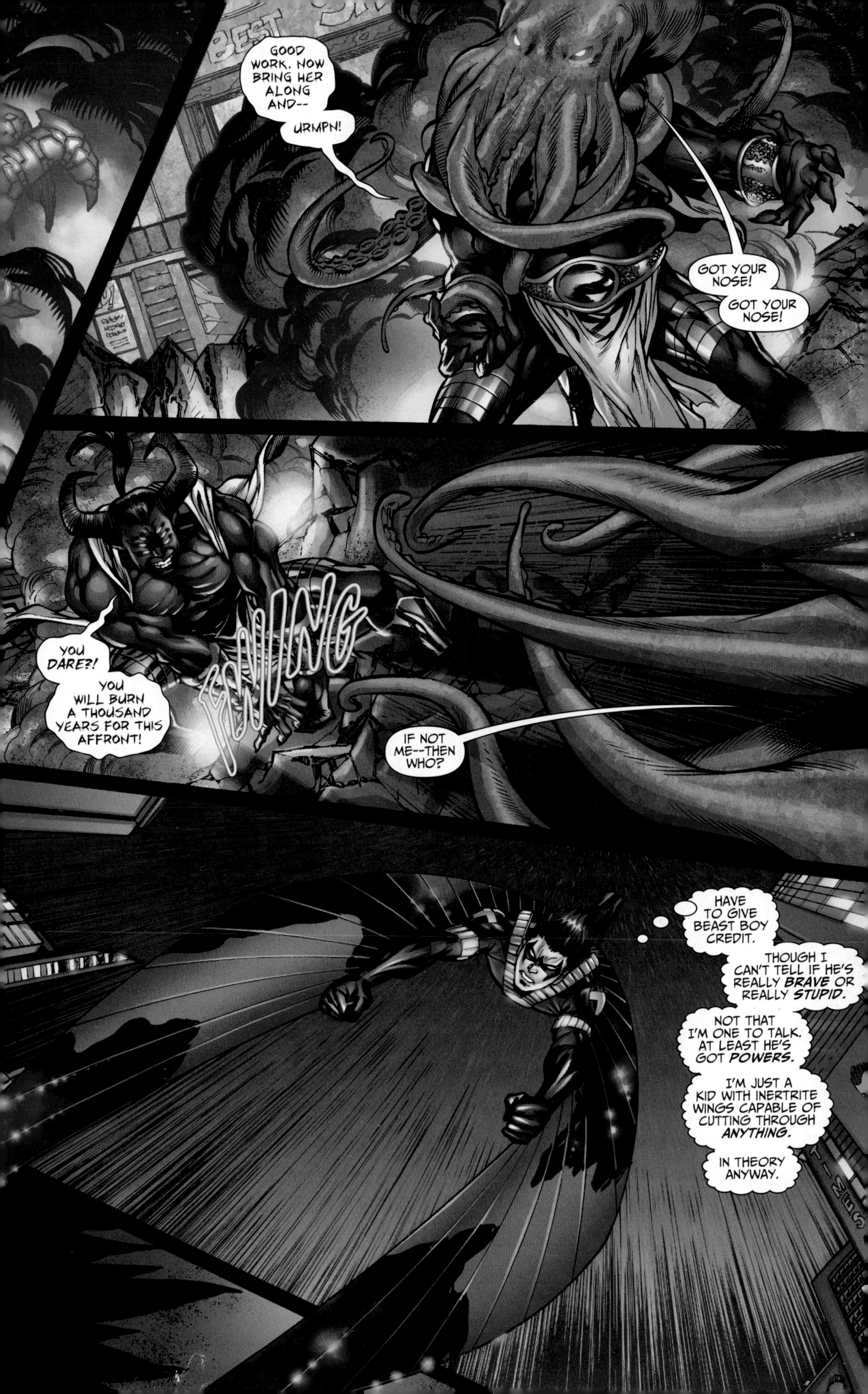
GOOD WORK. NOW BRING HER ALONG AND--
URMPN!
GOT YOUR NOSE!
GOT YOUR NOSE!
YOU DARE?!
YOU WILL BURN A THOUSAND YEARS FOR THIS AFFRONT!
FWING
IF NOT ME--THEN WHO?
HAVE TO GIVE BEAST BOY CREDIT.
THOUGH I CAN'T TELL IF HE'S REALLY BRAVE OR REALLY STUPID.
NOT THAT I'M ONE TO TALK. AT LEAST HE'S GOT POWERS.
I'M JUST A KID WITH INERTRITE WINGS CAPABLE OF CUTTING THROUGH ANYTHING.
IN THEORY ANYWAY.

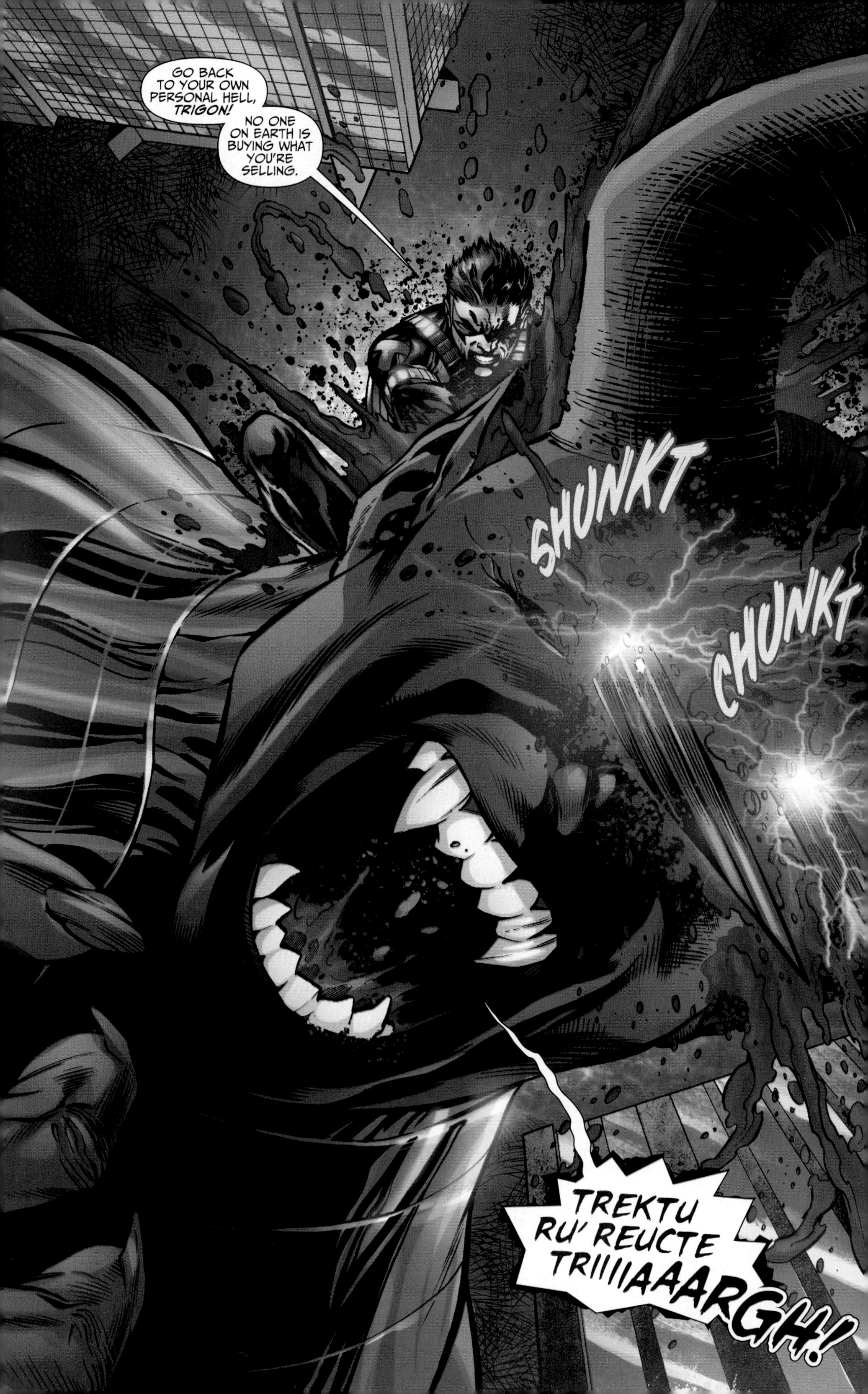
GO BACK TO YOUR OWN PERSONAL HELL, *TRIGON!*
NO ONE ON EARTH IS BUYING WHAT YOU'RE SELLING.
SHUNKT
CHUNKT
TREKTU RU' REUCTE TRIIIIAAARGH!

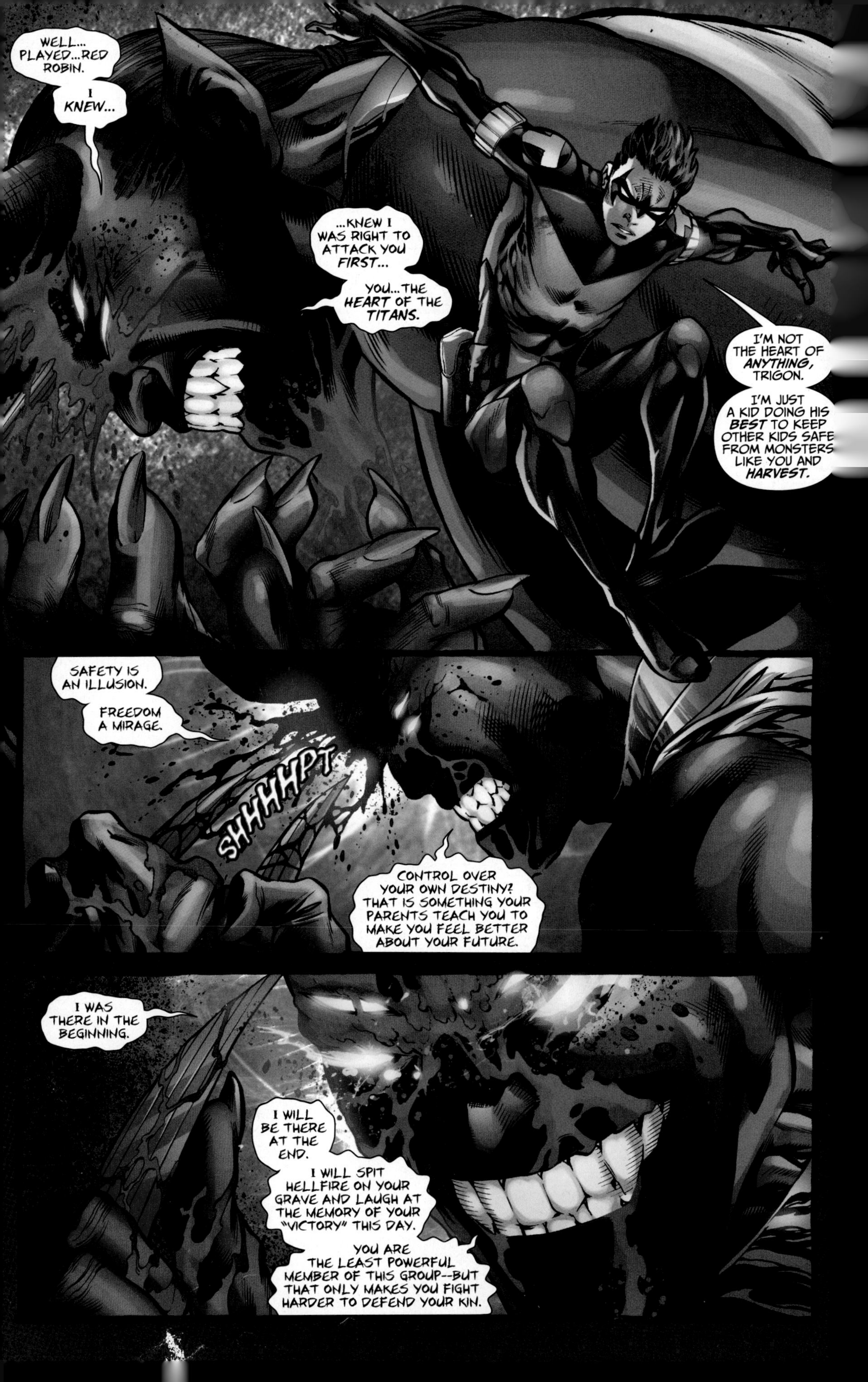

WELL... PLAYED...RED ROBIN.
I KNEW...
...KNEW I WAS RIGHT TO ATTACK YOU FIRST...
YOU...THE HEART OF THE TITANS.
I'M NOT THE HEART OF ANYTHING, TRIGON.
I'M JUST A KID DOING HIS BEST TO KEEP OTHER KIDS SAFE FROM MONSTERS LIKE YOU AND HARVEST.
SAFETY IS AN ILLUSION.
FREEDOM A MIRAGE.
SHHHHPT
CONTROL OVER YOUR OWN DESTINY? THAT IS SOMETHING YOUR PARENTS TEACH YOU TO MAKE YOU FEEL BETTER ABOUT YOUR FUTURE.
I WAS THERE IN THE BEGINNING.
I WILL BE THERE AT THE END.
I WILL SPIT HELLFIRE ON YOUR GRAVE AND LAUGH AT THE MEMORY OF YOUR "VICTORY" THIS DAY.
YOU ARE THE LEAST POWERFUL MEMBER OF THIS GROUP--BUT THAT ONLY MAKES YOU FIGHT HARDER TO DEFEND YOUR KIN.

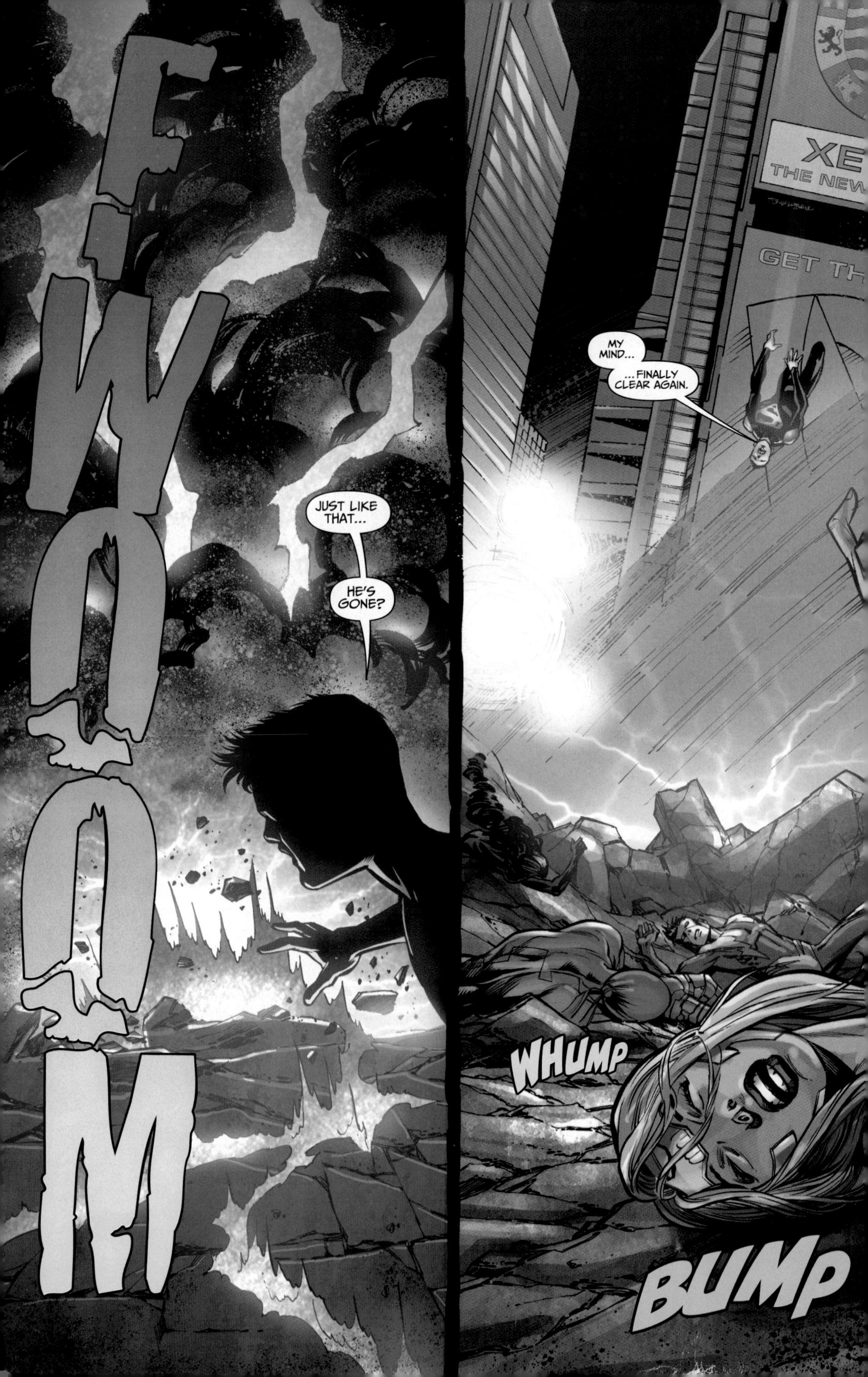
FWOOOM
JUST LIKE THAT...
HE'S GONE?
XE
THE NEW
GET TH
MY MIND...
...FINALLY CLEAR AGAIN.
WHUMP
BUMP

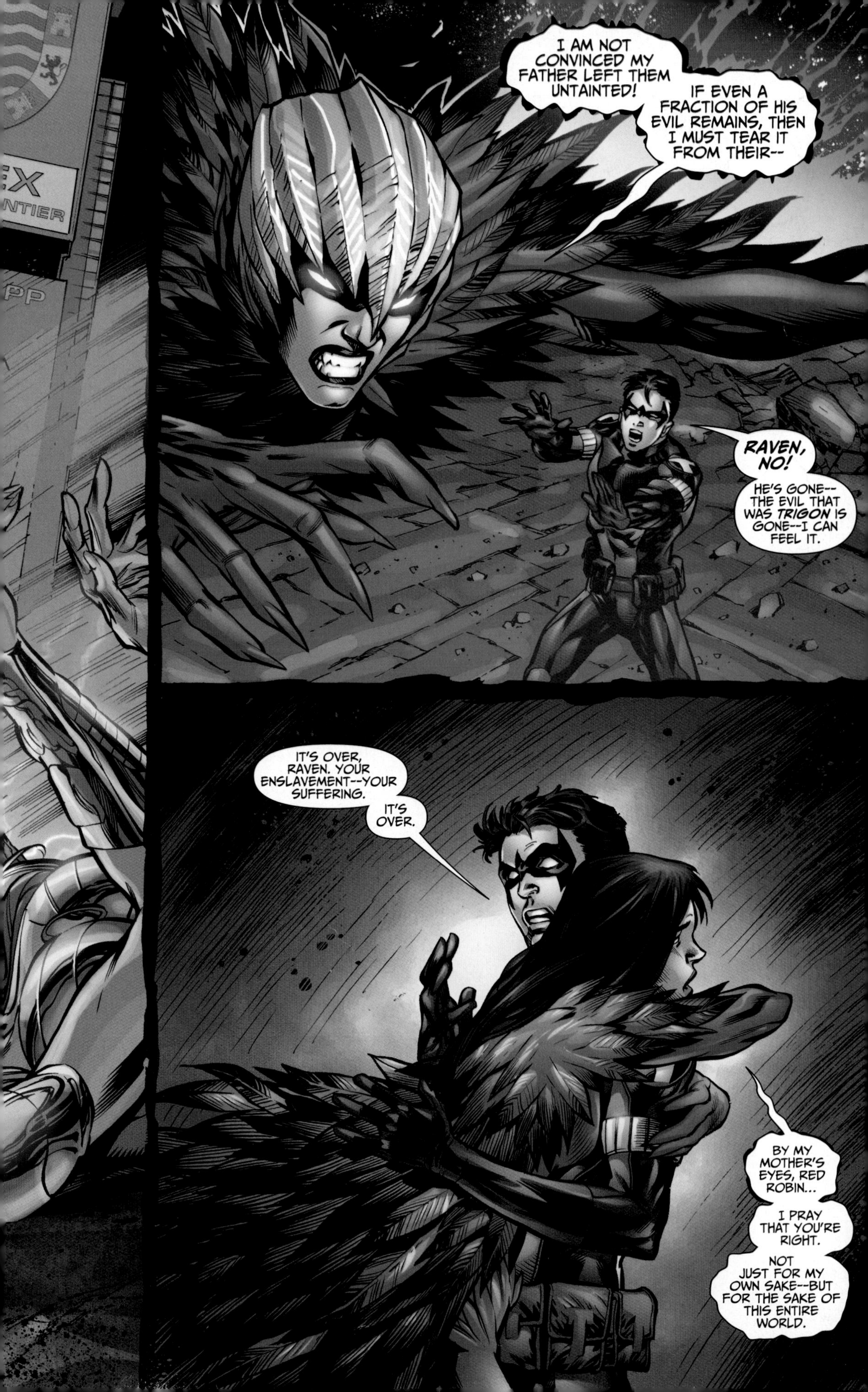
I AM NOT CONVINCED MY FATHER LEFT THEM UNTAINTED!
IF EVEN A FRACTION OF HIS EVIL REMAINS, THEN I MUST TEAR IT FROM THEIR--
RAVEN, NO!
HE'S GONE-- THE EVIL THAT WAS TRIGON IS GONE--I CAN FEEL IT.
IT'S OVER, RAVEN. YOUR ENSLAVEMENT--YOUR SUFFERING.
IT'S OVER.
BY MY MOTHER'S EYES, RED ROBIN...
I PRAY THAT YOU'RE RIGHT.
NOT JUST FOR MY OWN SAKE--BUT FOR THE SAKE OF THIS ENTIRE WORLD.

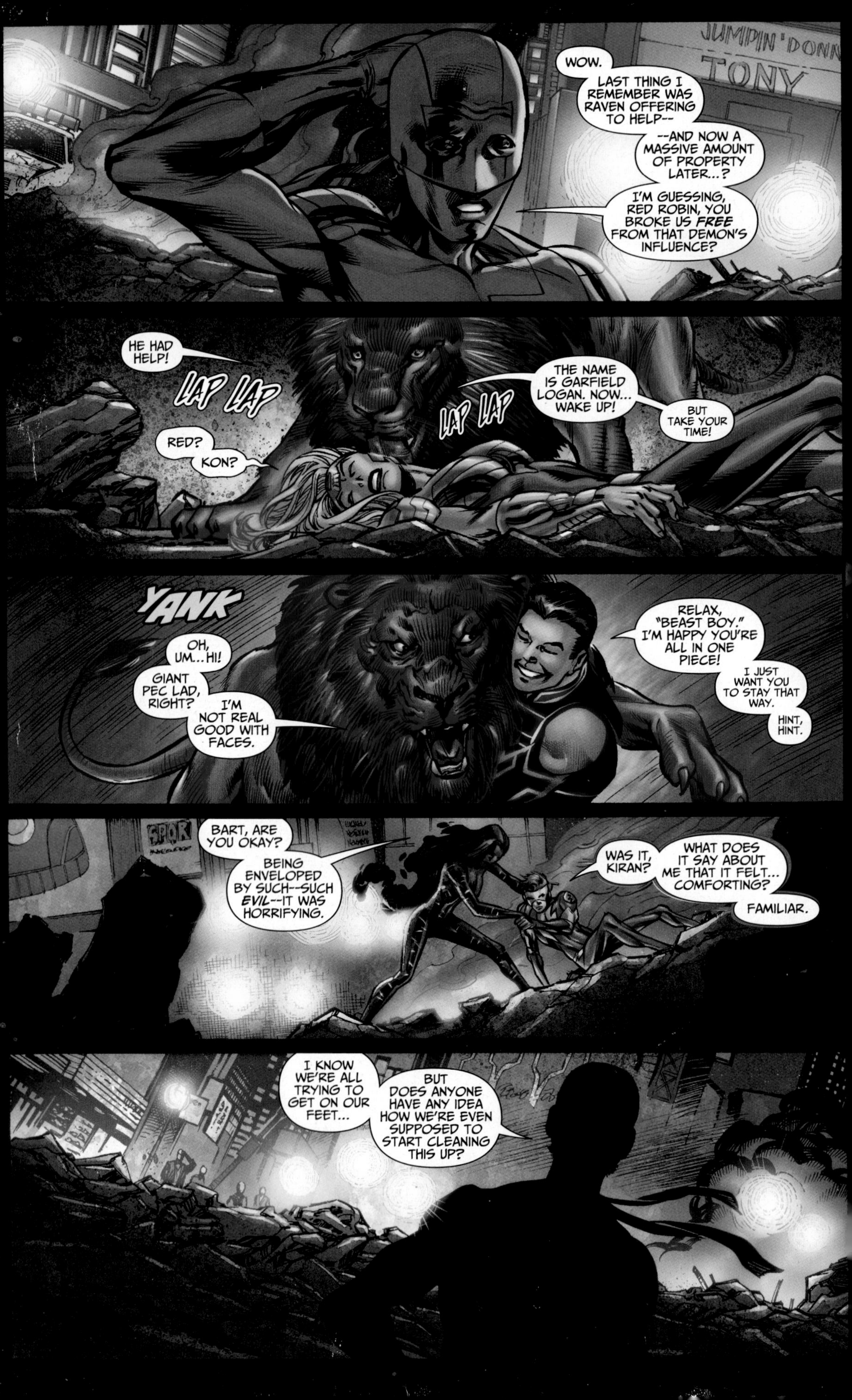
JUMPIN' DONN
TONY
WOW.
LAST THING I REMEMBER WAS RAVEN OFFERING TO HELP--
--AND NOW A MASSIVE AMOUNT OF PROPERTY LATER...?
I'M GUESSING, RED ROBIN, YOU BROKE US FREE FROM THAT DEMON'S INFLUENCE?
HE HAD HELP!
LAP LAP
THE NAME IS GARFIELD LOGAN. NOW... WAKE UP!
LAP LAP
BUT TAKE YOUR TIME!
RED?
KON?
YANK
OH, UM...HI!
GIANT PEC LAD, RIGHT?
I'M NOT REAL GOOD WITH FACES.
RELAX, "BEAST BOY." I'M HAPPY YOU'RE ALL IN ONE PIECE!
I JUST WANT YOU TO STAY THAT WAY.
HINT, HINT.
BART, ARE YOU OKAY?
BEING ENVELOPED BY SUCH--SUCH EVIL--IT WAS HORRIFYING.
WAS IT, KIRAN?
WHAT DOES IT SAY ABOUT ME THAT IT FELT... COMFORTING?
FAMILIAR.
I KNOW WE'RE ALL TRYING TO GET ON OUR FEET...
BUT DOES ANYONE HAVE ANY IDEA HOW WE'RE EVEN SUPPOSED TO START CLEANING THIS UP?

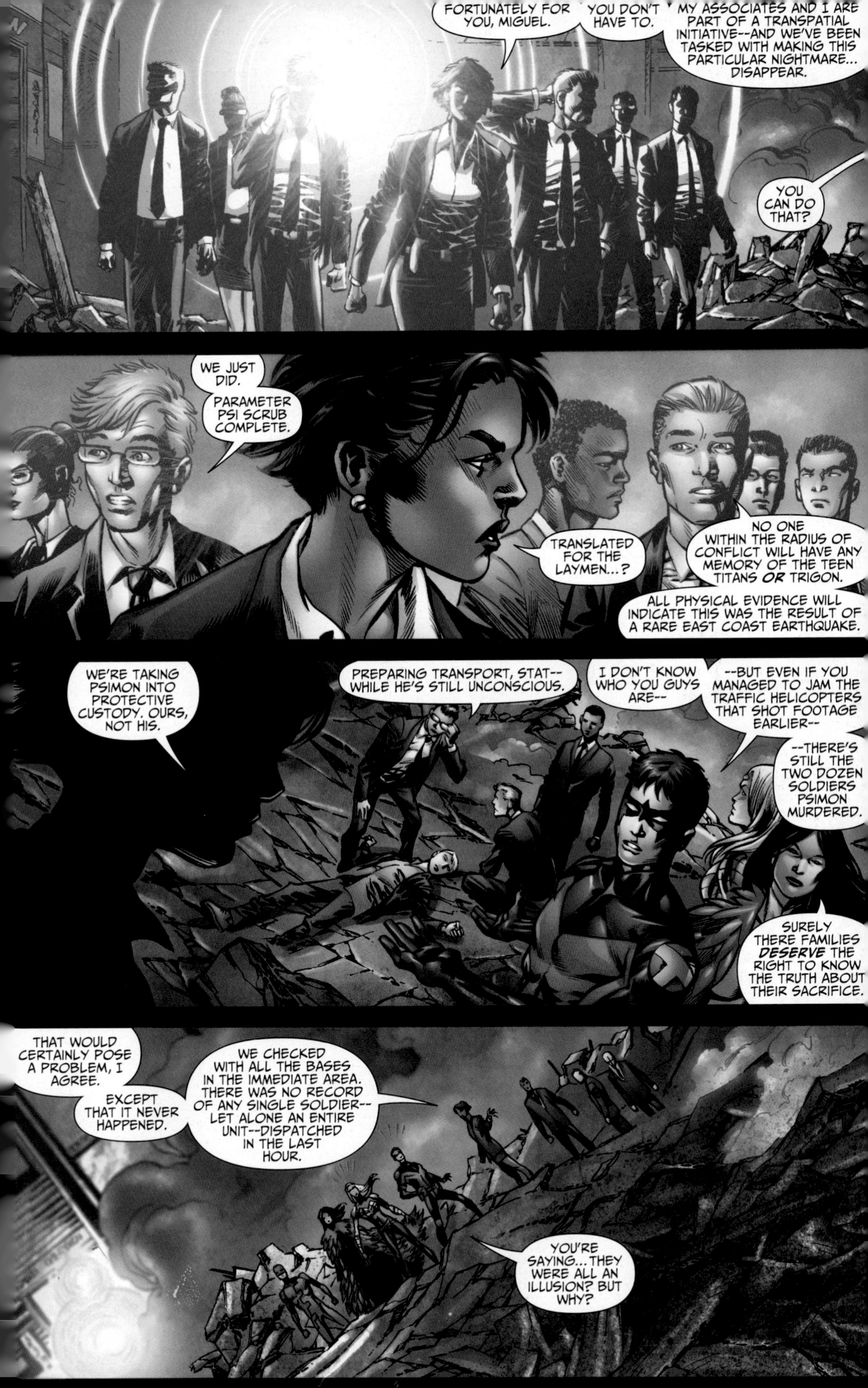
FORTUNATELY FOR YOU, MIGUEL.
YOU DON'T HAVE TO.
MY ASSOCIATES AND I ARE PART OF A TRANSPATIAL INITIATIVE--AND WE'VE BEEN TASKED WITH MAKING THIS PARTICULAR NIGHTMARE... DISAPPEAR.
YOU CAN DO THAT?
WE JUST DID.
PARAMETER PSI SCRUB COMPLETE.
TRANSLATED FOR THE LAYMEN...?
NO ONE WITHIN THE RADIUS OF CONFLICT WILL HAVE ANY MEMORY OF THE TEEN TITANS OR TRIGON.
ALL PHYSICAL EVIDENCE WILL INDICATE THIS WAS THE RESULT OF A RARE EAST COAST EARTHQUAKE.
WE'RE TAKING PSIMON INTO PROTECTIVE CUSTODY. OURS, NOT HIS.
PREPARING TRANSPORT, STAT-- WHILE HE'S STILL UNCONSCIOUS.
I DON'T KNOW WHO YOU GUYS ARE--
--BUT EVEN IF YOU MANAGED TO JAM THE TRAFFIC HELICOPTERS THAT SHOT FOOTAGE EARLIER--
--THERE'S STILL THE TWO DOZEN SOLDIERS PSIMON MURDERED.
SURELY THERE FAMILIES DESERVE THE RIGHT TO KNOW THE TRUTH ABOUT THEIR SACRIFICE.
THAT WOULD CERTAINLY POSE A PROBLEM, I AGREE.
EXCEPT THAT IT NEVER HAPPENED.
WE CHECKED WITH ALL THE BASES IN THE IMMEDIATE AREA. THERE WAS NO RECORD OF ANY SINGLE SOLDIER-- LET ALONE AN ENTIRE UNIT--DISPATCHED IN THE LAST HOUR.
YOU'RE SAYING... THEY WERE ALL AN ILLUSION? BUT WHY?

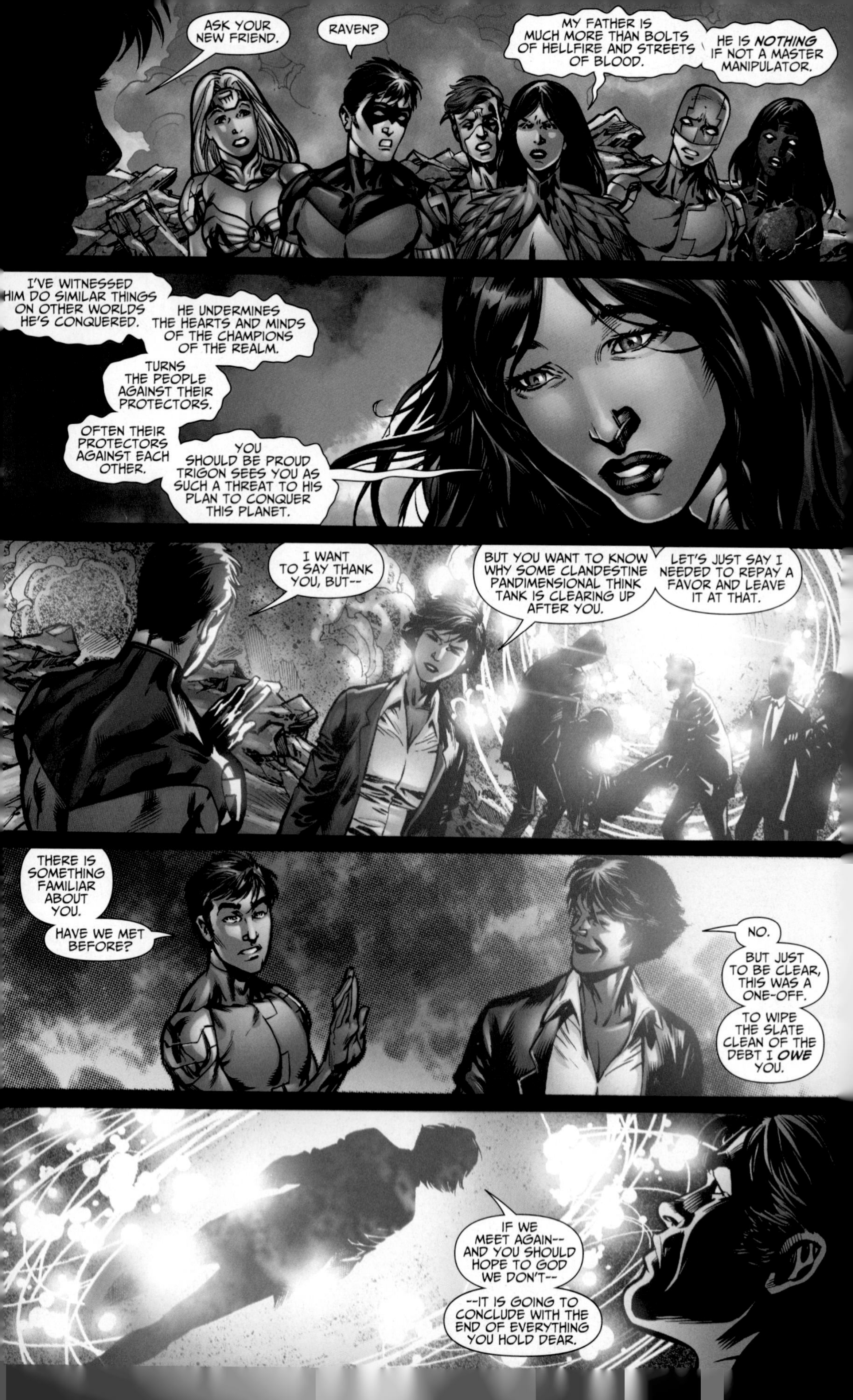
ASK YOUR NEW FRIEND.
RAVEN?
MY FATHER IS MUCH MORE THAN BOLTS OF HELLFIRE AND STREETS OF BLOOD.
HE IS NOTHING IF NOT A MASTER MANIPULATOR.
I'VE WITNESSED HIM DO SIMILAR THINGS ON OTHER WORLDS HE'S CONQUERED.
HE UNDERMINES THE HEARTS AND MINDS OF THE CHAMPIONS OF THE REALM.
TURNS THE PEOPLE AGAINST THEIR PROTECTORS.
OFTEN THEIR PROTECTORS AGAINST EACH OTHER.
YOU SHOULD BE PROUD TRIGON SEES YOU AS SUCH A THREAT TO HIS PLAN TO CONQUER THIS PLANET.
I WANT TO SAY THANK YOU, BUT--
BUT YOU WANT TO KNOW WHY SOME CLANDESTINE PANDIMENSIONAL THINK TANK IS CLEARING UP AFTER YOU.
LET'S JUST SAY I NEEDED TO REPAY A FAVOR AND LEAVE IT AT THAT.
THERE IS SOMETHING FAMILIAR ABOUT YOU.
HAVE WE MET BEFORE?
NO.
BUT JUST TO BE CLEAR, THIS WAS A ONE-OFF.
TO WIPE THE SLATE CLEAN OF THE DEBT I OWE YOU.
IF WE MEET AGAIN-- AND YOU SHOULD HOPE TO GOD WE DON'T--
--IT IS GOING TO CONCLUDE WITH THE END OF EVERYTHING YOU HOLD DEAR.

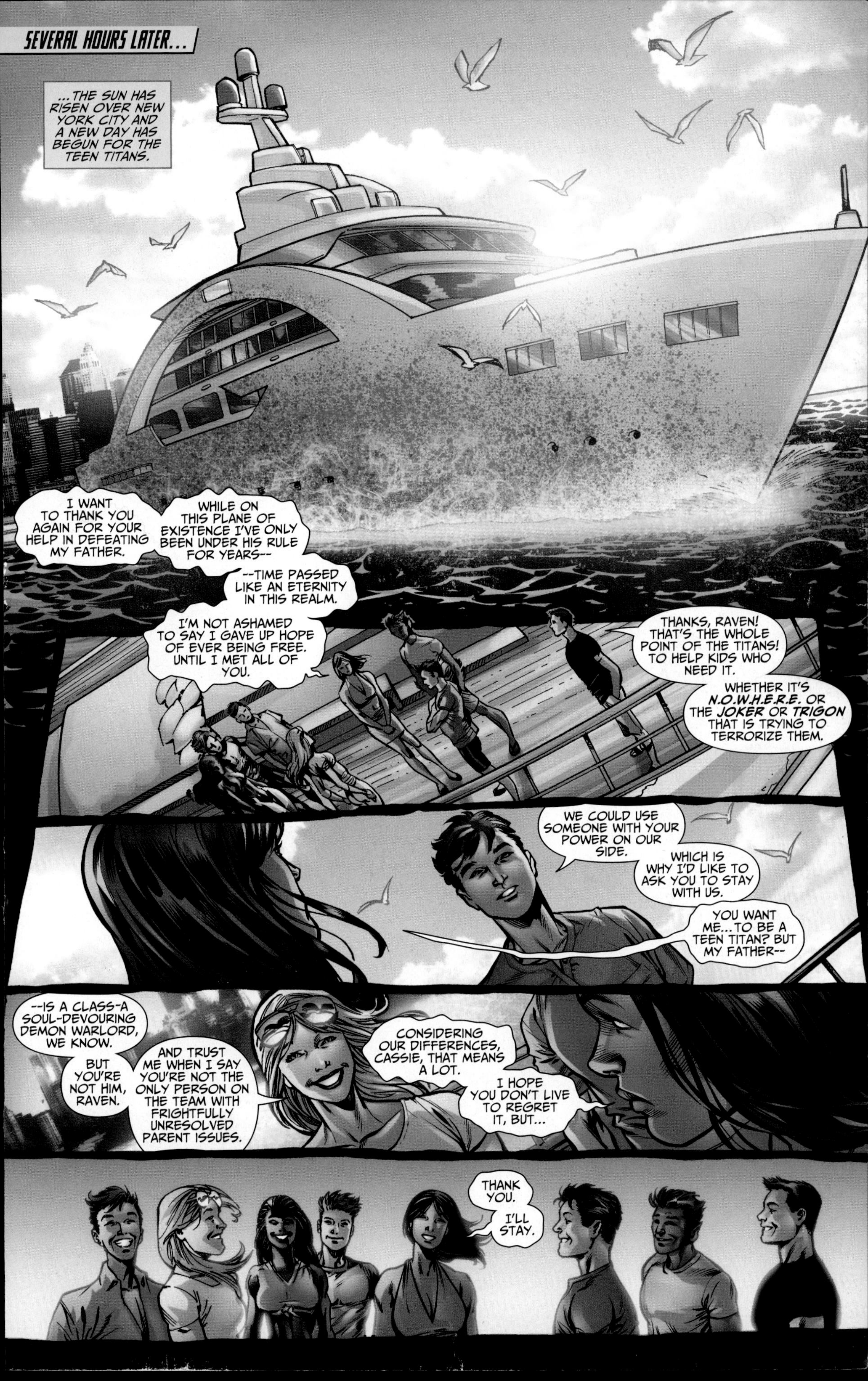
SEVERAL HOURS LATER...
...THE SUN HAS RISEN OVER NEW YORK CITY AND A NEW DAY HAS BEGUN FOR THE TEEN TITANS.
I WANT TO THANK YOU AGAIN FOR YOUR HELP IN DEFEATING MY FATHER.
WHILE ON THIS PLANE OF EXISTENCE I'VE ONLY BEEN UNDER HIS RULE FOR YEARS--
--TIME PASSED LIKE AN ETERNITY IN THIS REALM.
I'M NOT ASHAMED TO SAY I GAVE UP HOPE OF EVER BEING FREE. UNTIL I MET ALL OF YOU.
THANKS, RAVEN! THAT'S THE WHOLE POINT OF THE TITANS! TO HELP KIDS WHO NEED IT.
WHETHER IT'S N.O.W.H.E.R.E. OR THE JOKER OR TRIGON THAT IS TRYING TO TERRORIZE THEM.
WE COULD USE SOMEONE WITH YOUR POWER ON OUR SIDE.
WHICH IS WHY I'D LIKE TO ASK YOU TO STAY WITH US.
YOU WANT ME...TO BE A TEEN TITAN? BUT MY FATHER--
--IS A CLASS-A SOUL-DEVOURING DEMON WARLORD, WE KNOW.
BUT YOU'RE NOT HIM, RAVEN.
AND TRUST ME WHEN I SAY YOU'RE NOT THE ONLY PERSON ON THE TEAM WITH FRIGHTFULLY UNRESOLVED PARENT ISSUES.
CONSIDERING OUR DIFFERENCES, CASSIE, THAT MEANS A LOT.
I HOPE YOU DON'T LIVE TO REGRET IT, BUT...
THANK YOU.
I'LL STAY.

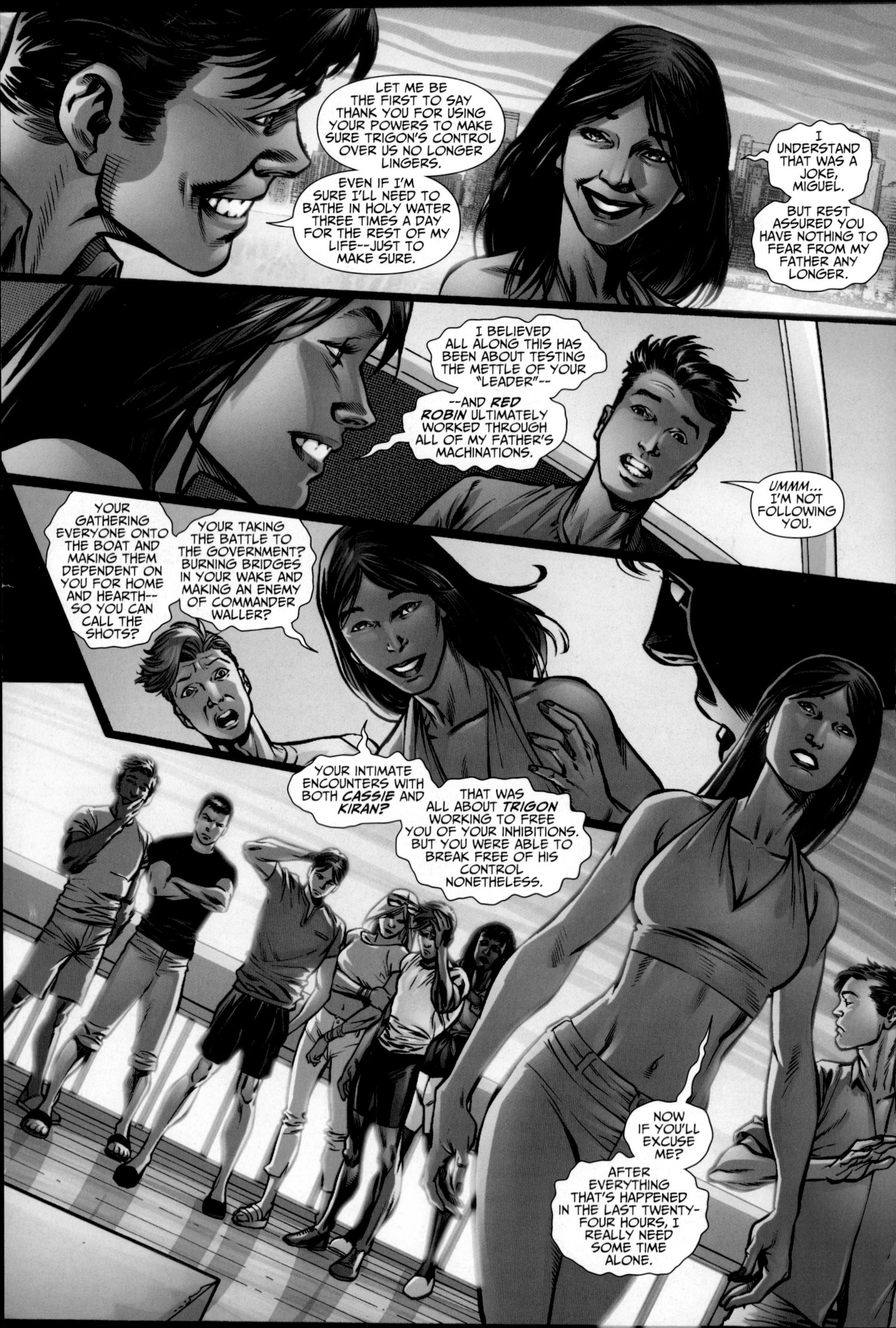
LET ME BE THE FIRST TO SAY THANK YOU FOR USING YOUR POWERS TO MAKE SURE TRIGON'S CONTROL OVER US NO LONGER LINGERS.
EVEN IF I'M SURE I'LL NEED TO BATHE IN HOLY WATER THREE TIMES A DAY FOR THE REST OF MY LIFE--JUST TO MAKE SURE.
I UNDERSTAND THAT WAS A JOKE, MIGUEL.
BUT REST ASSURED YOU HAVE NOTHING TO FEAR FROM MY FATHER ANY LONGER.
I BELIEVED ALL ALONG THIS HAS BEEN ABOUT TESTING THE METTLE OF YOUR "LEADER"--
--AND RED ROBIN ULTIMATELY WORKED THROUGH ALL OF MY FATHER'S MACHINATIONS.
UMMM... I'M NOT FOLLOWING YOU.
YOUR GATHERING EVERYONE ONTO THE BOAT AND MAKING THEM DEPENDENT ON YOU FOR HOME AND HEARTH-- SO YOU CAN CALL THE SHOTS?
YOUR TAKING THE BATTLE TO THE GOVERNMENT? BURNING BRIDGES IN YOUR WAKE AND MAKING AN ENEMY OF COMMANDER WALLER?
YOUR INTIMATE ENCOUNTERS WITH BOTH CASSIE AND KIRAN?
THAT WAS ALL ABOUT TRIGON WORKING TO FREE YOU OF YOUR INHIBITIONS. BUT YOU WERE ABLE TO BREAK FREE OF HIS CONTROL NONETHELESS.
NOW IF YOU'LL EXCUSE ME?
AFTER EVERYTHING THAT'S HAPPENED IN THE LAST TWENTY-FOUR HOURS, I REALLY NEED SOME TIME ALONE.

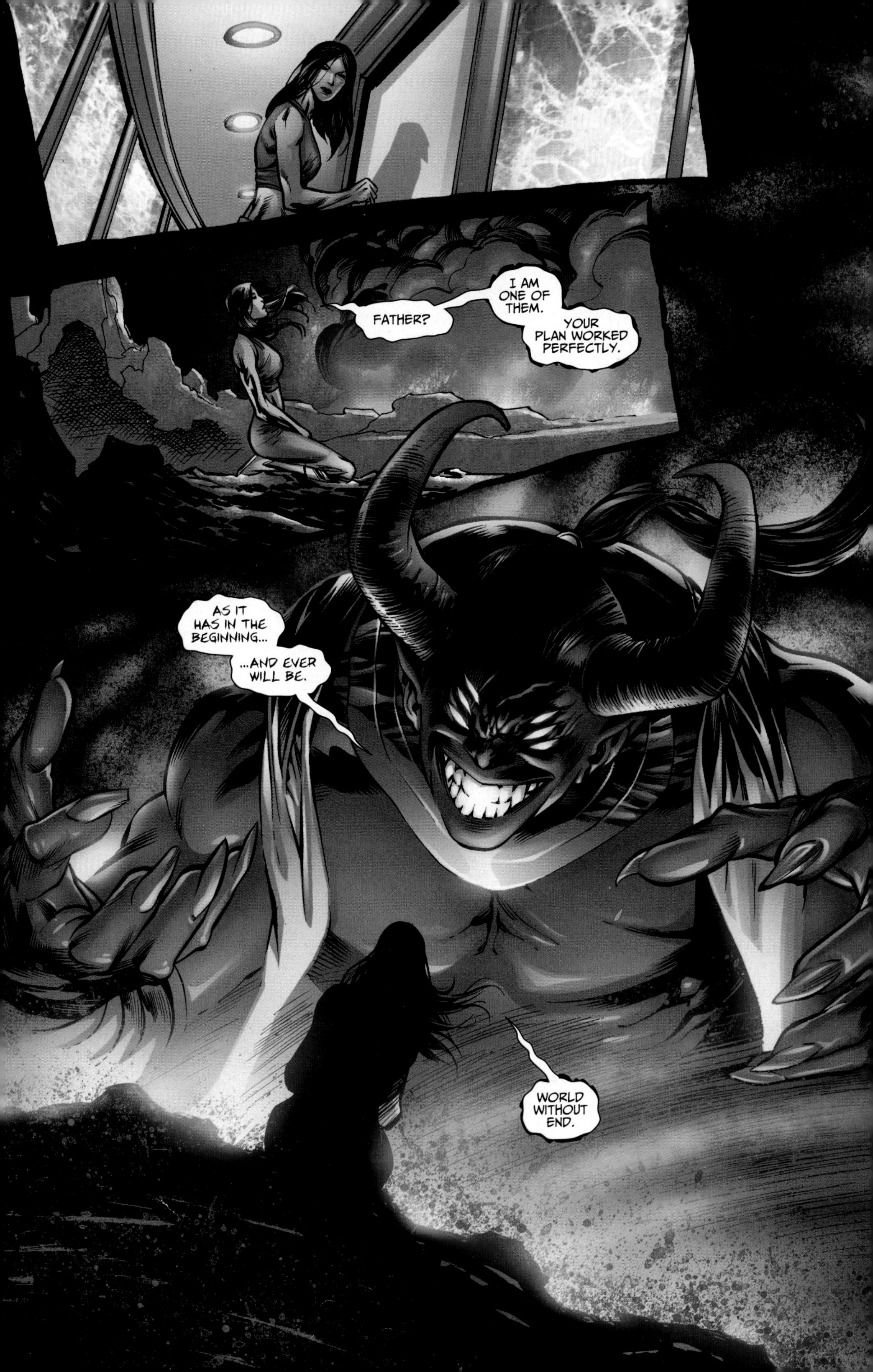
FATHER?
I AM ONE OF THEM.
YOUR PLAN WORKED PERFECTLY.
AS IT HAS IN THE BEGINNING...
...AND EVER WILL BE.
WORLD WITHOUT END.

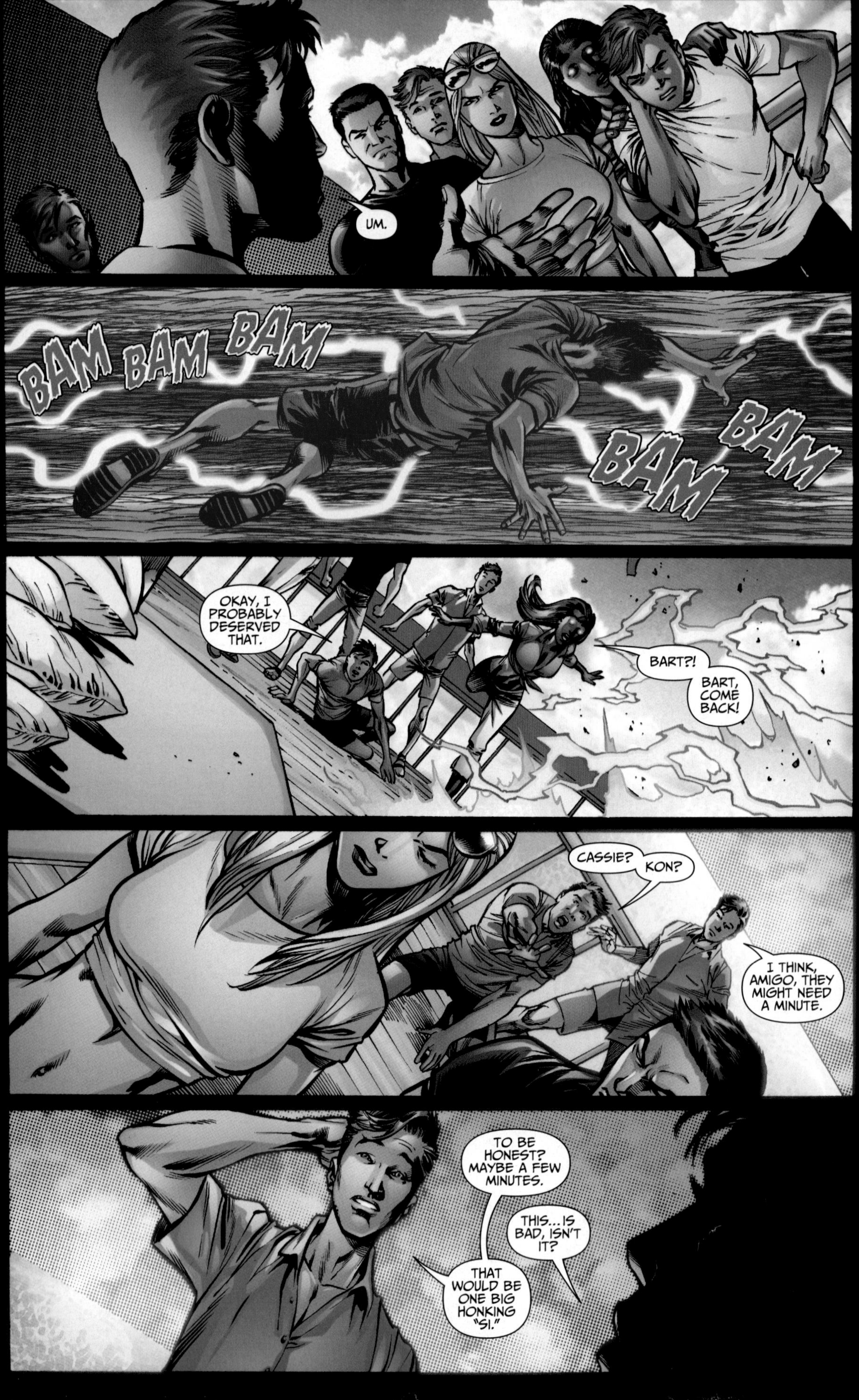
UM.
BAM BAM BAM
BAM BAM
OKAY, I PROBABLY DESERVED THAT.
BART?!
BART, COME BACK!
CASSIE?
KON?
I THINK, AMIGO, THEY MIGHT NEED A MINUTE.
TO BE HONEST? MAYBE A FEW MINUTES.
THIS...IS BAD, ISN'T IT?
THAT WOULD BE ONE BIG HONKING "SI."

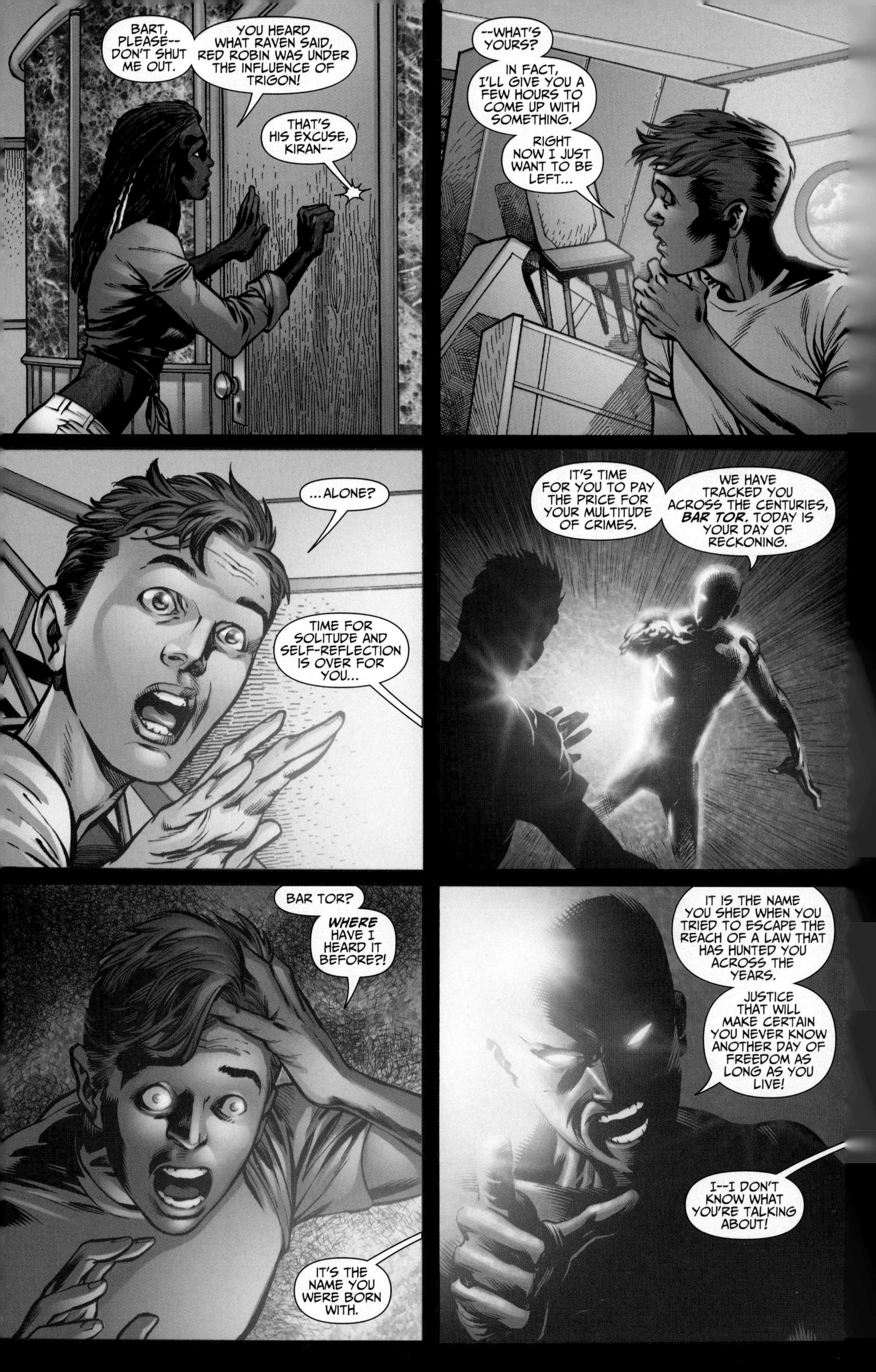
BART, PLEASE-- DON'T SHUT ME OUT.
YOU HEARD WHAT RAVEN SAID, RED ROBIN WAS UNDER THE INFLUENCE OF TRIGON!
THAT'S HIS EXCUSE, KIRAN--
--WHAT'S YOURS?
IN FACT, I'LL GIVE YOU A FEW HOURS TO COME UP WITH SOMETHING.
RIGHT NOW I JUST WANT TO BE LEFT...
...ALONE?
TIME FOR SOLITUDE AND SELF-REFLECTION IS OVER FOR YOU...
IT'S TIME FOR YOU TO PAY THE PRICE FOR YOUR MULTITUDE OF CRIMES.
WE HAVE TRACKED YOU ACROSS THE CENTURIES, BAR TOR. TODAY IS YOUR DAY OF RECKONING.
BAR TOR?
WHERE HAVE I HEARD IT BEFORE?!
IT'S THE NAME YOU WERE BORN WITH.
IT IS THE NAME YOU SHED WHEN YOU TRIED TO ESCAPE THE REACH OF A LAW THAT HAS HUNTED YOU ACROSS THE YEARS.
JUSTICE THAT WILL MAKE CERTAIN YOU NEVER KNOW ANOTHER DAY OF FREEDOM AS LONG AS YOU LIVE!
I--I DON'T KNOW WHAT YOU'RE TALKING ABOUT!

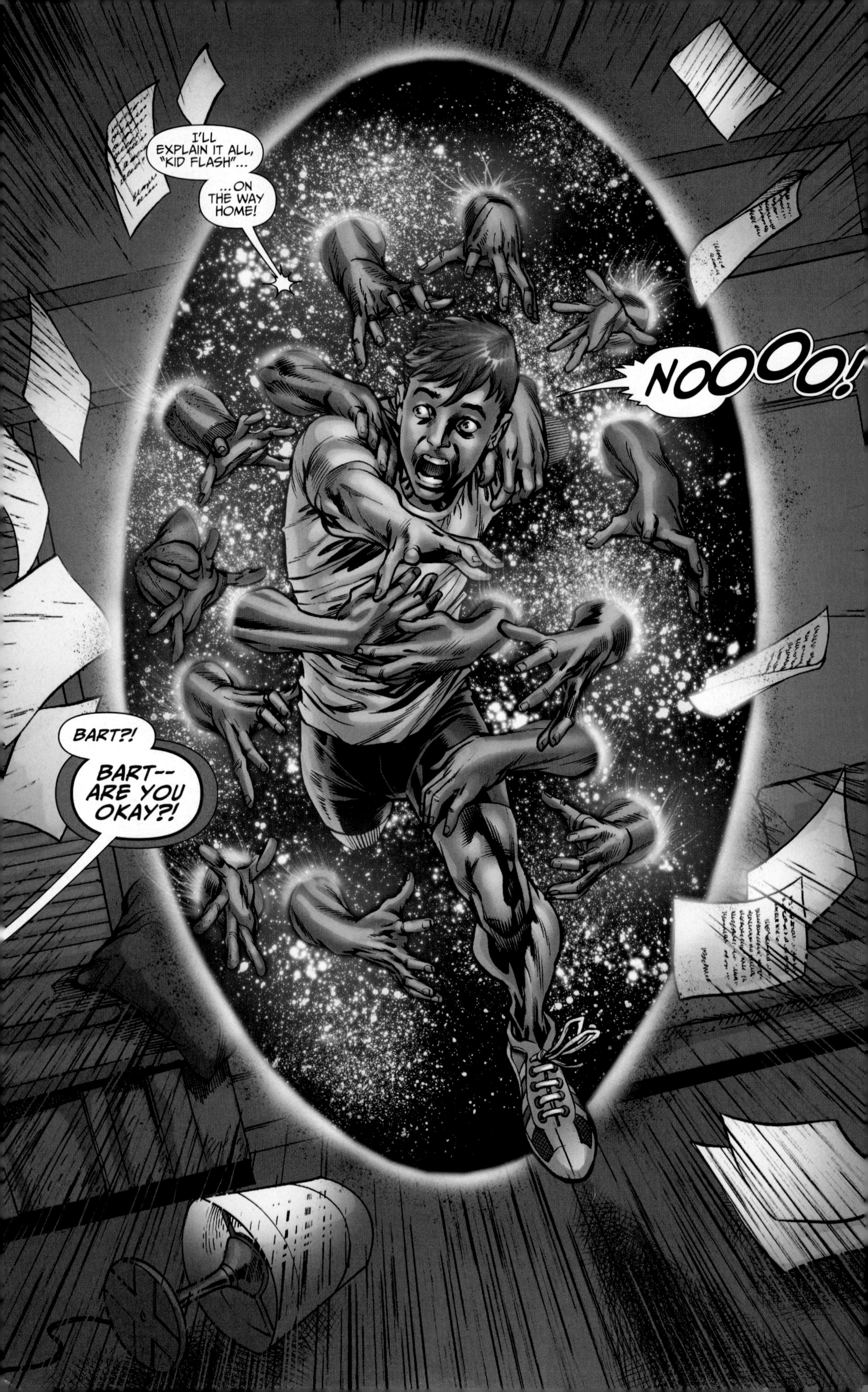

I'LL EXPLAIN IT ALL, "KID FLASH"...
...ON THE WAY HOME!
NOOOOO!
BART?!
BART-- ARE YOU OKAY?!

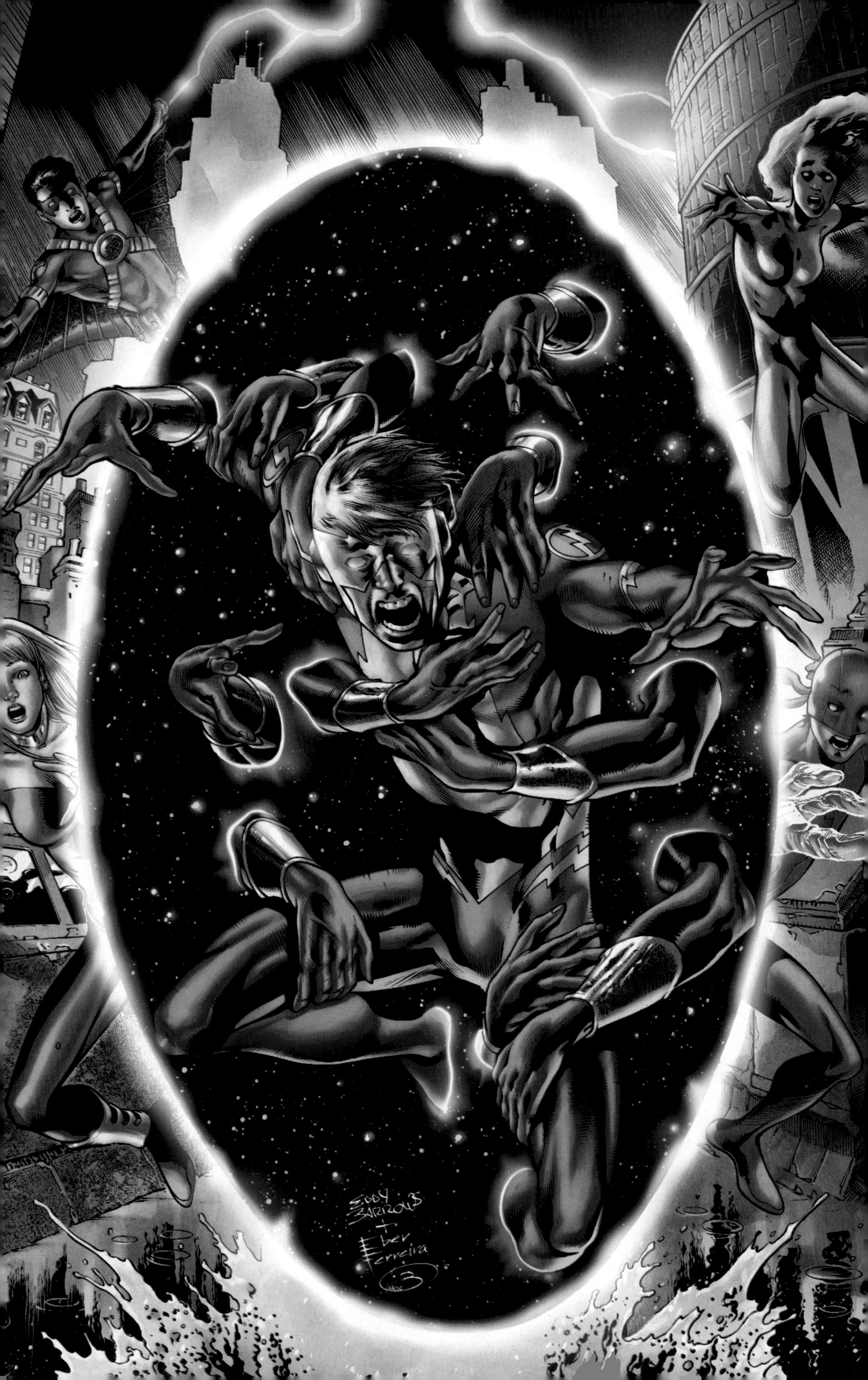
EDDY BARROWS
+
Eber Ferreira

HELLO, I MUST BE GOING!

SCOTT LOBDELL writer ROBSON ROCHA penciller WAYNE FAUCHER inker
cover art by EDDY BARROWS, EBER FERREIRA & BARBARA CIARDO

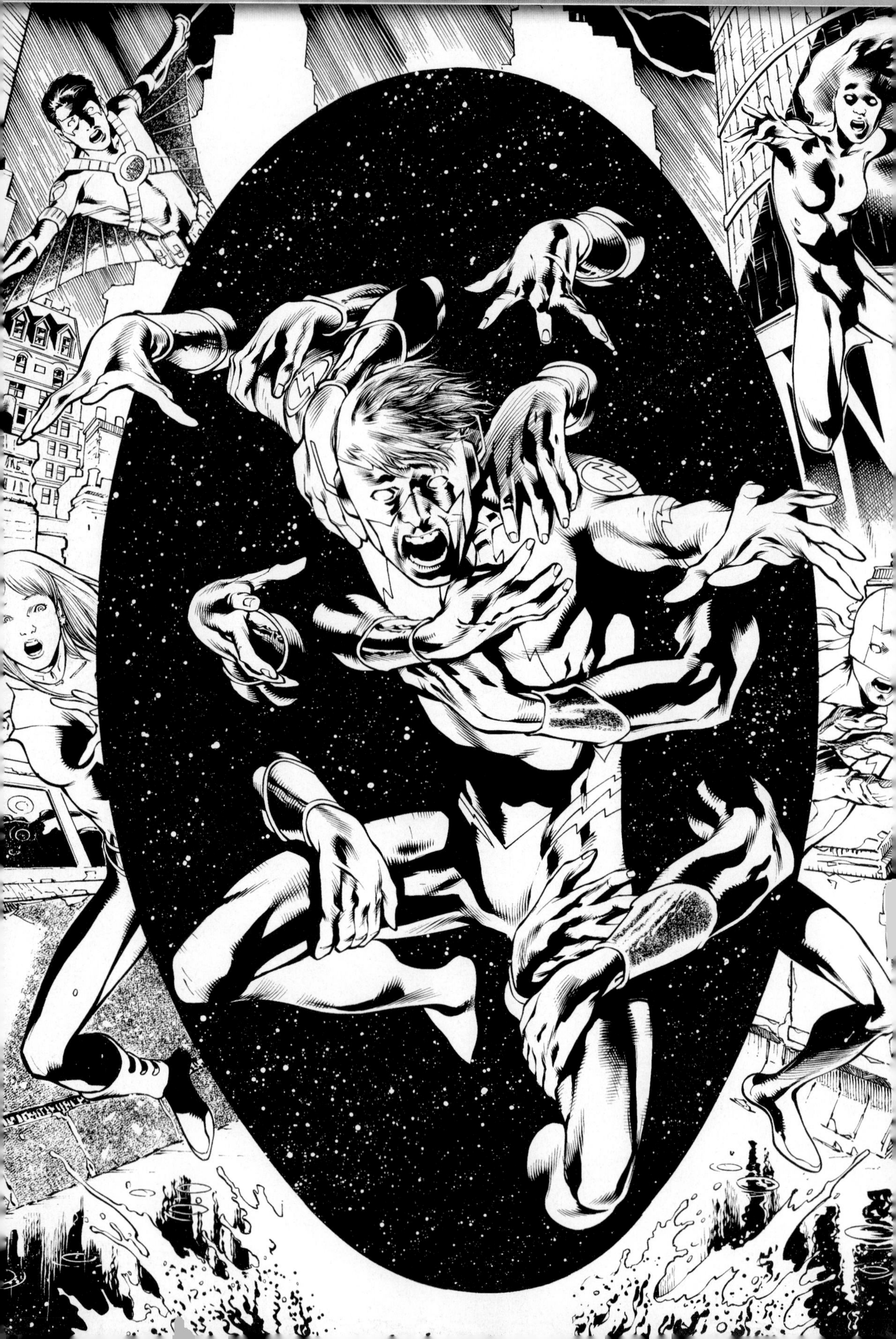

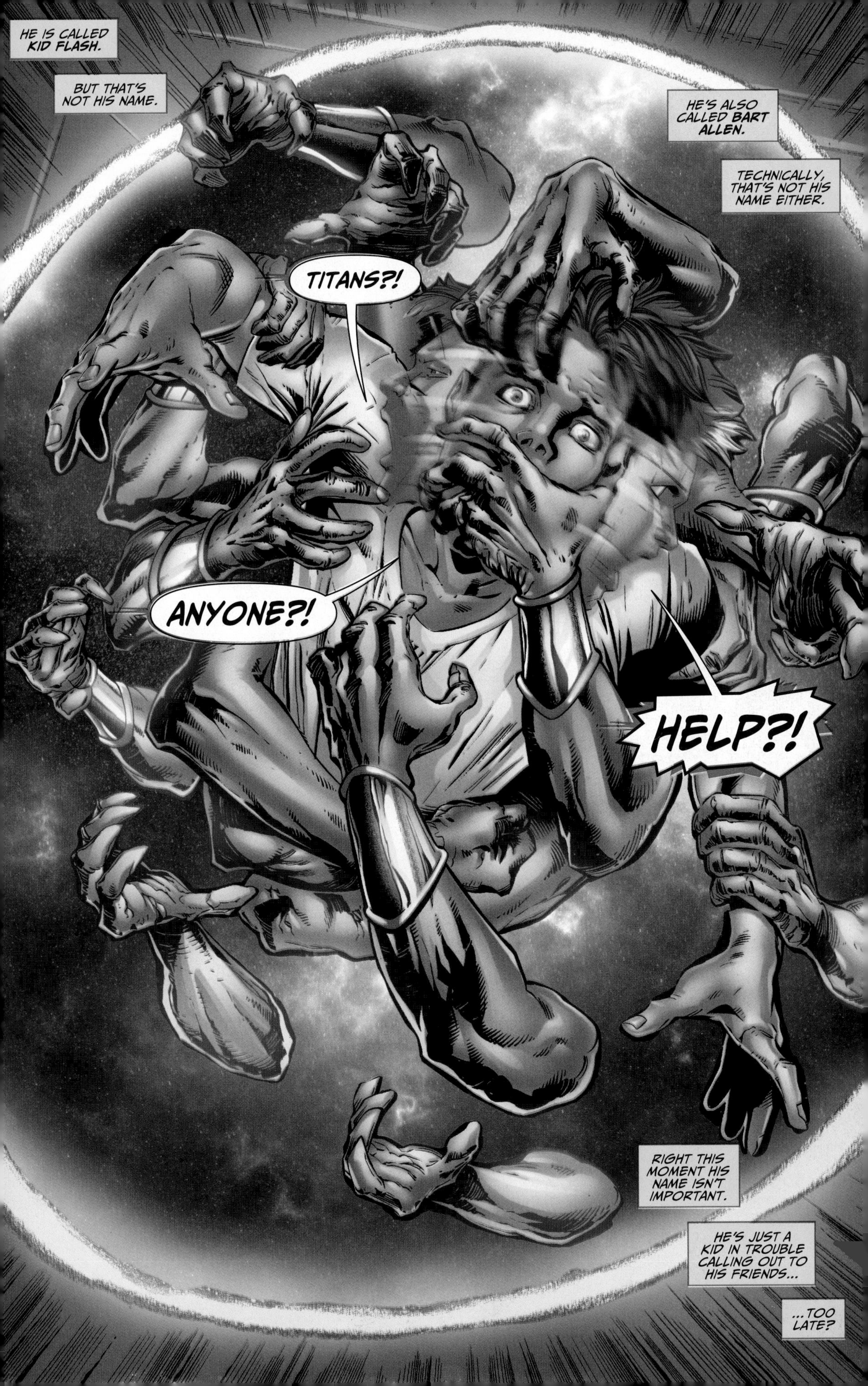
HE IS CALLED KID FLASH.
BUT THAT'S NOT HIS NAME.
HE'S ALSO CALLED BART ALLEN.
TECHNICALLY, THAT'S NOT HIS NAME EITHER.
TITANS?!
ANYONE?!
HELP?!
RIGHT THIS MOMENT HIS NAME ISN'T IMPORTANT.
HE'S JUST A KID IN TROUBLE CALLING OUT TO HIS FRIENDS...
...TOO LATE?

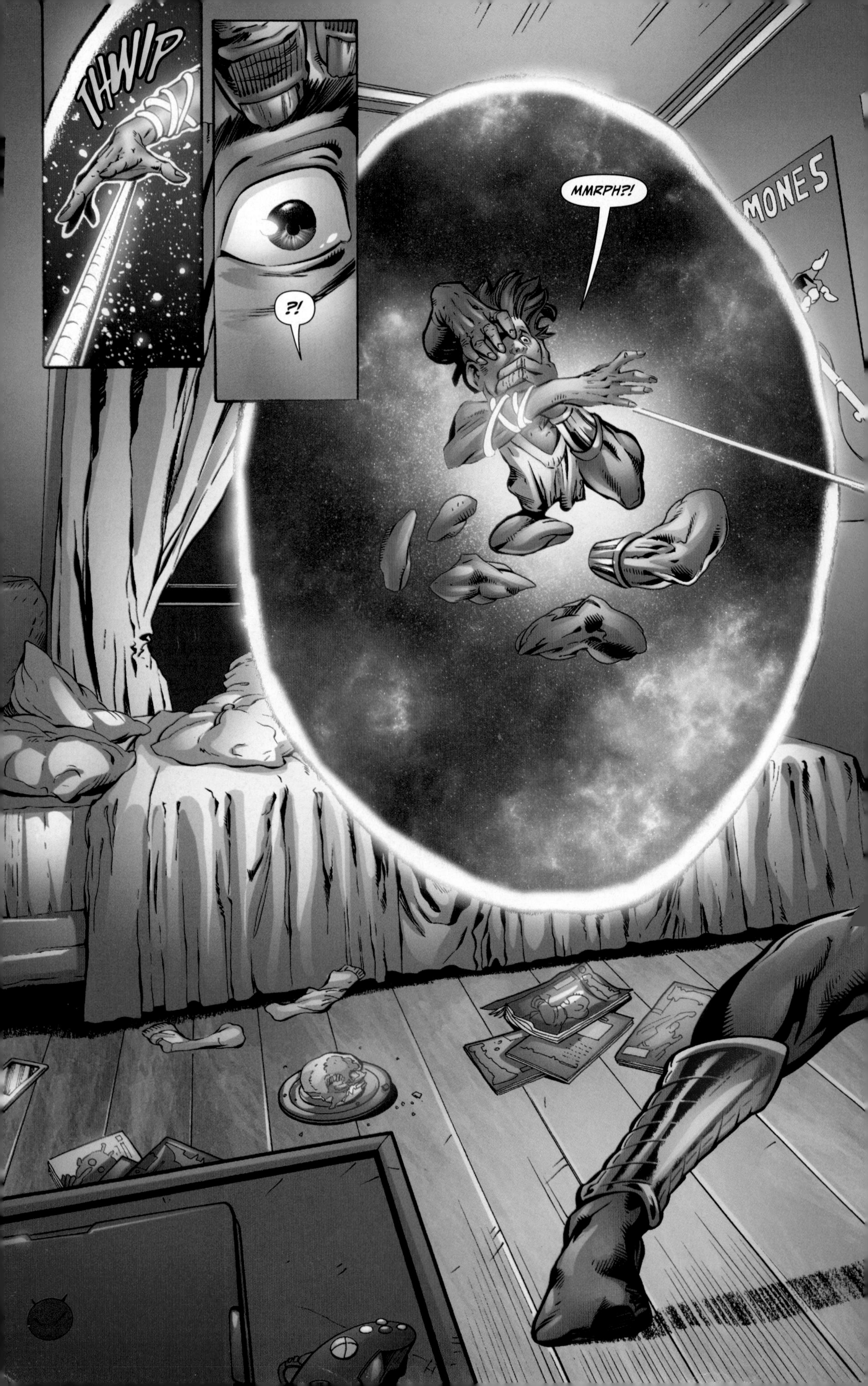
THWIP
?!
MMRPH?!
MONES

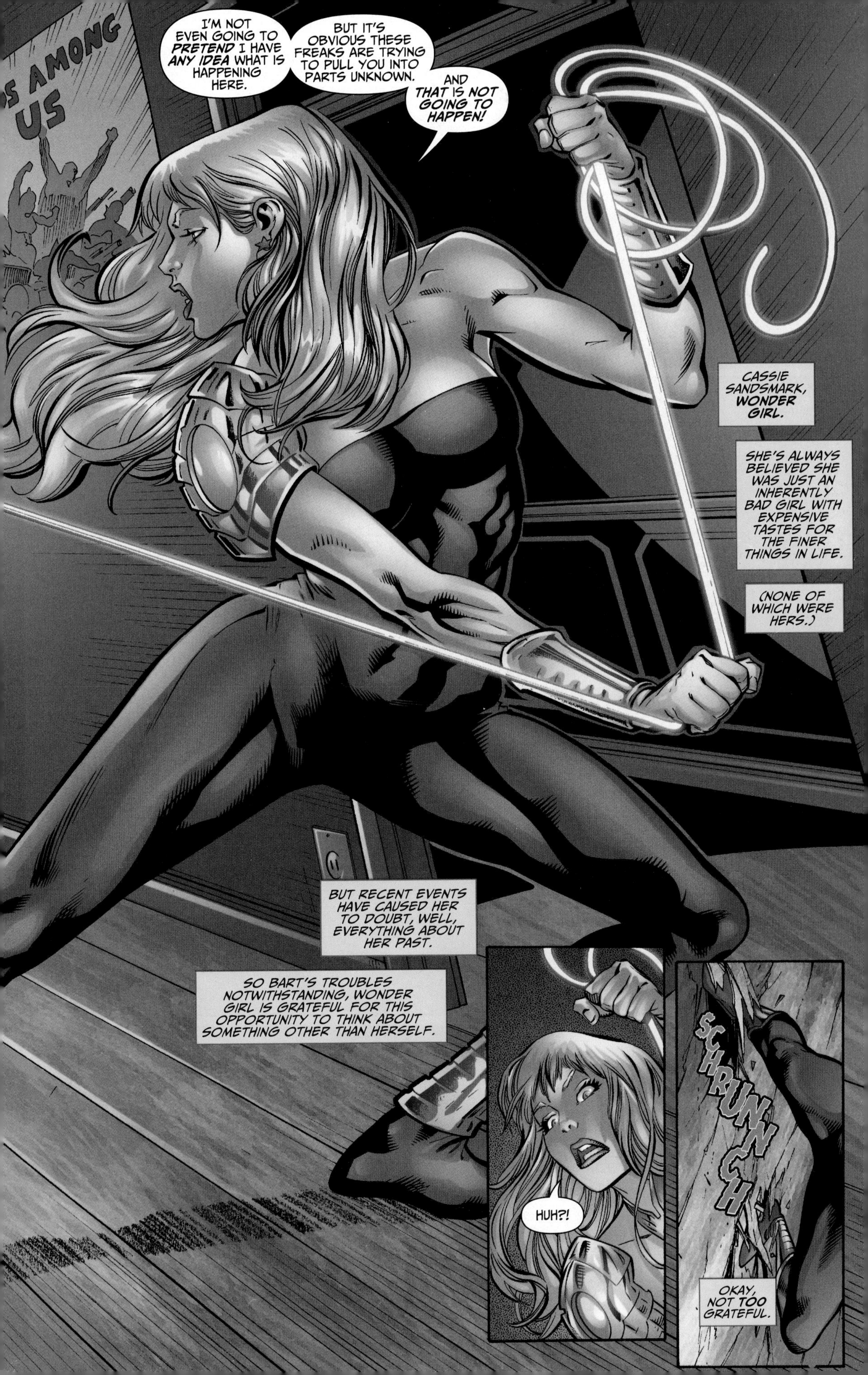

S AMONG US
I'M NOT EVEN GOING TO PRETEND I HAVE ANY IDEA WHAT IS HAPPENING HERE.
BUT IT'S OBVIOUS THESE FREAKS ARE TRYING TO PULL YOU INTO PARTS UNKNOWN.
AND THAT IS NOT GOING TO HAPPEN!
CASSIE SANDSMARK, WONDER GIRL.
SHE'S ALWAYS BELIEVED SHE WAS JUST AN INHERENTLY BAD GIRL WITH EXPENSIVE TASTES FOR THE FINER THINGS IN LIFE.
(NONE OF WHICH WERE HERS.)
BUT RECENT EVENTS HAVE CAUSED HER TO DOUBT, WELL, EVERYTHING ABOUT HER PAST.
SO BART'S TROUBLES NOTWITHSTANDING, WONDER GIRL IS GRATEFUL FOR THIS OPPORTUNITY TO THINK ABOUT SOMETHING OTHER THAN HERSELF.
HUH?!
SCHRUNNCH
OKAY, NOT TOO GRATEFUL.

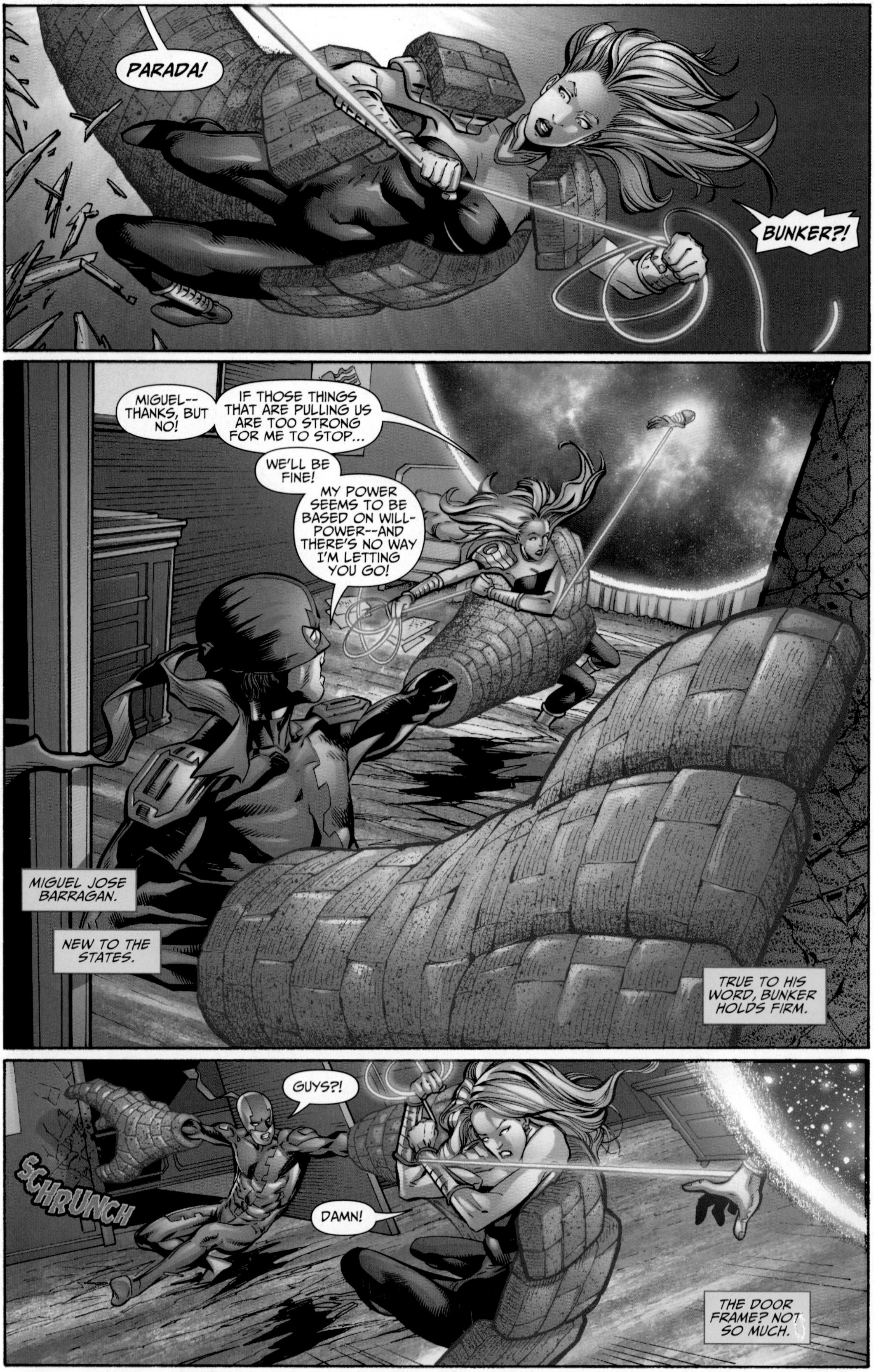
PARADA!
BUNKER?!
MIGUEL-- THANKS, BUT NO!
IF THOSE THINGS THAT ARE PULLING US ARE TOO STRONG FOR ME TO STOP...
WE'LL BE FINE!
MY POWER SEEMS TO BE BASED ON WILL-POWER--AND THERE'S NO WAY I'M LETTING YOU GO!
MIGUEL JOSE BARRAGAN.
NEW TO THE STATES.
TRUE TO HIS WORD, BUNKER HOLDS FIRM.
GUYS?!
SCHRUNCH
DAMN!
THE DOOR FRAME? NOT SO MUCH.

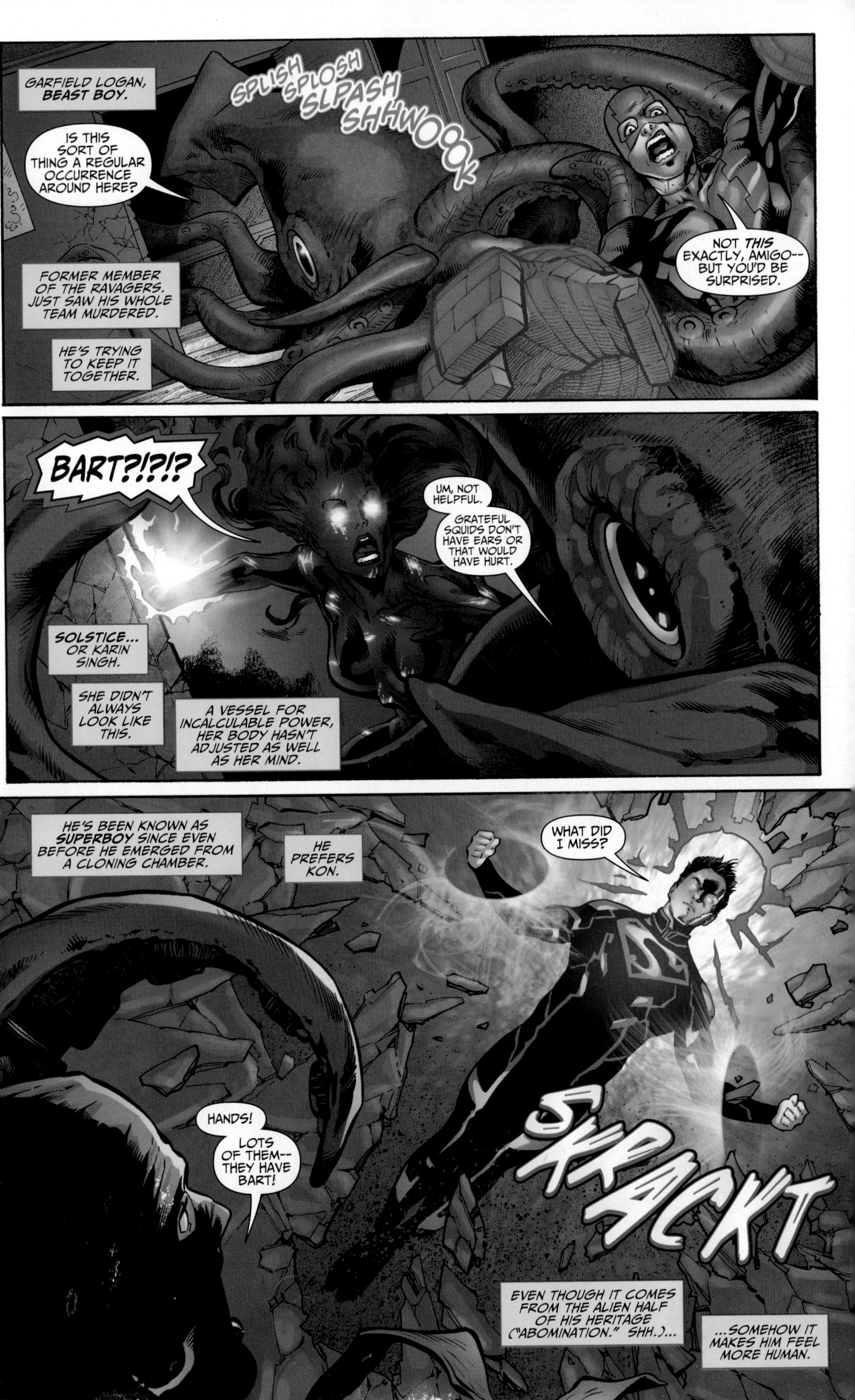
GARFIELD LOGAN, BEAST BOY.
SPLISH SPLOSH SLPASH SHHWOOOK
IS THIS SORT OF THING A REGULAR OCCURRENCE AROUND HERE?
NOT THIS EXACTLY, AMIGO-- BUT YOU'D BE SURPRISED.
FORMER MEMBER OF THE RAVAGERS. JUST SAW HIS WHOLE TEAM MURDERED.
HE'S TRYING TO KEEP IT TOGETHER.
BART?!?!?
UM, NOT HELPFUL.
GRATEFUL SQUIDS DON'T HAVE EARS OR THAT WOULD HAVE HURT.
SOLSTICE... OR KARIN SINGH.
SHE DIDN'T ALWAYS LOOK LIKE THIS.
A VESSEL FOR INCALCULABLE POWER, HER BODY HASN'T ADJUSTED AS WELL AS HER MIND.
HE'S BEEN KNOWN AS SUPERBOY SINCE EVEN BEFORE HE EMERGED FROM A CLONING CHAMBER.
HE PREFERS KON.
WHAT DID I MISS?
HANDS!
LOTS OF THEM-- THEY HAVE BART!
SKRACKT
EVEN THOUGH IT COMES FROM THE ALIEN HALF OF HIS HERITAGE ("ABOMINATION." SHH.)...
...SOMEHOW IT MAKES HIM FEEL MORE HUMAN.

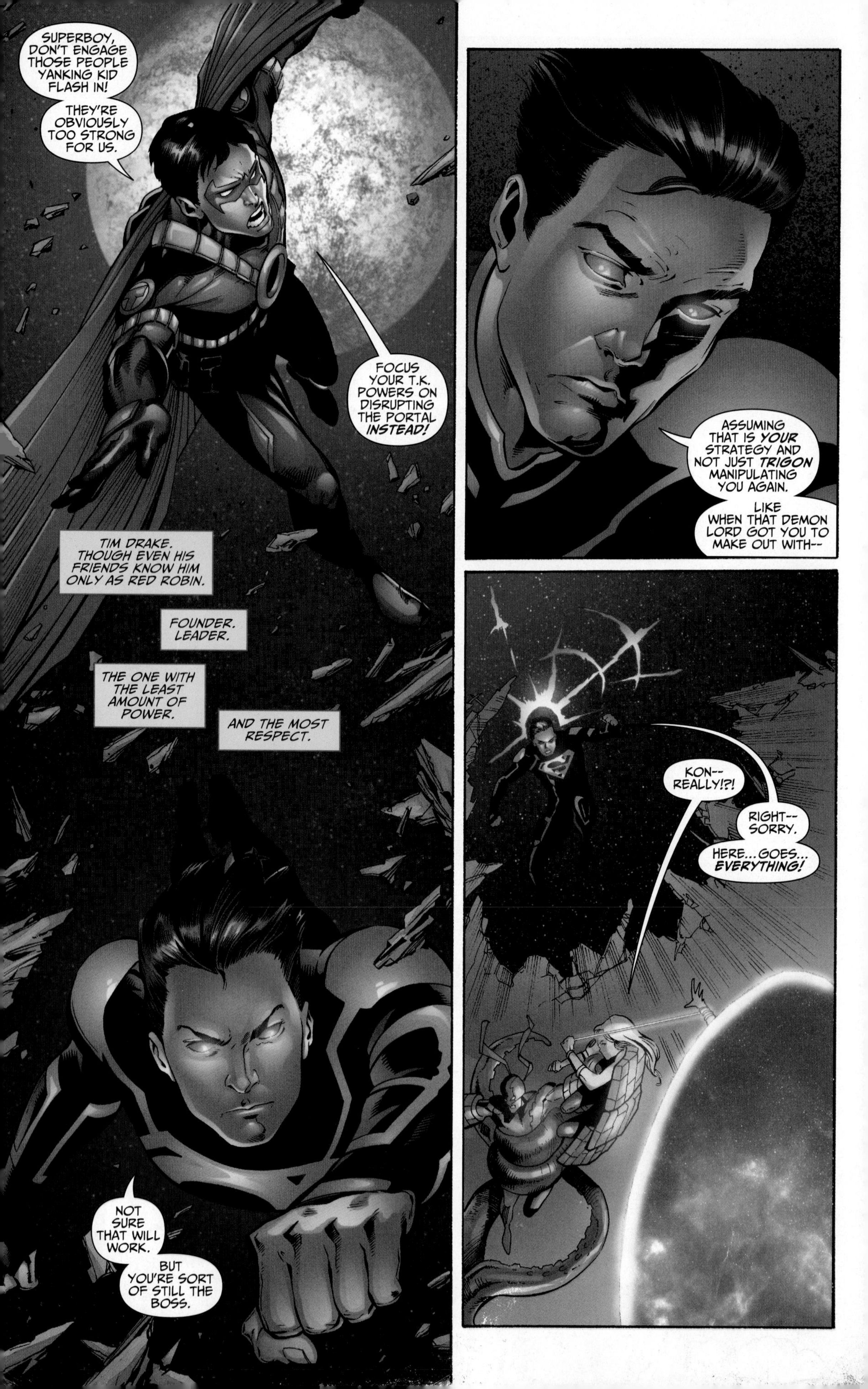

SUPERBOY, DON'T ENGAGE THOSE PEOPLE YANKING KID FLASH IN!
THEY'RE OBVIOUSLY TOO STRONG FOR US.
FOCUS YOUR T.K. POWERS ON DISRUPTING THE PORTAL *INSTEAD!*
TIM DRAKE. THOUGH EVEN HIS FRIENDS KNOW HIM ONLY AS RED ROBIN.
FOUNDER. LEADER.
THE ONE WITH THE LEAST AMOUNT OF POWER.
AND THE MOST RESPECT.
NOT SURE THAT WILL WORK.
BUT YOU'RE SORT OF STILL THE BOSS.
ASSUMING THAT IS ***YOUR*** STRATEGY AND NOT JUST ***TRIGON*** MANIPULATING YOU AGAIN.
LIKE WHEN THAT DEMON LORD GOT YOU TO MAKE OUT WITH--
KON-- REALLY!?!
RIGHT-- SORRY.
HERE...GOES... ***EVERYTHING!***

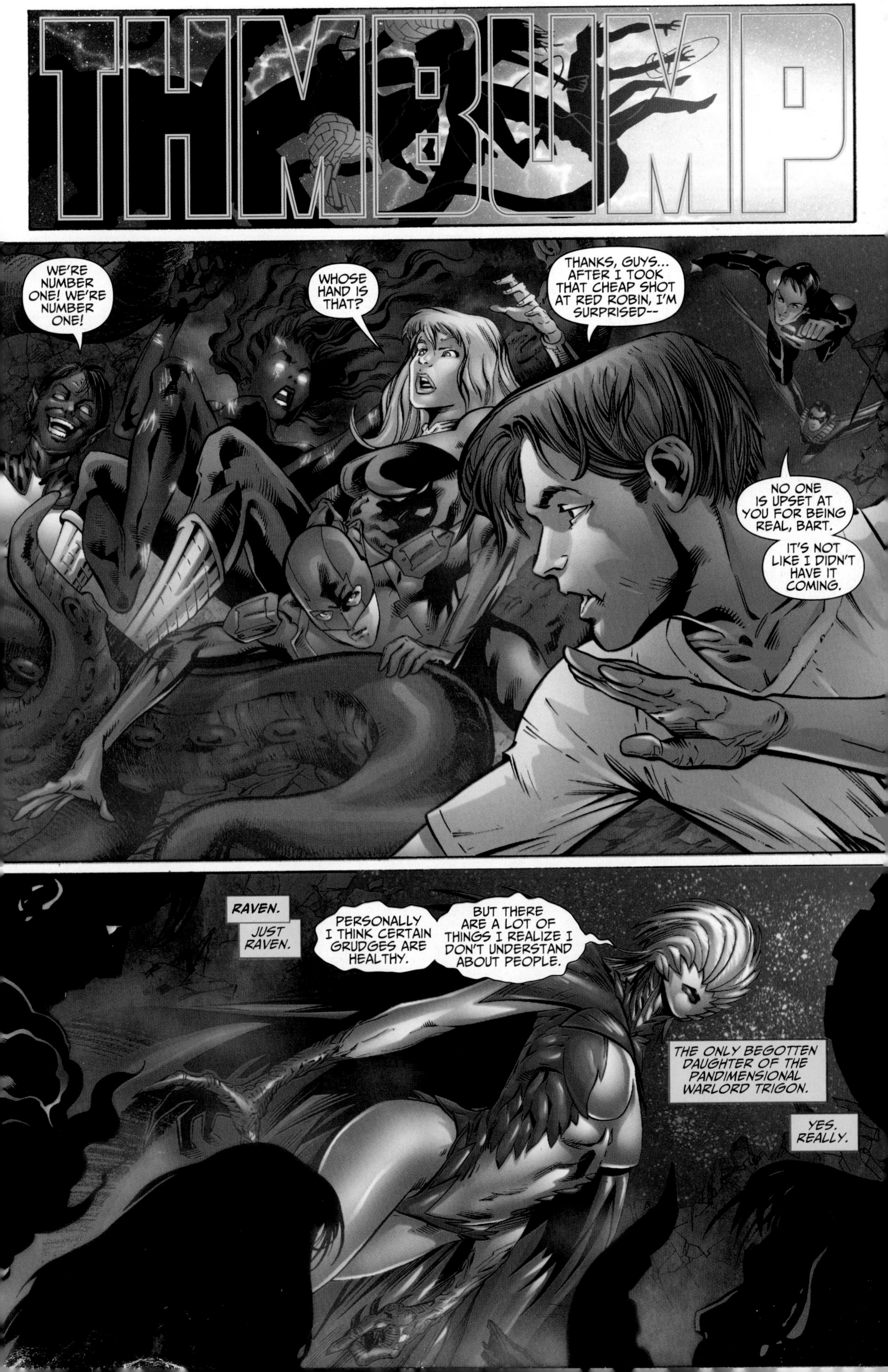

THMBUMP
WE'RE NUMBER ONE! WE'RE NUMBER ONE!
WHOSE HAND IS THAT?
THANKS, GUYS... AFTER I TOOK THAT CHEAP SHOT AT RED ROBIN, I'M SURPRISED--
NO ONE IS UPSET AT YOU FOR BEING REAL, BART.
IT'S NOT LIKE I DIDN'T HAVE IT COMING.
RAVEN.
JUST RAVEN.
PERSONALLY I THINK CERTAIN GRUDGES ARE HEALTHY.
BUT THERE ARE A LOT OF THINGS I REALIZE I DON'T UNDERSTAND ABOUT PEOPLE.
THE ONLY BEGOTTEN DAUGHTER OF THE PANDIMENSIONAL WARLORD TRIGON.
YES. REALLY.

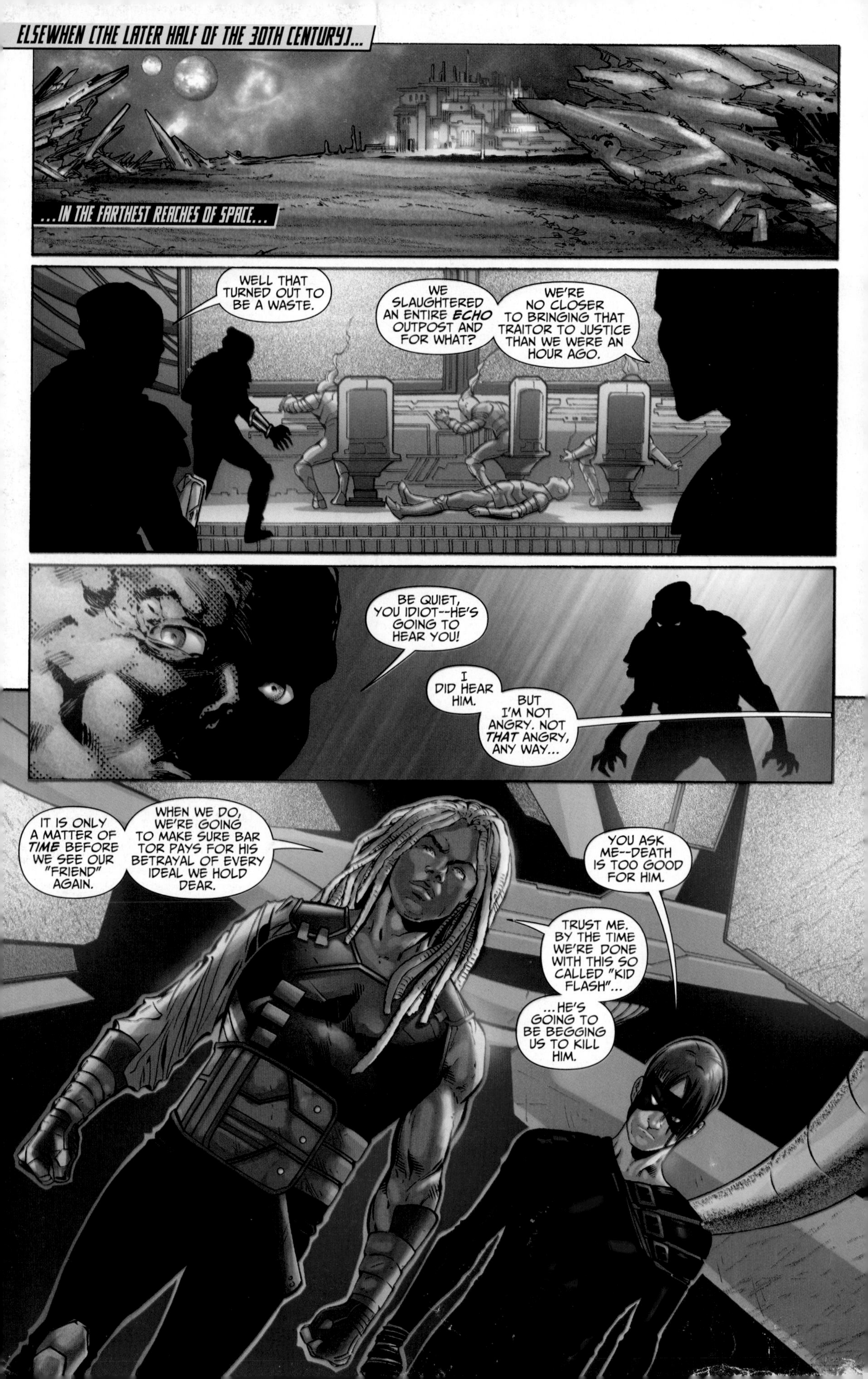
ELSEWHEN [THE LATER HALF OF THE 30TH CENTURY]...
...IN THE FARTHEST REACHES OF SPACE...
WELL THAT TURNED OUT TO BE A WASTE.
WE SLAUGHTERED AN ENTIRE ECHO OUTPOST AND FOR WHAT?
WE'RE NO CLOSER TO BRINGING THAT TRAITOR TO JUSTICE THAN WE WERE AN HOUR AGO.
BE QUIET, YOU IDIOT--HE'S GOING TO HEAR YOU!
I DID HEAR HIM.
BUT I'M NOT ANGRY. NOT THAT ANGRY, ANY WAY...
IT IS ONLY A MATTER OF TIME BEFORE WE SEE OUR "FRIEND" AGAIN.
WHEN WE DO, WE'RE GOING TO MAKE SURE BAR TOR PAYS FOR HIS BETRAYAL OF EVERY IDEAL WE HOLD DEAR.
YOU ASK ME--DEATH IS TOO GOOD FOR HIM.
TRUST ME. BY THE TIME WE'RE DONE WITH THIS SO CALLED "KID FLASH"...
...HE'S GOING TO BE BEGGING US TO KILL HIM.

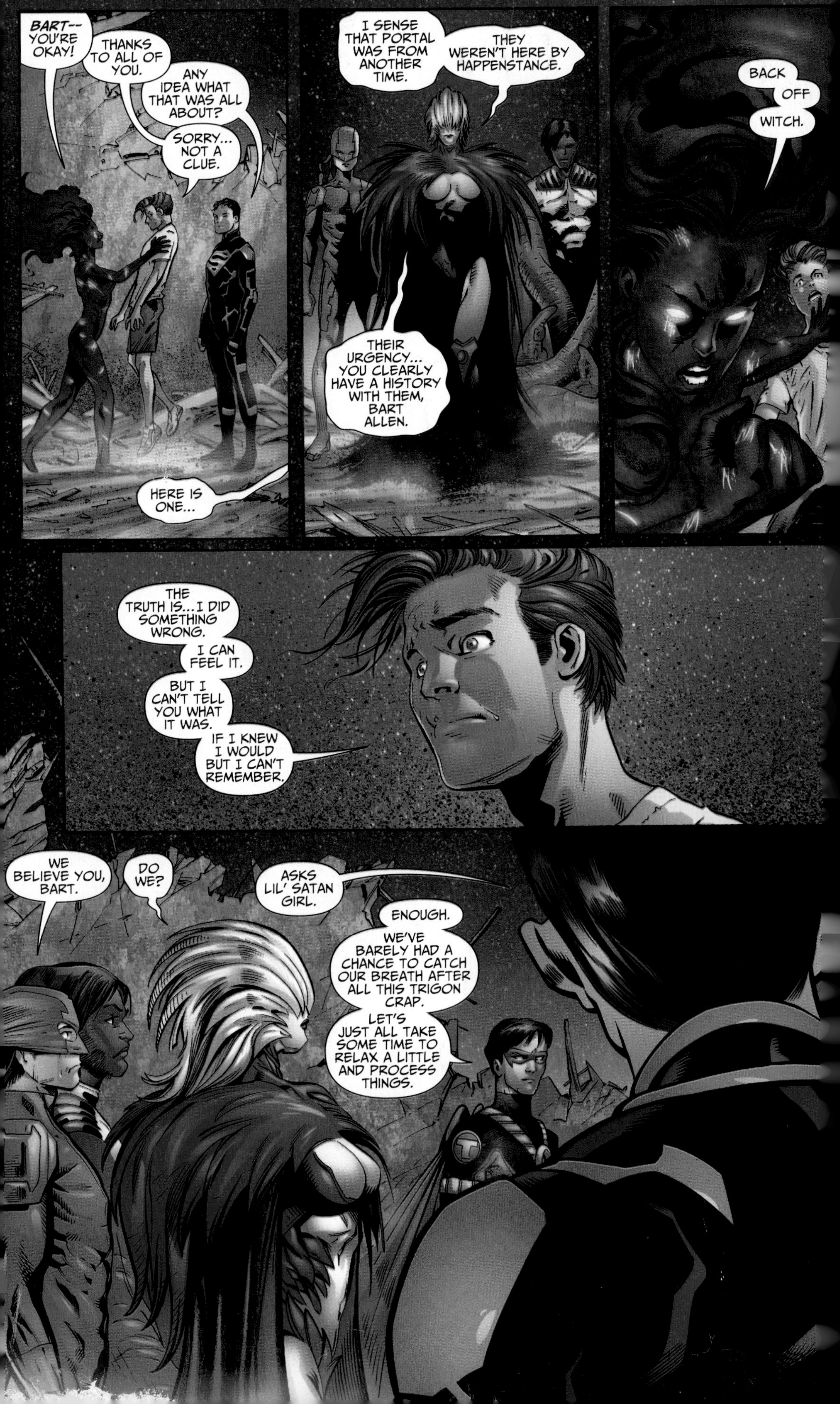
BART-- YOU'RE OKAY!
THANKS TO ALL OF YOU.
ANY IDEA WHAT THAT WAS ALL ABOUT?
SORRY... NOT A CLUE.
HERE IS ONE...
I SENSE THAT PORTAL WAS FROM ANOTHER TIME.
THEY WEREN'T HERE BY HAPPENSTANCE.
THEIR URGENCY... YOU CLEARLY HAVE A HISTORY WITH THEM, BART ALLEN.
BACK OFF WITCH.
THE TRUTH IS...I DID SOMETHING WRONG.
I CAN FEEL IT.
BUT I CAN'T TELL YOU WHAT IT WAS.
IF I KNEW I WOULD BUT I CAN'T REMEMBER.
WE BELIEVE YOU, BART.
DO WE?
ASKS LIL' SATAN GIRL.
ENOUGH.
WE'VE BARELY HAD A CHANCE TO CATCH OUR BREATH AFTER ALL THIS TRIGON CRAP.
LET'S JUST ALL TAKE SOME TIME TO RELAX A LITTLE AND PROCESS THINGS.

I JUST WISH YOU WERE HERE A FEW WEEKS AGO.

THIS USED TO BE REALLY FUN.

TRUST ME, AMIGO. AFTER EVERYTHING I'VE BEEN THROUGH--

--THIS ISN'T THAT BAD.

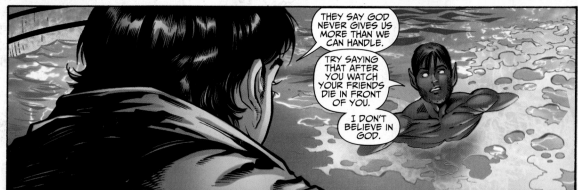

THEY SAY GOD NEVER GIVES US MORE THAN WE CAN HANDLE.

TRY SAYING THAT AFTER YOU WATCH YOUR FRIENDS DIE IN FRONT OF YOU.

I DON'T BELIEVE IN GOD.

WHY IS THAT VAGUELY COMFORTING?

CHIME

TAP TEP TAP

He's awake! He is asking for you!

INBOX MESSAGE

WHAT THE--?!

¡ESTA DESPIERTO! ¡ESTA DESPIERTO!

MI AMOR ESTA DESPIERTO!

I HAVE NO IDEA WHAT YOU'RE SAYING.

BUT I'M GETTING THE IMPRESSION YOU'RE HAPPY, SO...

YIPPEE?

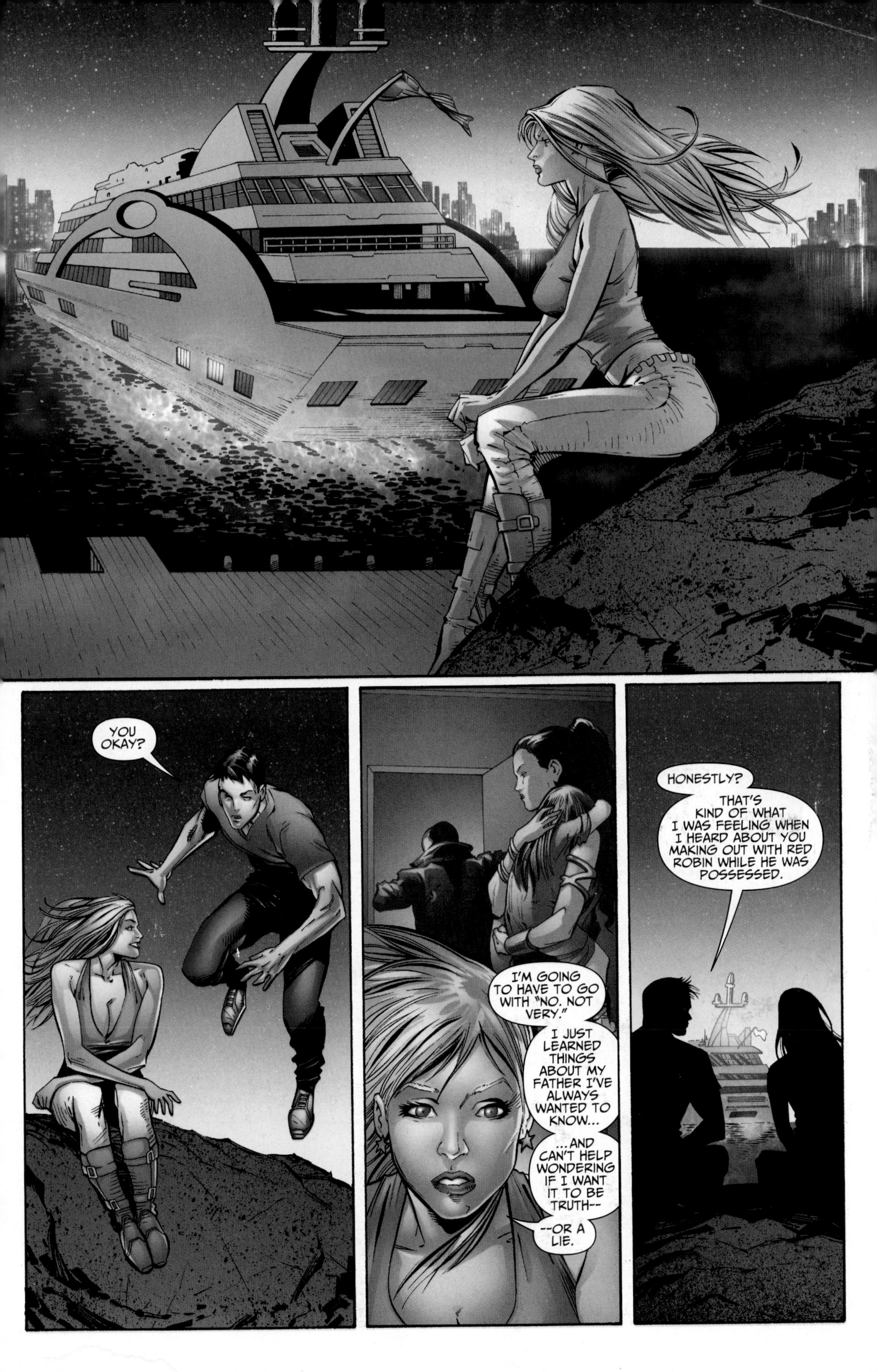

YOU OKAY?
I'M GOING TO HAVE TO GO WITH "NO. NOT VERY."
I JUST LEARNED THINGS ABOUT MY FATHER I'VE ALWAYS WANTED TO KNOW...
...AND CAN'T HELP WONDERING IF I WANT IT TO BE TRUTH--
--OR A LIE.
HONESTLY?
THAT'S KIND OF WHAT I WAS FEELING WHEN I HEARD ABOUT YOU MAKING OUT WITH RED ROBIN WHILE HE WAS POSSESSED.

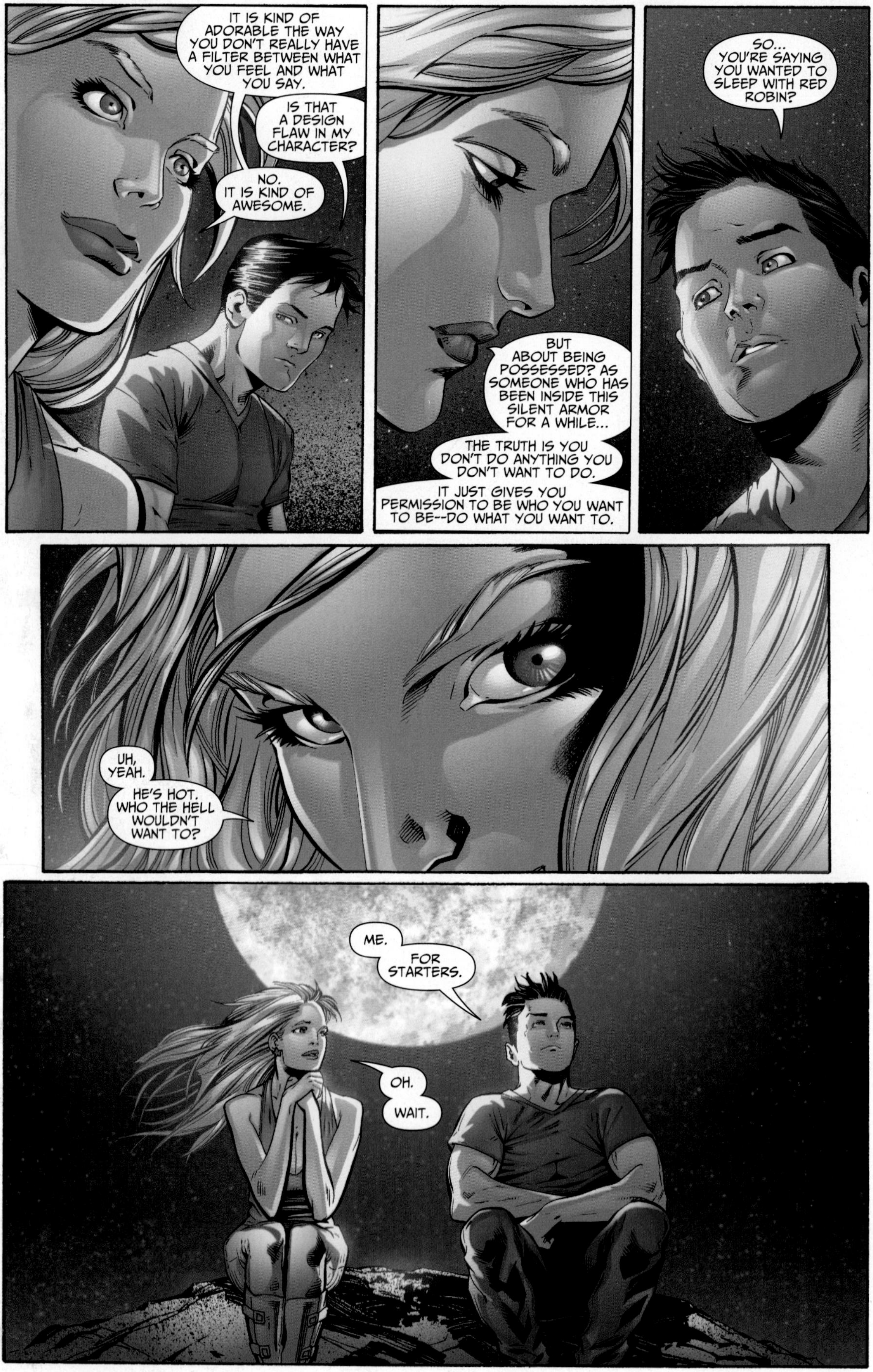
IT IS KIND OF ADORABLE THE WAY YOU DON'T REALLY HAVE A FILTER BETWEEN WHAT YOU FEEL AND WHAT YOU SAY.
IS THAT A DESIGN FLAW IN MY CHARACTER?
NO. IT IS KIND OF AWESOME.
BUT ABOUT BEING POSSESSED? AS SOMEONE WHO HAS BEEN INSIDE THIS SILENT ARMOR FOR A WHILE...
THE TRUTH IS YOU DON'T DO ANYTHING YOU DON'T WANT TO DO.
IT JUST GIVES YOU PERMISSION TO BE WHO YOU WANT TO BE--DO WHAT YOU WANT TO.
SO... YOU'RE SAYING YOU WANTED TO SLEEP WITH RED ROBIN?
UH, YEAH.
HE'S HOT. WHO THE HELL WOULDN'T WANT TO?
ME.
FOR STARTERS.
OH.
WAIT.

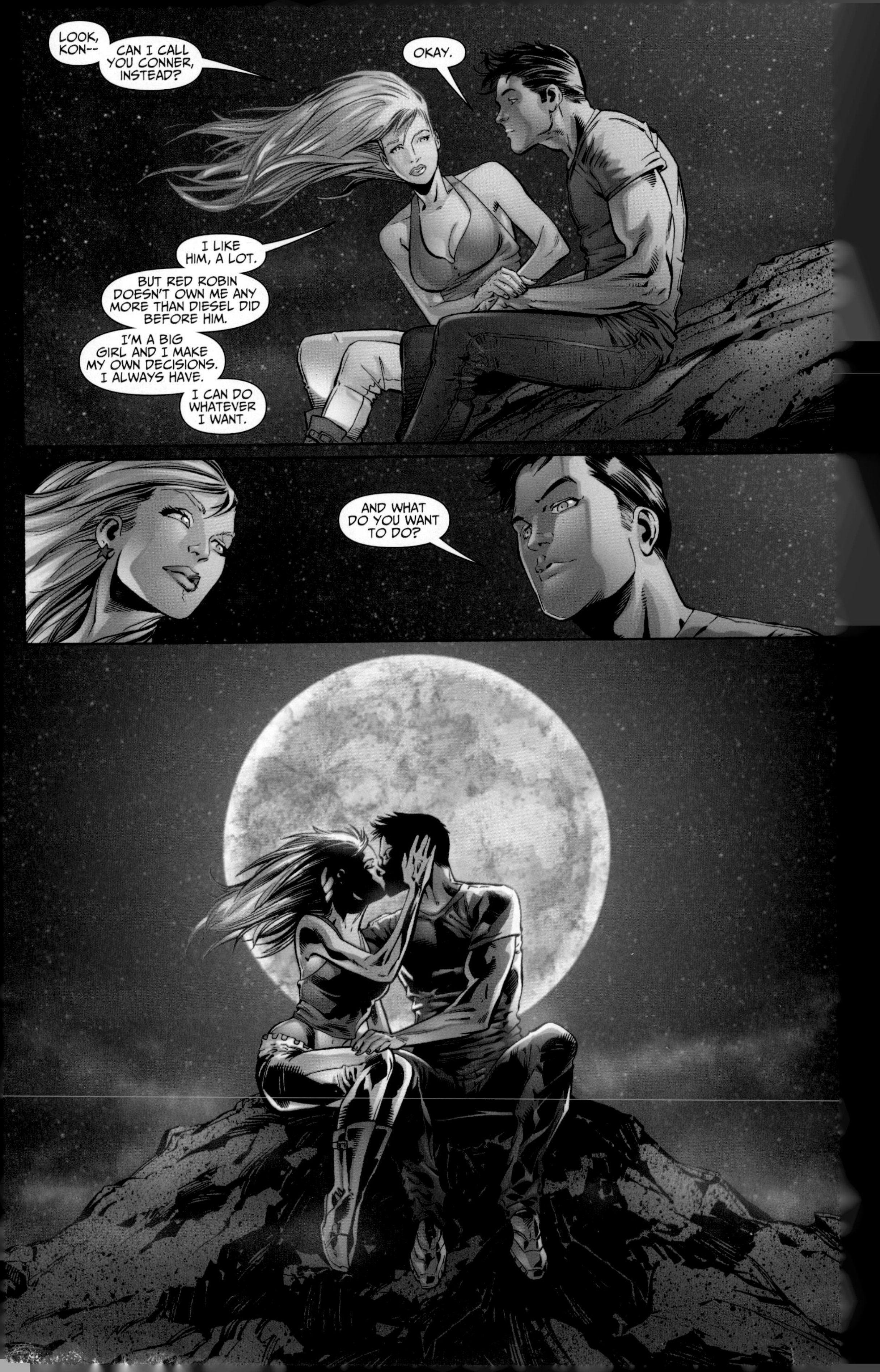
LOOK, KON--
CAN I CALL YOU CONNER, INSTEAD?
OKAY.
I LIKE HIM, A LOT.
BUT RED ROBIN DOESN'T OWN ME ANY MORE THAN DIESEL DID BEFORE HIM.
I'M A BIG GIRL AND I MAKE MY OWN DECISIONS. I ALWAYS HAVE.
I CAN DO WHATEVER I WANT.
AND WHAT DO YOU WANT TO DO?

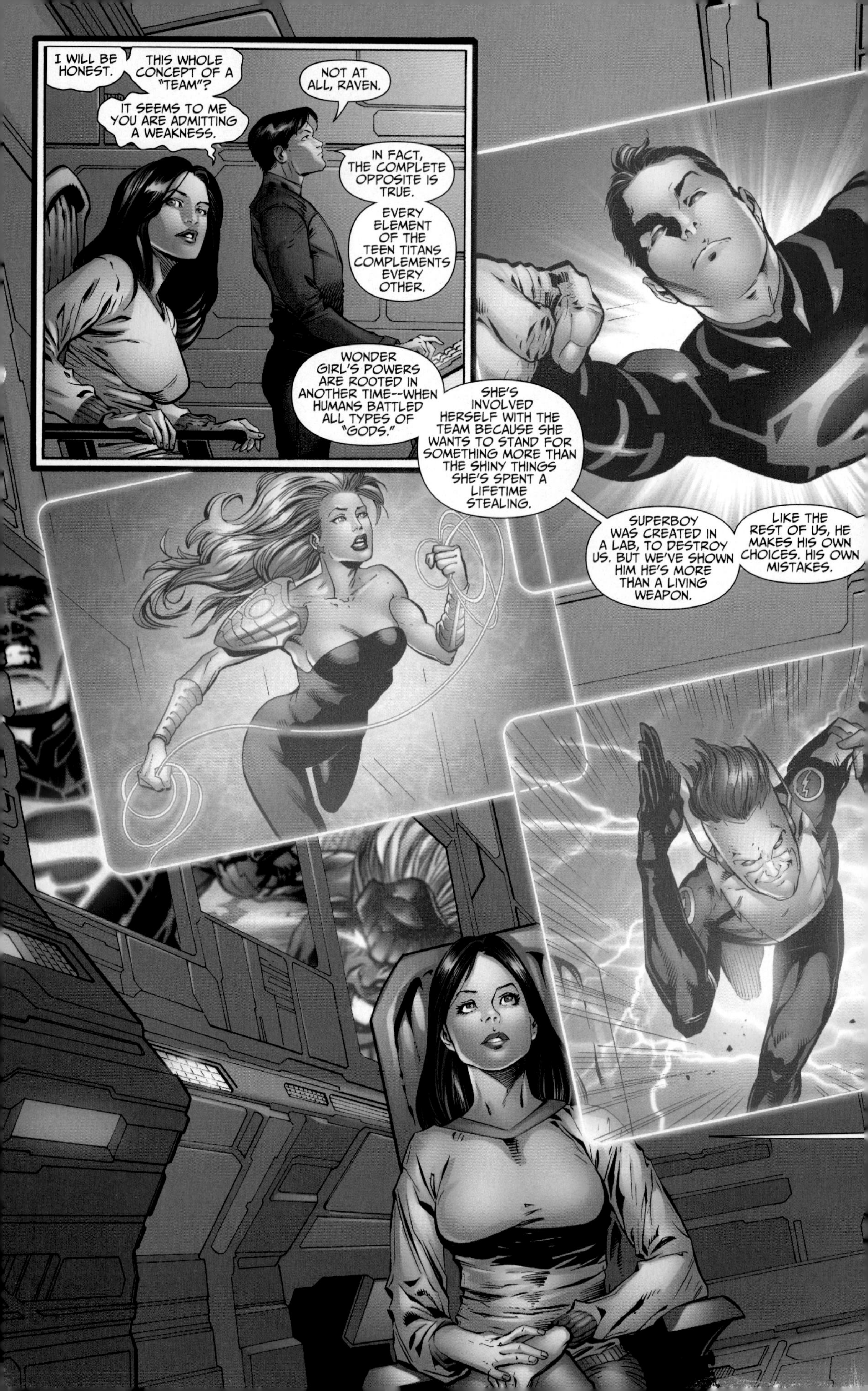
I WILL BE HONEST.
THIS WHOLE CONCEPT OF A "TEAM"?
IT SEEMS TO ME YOU ARE ADMITTING A WEAKNESS.
NOT AT ALL, RAVEN.
IN FACT, THE COMPLETE OPPOSITE IS TRUE.
EVERY ELEMENT OF THE TEEN TITANS COMPLEMENTS EVERY OTHER.
WONDER GIRL'S POWERS ARE ROOTED IN ANOTHER TIME--WHEN HUMANS BATTLED ALL TYPES OF "GODS."
SHE'S INVOLVED HERSELF WITH THE TEAM BECAUSE SHE WANTS TO STAND FOR SOMETHING MORE THAN THE SHINY THINGS SHE'S SPENT A LIFETIME STEALING.
SUPERBOY WAS CREATED IN A LAB, TO DESTROY US. BUT WE'VE SHOWN HIM HE'S MORE THAN A LIVING WEAPON.
LIKE THE REST OF US, HE MAKES HIS OWN CHOICES. HIS OWN MISTAKES.

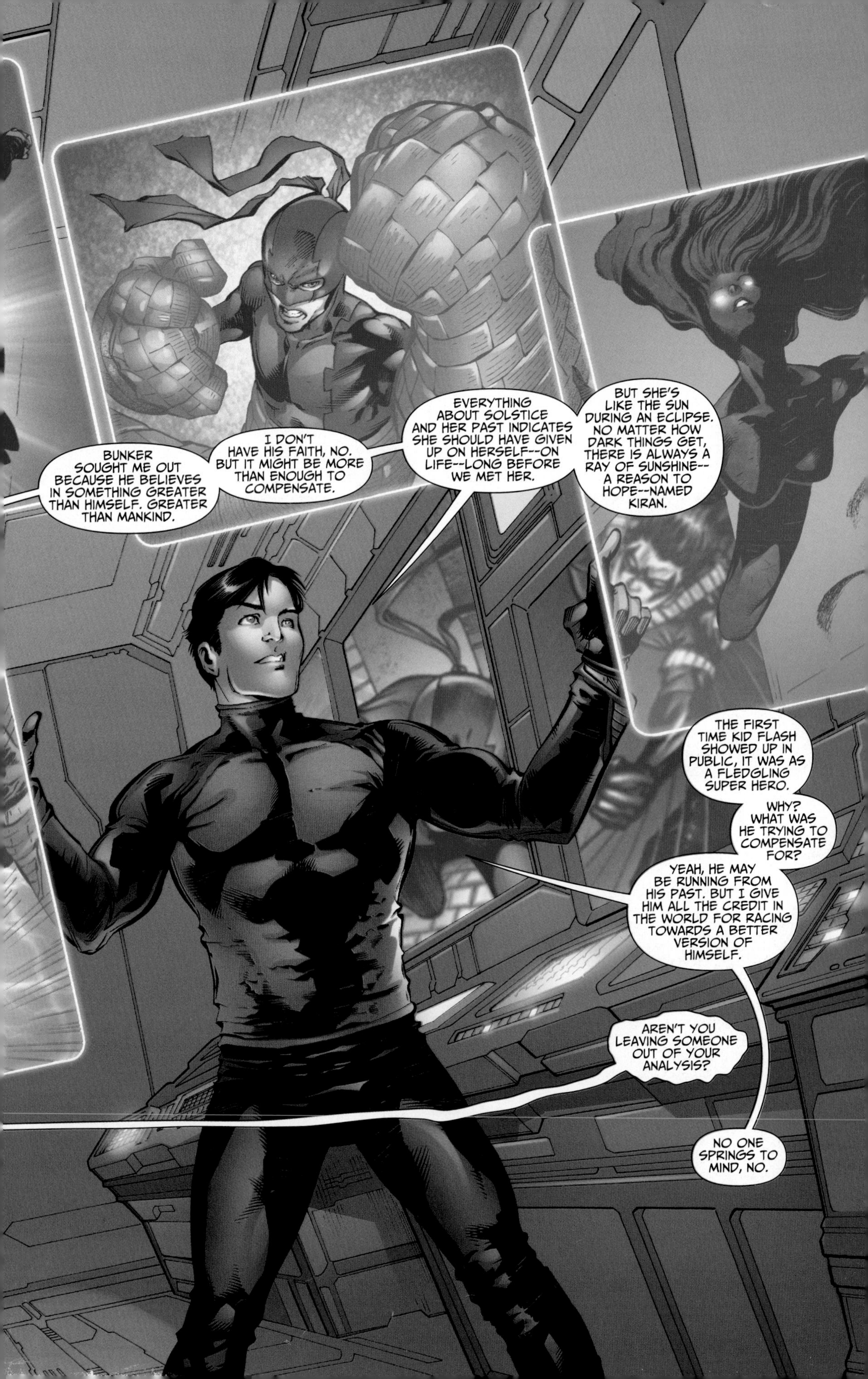
BUNKER SOUGHT ME OUT BECAUSE HE BELIEVES IN SOMETHING GREATER THAN HIMSELF. GREATER THAN MANKIND.
I DON'T HAVE HIS FAITH, NO. BUT IT MIGHT BE MORE THAN ENOUGH TO COMPENSATE.
EVERYTHING ABOUT SOLSTICE AND HER PAST INDICATES SHE SHOULD HAVE GIVEN UP ON HERSELF--ON LIFE--LONG BEFORE WE MET HER.
BUT SHE'S LIKE THE SUN DURING AN ECLIPSE. NO MATTER HOW DARK THINGS GET, THERE IS ALWAYS A RAY OF SUNSHINE--A REASON TO HOPE--NAMED KIRAN.
THE FIRST TIME KID FLASH SHOWED UP IN PUBLIC, IT WAS AS A FLEDGLING SUPER HERO.
WHY? WHAT WAS HE TRYING TO COMPENSATE FOR?
YEAH, HE MAY BE RUNNING FROM HIS PAST. BUT I GIVE HIM ALL THE CREDIT IN THE WORLD FOR RACING TOWARDS A BETTER VERSION OF HIMSELF.
AREN'T YOU LEAVING SOMEONE OUT OF YOUR ANALYSIS?
NO ONE SPRINGS TO MIND, NO.

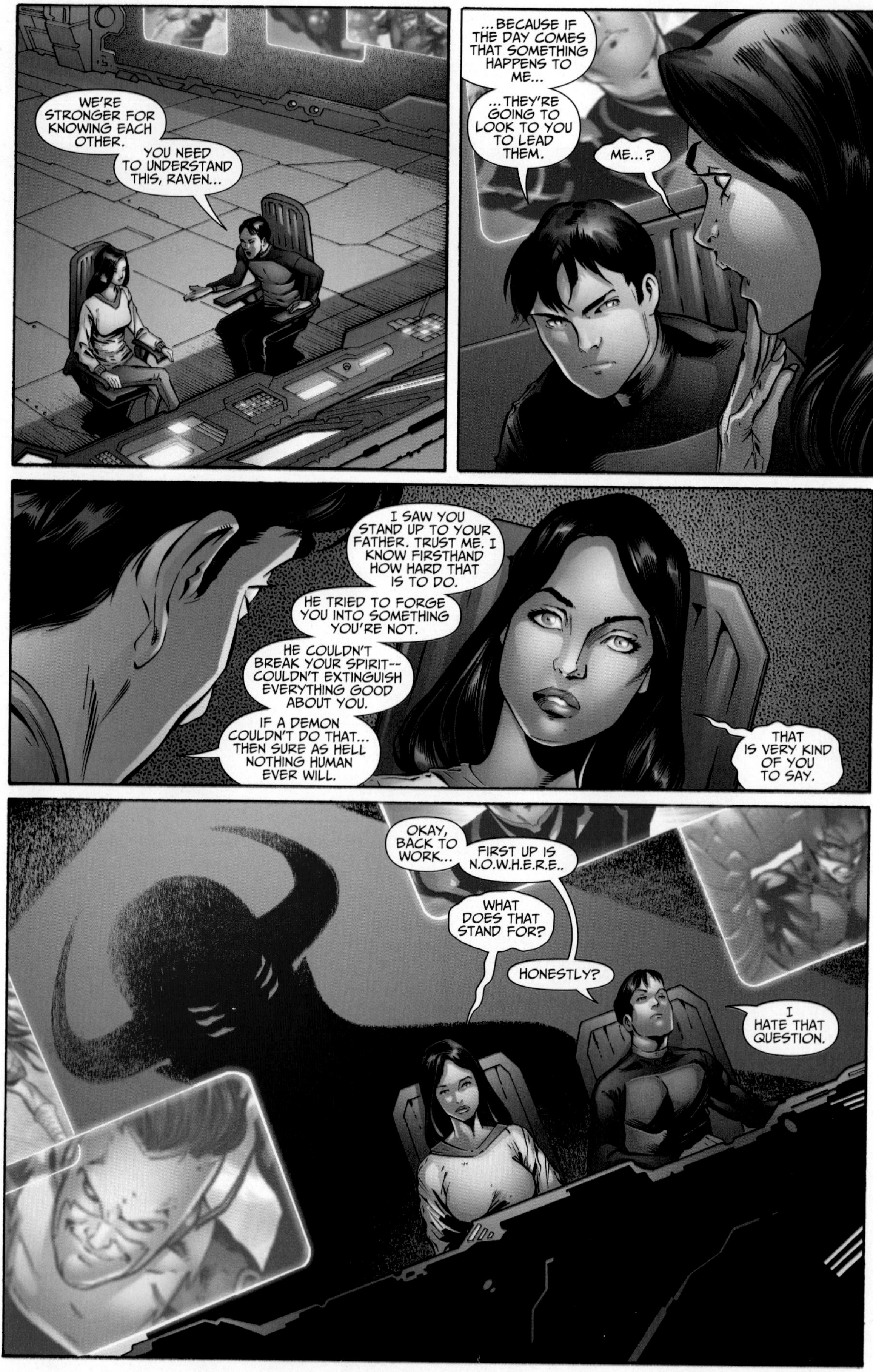
WE'RE STRONGER FOR KNOWING EACH OTHER.
YOU NEED TO UNDERSTAND THIS, RAVEN...
...BECAUSE IF THE DAY COMES THAT SOMETHING HAPPENS TO ME...
...THEY'RE GOING TO LOOK TO YOU TO LEAD THEM.
ME...?
I SAW YOU STAND UP TO YOUR FATHER. TRUST ME. I KNOW FIRSTHAND HOW HARD THAT IS TO DO.
HE TRIED TO FORGE YOU INTO SOMETHING YOU'RE NOT.
HE COULDN'T BREAK YOUR SPIRIT--COULDN'T EXTINGUISH EVERYTHING GOOD ABOUT YOU.
IF A DEMON COULDN'T DO THAT... THEN SURE AS HELL NOTHING HUMAN EVER WILL.
THAT IS VERY KIND OF YOU TO SAY.
OKAY, BACK TO WORK...
FIRST UP IS N.O.W.H.E.R.E..
WHAT DOES THAT STAND FOR?
HONESTLY?
I HATE THAT QUESTION.

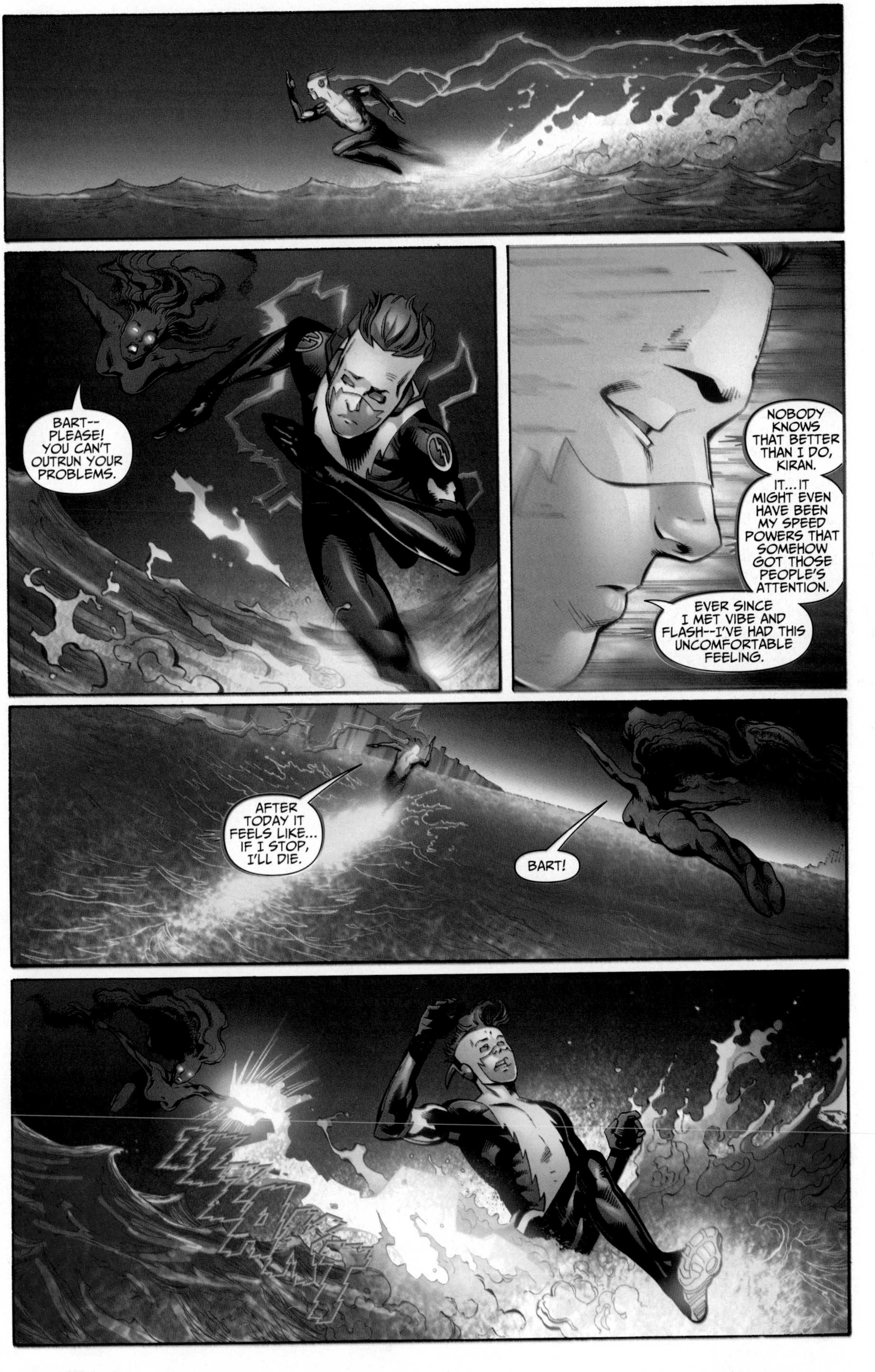
BART--
PLEASE!
YOU CAN'T
OUTRUN YOUR
PROBLEMS.
NOBODY KNOWS THAT BETTER THAN I DO, KIRAN.
IT... IT MIGHT EVEN HAVE BEEN MY SPEED POWERS THAT SOMEHOW GOT THOSE PEOPLE'S ATTENTION.
EVER SINCE I MET VIBE AND FLASH--I'VE HAD THIS UNCOMFORTABLE FEELING.
AFTER TODAY IT FEELS LIKE... IF I STOP, I'LL DIE.
BART!

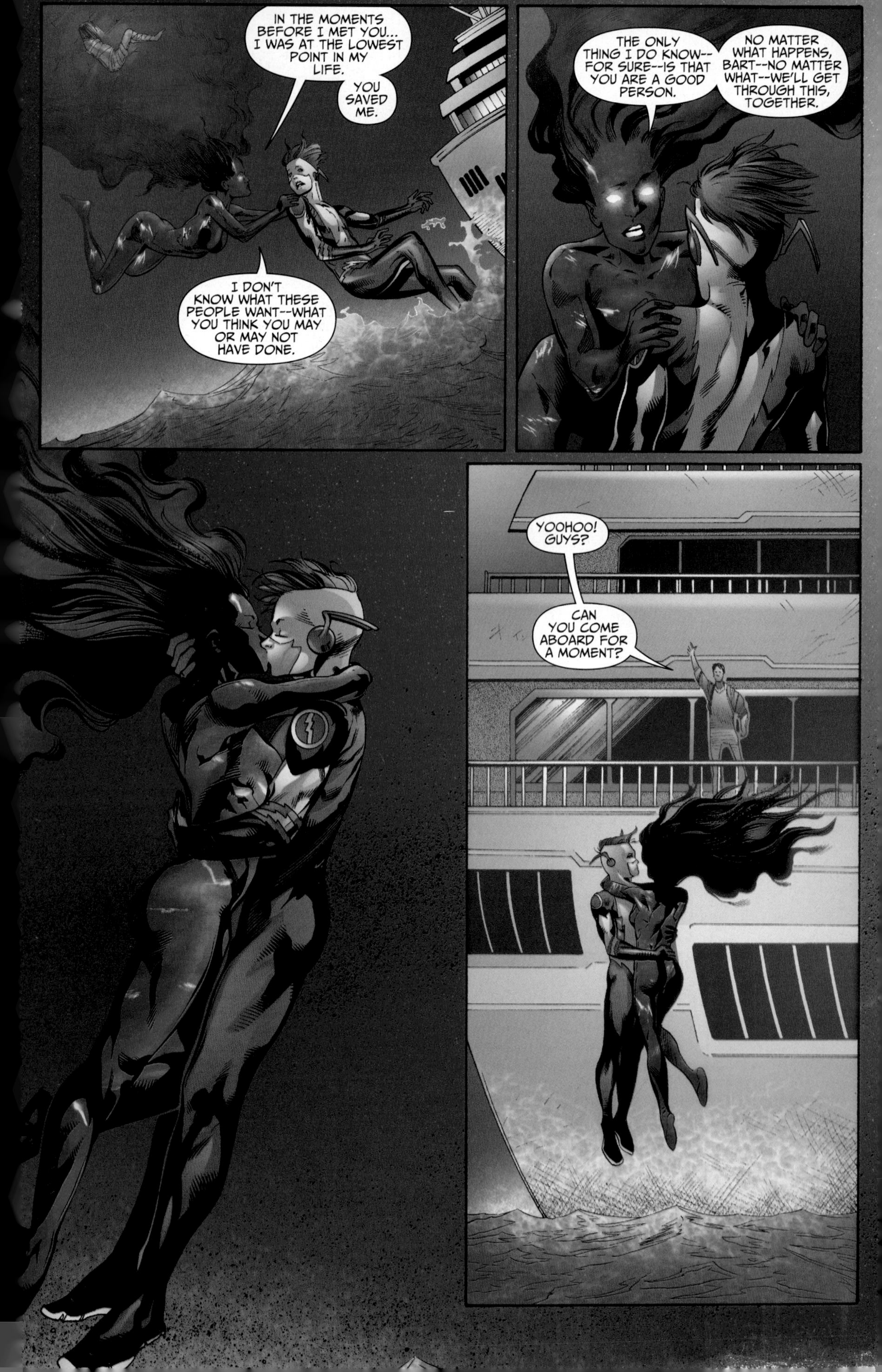
IN THE MOMENTS BEFORE I MET YOU... I WAS AT THE LOWEST POINT IN MY LIFE.
YOU SAVED ME.
I DON'T KNOW WHAT THESE PEOPLE WANT--WHAT YOU THINK YOU MAY OR MAY NOT HAVE DONE.
THE ONLY THING I DO KNOW--FOR SURE--IS THAT YOU ARE A GOOD PERSON.
NO MATTER WHAT HAPPENS, BART--NO MATTER WHAT--WE'LL GET THROUGH THIS, TOGETHER.
YOOHOO! GUYS?
CAN YOU COME ABOARD FOR A MOMENT?

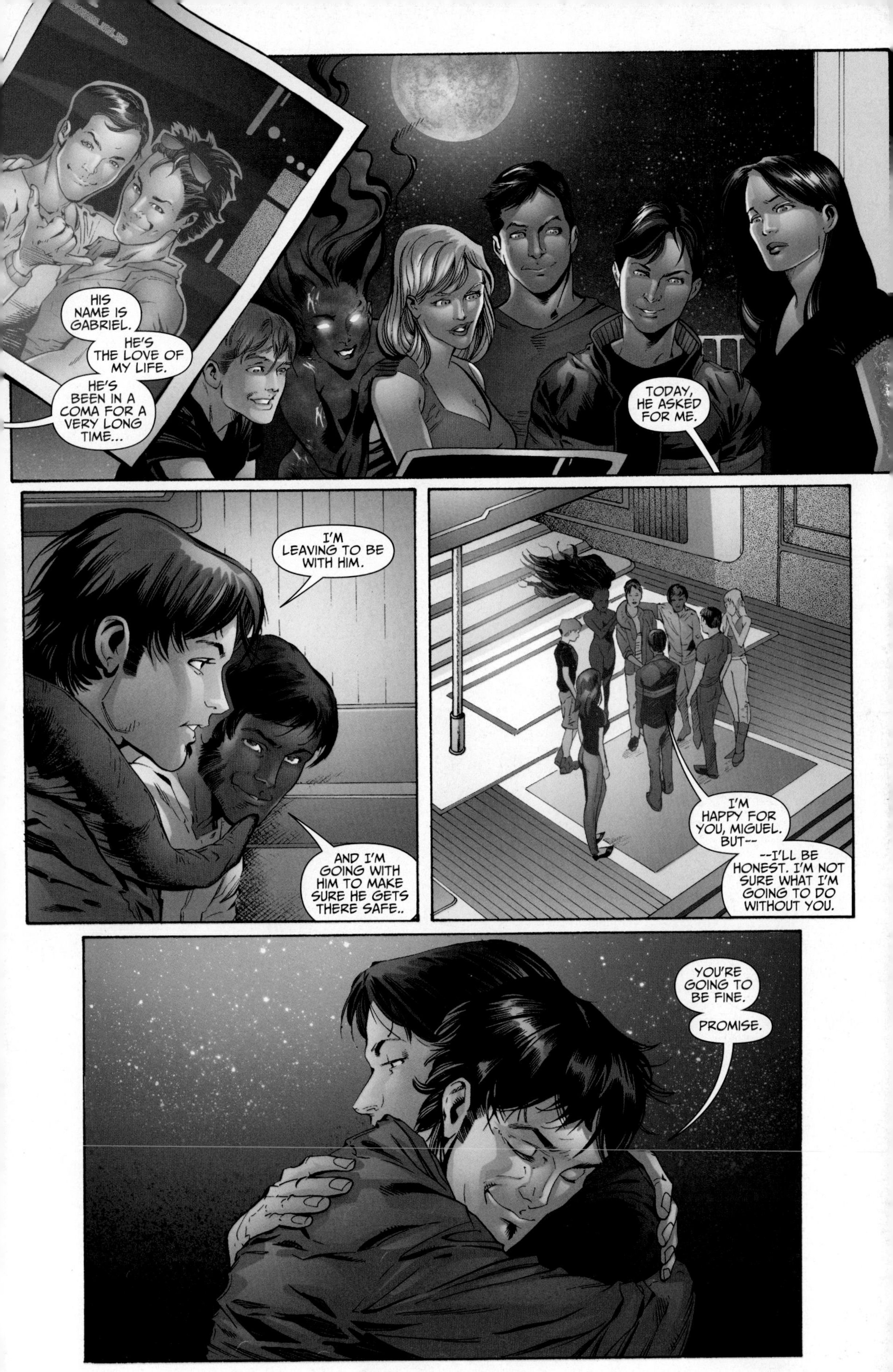
HIS NAME IS GABRIEL.
HE'S THE LOVE OF MY LIFE.
HE'S BEEN IN A COMA FOR A VERY LONG TIME...
TODAY, HE ASKED FOR ME.
I'M LEAVING TO BE WITH HIM.
AND I'M GOING WITH HIM TO MAKE SURE HE GETS THERE SAFE..
I'M HAPPY FOR YOU, MIGUEL. BUT--
--I'LL BE HONEST. I'M NOT SURE WHAT I'M GOING TO DO WITHOUT YOU.
YOU'RE GOING TO BE FINE.
PROMISE.

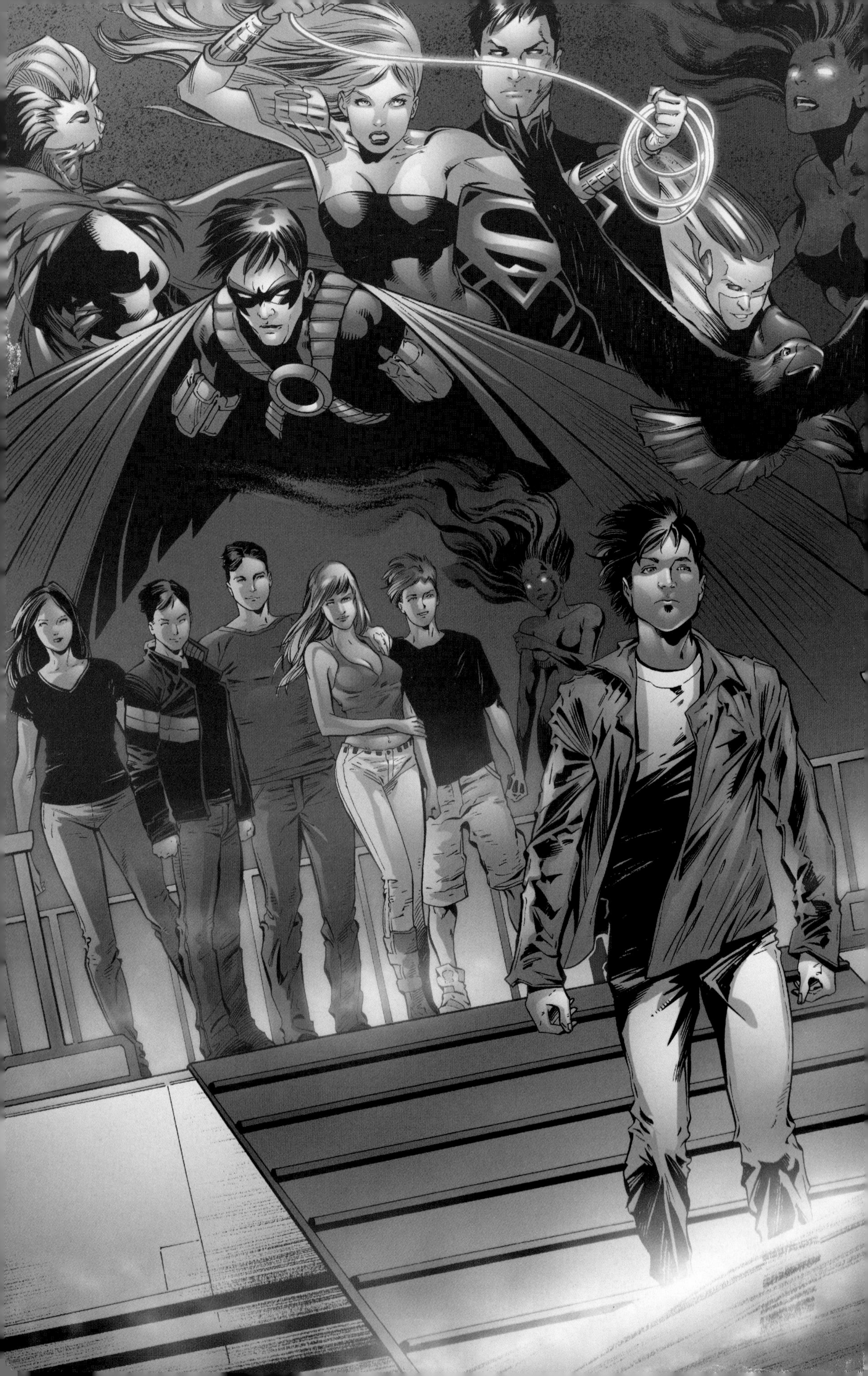

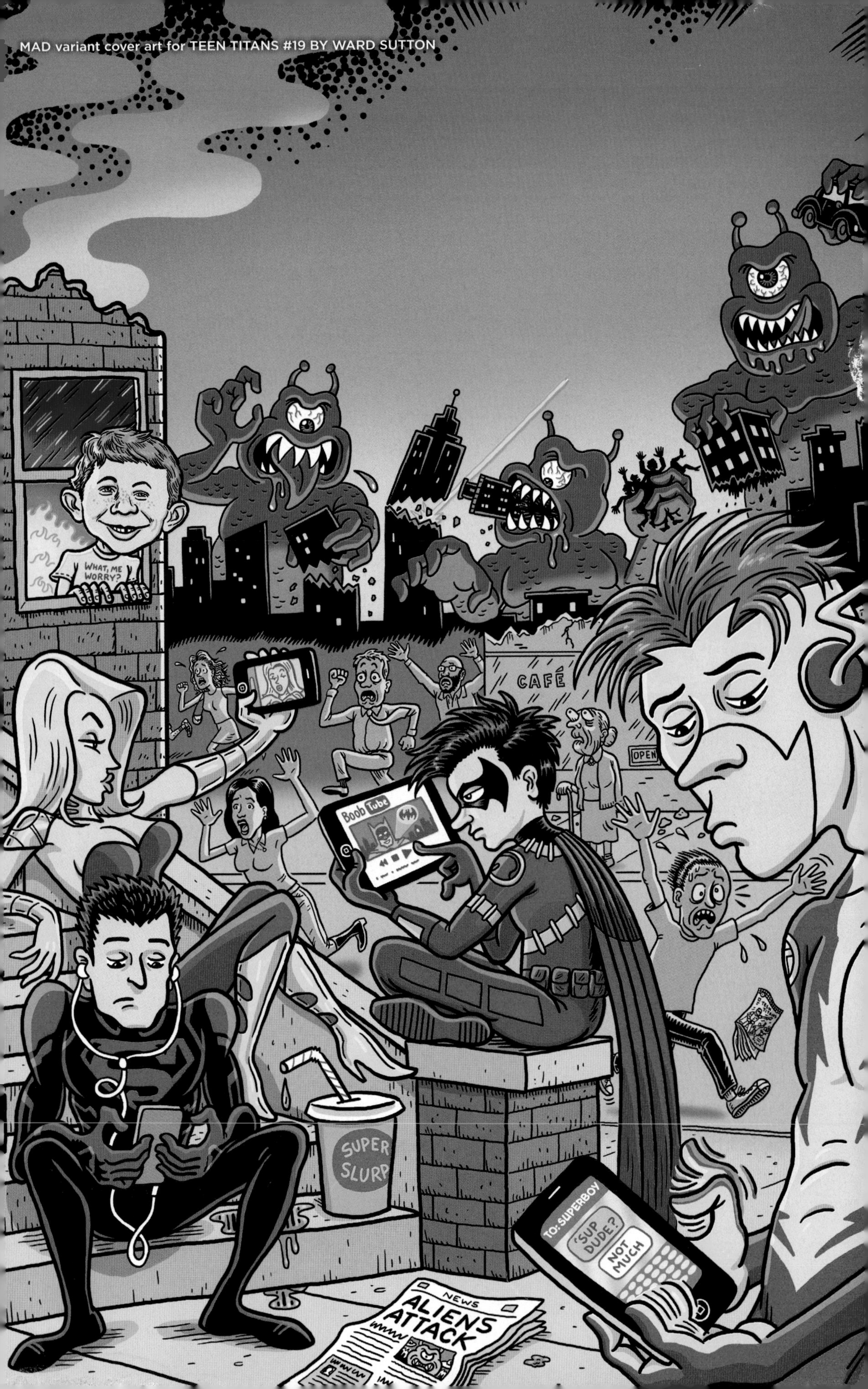
WHAT, ME WORRY?
CAFÉ
OPEN
Boob Tube
SUPER SLURP
TO: SUPERBOY
'SUP DUDE?
NOT MUCH
NEWS
ALIENS ATTACK
MAD variant cover art for TEEN TITANS #19 BY WARD SUTTON

Full spread cover art for TEEN TITANS #19 BY EDDY BARROWS, EBER FERREIRA & ALEX SINCLAIR

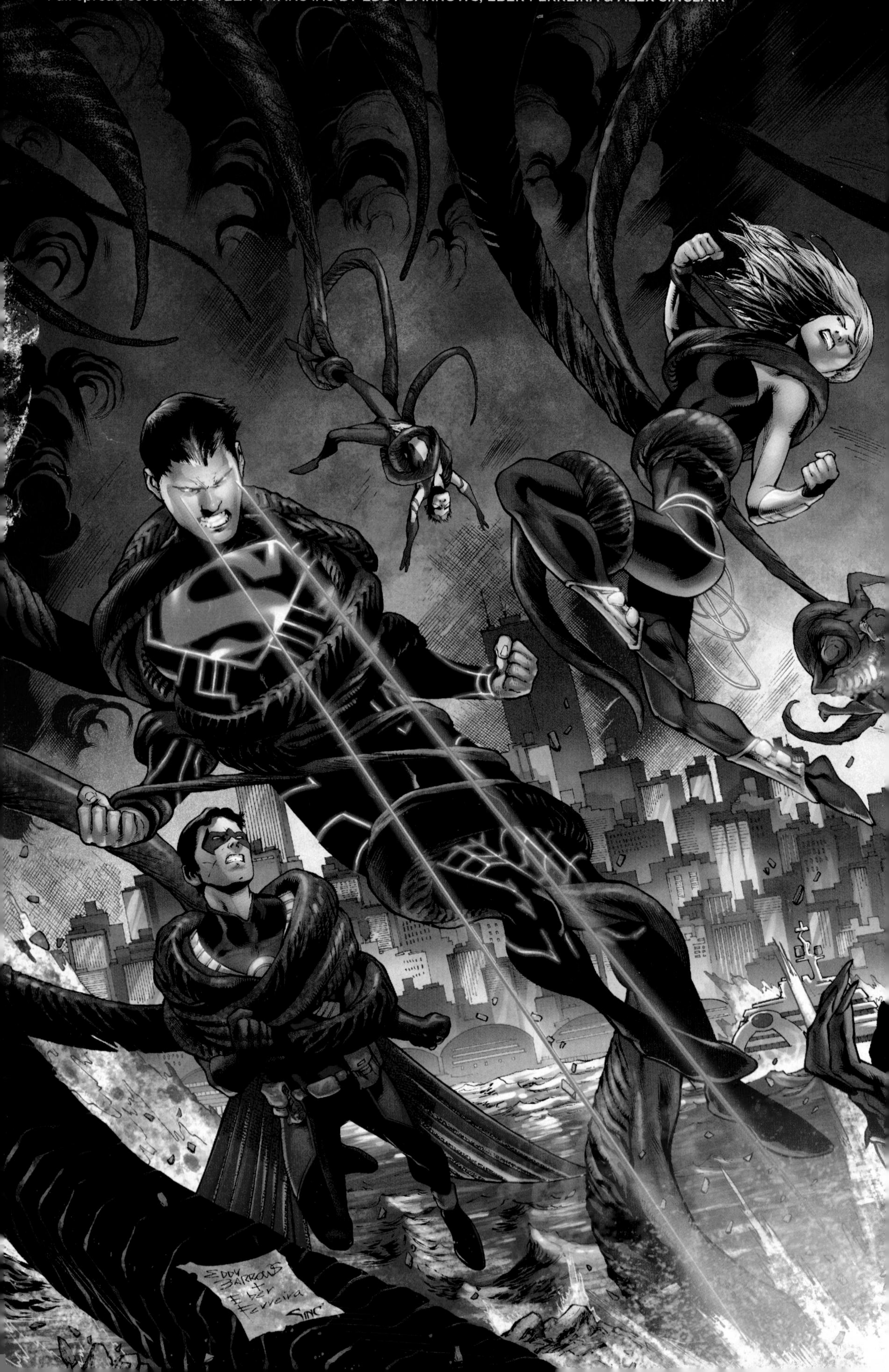
EDDY BARROWS + Eber Ferreira
SINC'

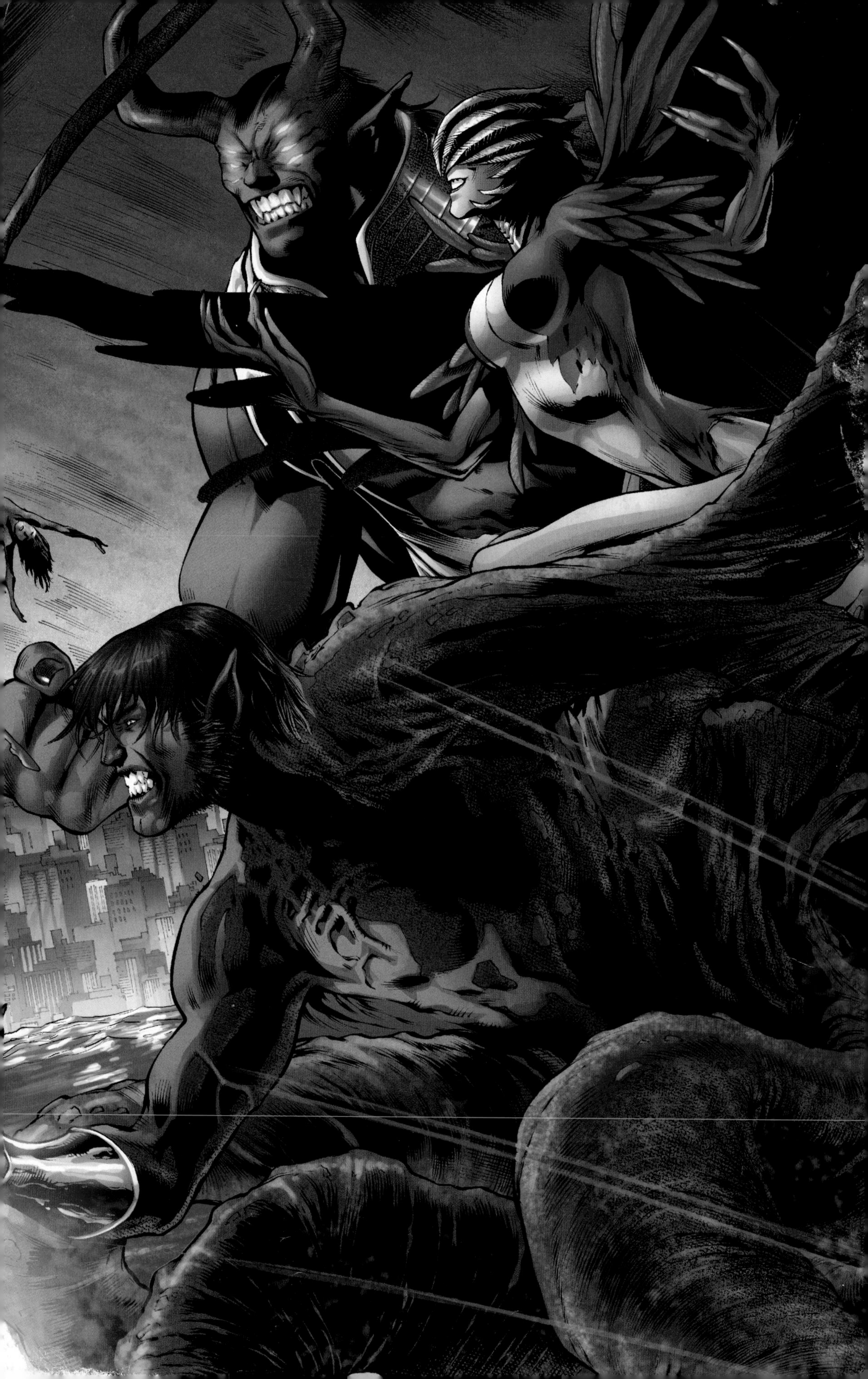

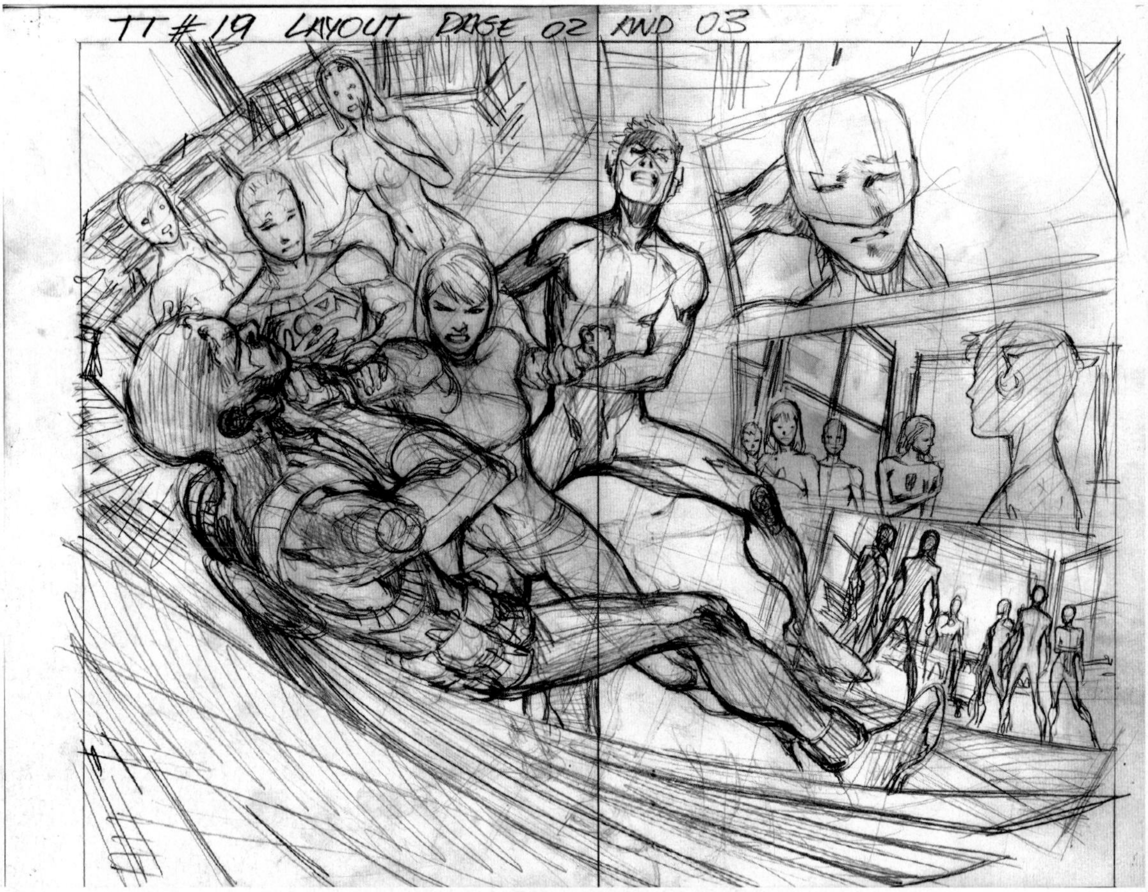
TT #19 LAYOUT PAGE 02 AND 03

Issue #19

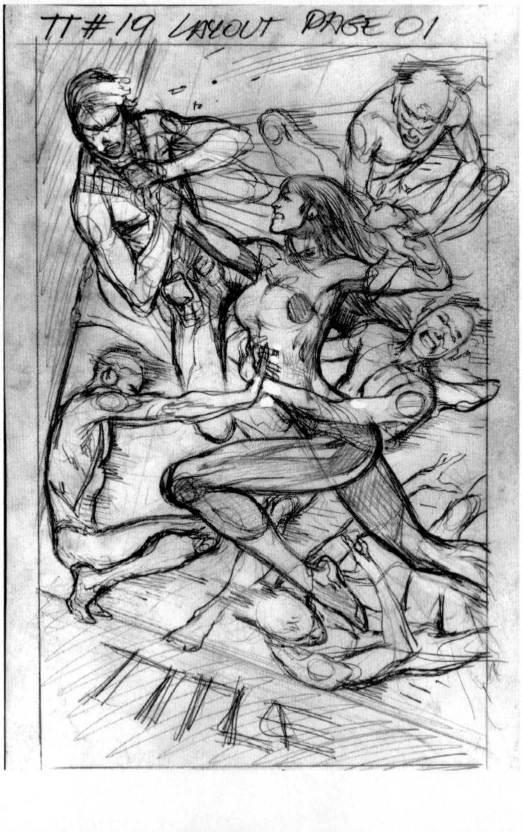
TT #19 LAYOUT PAGE 01

Issue #20

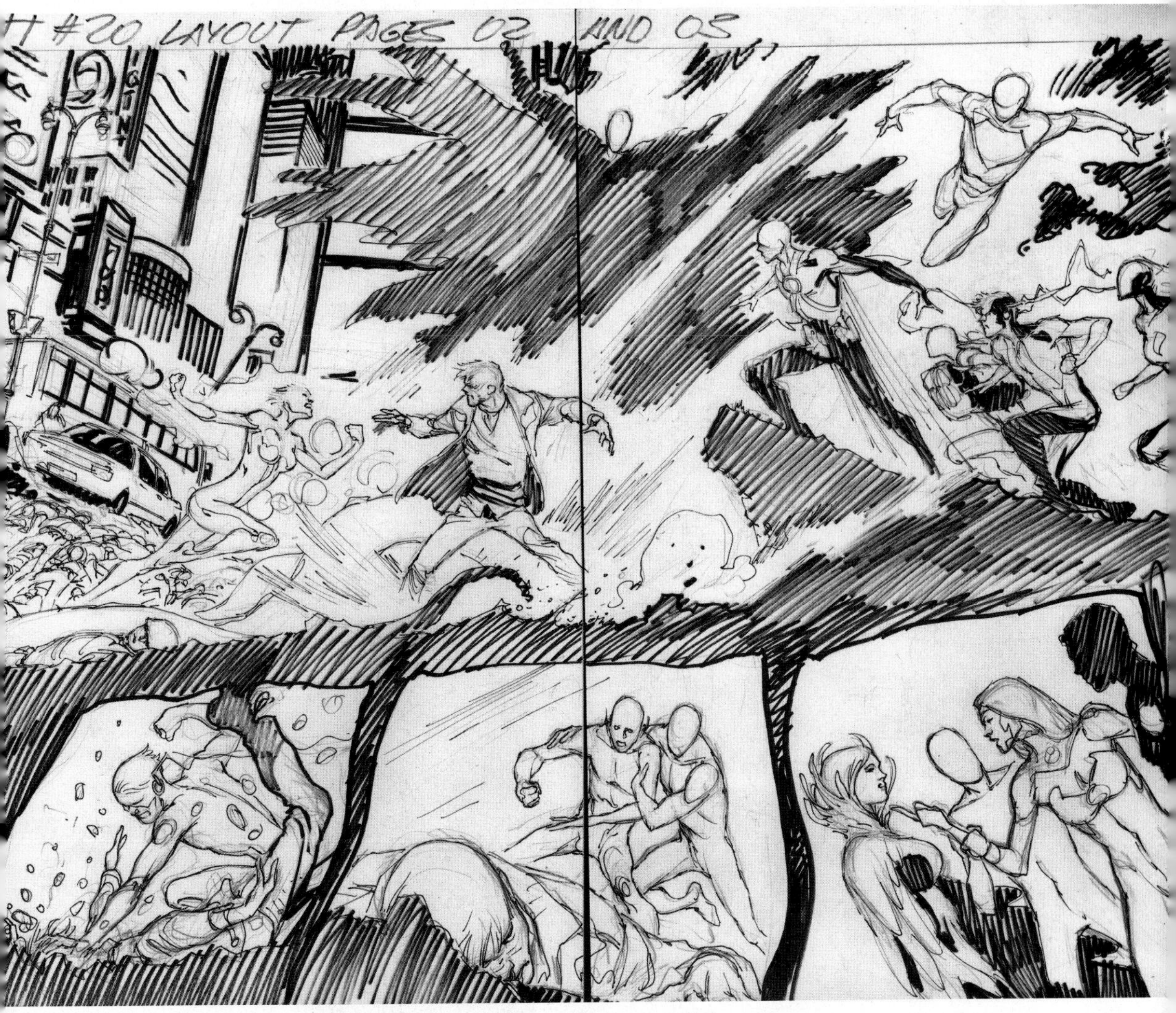
#20 LAYOUT PAGES 02 AND 03

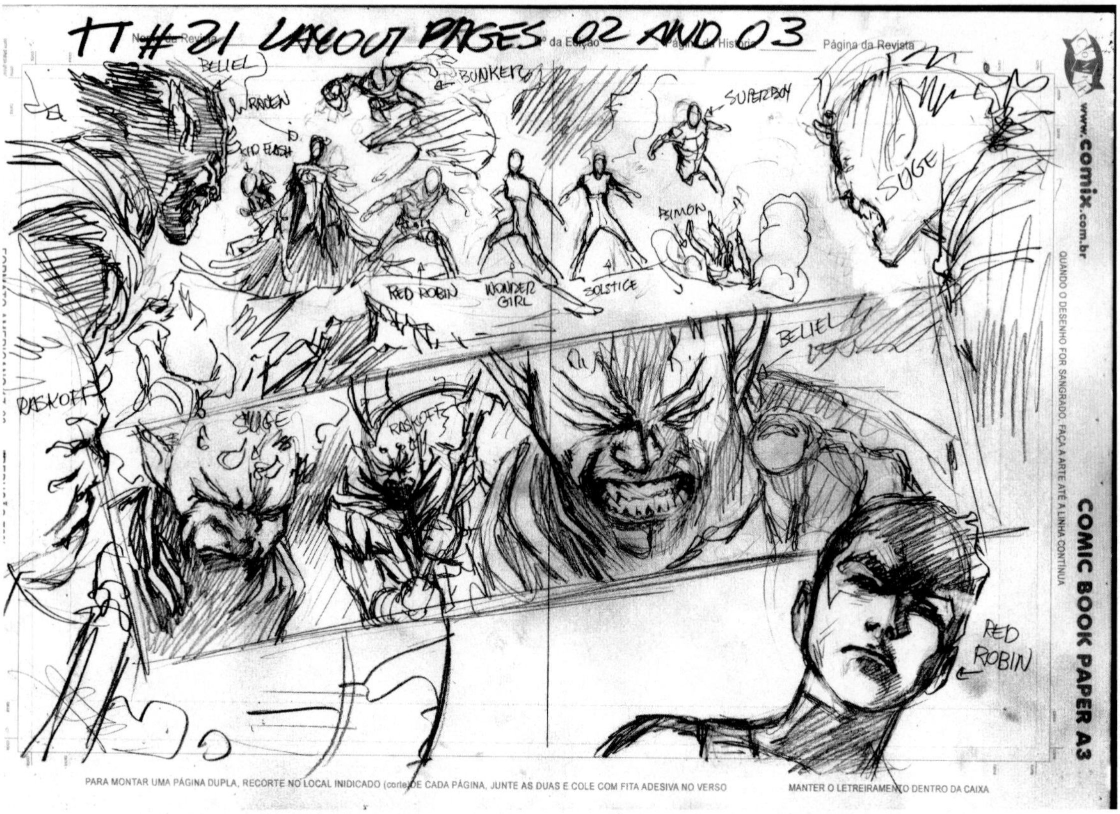
TT #21 LAYOUT PAGES 02 AND 03
Página da Revista
BELIEL
RAVEN
KID FLASH
BUNKER
SUPERBOY
SUGE
RED ROBIN
WONDER GIRL
SOLSTICE
BELIEL
RASKOFF
SUGE
RASKOFF
RED ROBIN
www.comix.com.br
QUANDO O DESENHO FOR SANGRADO, FAÇA A ARTE ATÉ A LINHA CONTÍNUA
COMIC BOOK PAPER A3
PARA MONTAR UMA PÁGINA DUPLA, RECORTE NO LOCAL INIDICADO (corte) DE CADA PÁGINA, JUNTE AS DUAS E COLE COM FITA ADESIVA NO VERSO
MANTER O LETREIRAMENTO DENTRO DA CAIXA

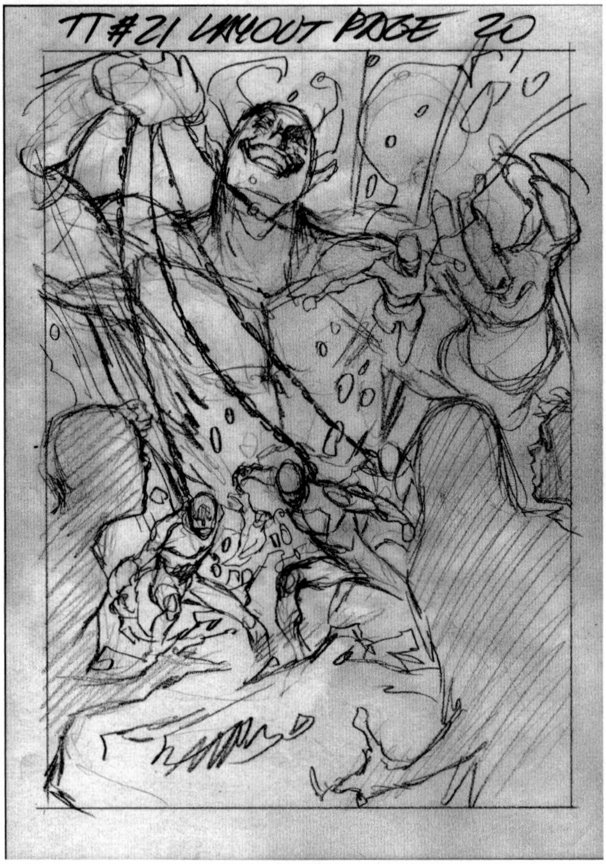
TT #21 LAYOUT PAGE 20

Issue #22

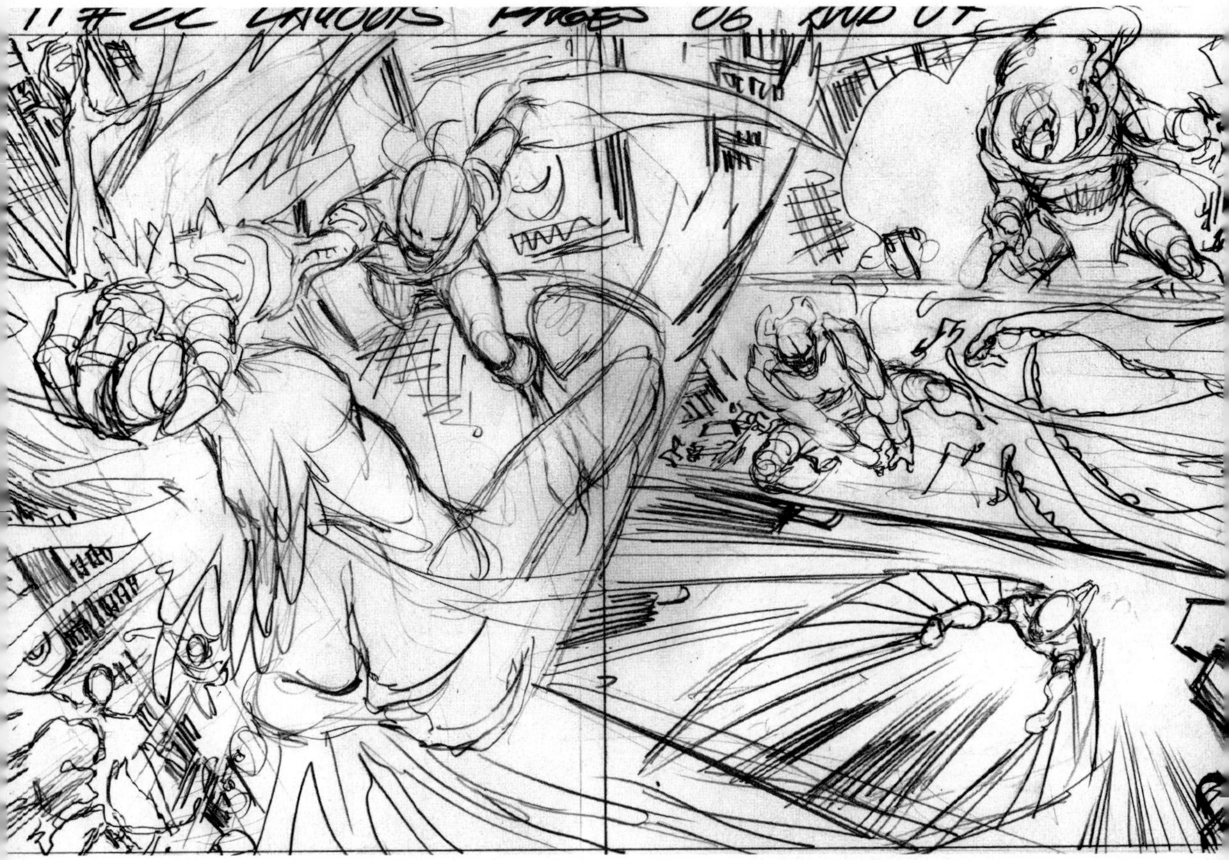

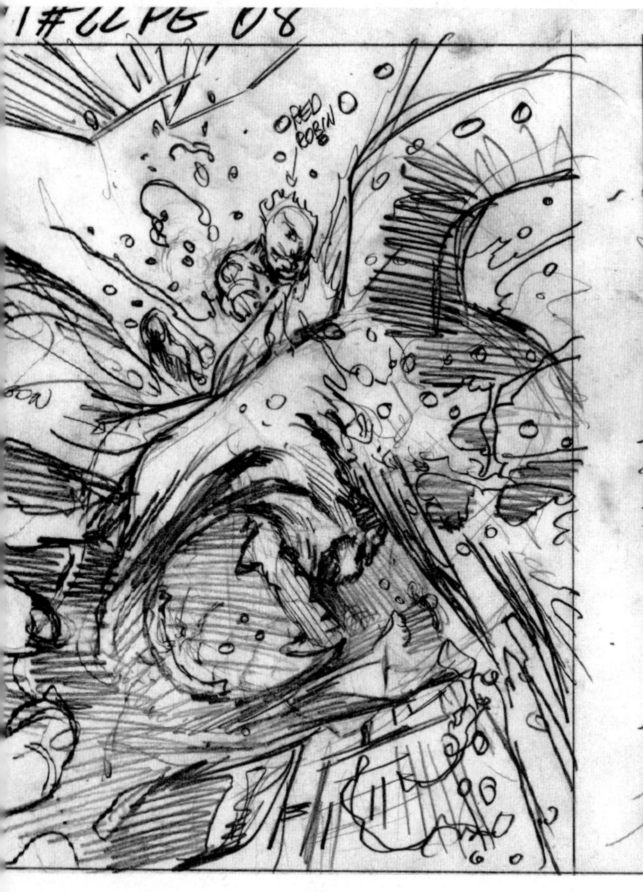
TT#22 PG 08
RED ROBIN

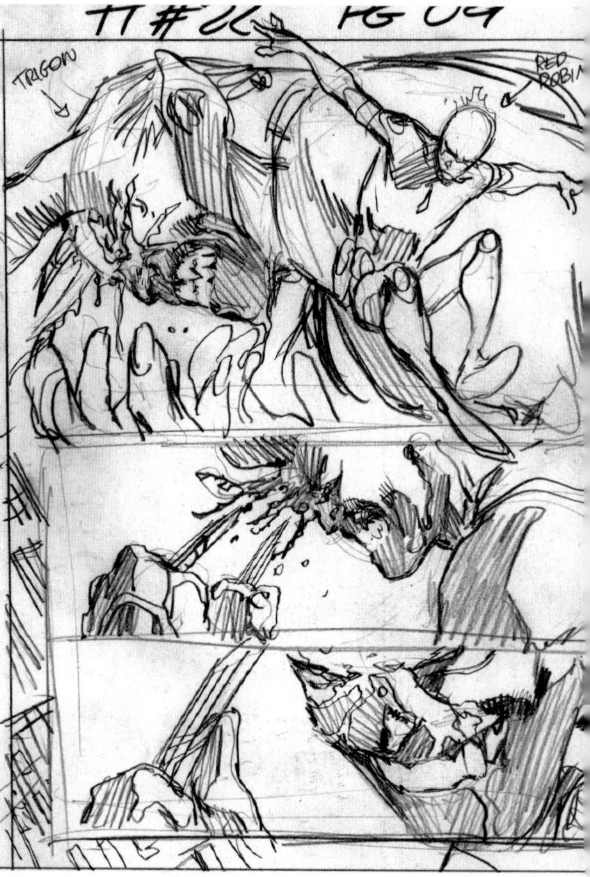
TT#22 PG 09
TRIGON
RED ROBIN